STORAGE   Art

JUL   1995

5x 9/03 2/04

STORAGE

D0743286

STORAGE

The
SPORTSMAN'S
Guide to
TEXAS

The
SPORTSMAN'S
Guide to
TEXAS

Hunting and Fishing in
the Lone Star State

DICK BARTLETT & JOANNE KRIEGER

Edited by DAVID BAXTER • *Texas Parks and Wildlife*

ILLUSTRATIONS BY JACK UNRUH

3 1336 03735 1799

TAYLOR PUBLISHING COMPANY
Dallas, Texas

Copyright 1988 by Richard Bartlett,
Joanne Krieger, and Jack Unruh

Published by
Taylor Publishing Company
1550 West Mockingbird Lane
Dallas, Texas 75235

All rights reserved.

No part of this book may be
reproduced in any form without written
permission from the publisher.

Library of Congress Cataloging-in-Publication Data
Bartlett, Dick, 1935–
   The sportsman's guide to Texas.

   1. Hunting—Texas.   2. Fishing—Texas.   I. Unruh,
Jack.   II. Krieger, Joanne.   III. Title.
SK131.B37   1988   799.29764   88–12183

ISBN: 0-87833-560-9

Printed in the United States of America

10 9 8 7 6 5 4 3 2 1

To the wildlife biologists,
technicians, and game wardens of the
Texas Parks and Wildlife Department,
without whom the state of Texas would
not be as nice a place to live.

A portion of the royalties of this book has been
dedicated to the Texas Parks and Wildlife Department.

Contents

Foreword

I first met Dick Bartlett out in the Glass Mountains near Alpine during a mule deer hunt. On that hunt I managed to bag a nice 12-point buck that turned out to be one of the better animals taken off the ranch that year. Dick helped me carry it down the side of a mountain, lashed to a length of water well sucker rod. I was pleased.

As I recall, Dick shot either a spike or a doe. He was pleased. We both came away from the hunt with a good feeling, but for two different reasons. At that point in my hunting career it was important to kill the biggest or the best. But Dick was way beyond me. The fellowship of the hunt and the beauty of West Texas were more important to him than the size of the deer, if he killed any deer at all.

His example has not been lost on me, and it's one that we have tried to get across in this book and in every issue of *Texas Parks & Wildlife* magazine—there's much more to the Texas outdoors than just the deer you kill, the quail you bag, or the fish you string.

In *The Sportsman's Guide to Texas,* we have photos of whitetails that will make a hunter's heart palpitate. But in the scheme of things, a Boone and Crockett white-tailed deer is no more nor less important than the birds of prey pictured in later chapters. We seek to influence sportsmen to transcend their special interests and develop a concern not only for the species they hunt, but also for all species whose value goes beyond food or trophies. We seek to instill in hunters and conservationists alike a more holistic view of wildlife.

In the epilogue Dick and co-author Joanne Krieger address key environmental issues facing Texas wildlife. The outdoor environment, they assert, is made up of many small, important parts, and the loss of any one of these parts would jeopardize the entire operation. We are wrestling here with the twin issues of consumptive and non-consumptive use of wildlife, that is, establishing a balance between the respective outlooks of traditional outdoorsmen who are interested in putting game on the table, and those who prefer to shoot a deer with a camera rather than a gun. *The Sportsman's Guide to Texas* champions that balance, treating wildlife in the rightful context of its relation to habitat and man.

DAVID BAXTER

Introduction

One in five Texans has a hunting or fishing license. This book is for these sportsmen, their children, and sportsmen from other states who join us by the thousands each year. *The Sportsman's Guide to Texas* is intended to help you become a better hunter, fisherman, observer, and protector of Texas wildlife.

Texas has more than a score of naturally occurring game animals: more white-tailed deer, more dove, more quail, more rabbits, more wild turkey, and more fishing variety than any other state. Ten million migratory waterfowl alone fly through each year, millions wintering in South Texas. Texas sportsmen enjoy world-class fishing and hunting year-round.

Yet, special knowledge and sometimes special lease arrangements are necessary to hunt and fish Texas productively. The *Sportsman's Guide* is the definitive source for outdoor instruction, covering everything from game to grill. The first chapter is designed to acquaint the reader with each of the ten ecological areas of the state. National and state parks, recreational areas, wildlife management areas, refuges, and national forests are identified, and a comprehensive lake and river guide is included, often with sportsman's commentary.

This is also a book for the dedicated conservationist who prefers binoculars or cameras to gun or rod. (For more information on how you can help support our valuable nongame resources, call the Texas Parks and Wildlife Department Nongame and Endangered Species Program tollfree at 1-800-792-1112.) Devoted wildlife enthusiasts or birders, like hunters themselves, are more than casual spectators of their environment. They are participants who desire to understand the environment from the perspective of the wildlife they seek.

Within the chapters on individual game species, we have indicated the ecological area hot spots for locating them, along with information on the beautiful, endangered, threatened, or protected species. If you are new to Texas or have tended to concentrate in just one area, this information will help focus your search for the exceptional hunt, fantastic fishing trip, or once-in-a-lifetime observation. When to hunt or fish each area, with information on seasons and regulations, is included, as well as good-to-know local customs.

Each chapter contains an *insights* section to help the sportsman use his powers of observation and reason to anticipate the patterns and instincts of wildlife. Wildlife behavior, reproductive cycles, food, water, and habitat requirements, ways in which you as an intruder may be sensed, and animals' typical reactions to danger are covered in detail. Knowing how wildlife will react under a variety of habitat changes, weather, or threatening situations not only increases the odds of success, but also vastly increases the quality of the hunting experience.

For the hunter or fisherman, the guide suggests appropriate gun or rod choices and covers handguns, primitive weapons, and fishing tackle. A special section concentrates on safe and skillful firearm handling. Wardrobe suggestions are covered as well as typical support systems, ranging from boats and four-wheel-drive vehicles to gun dogs. Comprehensive checklists in each chapter double as an outfitter's guide.

But it's the *expert techniques* section of each chapter that the already proficient hunter or fisherman will enjoy the most. This guide represents a distillation of the collective experiences of many knowledgeable Texas sportsmen as well as thorough research into the existing body of scientific knowledge. All the information gathered in these pages has been reviewed by professional wildlife specialists. It is complete, from pre-hunt reconnaissance to the techniques needed for taking specific fish and game. Each section ends with field dressing instruction and even recommends the appropriate Texas wine to complement an elegant menu.

The last chapter, focusing on the camp kitchen, contains a selection of traditional Texas recipes and a section on first aid.

One of the best features of the guide is immediately apparent—hundreds of wildlife photographs, often more difficult to come by than chicken fried venison, taken for *Texas Parks & Wildlife* magazine by our state's finest wildlife photographers. Beyond their aesthetic value, you will find these photographs very helpful in teaching the uninitiated about our birds, wild animals, and fish. You may very well see something that will surprise you, too.

We have found that even experienced guides are often not knowledgeable about nongame species and yet are constantly asked questions such as, "What kind of bird was that?" Such questions are typical of youngsters, who are naturally inquisitive. Their powers of observation are greatly enhanced by learning to discern between similar wildlife species, such as ducks.

Youngsters soak up this information, making the outdoors a wonderful place to build parent/child relationships centered on a mutual respect for nature. This guide will provide the parent with a rich lore of wildlife facts and the methods for instructing youngsters in technique and safety. This sharing and passing on of knowledge from one generation to the next is as much a part of the sporting tradition as the hunt itself.

Young sportsmen in Texas are required to take a course in hunter education which has its own study program. The *Sportsman's Guide*, while not designed to replace this formal study course, has been prepared as a primer or supplement to that program and provides suggestions for enriching the learning experience. The young hunter must learn the hunter's code as set forth here and in the state's program, which "demonstrates concern for other hunters, for wildlife, and for private property." The youngster must understand that the privilege of hunting is dependent upon all hunters behaving responsibly. They will come to learn what all mature sportsmen know: that the only acceptable way to hunt is the way that allows the

hunted an opportunity to avoid and escape the hunter within its natural habitat. This is called Fair Chase.

Theodore Roosevelt made the first case for Fair Chase in 1893, when market hunting was still legal. He stated, "The term 'Fair Chase' shall not be held to include killing a bear, wolf or cougar in traps, nor 'fire hunting,' nor 'crusting' moose, elk or deer in deep snow, nor killing game from a boat when it is swimming in the water, nor killing deer by any other method than that of fair stalking or still hunting."

In the '60s and '70s, the Boone and Crockett Club, principal keeper of big game records in North America, updated its fair chase definition to offset the advantages of motorized vehicles and electronic devices, two-way radios, power amplifiers for game calling, game fencing, and "coop shoots" of transplanted game. "Official Score Charts" of the club require that in addition to testifying that the hunter has complied with all applicable laws in the taking of game, he must also attest to taking the game in fair chase by signing an affidavit to that effect.

Although anti-hunters are a minority of the population, their political voice is enhanced by hunters' excesses and stupidities. Sadly, not every hunter is a sportsman. Therefore, it is important to spell out the distinct differences:

A true sportsman believes in fair chase. He only squeezes the trigger when he is sure of the shot, and he takes extremely good care of his meat, eating or sharing the edible game he shoots or catches. He often releases fish and always stops hunting when his table needs are met. "Enough is as good as feast." He is a good student of the animal or fish he seeks and is very knowledgeable about his overall environment. He is a conservationist, cherishes the land on which he hunts, supports wildlife management programs, and obeys all game laws. Many Texans place themselves in a "meat hunter" category because they don't seek trophies. If these hunters abide by the rules of fair chase and respect the game they pursue and the land on which they hunt, they are sportsmen.

A game thief, by contrast, does not believe in fair chase. If he thinks he can get away with it, this guy will spotlight deer or poach game, usually while trespassing. He loves to skillet shoot quail and dove, "telephone" bass, seine a tank clean of catfish, or use any technique he can come up with to accumulate as much meat as fast as possible. He usually takes good care of meat, and either uses it himself or sells it. Poaching—killing protected species, hunting out of season, or using illegal hunting techniques—has become a major threat to Texas wildlife. Game wardens are sorely outnumbered in the wildlife wars. If you see a game thief in action, report him by calling 1-800-729-GAME.

Undeniably, the most unforgivable transgressor is the slob hunter. His idea of fair chase usually has more to do with wine and women than fish and game. This guy has no respect for the game he pursues and cares little for the environment. His stock in trade is the discarded beer can.

He is often a hazard to others through his carelessness. He'll try ridiculous shots at what he considers trophy animals, but usually he doesn't have the requisite shooting skills to make such attempts. His idea of a trophy hunt is sitting in a stand over a baited field. If he has money, what he loves best is a guided pursuit of exotic livestock trapped within a game-fenced pasture. He usually is a road hunter. He may not know how to field dress an animal, and is seldom known to release fish. Such hunters are likely to employ a Gatling gun technique, resulting in multiple bullet holes in game. The gut shot is their specialty. These slob hunters have given all hunters a black eye.

This being said, perhaps the best thing about this guide is that you can dip into it when and where you wish, to plan hunts, gain insights, sharpen skills, or prepare a great meal. In the epilogue you are even invited to share some thinking about Texas conservation. It is the authors' strongly held belief that sportsmen are the backbone of support for all conservation efforts, yet they are too rarely heard.

Finally, many of our readers will especially enjoy matching their hard-earned knowledge against ours. One of the best things about the outdoors is the variety of ways in which individuals cope with, enjoy, and solve problems. We look forward to hearing from our readers and expanding our own knowledge. We hope that even the most accomplished hunters will find this work not only a useful reference book but also an entertainment—because Texas sportsmen are not always as serious as this introduction. We hunt because we are hunters. We hunt and fish because these are the most exciting participatory sports we know of—fulfilling, rewarding, and fun.

To the Hunt,
DICK BARTLETT
JOANNE KRIEGER

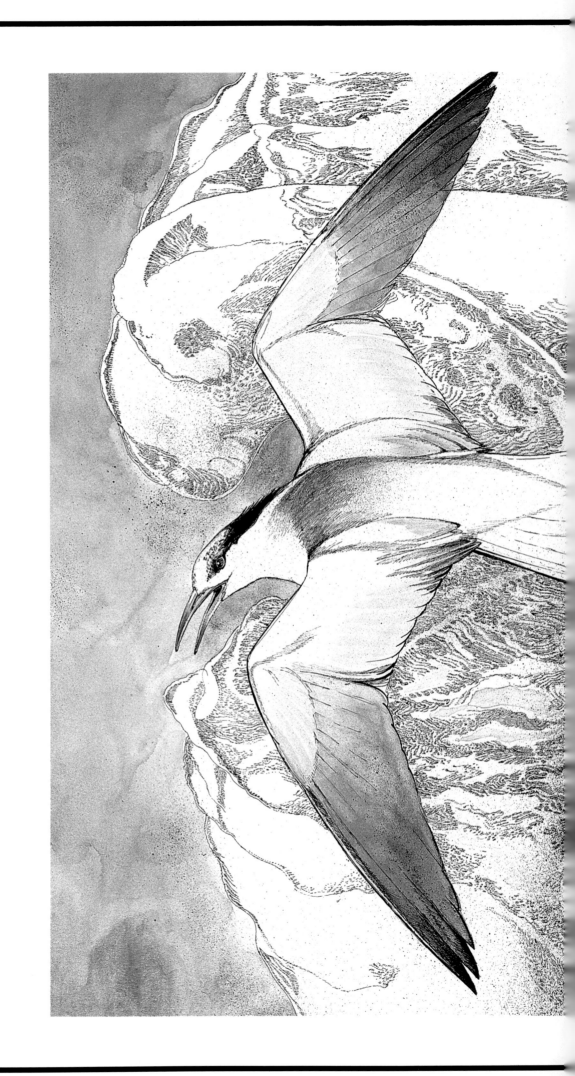

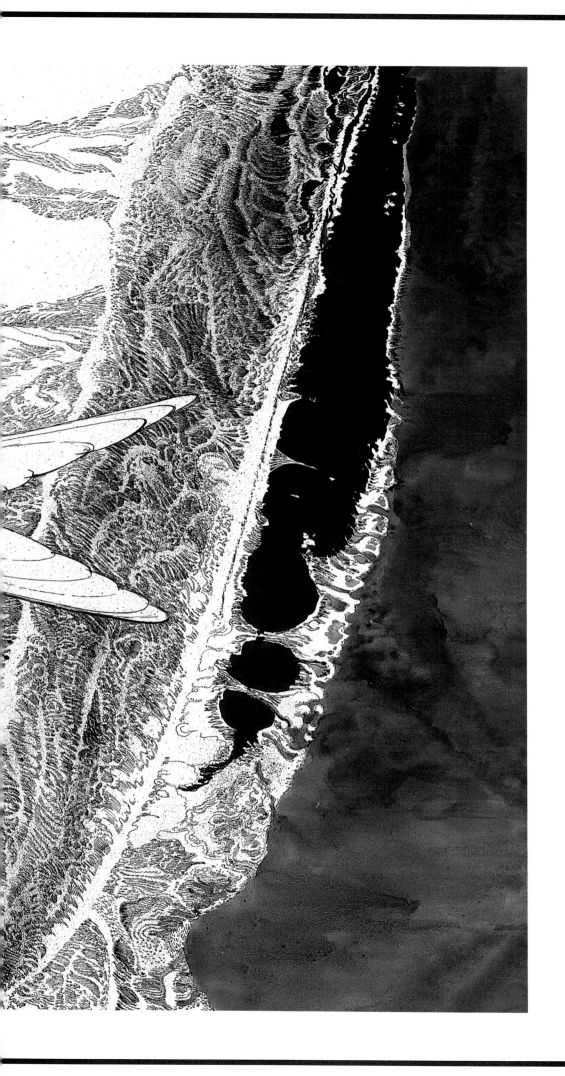

I

TEXAS
An
Ecological
Perspective

TEXAS—"Larger than the combined areas of Michigan, Wisconsin, Iowa, Illinois, and Indiana." "Larger than France," goes the litany as the newcomer politely stifles a yawn and thinks to himself, "So, Texas is big? I already knew that."

Sheer size has little significance. Antarctica and Alaska are bigger, and in some wildlife species, better. We don't have Dall sheep or penguins. What does have significance to the sportsman is the tremendous diversity of wildlife and plantlife found here. The state covers 267,338 square miles. Its mountains stand almost 9,000 feet tall. We have hundreds of miles of beaches, more than 80,000 miles of rivers, the largest desert in North America, tropical valleys, and millions of acres of prairies and canopied woodlands. Botanists tell us Texas has a thousand different soil series, 600 grasses, 4,000 species and subspecies of wildflowers.

To provide more in-depth understanding of the Lone Star State, we have used the previously established format of ten ecological or vegetational areas. Moving from east to west, descriptions of these areas provide insight into the state's rich geography and differing terrain. Even if you are completely new to the state, this format will quickly give you a feeling for the wildlife situation in each of these areas.

El Capitan, Guardian of the Guadalupes.

1. **Pineywoods**—Low-lying pine forests interspersed with grasslands. Includes the Big Thicket.
2. **Gulf Prairies and Marshes**—Tidewater marsh and salt grasses changing to bluestems and tall grasses inland, with some hardwoods along streams.
3. **Post Oak Savannah**—Oaks, elm, and pecan trees west of the forest region, slightly higher elevation.
4. **Blackland Prairies**—Prairies with oaks, pecan, elm, bois d'arc, and mesquite along streams.
5. **Cross Timbers and Prairies**—Alternating woodlands and prairies with vegetation varying according to sharp changes in soil and topography.
6. **South Texas Plains**—Brushlands or chaparral with subtropical dryland vegetation including small trees, shrubs, and cacti. Known as Brush Country.
7. **Edwards Plateau**—Woodlands extending to prairie with rolling terrain turning mountainous. Includes Hill Country.
8. **Rolling Plains**—Mesquite woodland and prairie with rugged, steep-sloped land. Includes Caprock Escarpment.
9. **High Plains**—Flat, nearly treeless Panhandle.
10. **Trans-Pecos**—Mountains, canyons, and deserts with only drought-resistant vegetation.

Surprisingly, much of Texas still is as it was, or close enough. This is the advantage of the size and remoteness of some of our wilder ecological areas. Most of the credit

for preservation goes to the fact that 90 percent of the state is privately owned, and the private owners, as a group, are good custodians of the land. They have found that the qualities that make land productive for crops, livestock, or game can be abused out of existence. Credit also goes to a wonderful parks system. In 1916, Mrs. Isabella Neff deeded six acres of Coryell County land to the state for "religious, educational, fraternal, and political purposes." This is now Mother Neff State Park, the prototype for a state parks system that at the end of the 20th century has reached more than 200,000 acres.

The Texas Parks and Wildlife Department (TPWD) is one of the finest in America. One of the reasons for its ascendancy is the TPWD's wildlife management areas. They are spread throughout the ecological areas and are living laboratories for scientific study. Many of them are also available for hunting, by permit, and are discussed in the chapters dealing with different game species.

A Texas summit meeting on predator controls.

Type II wildlife management areas offer hundreds of thousands of acres of public hunting to Texans. Annual permits may be purchased each August from TPWD offices at a very modest price. The permit allows access to all Type II units throughout the state, and often children may hunt free. Because of anticipated demand, drawings are conducted to determine the lucky hunters in certain units. Each permit purchaser receives a booklet describing the Type II WMA hunting units available for the upcoming season.

The Texas Parks and Wildlife Commission, the guiding force for TPWD, has a long-range objective to acquire much more state park land, waterfowl habitat, and white-winged dove habitat. Included in the goals are acquisition plans for nongame and ecologically sensitive habitat.

Also important are the efforts of the Texas Conservation Foundation and the Texas Nature Conservancy. The foundation was established in 1969 to act as trustee for donations of land like Mrs. Neff's. The Texas Nature Conservancy is a state affiliate of a national non-profit conservation organization. It acquires ecologically important lands and sometimes resells them to state and federal agencies.

A peregrine falcon hunts Padre Island beach.

In addition, Texas is part of a national park system. The National Wildlife Refuge system was established in 1903 by President/sportsman Teddy Roosevelt. In Texas, the refuges cover almost 200,000 acres. Big Bend falls within the National Park Service and has 740,000 acres. Also under the National Park Service are 76,000 acres in the Guadalupe Mountains, 130,000 acres of Padre Island beaches, and 85,000 acres in the Big Thicket.

Still more: There are 700,000 acres of national forest

Piers provide easy access to Gulf fishing.

land in East Texas. State forests cover another 7,000 acres. But after all this protected acreage is tabulated, sportsmen should note that nearly 50 percent of the unprotected natural areas of the United States are located entirely within the borders of Texas, making our state the most ecologically important in the nation.

Understanding the sportsman's Texas is a labor of love. It takes years to discover the resources of game or hunting and fishing possibilities. Size *can* be a barrier to understanding. It's amazing how many native Texans have never explored some of our most beautiful land, yet are completely conversant with midtown Manhattan or Paris. And while sportsmen also appreciate the diversions of Broadway and the Champs Elysees, sunset in the Chisos Mountains is, by far, the preferred experience.

THE RIVERS OF TEXAS

Rivers are the highways of exploration and the justifications of settlement. They provided early settlers not only an unfailing point of reference when traveling unfamiliar land, but also a dependable source of food, firewood, and water. Sportsmen, too, first come to know a new territory by its rivers, and this is particularly important in Texas. We have more than 80,000 miles of rivers, mainly flowing from the High Plains to the Gulf of Mexico. Before the set-

tlers built their own little dams, and before the U.S. Army Corps of Engineers went on the biggest dam building binge in history, a Panhandle thunderstorm's water would have flowed unimpeded 600 miles to the Gulf. The Medina River west of San Antonio was, in 1913, the first major Texas river to be dammed. By the mid-'80s, Texas' reservoir storage capacity reached near the 60 million acre-foot mark. One acre foot of water amounts to 326,000 gallons of water. Today, there are no major rivers without dams.

We have not segregated Texas rivers by ecological area since most run through more than one area, and the following list contains only the more well known. Only a few rivers, notably the Guadalupe, are crowded with canoes and rafts. A canoe/camping/fishing trip can be a soul-cleansing experience. One of the best times for exploring most Texas rivers, such as the Brazos, is during the early winter months, when fair-weather canoers are huddled around the fireplace. It's cool, no insects, and leaves have turned their vibrant shades. Dress options are similar to those suggested for deer hunters: rain gear and a full change of clothes is mandatory. Store spare clothing in a totally waterproof container, which you've tied to the canoe. In order to locate the more remote spots, to calculate distances, and plan ahead for campsites, we recommend

The Canadian River bisects Panhandle Plains.

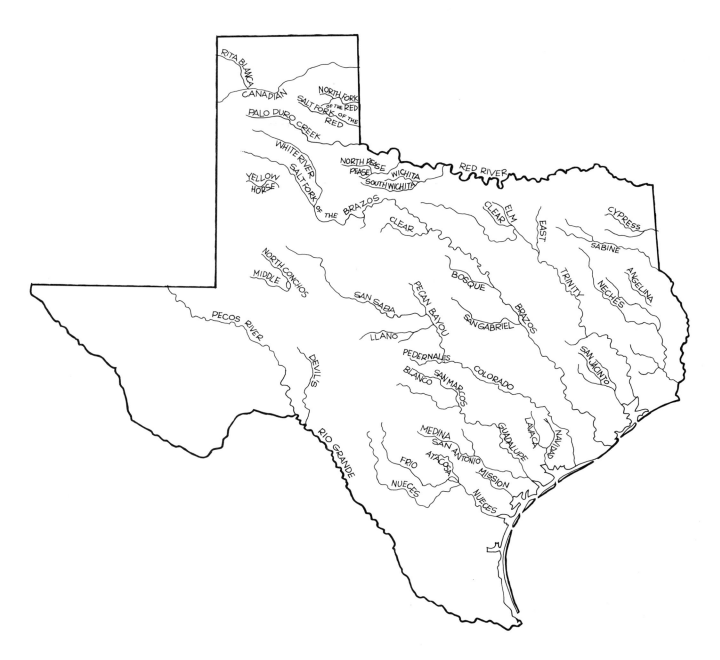

U.S. Geological Survey Topographical Maps. To purchase by mail, contact Distribution Section, U.S. Geological Survey, Federal Center, Denver, CO 80225. You must be quite specific as to the area wanted and scale desired. If possible, visit the Distribution Center in Denver. It's a fascinating place where the investment of a few dollars can enhance your appreciation and enjoyment of your favorite rivers, mountains, or deer lease.

Though rivers have become underutilized since access to fabulous fishing and boating has been made so easy on impoundments, bear in mind that the flowing river stream is public domain, but the banks are not. If you aren't within a public area, you could be trespassing by setting foot on the bank. Know where you are or stick to sand and gravel bars. Some rivers have dramatic level changes when dam waters are released, most have a danger of flooding, and others have white water hazards, so a little research is prudent. Newspapers in major cities publish river flow data for rivers such as the Rio Grande, Guadalupe, Colorado, and Brazos. TPWD can supply you with other sources for river flow information. Call the toll-free number, 1-800-792-1112.

TEXAS RIVERS

Angelina River—Headwaters near Lake Striker; scenic; black bass and catfish.

Atascosa River—Headwaters south of San Antonio; melds with Frio and Nueces at Three Rivers.

Blanco River—Headwaters near LBJ Ranch; this beautiful river winds through some of the most scenic Hill Country and joins the San Marcos River south of San Marcos.

Bosque River—Headwaters in Erath County; excellent white bass in spring.

Brazos River—Headwaters in Rolling Plains; scenic, especially below Possum Kingdom Lake Dam; water is very cool and clear below the dam since it's taken from the bottom of the lake; wide variety of fishing and canoeing; release rainbows.

Canadian River—Headwaters in New Mexico; forms Lake Meredith on way through Panhandle; was an interstate highway across the Panhandle in the 1850s; rich history.

Colorado River—Headwaters in High Plains; state's most dammed river; en route to the Gulf it forms many lakes, including Lake Buchanan, which features bald eagles in winter, and the Highland chain of lakes of the Hill

Country—Lake LBJ, Inks Lake, and Lake Travis. Breathtakingly beautiful canoe trips can be taken between dams. The almost 300 miles from Town Lake in Austin to the Gulf provide great canoeing and fishing.

Cypress River—Headwaters in Marion County; scenic, especially on 35-mile stretch between Lake o' the Pines and Caddo Lake State Park.

Devil's River—Headwaters near Barnhart; upper riverbed, which runs through some of our finest whitetail hunting in Val Verde County, is dry most of the year except for occasional high water runoffs. Lower portions flow year-round and join the Rio Grande near Amistad Reservoir.

Frio River—Headwaters in Real County; beautiful, clear, spring-fed river running through limestone bluffs. Many white-water rapids make it a canoer's favorite.

Guadalupe River—Headwaters near Kerrville; forms Canyon Lake near San Marcos, eventually joins San Marcos River near the historic town of Gonzales, then flows to the Gulf; rainbow trout stocking below Canyon Dam makes this stretch a sportsman's choice, along with the Guadalupe bass. There are many put-in/take-out canoe adventures along this river. Landowners have been at war with boaters for some years because inconsiderate canoers have despoiled the area with beer cans and litter. Don't set foot on a bank unless you know it's public property. Trespass laws will be enforced. Horseshoe Falls below Canyon Dam is extremely dangerous and should not be run under any circumstances.

Lavaca River—Headwaters near Hallettsville; joins Navidad River then flows into Lavaca Bay near Point Comfort.

Llano River—Headwaters in mid-Edwards Plateau; North and South Forks join near Junction; scenic, spring-fed river between Mason and Llano, joins Colorado River at Lake LBJ; offers excellent flathead catfish and Guadalupe bass, especially in the Castell area.

Medina River—Headwaters near Medina; between Medina and Bandera Falls there is white water with lots of chutes. River is very dangerous at high water.

Middle/Concho Rivers—Headwaters near Rankin; forms Twin Buttes Reservoir and Lake Nasworthy. Flows into the North Concho River, which in turn joins the Colorado. The North Concho forms O. C. Fisher Lake.

Mission River—Headwaters near Kenedy; begins as Medio Creek, enters Gulf at Copano Bay.

Navidad River—Headwaters near Schulenburg; joins Lavaca River en route to Gulf.

Neches River—Headwaters near Tyler; after forming Lake Palestine it flows to the Gulf. Much Texas history centers on this scenic, primitive river; canoe trip starts at Fort Teran and runs to Lake Bouton.

Nueces River—Headwaters in Edwards Plateau; headwater forks join near Ulvalde; river then flows through Cotulla. Spring-fed with excellent water quality. South Texas deer hunters have been known to take a break from staring down *senderos* to seek Stone Age artifacts along the Nueces and other South Texas sites. The famous Painted Pebble—a clue to the existence of a material culture in prehistoric times—was found on the Nueces in Zavala County. Many artifacts are found. Most are byproducts of lithic tool production, including flakes and bifaces. The Nueces enters Lake Corpus Christi then goes on to the Bay and Gulf.

Palo Duro Creek—Headwaters near Hereford; forms spectacular Palo Duro Canyon then joins the famous Prairie Dog Fork of the Red River.

Pease River and North Pease River—Headwaters in High Plains; North Pease forms Lake Copper Breaks then enters Red River in Oklahoma.

Pecan Bayou—Headwaters near Abilene; flows into Lake Brownwood then joins the Colorado near Goldthwaite.

Pecos River—Headwaters in New Mexico; this river is famed in western folklore with the "law west of the Pecos" being established at Langtry. For many years, white-tailed deer were unknown west of the Pecos, but they crossed and chased mule deer farther west. Ranches just west of the Pecos have some fabulous whitetail hunting now. The river enters the Rio Grande above Lake Amistad. There is a great 60-mile canoe trip downriver from Red Bluff Reservoir through sheer rocky cliffs in a primitive environment with rapids to run and caves to explore. Best in late spring and autumn.

Pedernales River—Headwaters near Fredericksburg; clear, scenic river with white-water canoeing during high water. Like most Hill Country rivers, there can be great danger after heavy rains. After flowing through the LBJ Ranch it joins the Colorado on the upper end of Lake Travis.

Red River—Headwaters in Rolling Plains; forms boundary between Oklahoma and a section of Arkansas. High water after long rains can make this river very dangerous. The protected, prehistoric-looking paddlefish is found here. It's the Cyrano of fish; 50 percent of its length is its flat bill.

- **Salt Fork of the Red River**—forms Green Belt Dam Reservoir near Amarillo.

Rio Grande—Headwaters in eastern Rocky Mountains; flows through New Mexico entering Texas near El Paso. Forms two major reservoirs as it flows to the Gulf: Amistad and Falcon. Float trips through the Big Bend National Parks' canyons, especially Santa Elena, Mariscal, and Boquillas, and the lower canyons east of the park rank high on the list for adventurous sportsmen. November to early March is best. You will float through sheer canyon walls where you can immerse yourself in one of America's most primitive wildlife areas.

Rita Blanca Creek—Headwaters in northwest corner of Panhandle; flows into Lake Rita Blanca near Dalhart then joins the Canadian River near Boy's Ranch at Tascosa.

Sabine River—Headwaters in upper blacklands; forms Lake Tawakoni near Dallas, flows to Logansport, Louisiana, where it becomes part of the state boundary and forms Toledo Bend Reservoir. Scenic for all its 200 miles, especially lovely below Toledo Bend. The canoer will discover majestic cypress trees, white sand bars, and, above all, solitude.

San Antonio River—Headwaters in Edwards Plateau. Sportsmen reentering civilization after a late November whitetail hunt in the Hill Country appreciate this river. It winds right through San Antonio and is especially beautiful when lit for Christmas. The River Walk is lined with establishments which market balms for the camp-worn sportsman. Joins the Guadalupe for flow to the Gulf.

San Gabriel River—Headwaters in Edwards Plateau; forms lakes Georgetown and Granger, then joins Brazos for run to the Gulf.

San Jacinto River—Headwaters in Blacklands; West Fork forms Lake Conroe, merges into Lake Houston.

San Marcos River—Headwaters in famous springs at San Marcos; in upper reaches, a clear river, but flows through highly developed areas until it joins the Guadalupe near Gonzales.

San Saba River—Headwaters near Eldorado; site of many Indian battles since it was in the heart of Comancheria. It can be canoed from famous Fort McKavett to where it joins the Colorado.

Trinity River—Headwaters in Rolling Plains.
- **Trinity Clear Fork**—scenic, sometimes completely canopied by pecan, cottonwood, and sycamore trees.
- **Elm Fork of Trinity**—starts at Lake Lewisville.
- **East Fork of Trinity**—forms Lake Ray Hubbard. The three forks join near Ennis and, after forming Lake Livingston, flow to the Gulf as the Trinity.

White River—Headwaters from New Mexico border; meanders through Plainview to form White River Lake near Crosbyton.

Wichita River—Headwaters of forks in Rolling Plains; forms Lake Kemp.
- **South Wichita River**—Joins North Wichita River near Lake Kemp.
- **North Wichita River**—Headwaters near Paducah; forms Lake Kemp.

Yellowhouse River—Headwaters in High Plains; forms a small chain of lakes known as Canyon Creek Lakes; flows through Lubbock.

TEXAS

Pineywoods

The old San Antonio road from Natchitoches, Louisiana, to Nacogdoches, Texas, introduced many an early 1800s Texas settler to the Pineywoods and prairies beyond. One such traveler was young Stephen F. Austin, who crossed the Sabine River at Gaines Ferry on the morning of July 16, 1821. The Austins were some of the first Anglo-American *empresarios* to receive land grants from Mexico and permission to form a colony. When Stephen Austin's feet hit Texas soil, the population of what is now the state was just a few thousand.

The Pineywoods ecological area, roughly 15 to 16 million acres, is a broad region of pine hardwood forests extending into Louisiana, Arkansas, and Oklahoma. In Texas the elevation ranges from 50 to 500 feet. Temperatures and humidity are high, with annual rainfall averaging from 35 to more than 50 inches. Early settlers avoided what they termed "pine barrens" and either moved on west or settled near the rich, fertile hardwood bottomlands of the Pineywoods. They also shied away from what became known as the "Big Thicket." Although the Thicket's boundaries have shrunk, it's still a dense, semitropical jungle with huge palmettos and vines unexpectedly juxtaposed with semi-arid desert. Above all, it remains a mysterious place of folklore and legend. In the early 1800s, Thicket settlers were primarily misanthropes who didn't want anything to do with other people, or they were scofflaws who needed an even more inaccessible hideout after the United States acquired the Neutral

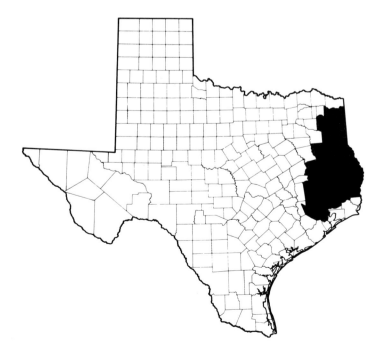

Ground on the Texas-Louisiana border from Spain in 1821.

Early Pineywoods settlers were primarily Anglo-Americans from the southern tier of states along with a fair number of Franco-American settlers from Louisiana. The Pineywoods teemed with game including passenger pigeons, eastern wild turkey, deer, buffalo, squirrels, waterfowl, and especially bears. When the early settlers began to run hogs, the bears' days were numbered. The bears retreated to the southern portion of what is now Hardin County, and the last reported bear kill was in 1928. Like UFO sightings, rumors and reports of Big Thicket bears are still heard, but, at best, these bears have slipped across from Louisiana. Today feral hogs abound in a bearless ecosystem.

The mysterious Big Thicket,
an ecological crossroads.

Now the Thicket is America's first national preserve, officially known as the Big Thicket National Biological Preserve. It is an ecotonal zone where different ecological areas collide; literally the biological epicenter of America where east meets west, north meets south. In stunning contrast, the megalopolis of Houston, with its futuristic glasswalled skyline, lies just a few miles southwest of the Thicket. For a few years Houston was capital of Texas, but in 1839 the capital was moved by Texas Republic president Mirabeau Lamar to its present site on the Colorado River.

The green-capped Pineywoods surround a myriad of lakes, from moss-draped Caddo to the timbered vastness of Toledo Bend. (Today the rich aquatic life of these lakes is threatened by acid rain, as is the lush woodlands foliage.) A good way to familiarize yourself with the area is to follow the blue and white road signs of the Texas Forest Trail, which mark a scenic loop through the Pineywoods. En route you'll find four national parks to visit and scores of outstanding state parks, such as the world-class park at Caddo Lake, which is spectacular in dogwood season.

Cypress trees and Spanish moss
adorn Caddo Lake in the Pineywoods.

Several timber companies permit public access hunting, and the Texas Parks and Wildlife Department (TPWD) oversees numerous state parks and Wildlife Management Areas (WMA). The major commercial timber species are loblolly, shortleaf, longleaf, and slash pines. The many hardwoods include oak, hickory, and maple. There's much to learn and enjoy in this area, the sportsman's focus being on freshwater fish, ducks, 'coons, and feral hogs.

Pineywoods Counties:
The following counties listed in the TPWD Hunting Guide are, for the most part, within the bounds of the Pineywoods ecological area. County lines may not follow precise vegetational or geological boundaries, but generally speaking, the sportsman will find similar hunting or fishing conditions in this ecological area.

Every Pineywoods county has a season on deer, squirrel, and quail unless an exception is noted.

PINEYWOODS COUNTIES

Angelina	Jasper	Rusk
Camp	Liberty	Upshur
Cass	Marion	Sabine
Cherokee	Montgomery	San Augustine
Gregg	Morris	San Jacinto
Hardin	Nacogdoches	Shelby
Harris	Newton	Trinity
Harrison	Panola	Tyler
Houston	Polk	Walker

PRINCIPAL LAKES OF THE PINEYWOODS *Where lakes are named for cities no specific location is given. Acreages are approximate and not all lakes are listed. Gamefish availability is variable. "Excellent" references are reserved for species which have been present in abundance for many years or have made the record books.*

Boykin Springs Lake—very small
–Angelina National Forest; stocked with rainbow trout in November.

Caddo Lake—32,000 acres
–Near Jefferson; black bass, white bass, bluegills, catfish, crappie, excellent chain pickerel.

Lake Conroe—15,500 acres
–black bass, channel catfish, excellent crappie, hybrid stripers, walleye.

Lake Gladewater—900 acres
–black bass, catfish.

Houston County Lake—
–Near Crockett; excellent black bass.

Lake Houston—12,000 acres
–black bass, bluegills, channel and flathead catfish, crappie, hybrid stripers.

Lake Jacksonville—1,300 acres
–black bass, excellent crappie, hybrid stripers.

Lake Livingston—90,000 acres
–black bass, striped bass, white bass, excellent catfish, crappie, hybrid stripers.

Martin Creek—5,200 acres
–Near Tatum; black bass, hybrid stripers, walleye, catfish.

Lake Murvaul—3,800 acres
–Near Carthage; excellent black bass, excellent bream, flathead catfish to 75 pounds, channel cats, crappie.

Lake Nacogdoches—2,200 acres
–black bass.

Lake O' the Pines—19,000 acres
–North of Longview; black bass, excellent bream, catfish, chain pickerel, crappie, hybrid stripers.

Lake Pinkston—800 acres
–black bass, bream, channel and flathead catfish, crappie.

Lake Raven—215 acres
–Huntsville State Park; family fishing; black bass, bream, catfish, crappie.

Lake Sam Rayburn—114,000 acres
–Largest impoundment entirely within state. Named for "Mr. Sam," former speaker of the U.S. House of Representatives.
–Near Nacogdoches and Lufkin; excellent black bass, spotted bass, striped bass, white bass, bream, excellent crappie, walleye.

Steinhagen Lake—14,000 acres
–Between Jasper and Woodville; black bass, excellent catfish, crappie.

Lake Striker—2,400 acres
–Near Henderson; black bass.

Toledo Bend—181,000 acres
–Largest impoundment in the South.
–Midway on Texas-Louisiana border. License reciprocity.
–excellent black bass, bream, catfish, excellent crappie, excellent hybrid stripers.

Lake Wright Patman—20,000 acres
–Near Texarkana; black bass, bream, channel cats, crappie.

PINEYWOODS STATE PARKS Make reservations if you plan an overnight stay. Ask for information from the listed town. Parks typically have a modest fee structure.

STATE PARK & LOCATION	CAMPING & RESTROOMS	FISHING	BOAT RAMP	MUSEUM EXHIBIT	HISTORIC STRUCTURE	NATURE TRAILS
Brazos Bend Needville	●	●				●
Caddo Lake Karnack	●	●	●			●
Daingerfield Daingerfield	●	●	●			●
Huntsville Huntsville	●	●	●	●		●
Martin Dies, Jr. Woodville	●	●	●			●

STATE PARK & LOCATION	CAMPING & RESTROOMS	FISHING	BOAT RAMP	MUSEUM EXHIBIT	HISTORIC STRUCTURE	NATURE TRAILS
Rusk/Palestine Rusk	●	●				
Sea Rim Sabine Pass	●	●	●	●		●
Tyler Tyler	●	●	●			●
STATE RECREATION AREAS						
Atlanta Queen City	●	●	●			●
Cassels/Boykin Jasper	●	●	●			
Lake Livingston Livingston	●	●	●			●
Martin Creek Park Tatum			●			
Sheldon Lake Houston	●	●				
STATE HISTORICAL PARKS & SITES						
Battleship Texas La Porte				●		
Caddoan Mounds Alto				●	●	
Mission Tejas Weches	●	●			●	
Sabine Pass Battleground Sabine			●			
San Jacinto Battleground Deer Park				●	●	
Starr Mansion Marshall				●	●	
Stephen F. Austin San Felipe	●	●		●	●	
Texas State Railroad Rusk				●		

STATE PARK & LOCATION	CAMPING & RESTROOMS	FISHING	BOAT RAMP	MUSEUM EXHIBIT	HISTORIC STRUCTURE	NATURE TRAILS
Washington-on-the-Brazos Washington				●	●	

NATIONAL FORESTS	COUNTY LOCATION	ACREAGE
Angelina	Angelina, Jasper, Nacogdoches, San Augustine	154,000
Davy Crockett	Houston, Trinity	162,000
Sabine	Jasper, Sabine, San Augustine, Shelby	184,000
Sam Houston	Montgomery, San Jacinto, Walker	158,000

STATE FORESTS	LOCATION	ACREAGE
Fairchild	Near Rusk	2,900
Jones	Near Conroe	1,700
Kirby	Near Woodville	600
Siecke	Near Kirbyville	1,700

STATE WILDLIFE MANAGEMENT AREAS	COUNTY LOCATION	ACREAGE
Special or regular permits or permission by registration requirements vary by season. Contact TPWD for current regulations: 1-800-792-1112.		
Alabama Creek	Trinity	14,500
(National Forest Area) Game typically hunted: Deer, archery and gun; feral hogs, archery; quail; squirrel; waterfowl; woodcock; gallinules; mourning doves; rabbits		
Dam B— Angelina Neches	Jasper, Tyler	13,500
Game typically hunted: Deer, archery and gun; feral hogs, archery and gun; quail; squirrel; waterfowl; woodcock; gallinules; mourning doves; rabbits		
Moore Plantation	Sabine	25,000
(National Forest Area) Game typically hunted: Deer, archery and gun; feral hogs, archery; quail; squirrel; gallinules; mourning doves; rabbits		
North Toledo Bend	Shelby	3,600
Game typically hunted: Deer, archery and gun; feral hogs, archery; quail; squirrel; gallinules; mourning doves; rabbits		

ECOLOGICAL AREA TWO

Gulf Prairies and Marshes

Goose hunters greet dawn on Gulf Prairie.

The first Old World explorer to set eyes on the Gulf Prairies and Marshes ecological area, was Amerigo Vespucci. The *Tabula Terre Nova* woodcut map, published in Strasbourg in 1513, clearly delineated the Gulf of Mexico he discovered. Several years after the publication of Amerigo's "Map of the New Earth," in 1519, Alonso Alvarez de Pineda mapped the entire Texas shoreline. After adding this territory to his map, Spain chalked up another claim to the vast New World and Alonso sailed on. The wildlife treasures of our Gulf Prairies and Marshes were left, for the time being, to the enjoyment of the Karankawa Indians.

The Gulf Prairies and Marshes encompass about 9.5 million acres from the Louisiana border to the northern end of Padre Island. The last 100 miles or so of the lower Gulf Coast are associated ecologically with the South Texas Plains, but insofar as the coastal features are concerned, they may be viewed in context of this ecological area.

The coastal prairie is a low-lying, 150-foot average elevation, slow-draining plain crossed by many rivers and streams flowing to the Gulf. The coast marsh is a narrow belt of low wetlands. The rainfall range is wide, from just 20 inches in the extreme west to 50 inches along the coast, with warm temperatures and high humidity. Large cattle ranches occupy much of the marsh area.

Pineda had discovered the mouth of the Mississippi River, but it took another 150 years or so for that mighty river to be explored and all of its immense basin claimed, not for Spain, but for France's Louis XIV by Rene Robert Cavelier, Sieur de la Salle. When the Spaniards discovered that La Salle had, in 1685, established a beachhead on the Texas coast, they set sail to restake their claim. But, because of confusion as to just which river was the Rio del Espiritu Santo, they didn't know exactly where to find La Salle. (We know today that La Salle's colony, named Fort St. Louis, was at Lavaca Bay.) After six expeditions by land and five by sea, the Spanish found the remains of the colony in 1689 and learned that La Salle had been murdered by his own men. Meanwhile, the search had much improved the maps of Texas' interior and coast, and even resulted in our state's name: "Texas" is said to be derived from an Indian's attempt to identify his tribe to the Spanish, using the word *tejas*, meaning friend or ally.

As soon as the Spanish assured themselves that La Salle was out of the picture, and after a half-hearted attempt to establish the first Spanish mission, Mission Tejas, they again left the Gulf Coast alone. Later Spanish

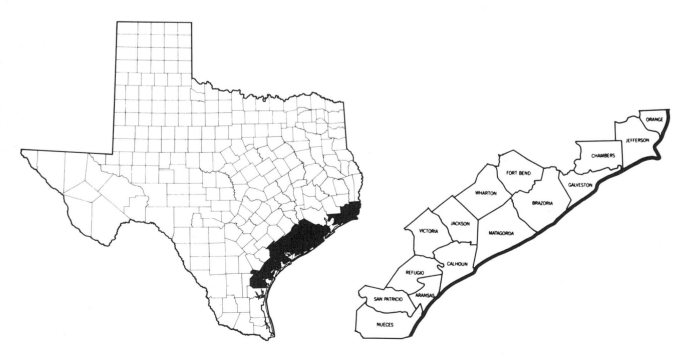

mission settlements came by land across the Rio del Norte, still leaving the coast clear for foreign intruders.

The Gulf Prairies and Marshes ecological area would later be the locale for many of the significant battles of the Texas War of Independence from Mexico, including the preludes at Anahuac and Velasco. The Irish, having established settlements at Refugio and Victoria—the crossroads of battle—suffered more loss of life than any other group. After the Alamo and Goliad, the war moved east, culminating in the Texas victory over Santa Anna at San Jacinto on April 21, 1836.

One of the first Texas-sized deals of the New Republic was to contract with the Mainz Society of Nobles in Germany to bring in settlers, who entered through the Gulf ports of Indianola near the site of La Salle's fort, Galveston, and Brazoria. The mosquito-plagued, low-lying coastal areas were regarded as unhealthy and, in fact, yellow fever and cholera were constant threats, so these immigrants moved inland as fast as they could to the Edwards Plateau ecological area. Since many of them came from truly beautiful homelands, our coast did appear desolate, and might still unless you can appreciate the harsher beauty of marshes and dunes.

Sportsmen revere this area for several reasons, including ducks, geese, spotted seatrout, and redfish. Nowhere in America is there such a concentration of shore birds, such huge populations of geese, so many varieties and numbers of ducks, and so many seatrout and redfish. More Texas coastal barrens are federally protected than those of any other state. The federal Coastal Barrier Resources System, established in 1982, protects the fragile, ecologically sensitive environment and prevents federal monies from being spent on areas at high risk of hurricanes and erosion.

Although the entire coast is exciting, including Matagorda Bay and Island, named aptly by the Spanish for the thick brush, there are very special places that all sportsmen should explore and enjoy. One is the Aransas National Wildlife Refuge, established in 1937, a 55,000 acre peninsula that is home for the famed whooping cranes as well as wild turkey, alligators, deer, javelina, coyotes, bobcats, feral hogs, and even cougar. It even has its pirate legend, as does Padre Island to the south. Historical references place Jean Lafitte here on a treasure-burying mission when he disbanded his crew. The other irreplaceable natural treasure is Padre Island National Seashore, the longest barrier island in our country. And the Anahuac National Wildlife Refuge, site of the San Jacinto battleground, is the winter home for hundreds of thousands of wild fowl. A great way to explore the area is to follow the blue and white Texas Independence Trail signs.

A channel cuts through coastal marsh in bloom.

GULF PRAIRIES & MARSHES COUNTIES

Aransas	Galveston	Orange
Brazoria	Jackson	Refugio
Calhoun	Jefferson	San Patricio
Chambers	Matagorda	Victoria
Fort Bend	Nueces	Wharton

PRINCIPAL LAKES OF THE GULF PRAIRIES AND MARSHES *Where lakes are named for cities or counties no further location information is given. Acreages are approximate and not all lakes are listed. Gamefish availability is variable. "Excellent" references are reserved for* species which have been present in abundance for many years or have made the record books.

Lake Corpus Christi—19,000 acres
–black bass, catfish, excellent alligator gar.
Lake Texana—11,000 acres
–Near Edna; black bass, catfish, walleye.

GULF PRAIRIES AND MARSHES PARKS Make reservations if you plan an overnight stay. Ask for information from the listed town. Parks typically have a modest fee structure.

STATE PARK & LOCATION	CAMPING & RESTROOMS	FISHING	BOAT RAMP	MUSEUM EXHIBIT	HISTORIC STRUCTURE	NATURE TRAILS
Galveston Island Galveston	●	●				●
Matagorda Island Port O'Connor	●	●			●	
Mustang Island Port Aransas	●	●				●
STATE RECREATION AREAS						
Bryan Beach Galveston	●	●				
Goose Island Rockport	●	●	●			●
Lake Texana Edna	●	●	●			
STATE HISTORICAL PARKS & SITES						
Fulton Mansion Fulton				●	●	
STATE FISH PIER						
Copano Bay Fulton		●				
Port Lavaca Port Lavaca		●	●			

STATE WILDLIFE MANAGEMENT AREAS	LOCATION	ACREAGE
Special or regular permits or permission by registration requirements vary by season. Contact TPWD for current regulations: 1-800-792-1112.		
Matagorda Island (Access by boat only)	Matagorda (Port O'Conner)	39,000
Game typically hunted: Deer, gun; quail; waterfowl; gallinules; mourning doves		
Murphree	Near Port Arthur	12,600
Game typically hunted: Waterfowl; rails; alligator		
Peach Point	Brazoria	8,600
Game typically hunted: Waterfowl; rails; gallinules		

ECOLOGICAL AREA THREE

Post Oak Savannah

Although we'll follow Stephen F. Austin across the Trinity River, he wasn't the first Anglo-American to discover the fertility of the Post Oak Savannah. Many GTT settlers were already in place. (The Yankee "Gone to Texas" label was applied to those who had emigrated to avoid debts or other troubles.) About 200 settlers in Red River Country in northeast Texas would eventually trek south to join Austin's "Old Three Hundred" in 1821. Land was offered in advertisements for 12½ cents an acre.

The Post Oak Savannah is approximately 8.5 million acres. Most classify the area as part of the true prairie. Frederick Law Olmstead, traveling through Texas on as-

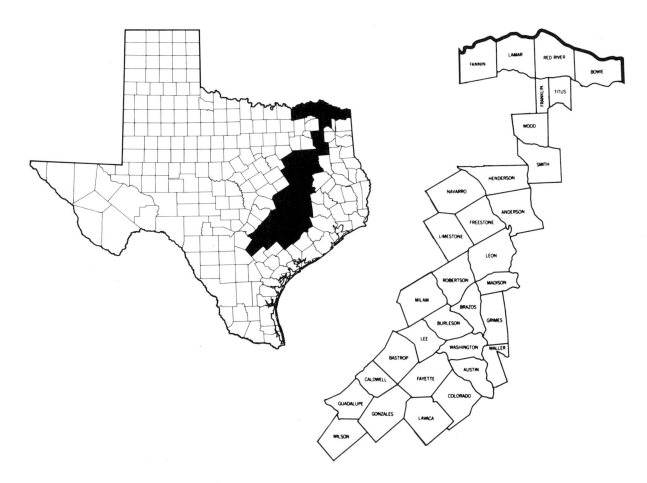

Open savannahs beckoned early settlers
as they emerged from the Pineywoods.

signment for the *New York Daily Times,* wrote in his journal on January 2, 1855, "After having been shut in during so many days by dreary winter forests [the Pineywoods], we were quite exhilarated at coming out upon an open country and a distant view . . . small prairies alternated agreeably with post oak woods." His journal was published in 1857 under the title *A Journey Through Texas.* Olmstead described his first camp across the Trinity: "For safety against our dirty persecutors, the hogs, we pitched our tent within a large hog yard, putting up the bars to exclude them." Later in the trip Olmstead reported killing several quail, "which are quite common," and seeing eastern wild turkey, deer, and geese.

Our research indicates that today this ecological area has a great many more trees than it had even in 1900, especially mesquite. Elevation ranges from 300 to 800 feet, and annual rainfall is 35 to 45 inches, with the rainy season in May and June. Today, most of the area is still in native or improved pasture, but you'll see the occasional farm.

The Trinity River was named by one of La Salle's manhunters, Alfonso de Leon, while he closed in on Fort St. Louis in 1690. Leon named it *El Rio de la Santisima Trinidad,* River of the Most Holy Trinity. It was a beautiful river then. Today, it remains the most polluted natural river in Texas, thanks primarily to the effluent of Dallas and Fort Worth, although as it runs through the Post Oak Savannah it is a focal point for much 'coon, squirrel, and deer hunting.

The meadow lands of the Post Oak Savannah, starting west of the Trinity and extending beyond the Brazos to the Colorado River, produced bumper crops of native American corn and garden produce. The area was ideally suited to settlement by Anglo-American emigrants from Missouri, Georgia, Alabama, Mississippi, Tennessee, and Kentucky because they knew how to grow the crops this

Trees have invaded the native
prairies of the Post Oak Savannah.

land could sustain and they knew how to settle a frontier. As it had elsewhere in southern America, cotton soon became king. From the original 1821 camp of 300 families, Austin's colony at Washington-on-the-Brazos expanded to about 9,000 by the '30s, and bales of cotton were flowing down river to Brazoria and Harrisburg. Today you'll see mainly cattle in the Post Oak Savannah, because cotton drained the land's fertility.

The planters who were established in the 1820s and '30s had come to own much of the finest land in Texas, wield great power, and exert a major influence on Texas customs. Despite the 1837 warning from Republic of Texas President Sam Houston, they continued in slave trading. By 1861 there were about 200,000 slaves in Texas. But in less than 50 years the source of power was emancipated—most read the "freedom papers" to their slaves on June 19, 1865. Many Texans celebrate "Juneteenth" to this day.

For a scenic overview of the ecological area, follow the blue and white Brazos Trail road signs. It's a beautiful drive. The impoundments that dot the area provide some of the finest freshwater bass fishing to be found anywhere.

POST OAK SAVANNAH COUNTIES

Anderson	Freestone	Milam
Austin	Gonzales	Navarro
Bastrop	Grimes	Red River
Bowie	Guadalupe	Robertson
Brazos	Henderson	Smith
Burleson	Lamar	Titus
Caldwell	Lavaca	Waller
Colorado	Lee	Washington
Fannin	Leon	Wilson
Fayette	Limestone	Wood
Franklin	Madison	

PRINCIPAL LAKES OF THE POST OAK SAVANNAH

Where lakes are named for cities or counties, no further location information is given. Acreages are approximate and not all lakes are listed. Gamefish availability is variable. "Excellent" references are reserved for species which have been present in abundance for many years or have made the record books.

Lake Athens—1,500 acres
–excellent black bass, excellent redear sunfish, walleye.

Lake Bastrop—900 acres
–black bass, bream, catfish, crappie.

Bob Sandlin Reservoir—10,000 acres
–Near Mt. Pleasant; backs up to Lake Cypress Springs and Lake Monticello; black bass, channel catfish.

Cedar Creek Lake—38,000 acres
–Near Kemp; black bass, excellent striped bass, catfish, excellent crappie, hyprid stripers, walleye.

Lake Crook—1,200 acres
–Near Paris; catfish.

Lake Cypress Springs—4,200 acres
–Near Mount Vernon; black bass, catfish, walleye.

Lake Fairfield—2,500 acres
–excellent black bass, bream, channel catfish, hybrid stripers.

Lake Fayette—2,400 acres
–black bass, blue and channel catfish, crappie, sunfish.

Lake Fork—27,690 acres
–Near Quitman; excellent black bass, channel catfish, crappie; may produce next world record bass.

Lake Limestone—14,200 acres
–excellent black bass, white bass, catfish, crappie.

Lake Mexia—1,200 acres
–black bass, excellent white bass, bream, excellent channel and flathead catfish, crappie.

Navarro Mills—5,000 acres
–Near Corsicana; excellent striped bass.

Lake Palestine—25,500 acres
–black bass, catfish, excellent crappie, redear sunfish, hybrid stripers.

Pat Mayse Lake—7,700 acres
–Near Paris; excellent black bass, striped bass, excellent crappie, hybrid stripers.

Lake Tyler—5,000 acres
–excellent black bass, excellent catfish, hybrid stripers.

POST OAK SAVANNAH PARKS Make reservations if you plan an overnight stay. Ask for information from the listed town. Parks typically have a modest fee structure.

STATE PARK & LOCATION	CAMPING & RESTROOMS	FISHING	BOAT RAMP	MUSEUM EXHIBIT	HISTORIC STRUCTURE	NATURE TRAILS
Bastrop Bastrop	●	●				●
Buescher Smithville	●	●				

STATE PARK & LOCATION	CAMPING & RESTROOMS	FISHING	BOAT RAMP	MUSEUM EXHIBIT	HISTORIC STRUCTURE	NATURE TRAILS
Dinosaur Valley Glen Rose	●	●		●		●
Palmetto Luling	●	●				●
STATE RECREATION AREAS						
Bonham Bonham	●	●	●			
Fairfield Lake Fairfield	●	●	●			●
Fort Parker Mexia	●	●	●			●
Lake Somerville Somerville	●	● (Deer hunting allowed by permit)	●			●
STATE HISTORICAL PARKS & SITES						
Confederate Reunion Grounds Mexia		●				●
Governor Hogg Shrine Quitman				●	●	
Stephen F. Austin San Felipe	●	●		●	●	●
Washington-on-the-Brazos Washington				●	●	
STATE HISTORIC STRUCTURES						
Monument Hill/ Kreische Brewery La Grange				●	●	●
Old Fort Parker Groesbeck				●	●	
Sam Bell Maxey House Paris				●	●	

STATE WILDLIFE MANAGEMENT AREAS	COUNTY LOCATION	ACREAGE
Special or regular permits or permission by registration requirements vary by season. Contact TPWD for current regulations: 1-800-792-1112.		
Caddo	Fannin	16,100
(National Forest Area—several tracts) Game typically hunted: Deer, by archery and gun; feral hogs, by archery; quail; squirrel; waterfowl; woodcock; gallinules; mourning doves; rabbit; coyotes; furbearers		
Engeling	Anderson	11,000
Game typically hunted: Deer, by archery and gun; feral hogs, by gun; turkey; squirrel; woodcock; gallinules		
Keechi Creek	Leon	1,500
Game typically hunted: Deer, by archery and gun; squirrel; waterfowl; woodcock; gallinules		
Pat Mayse	Lamar	9,000
Game typically hunted: Deer, by archery and gun; feral hog, by archery; quail; squirrel; waterfowl; woodcock; gallinules; mourning doves; rabbits; coyotes; furbearers		

ECOLOGICAL AREA FOUR

Blackland

Prairies

The Reverend Z. N. Morrell had planned a bear hunt at the falls of the Brazos with his Tennessee friend David Crockett and John Marlin in 1835. Davy didn't show up, but Morrell and Marlin found bear, mustang, deer, and buffalo abundant, and Morrell noted in his memoirs, "Our expectations as to the great value of the lands were fully realized. The country was all we could desire—lands very rich, range extraordinarily good, wood and water aplenty and the prospects for health very flattering." When the white settlers first arrived at the Falls of the Brazos they were astride the 97th meridian. TPWD wildlife experts say that everything west of this line was then home to the pronghorn antelope.

There are approximately 11.5 million acres in the

Blackland Prairies, including the San Antonio and Fayette Prairies. Elevations roll gently from 300 to 800 feet above sea level. The annual rainfall is 30 inches in the west to about 40 inches in the east, May being the wettest

Native prairie grasses grew scarce after farmers discovered the richness of Blackland Prairie soil. The native grasses shown here were preserved by the Texas Nature Conservancy in Clymer's Meadow north of Dallas.

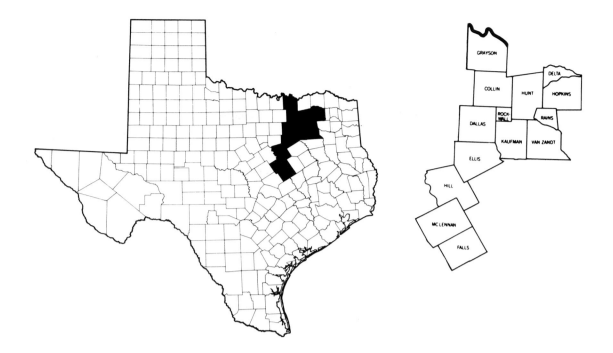

month. This area has been brought under intense cultivation, even to the extent of eliminating most fencerow habitat. The native vegetation was true prairie grass. Improved pastures have been established, seeded with grasses such as Dallis and common and coastal bermuda, as well as native grasses.

The Blackland Prairies run from San Antonio all the way to the Red River and are interspersed throughout the Post Oak Savannah. This fertile sea of grass astonished and pleased early settlers, many of whom were from worn-out Old South cotton plantations. They knew this land could grow cotton, with enough slaves, and when Texas joined the Confederacy on March 5, 1861, those dependent upon slave labor were especially ardent supporters. Despite the departure of over 60,000 who marched east to war, cotton production continued and bales were smuggled out through Galveston and across the Rio Grande to help fund the Confederacy.

The increased frequency of Comanche raids on settlements already weakened by the loss of fighting men made subsistence more urgent than farming. People had to eat. Hunting and fishing was of utmost importance. Buffalo and bear fat, hides, and meats were much needed, as were the meat and hides of deer. The river bottoms teemed with feral hogs. Quail, geese, ducks, opossums, rabbits, and squirrels rounded out the diet. The percussion rifle was popular until breechloading guns were introduced in the early 1860s.

The hunting pressure increased immensely after the Civil War; there were many more hungry people. It was time for the cowboy to ride through the Blacklands up to the Chisholm Trail to Abilene and place his indelible stamp on American culture. Cattle to feed Yankee cities was the answer to what ailed Texas in the late 1860s.

The bear and buffalo are long gone, like most of the other Blackland game, because almost all suitable wildlife habitat was lost to cultivation. The 1850s attitude that "game is ever in season" persisted until all the passenger pigeons were extirpated from the Blackland Prairies, Post Oak Savannah, and Pineywoods in the early 1900s, while market and millinery hunters came very close to leaving us a gameless ecosystem.

Texans continued to hunt and hunted hard despite the obvious decline in wildlife. Effective laws took until the 20th century, with passage of "The 1903 Act to Preserve and Protect the Wild Game, Wild Birds and Wild Fowl of the State."

Of the native grasses in the Blackland Prairies, over which Stone Age hunters pursued pronghorn antelope, less than 2,000 acres exist now, according to research by TPWD's Texas Natural Heritage Program. Without intervention this smidgen of prairie won't make it to 2000 A.D., its genetic wealth lost forever. Native grasses are the font for creation of new hybrid grasses on which the world may well depend. The Texas Nature Conservancy has acted to preserve Clymer's Meadow in Hunt County, the largest parcel of native grasslands left in the Blacklands.

Follow the blue and white signs of the Texas Lakes Trail and discover the true resources of this area, especially in great impoundments such as gigantic Lake Texoma and a host of other productive lakes. The Dallas metroplex has had such impact on the area that today, with the notable exception of great fishing and some dove, quail, and duck hunting, the Blacklands are mainly a drive-through to more game-abundant ecological areas.

BLACKLAND PRAIRIES COUNTIES

Collin	Grayson	McLennan
Dallas	Hill	Rains
Delta	Hopkins	Rockwall
Ellis	Hunt	Van Zandt
Falls	Kaufman	

PRINCIPAL LAKES OF THE BLACKLAND PRAIRIES *Where lakes are named for cities or counties, no further location information is given. All acreages are approximate. Gamefish availability is variable. "Excellent" references are reserved for species which have been in abundance for many years or made the record books.*

Lake Bardwell—3,500 acres
–Near Ennis; black bass, white bass, striped bass.
Lake Lavon—21,400 acres
–Near Dallas; black bass.
Lake Ray Hubbard—20,000 acres
–Near Dallas; black bass, excellent white bass, striped bass.

Lake Tawakoni—36,700 acres
–Between Wills Point and Greenville; excellent black bass, white bass, catfish, hybrid stripers.
Lake Texoma—89,000 acres
–On Texas-Oklahoma border north of Dallas; requires special Lake Texoma fishing license; black bass, excellent striped bass, excellent blue catfish, crappie.
Lake Waco—7,300 acres
–excellent crappie.

BLACKLAND PRAIRIES PARKS Make reservations if you plan an overnight stay. Ask for information from the listed town. Parks typically have a modest fee structure.

STATE PARK & LOCATION	CAMPING & RESTROOMS	FISHING	BOAT RAMP	MUSEUM EXHIBIT	HISTORIC STRUCTURE	NATURE TRAILS
Cleburne Cleburne	●		●			●
Eisenhower Denison	●	●	●			●
Lake Lewisville Frisco	●		●			
STATE HISTORIC STRUCTURES						
Eisenhower Home Denison				●	●	

STATE WILDLIFE MANAGEMENT AREAS	COUNTY LOCATION	ACREAGE
Special or regular permits or permission by registration requirements vary by season. Contact TPWD for current regulations: 1-800-792-1112.		
Granger	Williamson	11,100
Game typically hunted: Quail; squirrel; waterfowl; woodcock; gallinules; mourning doves; rabbits		

Cross Timbers and Prairies

It took the Spanish in the early 1600s to ignite the latent power of the Comanche. Stolen Spanish horses made the plains in Texas the Comanches' empire. Known as the "horse people," their equestrian culture was to control the plains for two centuries. But, unlike the Spanish, who were stalled in their conquest of the Southwest by the Comanche, the Indians found a more formidable foe in the Anglo-Americans. These settlers weren't going home to Spain; they *were* home.

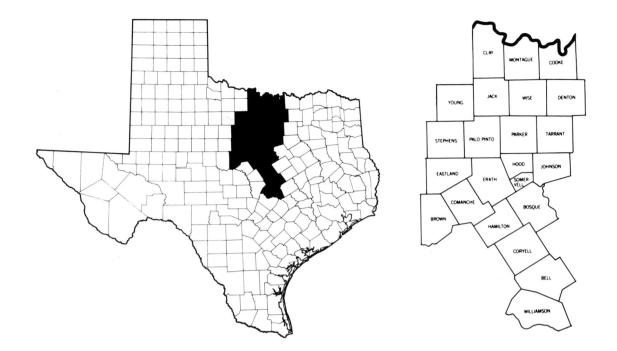

The settlers had found a beautiful land crisscrossed by the Brazos, covered with oaks and other timber woods, plenty of water, fertile soil for their corn, and deer and turkey everywhere. They weren't going to leave, and they were joined weekly by other tough Anglo-Americans. The Comanche Trail ran right through the Cross Timbers, and the many creeks that feed the Brazos have their ghosts of horribly slaughtered settlers and Indians.

The Cross Timbers and Prairies ecological area has about 17 million acres of rolling, hilly terrain, deeply cut with creeks and rivers, principally the Brazos. The average rainfall is 25 to 40 inches with April, May, and June the wettest months. This is primarily ranching country, although the better soil areas are cultivated. The area ranges from open savannah to dense brush, largely of post and blackjack oak.

Charlie Goodnight started his famous Goodnight-Loving cattle trail from Fort Belknap with his partner Oliver Loving. It followed the abandoned route of the Butterfield Overland Mail Stage to New Mexico, fording the Pecos at the Horse Head Crossing. The chuck box, derived from Goodnight's major invention, the chuck wagon, still serves as inspiration to expert camp cooks.

The area's largest city is, of course, Fort Worth, first settled by Ed Terrell in 1843. Camp Worth, built there in 1847 and named for Mexican War hero General William J. Worth, was later upgraded to Fort Worth. Fort Worth was just off the mainline Chisholm Trail and became a focal point for cowboys and cattle shipping.

Blue and white highway signs lead the interested sportsman through the Texas Fort Trail, which meanders through portions of the Rolling Plains and Edwards Plateau from its origin in the Cross Timbers. The post-Civil War Army forts ran from Fort Belknap on the Salt Fork of the Brazos west to Phantom Hill, down to Chadbourne on the Colorado River, south to McKenzie on the San Saba

River to Fort Terrell on the Llano River, Fort Mason, and finally Fort Clark.

Sportsmen will enjoy this area. It offers fantastic dove hunting, the finest turkey hunting in the world, and excellent duck hunting. Yankees have even discovered the turkeys of Brownwood and pay dearly for the privilege of participating in a spring gobbler adventure. Deer hunting is difficult because of limited visibility, but deer with huge body weights are regularly taken from the Cross Timbers. The Brazos offers great float fishing for bass and, during the winter, rainbow trout released by the TPWD as a bonus. Possum Kingdom Lake is one of the state's clearest and most scenic.

CROSS TIMBERS AND PRAIRIES COUNTIES

Bell	Eastland	Parker
Bosque	Erath	Somervell
Brown	Hamilton	Stephens
Clay	Hood	Tarrant
Comanche	Jack	Williamson
Cooke	Johnson	Wise
Coryell	Montague	Young
Denton	Palo Pinto	

PRINCIPAL LAKES OF THE CROSS TIMBERS AND PRAIRIES *Where lakes are named for cities or counties, no further location information is given. All acreages are approximate. Gamefish availability is variable. "Excellent" references are reserved for species which are in abundance or have made the record books.*

Lake Arlington—2,000 acres
–black bass, white bass, crappie.

Lake Arrowhead—13,500 acres
–Near Wichita Falls; black bass, excellent drum (gaspergou).

Hardwoods, lush prairies, and plentiful water mark the Cross Timbers.

Lake Belton—12,300 acres
–black bass, white bass, catfish, crappie, hybrid stripers.
Benbrook Lake—4,000 acres
–black bass, bream, catfish, crappie.
Lake Bridgeport—13,000 acres
–black bass, white bass, excellent blue, channel and flat-
  head catfish, excellent crappie, walleye.
Lake Brownwood—7,500 acres
–black bass, crappie, walleye.
Eagle Mountain Lake—8,500 acres
–Near Fort Worth; white bass, channel catfish, drum
Lake Georgetown—1,300 acres
–smallmouth bass, catfish, crappie.
Lake Graham—2,600 acres
–black bass.
Lake Granbury—9,000 acres
–excellent striped bass.
Granger Lake—4,400 acres
–black bass, channel catfish, crappie.
Lake Grapevine—7,330 acres
–Near Dallas; black bass, crappie.
Hubbard Creek Lake—15,000 acres
–Near Breckenridge; black bass.

Lake Lewisville—23,280 acres
–(Formerly known as Lake Dallas, then Garza Little Elm.)
–black bass, catfish.
Lake Monticello—2,000 acres
–excellent black bass, channel catfish, crappie.
Lake Palo Pinto—2,600 acres
–Near Mineral Wells; black bass.
Lake Pat Cleburne—1,600 acres
–black bass.
Possum Kingdom Lake—20,000 acres
–Near Graham; black bass, white bass, catfish, striped
  bass.
Proctor Lake—4,600 acres
–Near Comanche; black bass.
Lake Weatherford—1,200 acres
–black bass.
Lake Whitney—23,600 acres
–black bass, white bass, excellent striped bass (first spawn
  in Texas), bream, catfish, crappie.
Lake Worth—3,000 acres
–In Fort Worth; black bass, channel catfish, crappie.

CROSS TIMBERS AND PRAIRIES PARKS Make reservations if you plan an overnight stay. Ask for information from the listed town. Parks typically have a modest
fee structure.

STATE PARK & LOCATION	CAMPING & RESTROOMS	FISHING	BOAT RAMP	MUSEUM EXHIBIT	HISTORIC STRUCTURE	NATURE TRAILS
Lake Mineral Wells Mineral Wells	●	●	●			●
Mother Neff Moody	●					●
STATE RECREATION AREAS						
Lake Whitney Whitney	●		●			●
Meridian Meridian	●		●			●
Possum Kingdom Caddo	●	●	●			
STATE HISTORICAL PARKS & SITES						
Fort Richardson Jacksboro	●			●	●	●
Fort Parker Mexia		●				
STATE HISTORIC STRUCTURES						
Acton Acton					●	

South Texas Plains

"Mustang or Wild Horse Desert" was mapmaker Thomas Bradford's 1835 label for the blank space between the Nueces River and "Rio del Norte, also called Rio Bravo and Rio Grande." The void between the river borders made only vague reference to interior "salt lakes." Bradford had good data. By 1835 both mustangs and longhorns in unbelievable numbers were swarming in the Wild Horse Desert. Some estimates of the longhorn herds ranged from three million on both sides of the Rio to one million between the rivers.

Like the mustangs, cattle came with the Spaniards. These exotic imports thrived admirably *sin vaquero*. Records of early Spanish missions confirm the seed stock for the Texas longhorn herds. These European cattle, their progeny, and other imports found bovine utopia, with all they could eat and no enemies.

In the wild, longhorns were among the world's most challenging game animals, rivaling the famous Cape buffalo. Wild longhorns were touted in Richard Irving Dodge's *The Hunting Grounds of the Great West*, written from 1850s notes. "I should be doing injustice," said Dodge, "did I fail to mention as game the wild cattle of Texas. A footman is never safe when a herd is in his vicinity and every sportsman who has hunted quail in Texas will

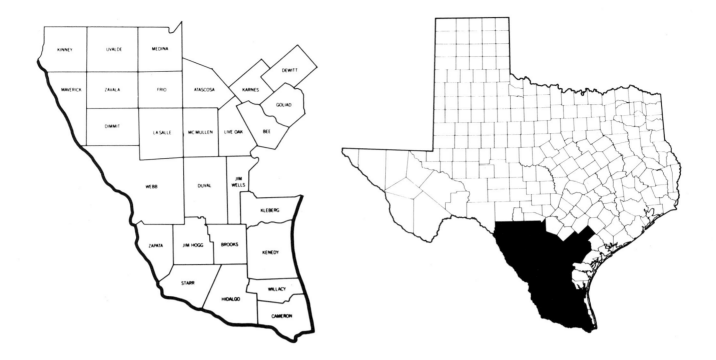

have experienced the uneasiness natural to any man around whom a crowd of longhorned beasts are pawing the earth tossing their heads in anger at his appearance." Wild cattle hunting was a lot more sport than coop-shooting buffalo.

There are about 20 million acres in the South Texas Plains ecological area. The topography is generally flat with some roll. Elevations range from sea level to 1,000 feet. Annual precipitation varies widely from 16 inches in the west to 35 on the coast. Cotulla, in the heart of *muy grande* whitetail country, recorded a blistering 2.82 inches of rain in 1917. The area was originally a savannah-type grassland, but many species of trees and shrubs, including mesquite, post, and live oak, have in-

Prickly pear cactus and mesquite
characterize the South Texas Plains.

creased. It's not for nothing that it's called Brush Country. It's almost impossible to see game unless you cut a swath through the brush, a *sendero*.

Texas was annexed to the Union in December, 1845. Five months later a skirmish at Brownsville precipitated the Mexican War.

"Old Rough and Ready" General Zachary Taylor was ready, having landed an army at the mouth of the Nueces near Corpus Christi in April, 1846. Taylor pushed south, winning two engagements and crossing the Rio Grande to occupy Matamoros. The South Texas Plains became known as the Desert of the Dead. General Winfield Scott replaced Taylor and led his 10,000 troops to triumph at the Halls of Montezuma. After the U.S. victory, the Treaty of Guadalupe Hidalgo, February 2, 1848, finally established the Rio Grande as the countries' border.

Richard King had arrived in 1847 at *El Paso de los Brazos de Santiago* to begin army riverboat duty with his friend Mifflin Kenedy. King and Kenedy went into business together, operating the paddlewheel steamers *Grampus* and *Comanche*, and the boats of M. Kenedy & Co. became major carriers for the lower Rio Grande valley. The Rio Grande was navigable then for some 250 miles. Today, you can barely navigate a canoe under the International Bridge at Matamoros.

In the fall of 1851, King set up a cow camp at a creek called Santa Gertrudis. His first ranch property, *Rincon de Santa Gertrudis*, measured three and a half Spanish leagues. At his death in 1885 appraisers counted 614,140 acres. Today, the King Ranch produces 25,000 beef calves a year—most the world famous Santa Gertrudis breed— and is comprised of 825,000 acres in four huge South Texas divisions. This adds up to 1,300 square miles, larger than the state of Rhode Island. Many sportsmen have hunting leases within the ranch. Some of the finest are found in the Encino division south of Falfurrias. The wildlife resources are fabulous, especially trophy whitetail, feral hogs, turkey, and quail. In effect, the ranch is also a preserve for nongame wildlife, and, in addition to lease fees, leasees are required to pay for the services of a full-time wildlife specialist to ensure good game management.

El Desierto de los Muertos, The Desert of the Dead, which occupied most of the South Texas Plains, was to again live up to its bloody name. The disbanding of the Texas Rangers after the Civil War allowed *banditos* free rein, and they would strike as far north as the San Antonio River, with much loss of life on both sides. The King Ranch alone reported losses of 30,000 head of cattle to these cattle rustlers.

The Texas Rangers were resurrected in 1874 and soon brought the border under control. Cattle then flowed up the trails to Kansas by the millions. The King Ranch alone reported driving more than 100,000 head up the Chisholm Trail between 1869 and 1884.

By 1877 the South Texas Plains had become peaceful,

Most of the South Texas Plains are known as The Brush Country to Texas hunters.

but still a challenge to man and beast. It remains so today. Larry McMurtry, in the opening lines of *Lonesome Dove*, captured the Brush Country essence: "The sun had the town trapped deep in dust; far out in the chapparal flats, a heaven for snakes and horned toads, roadrunners and stinging lizards, but a hell for pigs and Tennesseans."

Falcon Lake in Zapata County is a fishing hot spot, and for years Valley whitewing hunting has been an annual tradition with sportsmen. Most of the huge concentrations of doves have now been attracted south of the border, but the TPWD Commission is committed to a habitat establishment program to bring them back to Texas. The blue and white signs of the Texas Tropical Trail loop the newcomer through key areas.

Hunting leases in this area are *primo*, both in quality and cost, but by all measurements they're worth it when you've made contact with a first-class outfit.

SOUTH TEXAS PLAINS COUNTIES

Atascosa	Hidalgo	Maverick
Bee	Jim Hogg	McMullen
Brooks	Jim Wells	Medina
Cameron	Karnes	Starr
De Witt	Kenedy	Uvalde
Dimmit	Kinney	Webb
Duval	Kleberg	Willacy
Frio	La Salle	Zapata
Goliad	Live Oak	Zavala

PRINCIPAL LAKES OF THE SOUTH TEXAS PLAINS
Where lakes are named for cities or counties, no further location information is given. Acreages are approximate

and not all lakes are listed. Gamefish availability is variable. "Excellent" references are reserved for species which have been present in abundance for many years or have made the record book.

Lake Casa Blanca—1,700 acres
–Near Laredo; black bass, blue, channel, and flathead catfish.

Choke Canyon Reservoir—26,000 acres
–Between San Antonio and Corpus Christi on Frio River; black bass, white bass.

Coleto Creek Reservoir—3,100 acres
–Between Victoria and Goliad; black bass, catfish, crappie.

Delta Lake—2,000 acres
–Near Edinburg; black bass, catfish, crappie.

Falcon Lake—100,000 acres
–On Texas-Mexico border, Zapata County. Historic towns of Zapata and Guerrero were inundated by this lake. Mexican license required for fishing right bank of Rio Grande.
–Excellent black bass, striped bass, white bass, channel and flathead catfish, crappie.

Lake Medina—5,600 acres
–Near Bandera; black bass, catfish, crappie. (Lake tends to go dry, but once held excellent black bass.)

SOUTH TEXAS PLAINS PARKS Make reservations if you plan an overnight stay. Ask for information from the listed town. Parks typically have a modest fee structure.

STATE PARK & LOCATION	CAMPING & RESTROOMS	FISHING	BOAT RAMP	MUSEUM EXHIBIT	HISTORIC STRUCTURE	NATURE TRAILS
Bentsen-Rio Grande Mission	●	●	●			●
Choke Canyon Three Rivers	●	●	●			
Resaca de la Palma Cameron County	(White-winged dove hunting by permit.)					
STATE RECREATION AREAS						
Falcon Falcon Heights	●	●	●			
STATE HISTORICAL PARKS & SITES						
Goliad Goliad	●	●		●	●	●
Port Isabel Lighthouse Port Isabel					●	
STATE HISTORIC STRUCTURES						
Fannin Battleground Fannin					●	

STATE PARK & LOCATION	CAMPING & RESTROOMS	FISHING	BOAT RAMP	MUSEUM EXHIBIT	HISTORIC STRUCTURE	NATURE TRAILS
FISHING PIER						
Queen Isabella Port Isabel		●				

STATE WILDLIFE MANAGEMENT AREAS	COUNTY LOCATION	ACREAGE
Special or regular permits or permission by registration requirements vary by season. Contact TPWD for current regulations: 1-800-792-1112.		
Chaparral	Dimmit, La Salle	15,200
Game typically hunted: Deer, by gun; javelina, by gun: quail; mourning dove; coyotes		
Daughtrey	Live Oak, McMullen	25,000
Game typically hunted: Deer, by archery and gun; feral hogs, by archery; javelina, by gun; turkey; quail; waterfowl; sandhill crane; mourning dove; coyote		
Las Palomas	Valley	3,500
(Used for white-winged dove nesting habitat) Game typically hunted: Mourning dove; white-winged dove; chachalaca	(14 tracts in Willacy, Cameron, Hidalgo, Starr)	

ECOLOGICAL AREA SEVEN

Edwards Plateau

In 1831 Frederick Ernst, one of Texas' original German immigrants, established a farm at Mill Creek in northwestern Austin County and sent word back to his family at Oldenburg describing his farm and the land in "milk and honey" terms. Ernst had provided the impetus for the German immigration to Central Texas and the eventual settlement of the Edwards Plateau ecological area. Today, thousands of Texas sportsmen lease hunting rights from descendants of the early German settlers, and a knowledge of their heritage and history is essential to the quality of the landowner/hunter relationship.

The Edwards Plateau, named for *empresario* Haden Edwards, is the southernmost extension of the Great Plains and stretches from west of the Colorado to the Pecos, touching on the Rio Grande in Val Verde and Terrell counties in the far southwest corner. It contains about 24 million acres.

The Edwards Plateau is mainly range land with excellent mixtures of forage plants, which are ideal for deer.

North America's largest herds are found here. The northeastern portion of the plateau grades into mesquite-tobasa like the Rolling Plains. Rainfall varies from less than 14 inches in the west to more than 33 in the east. The area has seen many droughts and floods.

Settlement of the Edwards Plateau remained on the eastern boundary along the Austin, San Marcos, and San Antonio line until the Society for the Protection of German Immigrants in Texas was founded in Germany. The society, a group of aristocratic Germans, had negotiated the right to settle Germans on a tract of land that covered almost all the Edwards Plateau and the southern Comancheria, under the auspices of the Fisher-Miller Grant. Only Castell, established in 1847 on the Llano River between Llano and Mason, remains of the attempt to colonize this grant. When the Fisher-Miller Grant proved fraudulent, the thousands of German immigrants stranded from Indianola to Castell dug in right where they were. New Braunfels, Boerne, Fredericksburg, Llano, Mason, and many other settlements followed. These towns still reflect much of their German heritage.

Frederick Law Olmstead, who grumbled his way across the Pineywoods, Post Oak Savannah, and Blackland Prairies, visited the German settlements in 1854 but not before a few last verbal blasts at the Anglo settlers. "We asked if there was much game near? There were a great

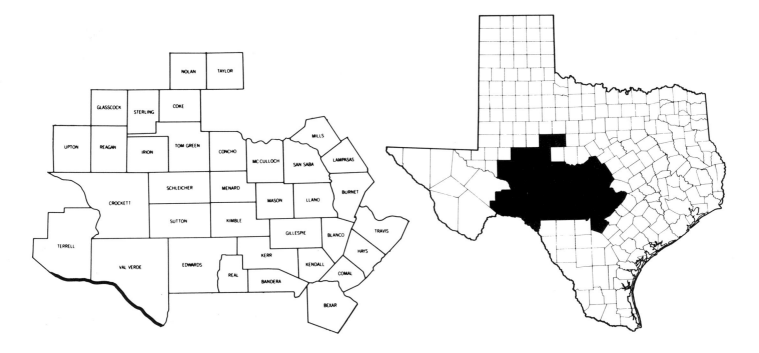

Edwards Plateau, home to more than
a million white-tailed deer.

many deer. He saw them every day. Did he shoot many?
He never shot any; 'twas too much trouble to hunt them.
When he wanted 'fresh,' 'twas easier to go out and stick a
hog . . ."

However, as he neared New Braunfels, Olmstead's commentary brightened. "The first German settlers we saw we
knew at once. The greater variety of the crops which had
been grown upon their allotments, and the more clean
and complete tillage they had received contrasted favor-
ably with the patches of corn stubble, overgrown with
crab grass which are the only gardens to be seen adjoin-
ing the cabins of the poor whites and slaves."

Olmstead had the good fortune to be in the Texas Hill
Country in early spring, a place where sportsmen are
compelled to return each year. "The beauty of the spring
prairies has never been and never will be so expressed,"
wrote Olmstead, after seeing his first fields of bluebonnets
laced with Indian paintbrush.

The Hill Country Bluebonnet Trail is a riot of color in
early April, marked by the familiar blue and white road
signs. Along the Colorado River above Lake Buchanan
you have a good chance of seeing American bald eagles
from November through March.

The Balcones Escarpment on the east marks the beginning of the picturesque Hill Country. In the heart of the
ecological area is the granite Central Basin centering on
Burnet, Llano, and Mason counties.

Elevations range from 100 feet to 3,000, and the surface is rugged, well drained, and crossed by many rivers
and streams. The Llano Basin is rock hound paradise, because the older sedimentaries have eroded to pre-
Cambrian rock—one of the few areas in North America
where this occurs. For years there were rumors of rich
gold and silver mines, fueled by traces discovered in the
area and legend.

San Antonio de los Llanos, renamed *San Antonio de
Bexar,* was established as a mission and fort in 1718. The
original mission chapel was converted to other uses and
nicknamed "the *Alamo.*" Today, San Antonio is a lovely,
romantic, cosmopolitan city that merges Old and New
World cultures in a way unique to the United States. It is
the largest city in the Edwards Plateau.

The sportsman will find incredible deer hunting
throughout the plateau. Trophy whitetail predominate in
the southwestern areas, particularly throughout Val Verde
County in the steep header-draws of Devil's River country.
Rio Grande turkeys abound, and in this part of the plateau blue quail and javelina are plentiful. Amistad Reservoir, at the tip of Val Verde County on the Rio Grande at
Del Rio, is one of America's finest fishing and waterfowling areas. Hill Country hunting produces lots of deer but
fewer trophy whitetails. Llano is known as the Deer Capital of the World. Deer hunter success ratios in this area
are close to one-on-one. No one goes home without venison.

Bluebonnets carpet Hill Country in early spring.

EDWARDS PLATEAU COUNTIES

Bandera	Hays	Reagan
Bexar	Irion	Real
Blanco	Kendall	San Saba
Burnet	Kerr	Schleicher
Coke	Kimble	Sterling
Comal	Lampasas	Sutton
Concho	Llano	Taylor
Crockett	Mason	Terrell
Edwards	McCulloch	Travis
Gillespie	Menard	Upton
Glascock	Mills	Val Verde
Tom Green	Nolan	

PRINCIPAL LAKES OF THE EDWARDS PLATEAU

Where lakes are named for cities or counties, no further location information is given. Acreages are approximate and not all lakes are listed. Gamefish availability is variable. "Excellent" references are reserved for species which have been present in abundance for many years or have made the record books.

Lake Abilene—640 acres
–black bass, catfish, excellent crappie, hybrid stripers.

Amistad Reservoir—67,000 acres
–Near Del Rio and Ciudad Acuna on Texas-Mexico border. Mexican license required for fishing right bank of Rio Grande. Name means "friendship."
–black bass, striped bass, bream, catfish, crappie, hybrid stripers, walleye.

Lake Austin—1,800 acres
–black bass, striped bass, white bass, crappie, hybrid stripers.

Brady Reservoir—2,000 acres
–black bass, crappie.

Lake Braunig—1,350 acres
–Near San Antonio; excellent black bass, channel catfish, (saltwater) redfish, hybrid stripers.

Lake Buchanan—23,000 acres
–Near Burnet; black bass, striped bass, excellent white bass, catfish, crappie, walleye.

Lake Calaveras—3,600 acres
–Near San Antonio; excellent black bass, blue, channel and flathead catfish, crappie, hybrid stripers.

Canyon Lake—8,200 acres
–Near San Antonio; smallmouth bass, striped bass, walleye.

Inks Lake—800 acres
–Between Burnet and Llano; excellent black bass, white bass, catfish, crappie.

Lake Lyndon B. Johnson—6,300 acres
–Near Kingsland; black bass, excellent white bass, catfish.

Lake Nasworthy—1,600 acres
–Near San Angelo; black bass, crappie, excellent hybrid stripers.

O. C. Fisher Lake—5,400 acres
–Near San Angelo; black bass, catfish, crappie, walleye.
Oak Creek Reservoir—2,000 acres
–Excellent black bass.
Spence Reservoir—15,000 acres
–Between Colorado City and San Angelo; excellent black bass, excellent striped bass.
Lake Sweetwater—650 acres
–black bass.
Town Lake—530 acres
–In Austin; black bass, smallmouth bass, excellent white bass, channel and flathead catfish, drum (gaspergou). (Excellent striped bass in the tailrace below the dam.)
Lake Travis—42,000 acres
–Near Austin; excellent striped bass, white bass, crappie.
Twin Buttes Reservoir—9,100 acres
–Near San Angelo; black bass, blue, channel and flathead catfish, walleye.

EDWARDS PLATEAU PARKS Make reservations if you plan an overnight stay. Ask for information from the listed town. Parks typically have a modest fee structure.

STATE PARK & LOCATION	CAMPING & RESTROOMS	FISHING	BOAT RAMP	MUSEUM EXHIBIT	HISTORIC STRUCTURE	NATURE TRAILS
Garner Concan	●	●				
Guadalupe River Bulverde	●	(Deer hunting by special permit, gun only) ●				●
Inks Lake Burnet	●	●	●			
Longhorn Cavern Burnet				●		
McKinney Falls Austin	●	●		●	●	●
Pedernales Falls Johnson City	●	(Deer hunting by special permit, gun only) ●				●
STATE RECREATION AREAS						
Abilene Buffalo Gap	●					●
Blanco Blanco	●	●				●
Kerrville Kerrville	●	●	●			●
Lockhart Lockhart	●					
STATE HISTORICAL PARKS & SITES						
Admiral Nimitz Fredericksburg				●	●	
Lyndon B. Johnson Stonewall				●	●	●

STATE PARK & LOCATION	CAMPING & RESTROOMS	FISHING	BOAT RAMP	MUSEUM EXHIBIT	HISTORIC STRUCTURE	NATURE TRAILS
Seminole Canyon Comstock	●			●		●
STATE HISTORIC STRUCTURES						
Fort McKavett Fort McKavett				●	●	●
Jose Antonio Navarro San Antonio				●	●	
Landmark Inn Castroville				●	●	●
San Jose Mission San Antonio				●	●	
NATURAL AREAS						
Enchanted Rock Fredericksburg	●					●
Hill Country Bandera			(camping permitted/no facilities)			
Lost Maples Vanderpool	●	●		●		●

STATE WILDLIFE MANAGEMENT AREAS	COUNTY LOCATION	ACREAGE
Special or regular permits or permission by registration requirements vary by season. Contact TPWD for current regulations: 1-800-792-1112.		
Walter Buck	Kimble	2,100
Game typically hunted: Deer, by archery and gun; javelina, by archery; quail; turkey		
Kerr	Kerr	6,500
Game typically hunted: Deer, by gun; turkey; mourning dove; exotics		

ECOLOGICAL AREA EIGHT

Rolling Plains

The Comanche Curtain of the 1860s was as much a barrier to westward settlement as the Iron Curtain is to western freedom seekers. Along this frontier fewer than 3,000 Comanches established an amorphous curtain of horror which stopped the white man dead. The Comanche was seldom in evidence on the Rolling Plains except for ephemeral puffs of smoke by day and coyote yips by night. When he was seen, usually on a full-moon night, the consequences were always violent.

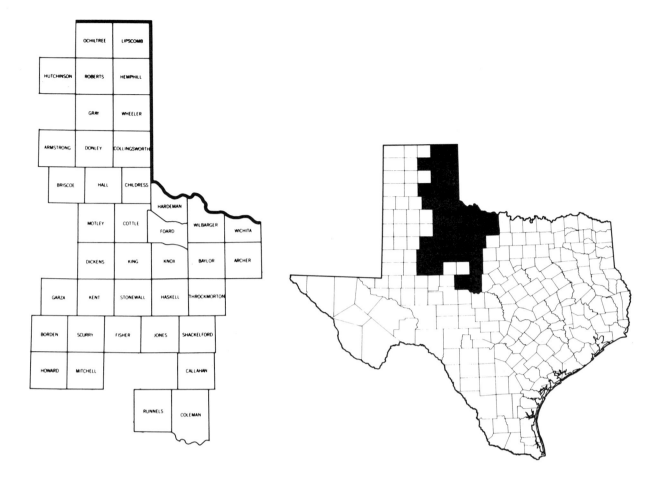

Caprock Canyon typifies the rough
terrain in the western Rolling Plains.

The Rolling Plains ecological area is about 24 million acres and is an extension of the Great Plains of the central United States. It is gently rolling country frequently broken by rough terrain and dissected by stream valleys flowing east to southeast. The Caprock Canyon State Park in Briscoe County will give you a good idea of the terrain. Annual rainfall ranges from about 22 inches in the west to 30 inches in the east. May and September are the rainier months.

More than 66 percent of the land remains in range, with large spreads such as the Swenson and Waggoner ranches still operating, and cattle are the main livestock. The original prairie vegetation included tall and mid-size grasses such as bluestem, grama and Indian grass, Canada wild rye, and western wheatgrass. Mesquite is a tough competitor for the range. You can tell when a rancher has struck oil or gas. His first act is to chain the mesquite off his pasture, then he adds new fencing, which he could not afford from livestock profits alone.

The 1860s Rolling Plains frontier ran from Fort Richardson at Jacksboro southwest through Fort Griffin to Fort Concho. Two symbiotic sets of players were on the proscenium, staged for a tragic drama that was to annihilate one set within the incredibly brief span of 20 years. Comanche and buffalo were arrayed against soldiers and hunters. Had not General Sheridan with his brave "Buffalo soldiers," the Fort Concho name for black troopers, and the buffalo hunters entered the scene, there's good reason to believe you'd need a passport and Comancheria visa to cross the Llano Estacado today.

Richard I. Dodge reported sighting a herd in 1871 that "contained not less than four million head." So long as there were buffalo the Comanche had a fighting chance. The Comanche wasted not even the bones, which were used for utensils. Sinews made bowstrings, dried chips provided cooking heat, hair made rope, blood was for drinking, stomachs for canteens, and hide for clothing and bedding. The rest was eaten.

When General Sheridan, with the help of market hunters, attempted to destroy the Comanche through wholesale annihilation of their food source, the Texas legislature tried to pass a bill to protect the buffalo. General

Binoculars are a must on West Texas big game hunts, such as this one west of Abilene.

Sheridan addressed the lawmakers, "Your prairies can be covered with cattle, and the cowboy will follow the hunter as a second forerunner of an advanced civilization." The General was right. The cattle herds moved on the Rolling Plains while the skinners peeled the last of the buffalo carcasses. The buffalo were slaughtered by America's first government subsidized hunters, and this helped set a deadly pattern that extended to the predator control programs of later years. Just one hunter, William F. Cody, firing his Springfield rifle named "Lucretia Borgia," killed 4,280 buffalo in 17 months.

Notes taken on the Capt. Randolph Marcy expedition of 1854 also foresaw the cattleman's era. Writing about the area around the Little Wichita River, chronicler W. B. Parker said, "Nothing can surpass the facilities of this country for stock raising, sufficient to mark Texas as the great stock-yard of our country in the future."

The famous Dodge City Trail ran from Bandera up to Dodge City, passing close to Fort Griffin, which boomed with the slaughter of buffalo, and sold more than $2,000 daily in ammo to the hunters. Cowboys took over for the buffalo hunters as the huge cattle drives came up the trail. Between 1867 and 1890 an estimated 10 million head crossed the Red River.

Sportsmen find great bird hunting in the Rolling Prairies, with the areas around Throckmorton and Haskell, to cite just two, producing outstanding dove and quail hunting. Lake Meredith, a 21,000-acre reservoir 40 miles northeast of Amarillo, is famous for its trophy walleye fishing. There are plenty of turkey, and deer are hunted in areas with suitable habitat. Waterfowl hunting can be spectacular here, too, and it is underutilized by sportsmen because of the distance most have to drive. Amarillo, headquarters for pheasant hunting, is the largest city in the Rolling Plains. Amarillo is located in the lower eroded plain breaks around the Canadian River, and therefore is technically not in the High Plains.

ROLLING PLAINS COUNTIES

Archer	Garza	Motley
Armstrong	Gray	Ochiltree
Baylor	Hall	Oldham
Borden	Hardeman	Potter
Briscoe	Haskell	Roberts
Callahan	Hemphill	Runnels
Childress	Howard	Scurry
Coleman	Hutchinson	Shackelford
Collingsworth	Jones	Stonewall
Cottle	Kent	Throckmorton
Dickens	King	Wheeler
Donley	Knox	Wichita
Fisher	Lipscomb	Willbarger
Foard	Mitchell	

PRINCIPAL LAKES OF THE ROLLING PLAINS

Where lakes are named for cities or counties, no further location information is given. Acreages are approximate and not all lakes are listed. Gamefish availability is variable. "Excellent" references are reserved for species which have been present in abundance for many years or have made the record books.

Buffalo Springs Lake—300 acres
–Near Lubbock; channel catfish, crappie, walleye.
Champion Creek Lake—1,600 acres
–Near Colorado City; excellent black bass.
Coleman Lake—2,000 acres
–black bass, catfish, crappie.
Lake Fort Phantom Hill—4,250 acres
–black bass, white bass, crappie, hybrid stripers, walleye.
Lake Greenbelt—2,500 acres
–Near Clarendon; excellent black bass, white bass, excellent channel catfish, crappie, excellent northern pike, hybrid stripers, sunfish, walleye.
Hords Creek Lake—510 acres
–Near Coleman; black bass, catfish, crappie.

Lake Kemp—20,000 acres
–Near Wichita Falls; black bass, crappie.
Lake Kirby—600 acres
–Near Abilene; black bass, excellent blue and flathead catfish, sunfish.
Lake Mackenzie—1,200 acres
–Near Canadian; black bass, catfish, crappie.
Lake Meredith—21,000 acres
–Near Amarillo (40 miles northeast); black bass, catfish, crappie, excellent walleye.
Lake Stamford—5,000 acres
–black bass, catfish, crappie.
Lake Thomas—8,000 acres
–Near Synder; black bass.
Miller's Creek Reservoir—2,400 acres
–Near Goree; black bass, blue and channel catfish, crappie.

ROLLING PLAINS PARKS Make reservations if you plan an overnight stay. Ask for information from the listed town. Parks typically have a modest fee structure.

STATE PARK & LOCATION	CAMPING & RESTROOMS	FISHING	BOAT RAMP	MUSEUM EXHIBIT	HISTORIC STRUCTURE	NATURE TRAILS
Caprock Canyon Quitaque	●	●	●	●		●
Copper Breaks Quanah	●	●	●	●		●
STATE RECREATION AREAS						
Big Spring Big Spring				●		●
Lake Arrowhead Wichita Falls	●	●	●			
Lake Brownwood Brownwood	●	●	●			●
Lake Colorado City Colorado City	●	●	●			
STATE HISTORICAL PARKS & SITES						
Fort Griffin Albany	●			●	●	

STATE WILDLIFE MANAGEMENT AREAS	COUNTY LOCATION	ACREAGE
Special or regular permits or permission by registration requirements vary by season. Contact TPWD for current regulations: 1-800-792-1112.		
Gene Howe	Hemphill	5,800
Game typically hunted: Deer, by archery and gun; turkey; quail; mourning dove		
Matador	Cottle	28,000
Game typically hunted: Deer, by archery; turkey; quail; mourning dove		

ECOLOGICAL AREA NINE

High Plains

Francisco Vazquez de Coronado was the first European to set foot on the Llano Estacado. He entered from the west, where the palisaded wall of the vast caprock escarpment inspired the name "Staked Plain," or Palisaded Plain. He did not drive stakes as he crossed the plains as some historians speculate. Indians were already there but, significantly, they were horseless.

In 1541 Coronado wrote, "I reached some plains with no more landmarks than if we had been swallowed up in the sea . . . there was not a stone, nor a bit of rising ground, nor a tree, nor a shrub, nor anything to go by. There is much fine pasture land, with good grass."

Explorers and settlers for centuries to come would echo Coronado's description of the High Plains, which is an upper plateau, 3,000 to 4,500 feet, and part of the Great Plains region. Playa lakes that "bespeckle the plains" are common, collecting water after heavy rains. The average rainfall is 15 to 21 inches, though many re-

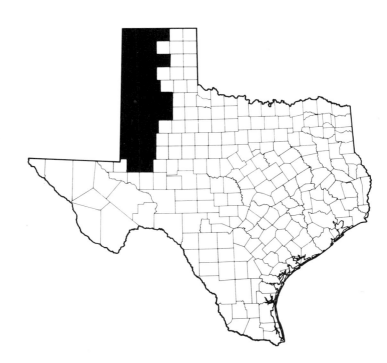

The giant escarpments of Palo Duro Canyon.

member the dust bowl days of the '30s following a terrible drought and poor farming practices. Native grasses are buffalo and blue grama, and the area, as noted by the pioneers, was free of brush. Today, mesquite and yucca are

Goose hunters in a pit blind on one of
the many playa lakes that dot the High Plains.

invaders and sand sage and junipers have spread out of the breaks. Some blame prairie dog control for the invasion of brush into pastures. Abundant at one time, prairie dogs are not dogs at all, but a species of small ground squirrel, which, to the horror of ranchers, eats grass. An 1850s estimate placed the statewide total in the 800 million range. Since the 1800s, prairie dogs have been shot, burned out, and poisoned nearly to extinction in efforts to save grass for cattle.

Also roaming the prairies were herds of wild mustang, antelope, gray wolves, and coyotes. Prairie chickens were noted as abundant in the 1840s, as were geese, ducks, and sandhill cranes, and they are all hunted today.

Three hundred years after the Spanish lost original mustang stock to Apaches and Comanches, John Gregg treated us to an update on the state of the Plains mustang in his classic sportsman's reference, *Commerce of the Prairies*. "Large droves are very frequently seen upon the Prairies, sometimes hundreds together, gambolling and curvetting within a short distance of the caravans," Gregg wrote in 1840. The only mustangs left in Texas today are those gambolling and curvetting in bronze.

Gregg described the "creasing" technique for capturing mustangs. The mustangs were shot through the upper neck above the vertebrae, and were roped while lying unconscious on the ground—but not every shot missed the spinal cord. Today, inexperienced deer hunters some-times lose accidentally creased animals when the presumably poleaxed whitetail suddenly springs to life and bounds away.

Today's most popular game in the High Plains is the pheasant, which established itself in the early 1940s. Because of the ruggedness of the Canadian River "breaks," which split the Panhandle, pheasants wouldn't migrate south. TPWD stocking programs south of the "breaks" have been very successful in spreading these great game-birds throughout the High Plains ecological area.

This area also shelters the fabulous *Arroyo Palo Duro.* Coronado is credited with being the first European to see the canyon. Later, Captain Randolph B. Marcy would stumble into it looking for the headwaters of the Red River. "The gigantic escarpments of sandstone," wrote Marcy, "rose to giddy heights of eight hundred feet upon each side and gradually closed in until they were only a few yards apart . . ." *Palo Duro* is Spanish for hardwood, descriptive of the canyon's vegetation.

Palo Duro Canyon State Park is awesomely beautiful. If you can tour immediately after a flood the tracks tell fascinating stories. Another worthwhile trip is to the Panhandle Plains Historical Museum at West Texas State University in Canyon, where the history of this area is brilliantly brought to life.

In 1874, the Palo Duro Canyon would be the site of the final Comanche defeat. Snaking his troops down a narrow trail into the Palo Duro Canyon and the last great Indian camp, Col. R. S. Mackenzie killed 1,051 ponies, making the people horseless, and thus powerless again after 200 glorious years of freedom on the plains.

Two years later, in 1876, Charles Goodnight, who since the '50s had driven Cross Timber cattle across the High Plains to New Mexico, led his cattle into the Palo Duro Canyon, built his dugout home (which stands today), and formed the JA Ranch. The cattle baron scene was set.

Ranches were unbelievably large. Even today land-owners talk casually in terms of multi-sections of land—640 acres a pop. The XIT Ranch at the turn of the century was three million acres. C. C. Slaughter's Lazy S was more than one million acres, and C. C. claimed 24 million acres as his brand's range—four million more than found in the entire High Plains ecological area.

Slaughter's biographer, Mary Whatley Clarke, took time to talk about windmills, indispensable to West Texas. "Keeping the windmills running on the big ranch was among the more onerous and risky tasks that the cowboys had. Alvin Harris was the official 'windmill man' . . . he kept 40 mills turning with the breeze. He traveled the ranch in a wagon pulled by mules that had plodded over the route from mill to mill so many times they worked without command." Hunters have long noted the importance of windmills to West Texas hunts as a water source for game.

Joseph F. Glidden's 1874 invention of barbed wire changed the High Plains forever. Its first effect was to create range wars between ranchers and nesters. These wars have been blown all out of proportion in Texas history, although in the northwestern states they were serious affairs.

There is an immensity to this land that commands attention. The blue and white highway signs of the Texas Plain Trail will loop you through the area. Your first reaction will probably be, "Boy, it's *flat*." Listen to Capt. Marcy as he first entered in 1854. "This evening we have another thunderstorm, accompanied by the most intensely vivid lightning I have ever seen. The whole artillery of heaven appears to be playing; and as the sound reverberates in the distance over the vast expanse of prairie, the effect is indeed most awfully sublime. Upon such an occasion one realizes truly the wonderful power and majesty of the Deity, and the total insignificance of man."

HIGH PLAINS COUNTIES

Andrews	Floyd	Midland
Bailey	Gaines	Moore
Carson	Hale	Parmer
Castro	Hansford	Randall
Cochran	Hartley	Sherman
Crosby	Hockley	Swisher
Dallam	Lamb	Terry
Dawson	Lubbock	Yoakum
Deaf Smith	Lynn	
Ector	Martin	

PRINCIPAL LAKES OF THE HIGH PLAINS *Where lakes are named for cities or counties, no further location information is given. All acreages are approximate. Gamefish availability is variable. "Excellent" references are reserved for species which have been in abundance for many years or made the record books.*
Buffalo Lake—1,500 acres
–Within Buffalo Lake Wildlife Refuge near Canyon; closed in waterfowl season; black bass, catfish, crappie.
White River Lake—1,800 acres
–Near Crosbyton; black bass, smallmouth bass, catfish, walleye.

HIGH PLAINS PARKS Make reservations if you plan an overnight stay. Ask for information from the listed town. Parks typically have a modest fee structure.

STATE PARK & LOCATION	CAMPING & RESTROOMS	FISHING	BOAT RAMP	MUSEUM EXHIBIT	HISTORIC STRUCTURE	NATURE TRAILS
Palo Duro Canyon Canyon	●			●		●
STATE RECREATION AREA						
Mackenzie Lubbock	●	●				

ECOLOGICAL AREA TEN

Trans-Pecos

West of the Pecos you enter the Chihuahuan Desert, the largest desert in North America. At Monahans it's sand dunes; at Guadalupe Peak you're at Texas' highest elevation. It's *terra incognito* to the multitudes, obscure and unloved by the unknowing. The Spanish certainly didn't love it and couldn't hold it for their empire. Apaches and Comanches took turns in command but couldn't hold it either.

Forts such as Stockton and Davis guarded the Trans-Pecos. '49er wagon trains lumbered through it en route to Sutter's Mill, California. The 19th-century stagecoaches lurched through where today interstate highway travelers speed past, unfortunately only seeing ugly creosote flats. To most, *El Despoblado,* which means the unpeopled, is still an accurate description if they think of the Trans-Pecos at all.

The Trans-Pecos ecological area covers about 19 million acres and has the wildest diversity of plants and animal and natural communities in Texas. Elevations range from 2,500 to 8,760 feet. The average annual precipitation is less than 12 inches, but increases at higher elevations, for example to 16 inches at Fort Davis. July and August have the highest average rainfall. Floods in the Big Bend send huge boulders crashing down stream beds, creating apocalyptic sight and sound. Don't camp in a dry stream bed.

Most of the land remains in native range in large ranch holdings, often equipped with helicopters and other modern aircraft. Livestock typically include cattle, sheep, and some Angora goats. Many types of vegetation exist including creosote-tarbrush desert shrub, grama, yucca, juniper, pinion pine, ponderosa, and even some oak forest.

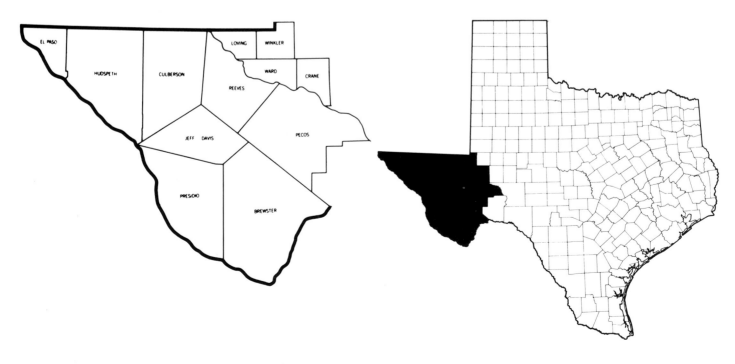

The Rio Grande cuts through towering canyons in Big Bend National Park.

The Mescalero Apache still roamed the farther reaches of the Guadalupe and Franklin Mountains in the 1850s. The agave, a small relative of the century plant, was to the Mescalero what buffalo was to the Comanche. The agave stores food for up to 20 years in preparation for reproduction, signaled by its 10- to 15-foot-tall stalk topped by a cluster of yellow flowers. Just after the stalk wilts the starch heart roots are at their maximum food value. The Apache baked these roots, buried within stone midden ovens, as their bread and potato equivalent. The midden stove circles are still to be found in the backreaches of the Guadalupes. The Apache also used agave leaves to make thread, fashioned needles from its thorns, and ground the seeds into meal. And, best of all, they fermented the sap to make mescal, which becomes tequila with a little more processing. The Apache ground up Mountain Laurel beans into their mescal for a kicker, often losing a ceremonial brave, since one bean can kill. Later, Apaches switched to peyote buttons for their "ghost dance" hallucinations.

Next came stagecoach lines with stops at every water hole. The Texas Rangers became a not-so-benign traveler's aid society. Ambushes by the Rangers, such as the one at Heuco Tanks in 1881, wiped out the Mescalero Apache.

Another water hole trap was sprung at Manzanillo on the western escarpments of the Guadalupe Springs by Lt. Howard B. Cushing on December 30, 1869. Cushing destroyed the Apache's vital necessities: huge stores of goods for shelter, clothing, and food, including 20,000 gallons of prepared mescal. This raid was the first of many into the mountains, a relentless Mescalero massacre.

Today, Manzanillo Springs or spectacular McKittrick Canyon in Guadalupe Mountains National Park can be good places to spot elk, but not the extinct Merriams. The ones you see are descendants of Rocky Mountain elk. Here elk are protected from man, but not from cougar, which eat them regularly. As they are throughout most of the Trans-Pecos mountain ranges, mule deer are plenti-

ful, and there are herds of antelope on the plains below. Farther back in the Guadalupes there are black bear.

Today there is more desert than there was in the 1800s. Cattle in the huge grazing herds such as those of Charles Goodnight and Oliver Loving simply destroyed the topsoil root structure. Cattle didn't graze the pasture bare, they stomped it to a stony death.

By the 1850s the Texas map was lashed with trails from east to west, north to south except for an area surrounded on three sides by the Rio Grande in present Brewster and Presidio counties, which appeared blank on most early maps. At that time the only known trail through this area was the Comanche Trace. The Sierra Del Carmens Mountains guard the east, the Chisos the north.

The Chisos Mountains are in Big Bend Park, one of America's natural wonders. This is one place where a geologist can study Paleozoic, Mesozoic, and Cenozoic rock, taking him from the trilobites of Cambrian to the mammoths of the Pleistocene. The limestone varieties are rich in fossils, the rock strata wonderfully exposed. Only pre-Cambrian and older rocks are not immediately accessible, but you can unearth them near Van Horn and in Llano County. Cinnabar (mercury), silver, and lead mines, as well as hot springs, are scattered throughout the Big Bend.

The view from the western side of the Chisos Mountains at sunset is *muy bonito*! There is a beautiful campsite in the Chisos Basin overlooking the Mexican state of Chihuahua through what is called "the window."

Strange lights sometimes are seen in the Chisos giving rise to the "Indian spirit ghost" legend. ("Chisos" does not mean "ghost," but rather is taken from the name of an Indian tribe.) The eerie glow is probably foxfire from rotting wood or reflections of light from flecks of minerals embedded in the rocks. The Glass Mountains to the north have this same peculiar light-reflecting quality, thus their name. Cougar, mule deer, and small, wild black bees that produce a marvelous honey from cactus flowers still grace the Big Bend.

Trans-Pecos mountains and deserts provide rugged habitat for a diversity of plants and animals.

One of the longest but most spectacular of the blue and white highway loops is the Texas Mountain Trail, which covers most of the Trans-Pecos. Highly recommended is a stay at Indian Lodge in Davis Mountains State Park, but call well ahead for reservations, especially for late April and early May, when the desert flowers are apt to be in bloom.

The McDonald Observatory, one of the nation's premier space observatories, is nearby in the Davis Mountains. The conditions here are ideal for studying astronomy, with low humidity, no air or light pollution, and enough elevation to reach thinner atmosphere. On a moonless night, stars overpower the naked eye. Night travelers could almost always navigate by Polaris and tell time by the position of Ursa Major and other constellations. This area is also under major meteorite belts, and in late November meteor showers often fill the sky with heavenly fireworks.

Like the Big Thicket, the Trans-Pecos is an ecotonal zone, where different ecological areas come together. Survivors of the Ice Age, such as the Big Bend gecko, are found in the rare springs, as are frogs that live underground for all but two weeks a year, and lizards that reproduce without intercourse.

Aside from the annual Terlingua chili cookoff, the main attractions for hunters are antelope, desert mulies, blue quail, and Rio Grande turkey. Just west of the Pecos some trophy whitetail hunting is also found. The hunting is rugged, requiring the best in vehicles, even horses to recover game, and good camp cooks since facilities are do-it-yourself. There are two very special offseason thrills available: spring desert flowers and a raft ride down the rain-swollen Rio through Santa Elena Canyon.

TRANS-PECOS COUNTIES

Brewster	Hudspeth	Presidio
Crane	Jeff Davis	Reeves
Culberson	Loving	Ward
El Paso	Pecos	Winkler

PRINCIPAL LAKES OF THE TRANS-PECOS *Where lakes are named for cities or counties, no further location information is given. Acreages are approximate and not all lakes are listed. Gamefish availability is variable. "Excellent" references are reserved for species which have been in abundance for many years or in the record books.*
Lake Ascarte—43 acres
–Vicinity of El Paso; black bass, channel and flathead catfish, black crappie, sunfish.
Lake Balmorhea—500 acres
–black bass, bream, catfish.
Red Bluff Lake—11,700 acres
–Near Pecos; black bass, catfish.

TRANS-PECOS PARKS Make reservations if you plan an overnight stay. Ask for information from the listed town. Parks typically have a modest fee structure.

STATE PARK & LOCATION	CAMPING & RESTROOMS	FISHING	BOAT RAMP	MUSEUM EXHIBIT	HISTORIC STRUCTURE	NATURE TRAILS
Davis Mountains (Indian Lodge) Fort Davis	●			●		●
Monahans Sandhills Monahans	●			●		
STATE RECREATION AREA						
Balmorhea Toyahville	●					
STATE HISTORICAL PARK						
Hueco Tanks El Paso	●					●

STATE PARK & LOCATION	CAMPING & RESTROOMS	FISHING	BOAT RAMP	MUSEUM EXHIBIT	HISTORIC STRUCTURE	NATURE TRAILS
STATE HISTORIC SITES & STRUCTURES						
Fort Lancaster Sheffield				•	•	
Fort Leaton Presidio				•	•	
Magoffin Home El Paso				•	•	
NATURAL AREA						
Franklin Mountains		(No facilities; pedestrian access only)				

STATE WILDLIFE MANAGEMENT AREAS	COUNTY LOCATION	ACREAGE
Special or regular permits or permission by registration requirements vary by season. Contact TPWD for current regulations: 1-800-792-1112.		
Black Gap	Brewster	100,000
Game typically hunted: Deer, by archery and gun; javelina, by gun; quail; mourning dove; white-winged dove		
Elephant Mountain	Brewster	23,000
Game typically hunted: Deer, by archery and gun; pronghorn antelope; javelina, by gun; quail; mourning dove		
Las Palomas	Presidio	(very small)
Ocotillo unit (White-winged dove nesting habitat—sometimes made available for dove hunting)		
Sierra Diablo	Culberson	7,800
Game typically hunted: Deer, by gun		

THE BIG BEND RANCH

In late 1988, the 215,000-acre Big Bend Ranch was purchased by the Texas Commission of Parks and Wildlife. The ranch encompasses some of the last wilderness land in North America, primitive land cut through by huge canyons and arroyos, and dotted with giant mesas. It stretches for 28 miles between Lajitas in the Big Bend National Park and Presidio. In the 1990s, the Big Bend Ranch will become one of the premier wilderness experiences for Texans and all Americans.

II

DOVE

DOVE

In late summer, Texas outdoorsmen begin the great annual hunt ritual—getting ready for dove season. The traditional opening day, the first of September, usually means 100-degree weather, but this neither dampens enthusiasm nor daunts anticipation. Although many dove hunters hunt no other game, all hunters hunt dove if they can. It's the way we start our hunting year.

The most abundant game bird in the nation, mourning dove populate each of our 48 contiguous states, including the 254 counties of Texas. The national dove population is placed at 500 million. Some 50 million doves, or approximately 10 percent of the total population, are shot each season according to national harvest estimates. Eight out of ten doves die of natural causes each year, so hunting is not a major factor in mortality rates.

To some, dove hunting raises the specter of the tragic extinction of the passenger pigeon, of which the last Texas specimen was spotted in 1900. As recently as the 1860s, flights of passenger pigeons numbered in the millions and roosts covering one thousand acres were reported in Henderson County southeast of Dallas. Eyewitnesses recalled the pigeons devastating trees and crops.

But the slaughter of these pigeons cannot be compared to modern sport hunting, because pigeon hunters often struck the roosts or nesting colonies at night, when the birds were most vulnerable. These hunters did not use guns, but rather lamps, nets, and sticks to bring the birds out of the field by tote sackfuls. Shooting the birds, in fact, was considered poor form, not because of the lack of sportsmanship, but because shooting disturbed the roost and caused the pigeons to fly away, frustrating those using the much more efficient lamp-and-sack techniques. While diseases such as trichomoniasis and unlimited market shooting also took their toll, the real wipeouts were nocturnal or nesting colony events.

When the last passenger pigeon in captivity died at the Cincinnati Zoo on September 1, 1914—ironically the date set in Texas as opening day of dove season—the stage was set for the establishment of federal laws covering all migratory birds. These laws have helped assure that, despite the tremendous loss of natural habitat, huntable populations of other migratory birds exist today.

Now if all hunters were infallible shots, doves too would be on the endangered species list. But, the national average of hunter-harvested doves is a rousing three birds for every *box* of 25 shells fired. There are several reasons for this, mainly the flaring acrobatic performance of the dove itself. Suffice it to say that unless you count the birds yourself, never trust a bragging dove hunter—he will lie about other things, too.

Mourning doves usually occur in good concentrations throughout the state. Great shooting can often be had within sight of the office towers of Dallas or Houston, wherever there's lots of small grain. The real hot spots are in the Rolling Plains, Cross Timbers, Hill Country, and Brush Country. The vast grain fields of West Texas are a magnet, supporting large native populations and attracting huge flights of "Kansas birds," the catchall phrase for all migrant doves.

With the onset of cold weather many native birds from our northern counties migrate toward the Mexican border. Texas is in a natural location to capitalize on the southern migrations, when dove congregations from up north stop through on their exodus south. Along our border, especially in the Brush Country, we have the white-winged dove. And, in the Rio Grande Valley, there's the white-tipped dove. However, hunting pressure, loss of nesting cover, and changing feed and weather patterns have created erratic hunting. What used to be an annual pilgrimage to the Texas border counties and the Valley has now turned into an international adventure into Mexico for those with the time and money.

DOVE INSIGHTS

MOURNING DOVE "Gray Ghost" is what many call the mourning dove, an allusion to the bird's overall color and elusive flying. The dove's streamlined body, tapered tail, and raked-back wings compare to those of a jet fighter. Look for a pinkish tinge on the underside. In flight, there's an illusion of white on wingtips, but nothing like the white patches of the whitewing.

Relatively small birds weighing only four ounces or so, mature doves surprisingly average more than a foot in length with a wingspan of 16 inches. More than 50 percent of a bird in flight is tail feathers. Feathering doves is common because they can take a great deal of shot aft and not be the worse for it.

Listen for a fluttery, high-pitched whistle when doves fly from their roost. The mourning dove's rapidly beating primary feathers also create a soft whistle in normal flight. You may hear its mournful-sounding coos, a territorial or courtship call of both sexes, from the roost during hunting season.

A 15-mile-per-hour tail wind enables doves to hit speeds up to 60 miles per hour downwind, the speed at which skeet targets leave the house. This speed combined with great maneuverability and small target size explains why the ammo makers of America should erect a monument to our most plentiful game bird. In addition, mourning doves may hatch up to six broods in a good breeding season, that is, a spring and summer with ample but not too much rainfall. Typically, two eggs are laid, requiring a two-week incubation period. Unlike many other game birds the chicks are born featherless, but they are ready to leave the nest in two weeks or less. An indicator of a good season is the oft-heard Texas phrase, "They must've paired twice," though this is actually the norm, not the exception. A dove couple will usually hatch and raise four young in an average season. This is all the more impressive if you have ever seen the flimsy nests mourning doves build, nothing more than a platform of twigs.

WHITE-WINGED DOVE Whitewings are about 25 percent larger than mourning doves, stockier, and their tails are more rounded. Conspicuous white patches on the wing coverts provide the most distinct identification. The whitewing's feathers carry a hint of brown and are a darker gray than the mourning dove's.

The streamlined mourning dove
is a fast, elusive target.

Distinctive wing patches
identify the white-winged dove.

Unlike its smaller and paler cousin, the white-winged dove is a silent flier and not quite so much the acrobat. These doves are capable of doing up to 45 miles per hour in level flight and are great downwind fliers.

WHITE-TIPPED DOVE Also known as the white-fronted dove, this nonmigratory dove is most numerous in the Lower Rio Grande Valley but is expanding its range in South Texas. Slightly larger than whitewings, these doves are difficult to distinguish from mourning doves in flight. Their namesake white-tipped tail is a poor in-flight identifier since whitewings, mourning doves, and whitetips all

The white-tipped dove, also known as the white-fronted dove, is native to South Texas.

have white-tipped tails. However, the cinnamon colored underwing linings readily identify a whitetip in hand. Another distinguishing characteristic is the dove's habit of flying low. Its low-pitched call sounds like someone blowing across the mouth of a soda pop bottle, hence another common name, "jug blower."

As with other game, the hunter has the responsibility of identifying harvestable birds; only the mourning, white-winged, and white-tipped doves may be legally taken under state and federal regulations. Six other native doves or pigeons—all members of the family *Columdidae*, and all found in Texas—are protected. The protected six include the common ground dove, which ranges from sea level to 4,000 feet across the southern half of the state, and the tame little Inca dove, which prefers to live near human habitations. Both are all of an ounce in weight. Two other rarely seen ground doves are the ruddy ground dove, sometimes spotted in the Valley, and the blue ground dove, found also in South Texas.

Rounding out our protected dove list are the red-billed and band-tailed pigeons, both about the size of a domestic pigeon. The red-billed is just that, with a whitish tip. He lives in the Valley area of South Texas. The beautifully

The common ground dove is one of six protected doves.

marked bandtail breeds from 1,500 to 9,000 feet in the Trans-Pecos mountains of Davis, Glass, Chinati, Chisos, and Guadalupe.

Two additional species were introduced and are currently unprotected by state and federal laws. These include the rock dove and the ring-necked dove. The rock dove or domestic pigeon that you see on viaducts, park benches, and window ledges is a large, plump dove with a white rump patch and all sorts of purple-gray markings and colors. These doves don't roost in trees. The ring-necked dove is an escaped cage bird that is sometimes seen at backyard bird feeders.

Almost all small grains, both wild and cultivated, appeal to dove. They adore doveweed and will fly a mile for a sunflower seed. They thrive on ragweed, pokeweed, crab grass, even pine cone seeds. Maize and corn, sorghum, wheat and rye, millet, soybeans, peanuts, and peas will draw doves by the droves. Sometimes you'll notice doves flying into what appears to be a freshly plowed field. Though all you can see is dirt, the birds see a field recently seeded, often with wheat or rye—the doves are doing the farmer no favors. If you're hunting on a day lease or other areas unfamiliar to you, assure yourself that you are not hunting over a baited field, since this is an illegal way to hunt migratory birds. In Texas it's legal but not sportsmanlike to hunt native, nonmigratory game such as quail over bait.

In addition to food, water, and rest, doves must have gravel to live. They take the small stones into their craws (gizzards) to help grind grains before digesting them. Feed, water, gravel, and roost areas are visited by doves on a habitual basis. Hunters describe these habits as *patterns*. Local birds are remarkably patterned, but even migrating visitors, given a few days in an area, will develop patterns for feeding, graveling, watering, and roosting.

Depending upon the part of Texas where you find him, your dove will wake from a roost in mesquite brush or citrus, pine, or oak trees. If it isn't raining, which keeps him on the roost, he'll fly hungrily to the nearest grain source. Breakfast time is just at daybreak, so hunters need to be in position by first light. Just remember, shooting hours are from one-half hour before sunrise until sunset. Your local newspaper will publish the official times of sunrise and sunset. The thoughtful hunter will clip the information and carry it with his license to stop debates with fellow hunters as to quitting time.

Doves feed in the morning and usually go to water before returning to nap on their roost during the midday heat. By midafternoon, doves are hungry again and head for grain. If patterns are established, they will often fly right down a fence line or tree line, since these provide navigational aids in their food search. If there is a tall, preferably dead tree nearby, get close. Doves will aim for this tree and sit a spell surveying the grain field. High lines also serve as dove sentinel posts.

Doves tend to feed as late as possible, depending on the light. Late afternoon shadows and overcast skies send them toward gravel and water. Stock tanks with gravelly banks, muddy water, and a little distance to the surrounding underbrush and trees are ideal for the dove. His next stop is the roost, and again he may well have a tendency to fly home along a fence or tree line.

PREPARATION FOR

THE DOVE HUNT

TEXAS PREFERRED GUN SELECTION The 12- or 20-gauge over/under with improved cylinder and modified choke is a good choice. A 12- or 20-gauge, pump modified choke is perhaps the all-time favorite, but the over/under with the typical barrel selector is better because you have a choice of loads.

In early season, #8s in a 3¼ dram, 1⅛ ounce shot are ideal for 12-gauge with 2½ dram; 1 ounce shot for 20 gauge. Later you may wish to switch to #7½s, but we suggest you stick to the same powder load since your instincts and hand-eye coordination should now be familiar with the time it takes to get the shot to the bird.

Since dove shooting creates many empty shell casings, always pick up your shells. Even if you are not a reloader, you can give the empties to a reloader. Shells left on the ground are not only unsightly, but also cause serious and sometimes fatal digestive problems in livestock.

Many dove shots will be crossing, so our water hose shooting method is highly recommended. Your objective is to spray the bird with shot. Start the swing from behind the bird, swinging through the tail, then the head. When you see daylight, pull the trigger while continuing the swing. Keep your eyes riveted on the bird through the entire process and continue to focus on him as he falls. Mark the spot and walk straight to it. This is important in rough cover. If the bird is falling into a clear space it's all right to get on another bird and start over, but only if you're 100 percent sure of finding the first one.

DOG SELECTION It is unusual for the dove hunter to own a dog solely for dove hunting. The more typical scenario is a hunter who enjoys getting the dog, a retriever breed such as a Labrador or golden, into the field for some exercise and help.

Labradors make great dove dogs. Trained to stay still, they don't spook incomers. They'll mark down birds on command and go right to them for quick pick up. All this makes you much more efficient since you can keep an eye on the sky and feel free to take a double. Other retrievers and pointers can also work.

WARDROBE SELECTION Preparation for Texas dove hunting requires that you pay special attention to comfortable clothing. The heat's liable to approach the three digit range. Select lightweight gear with nylon mesh and preferably camouflage cotton T-shirts paired with khaki pants or jeans. Camouflage is not essential in the early part of the season if you wear muted, neutral colors such as khaki. But camo can make a three- or four-yard difference later on when birds flare more. Laceless boots which let air circulate or jogging shoes are recommended over traditional, heavy leather hunting boots. Top off your dove hunting wardrobe with a camo gimme hat or dark straw cowboy hat to shade your face. The flash of sunlight off exposed skin has spooked more doves than glare from gun barrels.

Comfort has a direct relationship to good dove hunting —in fact, to all good hunting. The uncomfortable hunter who squirms and wiggles, who moves at all, will simply not collect game. Start the season off right with doves. Wear whatever works for you, even if it's a raggedy T-shirt air conditioned with holes. Practice patience and staying still from the first day of this year's hunting season. Remember you want to keep cool and blend in with the scenery.

The effective dove hunter waits calmly in a pose of suspended animation until timing for the first shot is as perfect as it's going to get. Remember, bad shots often shoot too soon or too late.

GEAR SELECTION Don't underestimate the importance of your camp stool; without it you're apt to be miserable. Some commercially available stools have insulated pockets which help keep water cool. These are great if you've pre-iced a canteen or thermos. Your stool should have another pocket available for carrying spare shells. Be sure the stool has a comfortable carry strap; if not, add your own jury rig.

Take along an easy-to-wear, belt-type bird-and-shell bag, which is much cooler than a vest. Two other musts for a dove hunt include game shears—they make wing removal quick and neat—and plenty of insect repellent. In the early season douse yourself with insect repellent, giving extra attention to your pants legs and waist. Don't sit in the grass, especially Johnson grass or Bermuda grass, or the chiggers will have you looking like you were peppered with #8s at close range. If you're hunting under trees be alert for ticks.

Have your gun and gear packed so that nothing critical is overlooked. The social nature of a dove hunt often requires frequent transfers of equipment, so always check your own gear after a vehicle switch.

DOVE HUNTER'S CHECKLIST
Hunting license
White-winged dove stamp for whitewing and
    whitetip hunts
Binoculars—for pre-season reconnaissance only
12- or 20-gauge shotgun
#8s in trap load, #7½s late season

Shooting glasses
Canteen or thermos with pre-chilled water
Camp stool
Insect repellent
Sunscreen
Camouflage gimme cap or dark straw hat
Cotton camouflage T-shirt
Mesh jacket
Jeans or cotton khaki slacks
Lightweight, laceless boots or ultra light canvas
    shoes
Dark socks
Bandana or neckerchief
Game shears
Pocket knife
Zip-type plastic bags
Milk cartons
Small cooler with ice and after-hunt beverages
Alarm clock
OPTIONS:
12 dove decoys
Dove call
Fishing gear in case the opportunity strikes

TECHNIQUES THE

EXPERTS USE

Unlike most hunting sorties, dove hunts are often social events. A group of hunters enhances the quality of the hunt since the birds can be kept moving, allowing many hunters to maintain their miss ratio.

Tuning up on the skeet range is also more fun as a social event. Invite fellow hunters to share an entire skeet field for a couple of hours one afternoon. Forget skeet protocol. No dove ever appeared at the command, "Pull," nor from the high or low house. Instead, have each hunter stride up to a station, gun on safety and off the shoulder, as someone behind releases the clay pigeons at will. Release all doubles except for the last station. This "walk up and shoot" method is good practice for the field.

Hunting with a group makes locating birds easy. Friends triangulate and mark downed birds, pick them up, dispatch cripples, and otherwise police the area for one another. In the field after the hunt, team effort makes short work of cleaning birds. Finally, a dove feast the evening of the first day's hunt is an especially grand occasion when shared with good friends.

LOCATING DOVES Reconnaissance is the earmark of an expert. Often, the area to be hunted is proscribed by lease or other arrangements. Nevertheless, scouting dove flight patterns makes for a more productive hunt every time. Scouting becomes particularly important if there has been a recent rain. Rain scatters the birds and disrupts certain parts of the normal pattern, such as the need to fly to water. One pattern always remains, barring an absolute downpour: the flight from roost to feed. We have had fantastic hunts in drizzle and fog by finding a feeding field. Spurred perhaps by the instinct that they may not be able to feed because of barometric pressure change, gloomy overcast skies, or drizzle, the birds will often persist in flying into such fields with almost no regard for early season hunters.

Placement around a field or stock tank is another mark of the seasoned hunter. As larger numbers of birds begin leaving the field in the afternoon, it's time to set up at stock tanks. This is particularly true if it's a dry season. Conversely, heavy rain can stop tank shooting cold. After studying flight paths inbound, place hunters on tree lines near tall, dead trees; cover flyway gaps to stock tanks. Avoid placing hunters where the logical shot would put a downed bird in heavy cover or in the water. Rather, hit birds so they drop in a roadway or clear area. Hunters who are the better shots should be in locations where shot placement is important. Teamwork is important, and you are noted as a considerate hunter if you don't grab the obvious best place every time, but rather work with the group to ensure coverage of the field or tank.

In positioning yourself, don't get too far under a tree or

The opening day of dove season is one of the great social events in Texas.

into brush where your vision or field of fire is restricted. Many birds are missed because they aren't seen until it's too late to get on them. Doves are not as smart as they are tricky. So long as your silhouette is broken by brush or trees and you're somewhat shaded, you'll be unnoticed.

If you feel energetic, you may wish to jump 'em up during the midday roost. This has three disadvantages however: It's hot, you'll miss most birds as they fly out ahead of you, usually putting heavy cover between them and you, and you run the risk of scaring large numbers of birds off a roost that will later furnish great shooting in the grain fields and/or stock tanks nearby. But, it's sporting shooting requiring endurance and skill. Remember, when they first leave the roost, the birds will almost always drop, much like planes off a carrier deck, and you'll be shooting over them if you're not careful.

The mark of a professional is the effort he makes to locate downed birds and the frustration he feels when he doesn't find them. Watch a veteran near heavy brush or over water. He won't take a shot that allows a downed bird to fall into heavy cover or water, unless just at the edge.

In fact, taking shots that drop doves at pre-selected landing areas—say on your side of the fence or at the water's edge—is considered a sign of sure skill among good hunters. But, don't leave a bunch of downed birds out there expecting to find them all. After reloading, walk quickly to the spot where you believe the bird hit the ground, and look for feathers. Stop short and really eye the ground, because often you'll have the line right, but not the distance. If you've walked the maximum distance at which the bird may have fallen and you're on line, drop your bandana and begin circling. When birds drop from other guns, take a quick look to give your partner a triangulation.

Unless you have an unusually fine sense of distance, it's a great idea to place a dove-sized object, such as a stick about 12 inches long with the depth of a dove, out at 40 yards. This is your optimum shooting distance. Beyond that the going is bound to be dicey. With incoming birds, shoot first at this optimum distance then take other shots as the flight sweeps in. Many greenhorns wait until the flight is right on them, then they have a difficult overhead angle for the first shot and usually no second shot.

Be in position early for both morning and afternoon hunting. Hunters walking around unnecessarily disturb flight patterns, especially later in the season when the doves are more nervous after being shot at for a few weeks. When changing flight patterns is desirable, dove decoys are very effective. Decoys placed high in dead trees near a stock tank or at the edge of grain fields are excellent. In a pinch they can be placed on barbed wire fences. They do work, and work better when there's quite a bit of shooting activity around your field and neighboring fields. The doves need a sense of reassurance that this is a safe place to feed, and your decoys will accomplish this.

Dove calls are less effective in altering dove flight paths, but used in conjunction with decoys there are some minimal benefits, the best of which is probably just keeping the hunter concentrated on the birds.

FIELD DRESSING Once you've bagged your limit it's best to dress your doves in the field. TPWD regulations require that one wing be left on field-dressed migratory birds taken in the South Zone, and on birds imported from Mexico. This helps game wardens enforce limits on doves since mourning, whitewing, and white-tipped doves are legal in the South Zone.

When cleaning doves we like to select secluded areas to minimize litter. Game shears to clip off wings speed the process and help save city-soft hands. The decision is yours to pluck or skin, often called breasting. Although the plucking option is by far the best for most game birds, with doves it's not essential, and it is certainly more time consuming if a large party of hunters get their limit.

In breasting the birds, simply insert your thumb under the breast bone and pop out the breast. Dove hearts make a savory addition to sauces, so if daylight and time permit, you ought to save them. Always take along a couple of large lock-and-seal plastic bags for storing and transporting your dressed doves. It's a good idea to have a couple of these bags in your pocket ready for use on an extremely hot day, when you may want to clean doves right away and store them with your cool water. This will improve the quality of the meat.

Unless you plan to cook your doves within two or three days, we suggest you freeze them in water-filled milk cartons. This storage method will preserve your doves up to 10 months.

Rolling Plains Menu

·

Minted Cantaloupe Balls
Baked Dove Breasts
Pioneer Noodles
Dill Bread
Scottish Shortbread

·

Llano Estacado Chenin Blanc

INDIAN BLANKET/Firewheel. *Gaillardia pulchella*. Rich red and yellow ray flowers, the amount of red in the center and yellow on tips varies from plant to plant. Drought-resistant, grows with blanket-like density on prairies, fields, and woodlands. Annual, April through June.

Minted Cantaloupe Balls

SERVES 8

Melons and mint were available to early settlers. Where they had a problem was in chilling! Melons become ripe just as dove season opens. Pick them ripe off the vine and chill them in a washtub of ice for a camp treat.

1 cup freshly squeezed orange juice
1/2 cup sugar
1 lime
   enough fresh lemon mint leaves, crushed,
     to fill 1/4 cup
6 cups cantaloupe balls

PREPARATION

1. Combine orange juice, sugar, lime juice, and mint leaves in a pan.
2. Cook over low heat, stirring constantly.
3. Bring to boil. Remove from heat. Chill.
4. Strain cooled juice over melon balls and chill overnight.

Baked Dove Breasts

SERVES 8

18 dove breasts
   dove hearts, diced
1 medium onion, diced
24 fresh mushrooms, sliced
2 tablespoons butter
2 tablespoons flour
2 tablespoons corn oil margarine
1 clove garlic, crushed
2 cups milk
1/2 cup celery, chopped
   rosemary
   oregano
   salt
   pepper
1 tablespoon darkening agent such as
   Kitchen Bouquet
1 8-ounce container sour cream

PREPARATION

1. Preheat oven to 325 degrees.
2. Wash dove breasts, arrange in large baking dish, leaving room around each breast.
3. Saute dove hearts, onion, and mushrooms in butter.
4. In another pan melt margarine, then add flour. Stir with whisk until blended.
5. Add milk, garlic, spices and celery, continue stirring and simmer two minutes. Add darkening agent for color.
6. Pour both mixtures over doves in baking pan. Cover pan with foil.

7. Bake for 60 minutes.
8. Add sour cream, stir, and turn doves.
9. Bake, uncovered, another 20 minutes.

Pioneer Noodles

SERVES 6 TO 8

3 eggs, beaten
3 tablespoons milk
1/2 teaspoon salt
3 cups flour, more or less as needed

PREPARATION

1. Mix eggs, milk, and salt.
2. Add flour to make stiff dough. Knead to combine.
3. Roll out very thinly on a floured surface.
4. Roll up loosely, cut slices about 1/4-inch wide.
5. Unroll, cut into desired lengths.
6. To dry, spread out on cloth for two hours or more.
7. Store in sealed container.
8. To cook, drop noodles into boiling water, cook uncovered until al dente, no more than ten minutes.

Dill Bread

YIELDS 1 LOAF

   hot water
1 cup cottage cheese
1 package dry yeast
1 tablespoon butter, softened, plus butter
   for brushing top of loaf
1 tablespoon sugar
2 teaspoons dill seed
2 tablespoons minced onions
1/4 teaspoon baking soda
1 egg
2 1/4 cups flour
   peanut oil
   salt to taste

PREPARATION

1. Warm mixing bowl by allowing hot water to stand in it.
2. Pour 1/4 cup of water into measuring cup and let stand until lukewarm.
3. Warm cottage cheese, preferably over double boiler.
4. Pour water out of mixing bowl. Pour in 1/4 cup of lukewarm water.
5. Add yeast, stir until dissolved.
6. Blend in 1 tablespoon butter.
7. Add warmed cottage cheese to yeast mix.
8. Stir in sugar, dill seed, onion, baking soda, and salt. Add egg and beat.
9. Add flour. Stir until all flour is moist.

10. Knead mixture until it appears smooth. (Add a little more flour only if necessary.)
11. Wipe a little peanut oil over top of dough.
12. Cover and let rise in a warm place until almost double. (60 minutes or so.)
13. Punch down. Place in large loaf pan. Allow to rise in a warm place again for 40 minutes or until doubled.
14. Preheat oven to 350 degrees.
15. Bake for 40 minutes or until bread sounds hollow when tapped.
16. Brush with melted butter.

Scottish Shortbread

SERVES 4 TO 6

½ pound butter, softened
¾ cup sugar
3 cups flour, sifted
¼ cup cornstarch

PREPARATION

1. Preheat oven to 350 degrees.
2. Cream butter and sugar. Add flour and cornstarch.
3. Mix with hands until no dough sticks to the sides of the bowl.
4. Place dough in 8-inch pie pan and pat out evenly, to about ½-inch thickness.
5. Prick dough with fork to make serving sizes when done.
6. Bake for 20 minutes or until edges start to brown.
7. Remove from pan and break on pricked lines.

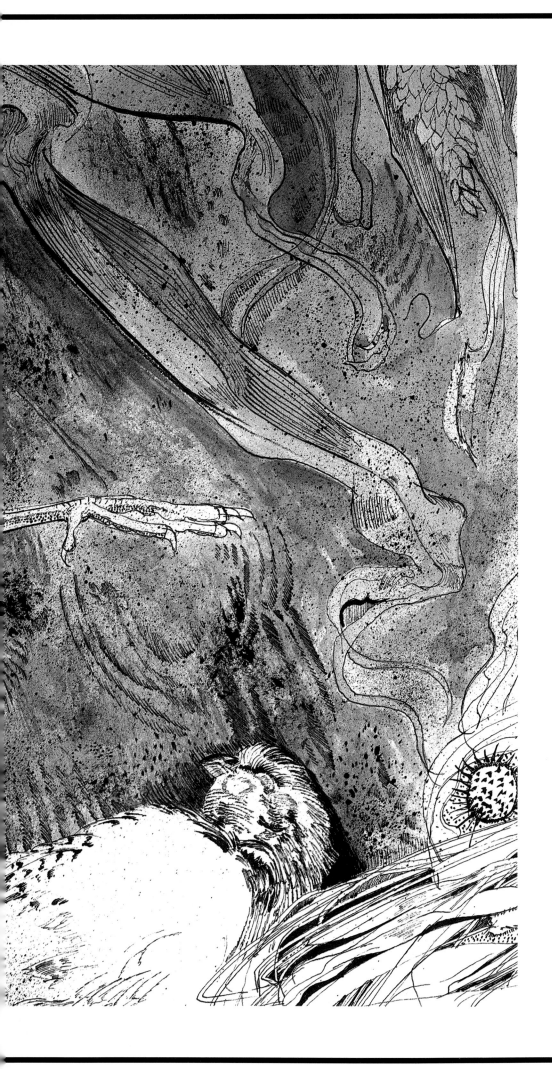

III

QUAIL

QUAIL

This little bobwhite, the Old Man told me, was a gentleman, and you had to approach him as gentleman to gentleman. You had to cherish him and look after him and make him very important in his own right, because there weren't many of him around and he was worthy of respectful shooting. The way you handled quail sort of kicked back on you.

—Robert Ruark
THE OLD MAN AND THE BOY

Texas is serious quail country, and our little bobwhites are cherished. But Texas quail hunting is definitely a walk on the wild side compared to most of the country. Forget the starchy white shooting jackets, mule-drawn refreshment wagons, manicured fields, and well-groomed saddle horses of Southwestern Georgia plantations. It's best to think more about rattlesnakes, leggings, brush-tough dogs, and protective clothing that can take a beating.

Although Texas has bird ranches and Pineywoods hunting reminiscent of hunting east of the Mississippi, the elegant approach is virtually nonexistent. The pursuit of Texas quail takes hunters through diverse and rugged terrain, from the Pineywoods, to the arid deserts and mountains of the Trans-Pecos, and many thorny places in between.

Quail season is fairly long, normally running from the first of November through late February. Texas hunters have the option of hunting for three species: bobwhite, Gamble's, and scaled or blue quail.

Though you may travel in a group to a quail hunt, it's a sport for twosomes. Any extras ought to be dogs. If you're shooting over someone else's dogs, never issue commands or you'll never hunt with those dogs again. When quail rise and fly low over the dogs, or a dog breaks and chases quail along your line of fire, hold your fire. Sound a warning if the greenhorn next to you looks as if he's about to dust a dog. Also, it's the rare bird dog owner who'll be happy if you pop a rabbit breaking in front of the dogs, since curing rabbit fever is one of the dog handler's main chores. Resist the temptation to take any other game while quail hunting over dogs.

Improper gun handling causes the most serious breaches of etiquette in the field. You'll never want to hunt again with an ungentlemanly character who insists on pointing his gun at your head while he's either carrying or loading it—any time. There's one bad habit that marks you as a greenhorn immediately and will not be tolerated by your partner—taking your gun off safety before the covey rises. That "safety off" click scares experienced hunters into a state of paroxysm when walking up to a point.

Greedy hunters, especially those who shoot birds flying across a partner's clear field of fire, are most unwelcome on the quail hunt. Take only *your* birds, even if you have to stop shooting.

Quail hunting is for twosomes—any extras should be dogs.

Devoted bobwhite hunters are dedicated foremost to their dogs. Bobwhite hunters spend far more time discussing and cussing their dogs than the quarry. They assume the quail will perform much as always; a reasonable bet, even in Texas. Bobwhites will generally hold in a covey since they hate to fly, although as a season wears on they typically flush wilder. They can usually be pointed by well-trained dogs and worked as singles, because once in the air they seldom fly any farther than the length of a couple of football fields.

Blue quail hunts are different; dogs play little part in much of this hunting except in the Brush Country and other areas where bobs and blues run together. It comes as a shock to many an eastern-trained quail hunter that blue quail are actually shot on the ground. And then, it's also considered perfectly sporting to just kick 'em up; often it's the only way to hunt them. This is so contrary to a good bobwhite hunter's training and sense of sportsmanship that the very mention of it is enough to start a brouhaha between eastern and western hunters.

While bobwhite hunters prefer #8s or even #9 field loads, blue quail hunters go to #7½ high brass, even #6s, because shots are generally longer and most often travel through brush. Also, the blue is tougher to bring down in the air than a bob, because shots are longer, feathers thicker, and the birds larger.

QUAIL INSIGHTS

BLUE OR SCALED QUAIL   This bird's blue-gray breast feathers are tipped in black, giving the illusion of scales. Texans call him a blue quail, though in our state he usu-

Black-tipped, bluish-gray breast feathers give the illusion of scales on the quail Texans call blue.

ally has a chestnut-brown belly. A white-tipped crest graces the head.

Blue quail eat more insects than other quail, which accounts for their ability to range far from water. The body fluids of bugs sustain blue quail, making them less dependent upon traditional water sources. They can also obtain water from prickly pears, particularly the tunas. They will go through, under, and around brush or other obstacles rather than flush into flight. If they do fly they sail down quickly into the most dense cover.

Their nesting period extends later into the summer than that of the bobwhite; a need for summer rain triggers nesting in their arid, desert habitat.

In the fall, blues usually form large coveys of 40 or more, and at night roost on the ground. They are more prone than bobwhites to loaf in trees at midday, and if pressured by a predator will often escape by tree sitting.

Blue concentrations are heaviest in the Trans-Pecos and Brush Country. They overlap with bobs in the Brush Country, the extreme western range of the Hill Country, and in southern portions of the High Plains. In these areas the birds may interbreed.

GAMBLE'S QUAIL Trans-Pecos hunters may glimpse a handsome gray-backed quail with a black, erect plume waving merrily in the air. If so, he's seen a Gamble's quail, legally huntable, but rarely found in the skillet. He's sometimes called the desert quail. The male will have a black forehead and throat giving him a regal appearance. Like the scaled quail, Gamble's quail tend to form large coveys of 40 or more birds. They favor the same desert shrub habitat and have a high tolerance for altitude. A key to their abundance is precipitation. The Chihuahuan desert must turn green in order for their reproduction cycle to be stimulated. No rain means no breeding that season.

Erect, black plume identifies the rarely hunted Gamble's quail.

One of the first Americans to note the desert quail, long known to Spanish explorers, was naturalist Dr. William Gamble, who explored the Southwest in the early 1850s.

Like the blue quail, the Gamble's prefers to escape by foot rather than freeze, hide, or burst into the air.

The bobwhite's beautiful plumage provides superior camouflage, but not on a perch.

BOBWHITE QUAIL Bobs have beautiful plumage. Their back feathers reveal a flow of rich brown tones from gumbo to sandy loam. This natural camouflage makes them difficult to see. Bobwhites are one of our smallest game birds. If conditions suppress their scent, your dogs will have a most difficult time finding Mr. Bob.

Bobwhite habitat varies widely from the more traditional southern Pineywoods, to the rugged and rocky Hill Country, or the tamer Rolling Plains areas. Like all other quail hunting, the best bobwhite hunting is often along shady fence rows, creek bottoms, and rough draws. Quail always seek cover such as briars or vines. They gravitate to ranch and farm land where they can find available water and stock tanks. Bobwhites like to eat small grains and they're partial to the farmer's maize, millet, and soybeans. Natural feed includes croton, ragweed, broomweed, sunflowers, bundle flowers, sumac, and beggarweed.

MONTEZUMA QUAIL Long ago dubbed the "fool's quail," this plump little fellow has had a difficult time with nicknames. His other names are the purely descriptive "harlequin quail" and "Mearns' quail." It's said that Col. Edgar Mearns, called a Southwest explorer though his visits took place as late as the late 1800s, shot everything—including quail—with a rifle, which again supports the "fool's quail" opprobrium. Actually, "fool's quail" comes from the fact that this bird almost refuses to budge. He'll sit so tight you can pick him up. But when he finally flies he's almost twice as fast as a bobwhite. At moments such as these the hunters of old themselves looked foolish. These quail are found only in the extreme southeast sector of the Trans-Pecos and at higher elevations along the Mexican border.

The Montezuma quail is short tailed, and the male has a distinctive facial paint pattern, looking for all the world like an Apache on the warpath. His breast is polka dotted and his call has been rudely described as a "quavering, descending whinney," which doesn't help his image a bit. The bird is not hunted today in Texas.

More is known about quail, from habitat to habits, than any other game bird. However, in Texas, all the research in the world boils down to just one important element when forecasting the quality of the upcoming hunting season: *rain*, especially in the autumn. There's practically no such thing in Texas as too much rain. An exception to this would be in the coastal counties where heavy rains can wash out quail nests. Gauge your probable bobwhite hunting prospects on the amount of rainfall. Rain is essential to grain and wild seed production as well as encouraging the insect population, a heavy component of young birds' diets. Late winter storms, disease, or a terrible summer drought can all affect the next season's hunt.

Quail are naturally gregarious. They need their covey for survival, to find food, to warn of danger, to escape enemies, establish and defend their range, propagate in the spring, and even to keep warm. A quail alone is a wretched creature, most often a male, and his piercing "bob-white" call is a lament to loneliness. First, he's upset because he lacks female companionship during the spring breeding season, and he's really upset as autumn approaches and no covey will accept him. In late summer, desperation sets in as coveys composed of paired adults and their young accept other adults with young, but not him! More and more plaintive "bob-whites" rend the air.

In October, coveys begin to form in earnest during what some call the fall shuffle. But the covey must be just the right size—and above all congenial. Harmony is health and happiness to a covey. A lot of quail bravado fills the air. Quail are at war with beak-to-beak battles, intra-covey uprisings, and internecine police actions. Several coveys may engage one another over territorial rights. The weak are killed or banished, the winners band together forming coveys that will not associate with other coveys until winter is almost done. Many a sportsman has watched coveys come to quail feeders on different schedules. Should one group arrive while another is feeding, the norm is for the new arrivals to wait and the feeding quail to move out on the double. This behavior starts to change when spring heralds the breeding season and the spring dispersal begins, which ultimately breaks up the covey into independent breeding pairs. Once a covey has established feeding territory, it's likely to keep coming back. We have hunted the same coveys for more than 20 years on one modest ranch in the Hill Country.

Quail coveys usually feed together, staying close, but with scouts out to warn of predators. Their range for feed also varies with the amount of rainfall. If you have a dry year the range will be wider. The birds will not stop during the morning and evening feedings until their crops are full. Quail generally take cover, especially in the early season, when it's blazing hot. Around 3 p.m. they venture out to feed, returning to roost at sunset. You'll often find quail roosts smack dab in the middle of a field in fairly short grass. This is for protection from predators, because being out in the clear in open cover enables the birds to fly or run at will to escape. Pushed by a bobcat or other predator, quail will even take temporary refuge in trees.

More than 80 percent of quail die each season due to natural causes. There's really no such thing as carrying a good quail crop over to the next season, since rain is the primary determinant. However, retaining coveys is an element that can be affected by hunters. Covey size seems critical with bobwhites, and most November coveys contain a dozen birds or more. Our practice is to try to leave at least eight birds. This isn't much margin, but leave eight, no matter what, so some of the birds will breed and hatch more quail for next year. As the season wears on, covey size will decrease, on average, by a bird or two per month, so that by season's end in February the coveys are already perilously close to the eight-bird survival level. Quail roost in a circle, so if you cut a covey down to much fewer than eight birds, you rob them of enough community warmth for surviving the winter. Aside from ensuring warmth, covey size works as additional protection against intruders. The whir of a covey rising is nature's design for startling predators. The surprise of that sound works well on men, too.

Quail roost in a circle
for protection and warmth.

PREPARATION FOR

THE QUAIL HUNT

TEXAS PREFERRED GUN SELECTION   A classic quail hunter's choice is the 20-gauge, 3-inch mag over-under or side-by-side, either bored skeet and improved cylinder, or improved and modified. A lightweight auto-loader, choked improved cylinder is more efficient, as it allows five shots for less carrying weight. These guns work well throughout the state for everything from close shooting in the Pineywoods to the wide open stuff in the High Plains. We give the edge to the over-under magnum, as it allows you to beef up your firepower with 3-inch shells if conditions and wildly flying birds demand. A lightweight, quick pointing gun is the quail hunter's choice.

For early season hunting, #9s or #8s are the best shot; move to #7½s in mid-season because the birds' feathers thicken. They will also flush sooner, making longer shots the norm. Bobs are thin-skinned and often just a smattering of light shot will down them. A high percentage of shots are at flushed birds going away from you, requiring that you hold on the bird. In level flight quail are moving at only 25 miles per hour, compared to a mourning dove flying at about 60 miles per hour with a tail wind; so unless a tail wind is moving the bird, right angle and even crossing shots don't require much lead.

DOG SELECTION   Quail dog selection comes down to matching the dog with the hunter's shooting style, personality, and even his lifestyle.

If you're an open country quail hunter and enjoy playing the role of drill instructor, the long-ranging pointers are for you. If you're mainly a heavy cover hunter, then the Vizsla or Brittany are good options. If your family has a vote in the matter, they'll elect the latter, since they're easier-going, friendly dogs.

English setter on bobwhite point.

The next matter of consideration is price. You should get what you pay for in a bird dog. Once you've made your selection you'll probably have further investments in general upkeep, but mostly in time spent ensuring the dog minds. You want a dog that will obey, hold your coveys, and not eat your birds. If your dog always breaks, he's not worth what you paid for him.

Acquiring your first bird dog is a major step, and individual sportsmen's criteria for selecting dogs will vary. Once you are an expert you may wish to re-rank the following to put more emphasis on qualities that make a champion rather than those that make for a pleasurable companion.

Bird Dog Assets
1. **Sociability**—with both humans and other dogs. A personality that fits with yours.
2. **Trainability**
3. **Desire and Determination**
4. **Range**—It's nearly impossible to train a dog to range farther, but he can be trained to range closer in.
5. **Stamina**—Unless you can afford a whole pack, you won't want to "re-dog" too often in the field.

The selection process starts with a knowledge of the dog's background. The primary source is the *Field Dog Stud Book* (American Field Publishing). Dogs that have what breeders call "pre-potent" sires are likely to yield dogs with good field trial and hunting potential. Pre-potent champions within a line are wonderful predictors and wonderfully expensive, too. But, be prepared to invest a princely sum because to chintz here is to open yourself to many months of misery, culminating in an embarrassing and non-productive hunt.

Finally, our selections omit many fine choices due to our concentrating on what present-day sportsmen rank useful for Texas hunting. More research by the would-be dog handler is definitely recommended.

English Pointer
The English pointer is the number one quail dog in Texas. The sturdy brown and white, ticked or spotted bird dog is bold, with a mind of his own, and a lot of spirit. It takes a hunter with similar qualities to bring out the best in this dog.

Endurance gives the English pointer an advantage over other quail dogs. This dog has the ability to cover wide ranges, an important quality for Texas quail hunts where it's not uncommon to cover 1,000 acres in a hard day of hunting. The dog's short hair helps him out in thick cover.

A weakness, only overcome by a great deal of off-season work, is retrieving. Frequent commands of "dead bird here" are required for the typical pointer. He's ready for the next adventure.

Some of the finest working pointers are bred in Texas, where thousands participate in field trials. These are usu-

English pointer delivers the goods.

motto, from ground trailing to fetching. The shorthair requires firm, decisive training and field commands.

Brittany Spaniel

Forget the "spaniel" connotation; the Brittany is bright and a darned good pointer. His longhaired coat gives him the same hunting disadvantage as the setter in Texas. The Brittany is best deployed against pheasant and woodcock, but many hunters use him to seek out quail in tight cover. One hunter we know works with six Brittanies, hunting a pair at a time, switching off when they're fatigued. The Brittany is a sweet-tempered dog and great as a pet, not to be yelled at in training or in the field. The smaller size and affectionate nature of these attractive white-and-liver-spot-coated dogs make them good candidates for pets as well as hunting partners.

ally heavily attended events, fun for the family and competitive to the extreme. Field trials are normally open to dogs of all ages; they include National Bird Hunters Association events, and often feature national "shoot-to-retrieve" trials where fully trained dogs point, honor, and retrieve.

English Setter

Outside of Texas, the English setter usually gets the "most popular" vote among the pointing breeds, although English pointers dominate field trials. Like the best picks in the old high school annual, good looks and personality count for many setter votes. You just want to be around this guy with his silky, soft coat, feathery tail, warm, gentle, and affectionate nature. This list of qualities goes on to include trainability—with the sometime exception of retrieving—and other natural attributes of great value. He's an airborne scent master whose pointing instincts are legendary and whose exploits at putting game birds in the bag have long been extolled.

Nonetheless, the English setter is still a runner-up in Texas. Setters suffer in Texas heat. In addition, the care their long hair requires, their weakness on running birds, and their medium range make them less than optimum for Texas terrain.

Where cover and coveys are thick, close-hunting Brittanys are a good choice.

German Shorthair

The German shorthair is a hunter's hunter. Perhaps the only reason he doesn't get top billing is that he doesn't look too stylish working. With his nose constantly vacuuming the ground, he's not only scenting the bird, he's also smelling for food. The typical shorthair doesn't range quite as far as the pointer, but he'll get the job done, hour after hour after hour. The shorthair has every bit as much stamina as the pointer, despite the heat. He's a tough dog and he beats pointers and setters hands down at the retrieving game. "Put the bird in the game vest" is his

Vizsla

The Vizsla, a Hungarian dog, is similar in many ways to the shorthair. One of the most versatile hunting dogs ever bred, the Vizsla's hunting tradition goes back more than 1,000 years. Typically a close-ranging dog, the Vizsla tends to pick close-holding birds and is a good choice for heavy cover quail hunting. He excels at the retrieving end of the business, and he can also be readily used for hunting other game such as pheasant and woodcock. The Vizsla makes a great family dog.

It's wise to protect your bird dog investment in the field, which is likely to be some of the rocky road terrain we've been discussing. In some of our more treacherous areas of dense brush, cactus, burrs, and rocks, you should take extra precaution in caring for your dog's feet.

Old innertube pieces make excellent dog boots. Cut rectangles large enough to cover paws. Punch holes in the corners and tie them on with leather thongs. Then wrap the thongs in place with duct tape, carrying the wrap up the leg to hold the thongs securely. Check your dog's paws frequently during the hunt. Also be sure to have water available for the dogs. Many areas simply do not have a lot of accessible ground water. Dogs don't have sweat glands to help them keep cool in hot weather, so give your dog a break and wet his belly down to cool him off on dog days. Rub him all over with cool water when he's really panting.

Texas distances call for careful consideration of dog transportation. Again, the best bet is to go first class with a well-ventilated trailer that will hold four or more dogs. Choose one with a compartment for feed, water, and assorted dog gear. Another way to go is a dog box that fits in your pickup bed. The worst option is to throw the dogs in with you in your station wagon. Sixty-pound pointers can be all too present on a long drive.

WARDROBE SELECTION   Quail hunting requires the most versatile clothing selection of all Texas outdoor sports. The layered look is always in when it comes to quail hunting.

Regardless of the season, dress to peel. Just add warmer layers as you get into January and February, particularly in the High Plains. Chill factors there have registered at 40 degrees below. Outerwear which you can tie around you or stuff in a sack is smart.

Your boots are your most important wardrobe item. Go first class with footwear; you can't hunt with sore feet. Just remember to break in your boots before you begin a 15-mile trek behind the dogs. Equally important over much of Texas during warm weather are leggings for snake protection. We favor the heavy canvas type over plastic sleeves although the plastic gives better protection. Don't cut or overheat a snake bite victim—man or dog—but get him immediate medical attention. The best first aid for snake bite is a set of car keys. (For more on emergency snake bite treatment when you're far removed from medical attention, see Chapter XIII.)

Brush pants, those made from cotton twill with nylon patches on the thighs, are highly recommended, especially in the western ranges. In pants, shirts, and jackets, go for snag-resistant, breathable fabrics.

During most of the quail season a lightweight, white, straw cowboy hat is ideal headgear. Your partner will be able to see it easily. Add international orange to your outfit when hunting with greenhorns. A felt or beaver cowboy hat, again in a light color, is the logical choice for late season.

GEAR SELECTION   Essential items include a lightweight but rip-proof game vest, game shears, whistle, and pocket knife. You might also add tweezers for paw treatment en route. Sometimes a cactus will jump right in front of you, making those tweezers welcome for your hide, too. In early season, we do a thorough job of dosing insect repellent on ankles, legs, and waistbands. Carry a small container of meat tenderizer to cope with fire ant bites, bee stings, and other insect attacks. Chewing tobacco works fairly well on bites, if you so indulge.

You'll want zip-type plastic bags in your game vest. Depending on your hunt plan, a small canteen may also be important. But carry as little weight as possible. You're going to walk more than usual, and over very tiring terrain. By the end of the day, even one shotshell can be too much. Don't overload on shells. Unless you're an awful shot, a box should do. This is another reason, by the way, for selecting 20-gauges or even 28s over the weighty 12s.

QUAIL HUNTER'S CHECKLIST
Hunting license
20-gauge shotgun
Bobwhite: #9s in early season,
           #8s or #7½s in late season
Blue Quail: #7½s and #6s
Game and shell vest
Lightweight rain gear, two piece
Lightweight T-shirt
Cotton twill shirt
Lightweight down vest
Brush pants
Straw cowboy hat—early season
Felt cowboy hat—late season
Hiking boots
Protective leggings
Wool socks
Canteen
Whistle
Insect repellent
Meat tenderizer
Zip-type plastic bags
Small ice chest
Game shears
Tweezers
Pocket knife
Alarm clock
Supply of innertube dog booties
Duct tape
Dog food
Water supply for dogs

TECHNIQUES THE EXPERTS USE

For many hunters, the early dove season (before the opening of quail on the first Saturday in November) is an ideal time to scout for quail. Without taking along a gun, you can give the dogs a good workout and locate birds as well. Pointing breed dogs could interfere with a dove hunt, so a better bet might be to simply take some time out to kick up birds while crisscrossing over pastures. Be sure to work typical quail cover.

Weather conditions can seriously affect your hunt. If it's too dry the dogs wouldn't find a bobcat's den at 20 paces. Too wet, same problem. Wind can blow scent to or away from the dogs, so try to hunt into the wind when it's blowing, which is usually all the time in West Texas. Both extreme heat and cold present special problems for dogs. You may wish to carry a light tin sauce dish with you for watering dogs if it's far between stock tanks on a hot day. Keep spare blankets for use in the dog trailer on bitter cold days. We've slept with the dogs on many a January night in West Texas, much to the amazement of motel operators.

BOBWHITE GUNNING TECHNIQUES To hit a bird it's essential to pick out a single bird from any flight, flock, gaggle, or bunch. This technique is most difficult to master on quail. The covey rise triggers something in the hunter closely related to paralysis, followed by a serious case of indecision or over-reaction, either one of which is good news for the quail. Shooting at the flock is the major error. But failing to settle in on a bird quickly can lead to a pick-and-choose approach, netting zero birds.

With a dog on point, the expert will stride to the point, gun held at the Army's port arms position, safety on, gun barrel pointed away from his companion. Don't sneak up. Don't sprint up. Just go right in, paying attention to your partner's position. Don't walk in front of him. Don't look down for the birds. Try to ensure that both of you have a shot and that you are covering the logical flight paths of the point area. Look straight ahead toward where you anticipate the covey rise. Even experienced quail hunters make the sneak-and-stop mistake while hoping for better position. They wind up not being in position when the covey rises. Forget it. Go straight in.

The main thing to keep in mind is that you have a lot more time than you think. Despite the noise and fuss, quail are not fast flyers. They get up quick, but you have all the time in the world to get off at least two well-considered shots at individual birds. Keep on the first bird until you're sure he's down. Mark him well before taking number two. This takes split seconds, and you have the time.

Covey fluster induces another instinctive reaction: shooting at birds that are too close. It's like trying to hit with a .22. You have time. Quail fly low, slow, and straight. Let them go on out a bit, and for heaven's sake don't position yourself between the birds and the flight path they're likely to cover with the thought that you're "heading them off at the pass."

SCALED QUAIL HUNTING TECHNIQUES Hunting for scaled quail, a.k.a. blue quail, requires some getting used to, especially as the birds are often hard to locate. Good blue hunters, however, have usually done some reconnaissance during deer season, marking various coveys.

Look for the blue's topknot moving through heavy cover. If you see one, you're apt to see many. Coveys of 40 or more are not uncommon in good seasons. If you're without a dog, like most blue hunters, start after the covey at your top speed. Don't hesitate. The closer you get, the better your chances of nailing one or more. With luck, you'll scare the covey into the air, where you have your best prospects. More likely, you'll be taking very difficult shots through heavy cover at birds running wildly on the ground. This is extremely sporting hunting, and a day of rough and tumble running over rocky terrain, up and down steep draws, through heavy brush, cactus, mesquite, and thorn bushes will ensure your aerobics for the day.

In the more easily negotiable areas of the blue's terrible terrain, hunters use dogs successfully in conjunction with good paw protection. Dogs come in handy for pointing and retrieving, but the problems usually outweigh the advantages in rugged blue quail country, because most pointing breeds are frustrated by birds running long distances on the ground.

FIELD DRESSING Texans have two schools of thought on how best to field dress quail. Most quail eaters prefer to take the little extra time required to pluck the birds; others remove the skin entirely. The skin imparts flavor, and fats in the skin help retain moisture. Either method is faster when you use game shears. Cut off the legs at the first joint above the foot, cut right down the back, and remove the entrails. Rinse out the cavity carefully. Don't carry undressed birds all day in a hot game vest. Take a break, clean out the birds, place them in zip-type plastic bags, and get them on ice as soon as possible. (If you plan to mount a prize bird and can't take it to a taxidermist within a day or two, freeze it.)

Cross Timbers and Prairies
Menu
·

Marinaded Tomatoes, Sweet Peppers
and Onions
Quail with Pecans and Grapes
Baked Acorn Squash
Whiskey Custard Pie
·

Oberhellman Chardonnay

BLACK-EYED SUSAN. *Rudbeckia hirta*. Single yellow flowers at the ends of many
rough, hairy branches. Grows one to two feet tall in carious soils—prairies
and woodlands. Annual or short-lived perennial, May through September.

Marinated Tomatoes, Sweet Peppers, and Onions

SERVES 4 TO 6

1 cup vinegar
1/2 cup water
1/3 cup sugar
2 teaspoons dried mustard
1 teaspoon celery seed
   dash cayenne pepper
   salt to taste
   freshly ground black pepper
1 green pepper, sliced
1 yellow pepper, sliced
1 yellow onion, sliced
6 tomatoes, peeled and sliced

PREPARATION

1. Combine all liquids and spices and bring to boil. Reduce heat and cook about 10 minutes. Stir occasionally.
2. When cool, pour over tomatoes, peppers, and onions. Chill overnight.

Quail with Pecans and Grapes

SERVES 4

8 quail
   salt to taste
   freshly ground black pepper
   flour
4 ounces butter or margarine
1 cup water
1 cup seedless green grapes
4 tablespoons chopped pecans
1 tablespoon lemon juice
2 tablespoons white wine
8 thick slices bread, a.k.a. "Texas Toast,"
   crusts trimmed, fried crisp in butter or
   margarine

PREPARATION

1. Rub quail inside and out with salt and pepper. Dredge in flour.
2. Melt butter in skillet. Brown quail on all sides.
3. Add water and lemon juice, cover tightly. Simmer for 15 minutes or until tender.
4. Add grapes and pecans.
5. Stir in wine. Cook for 2 more minutes.

Serve the quail on Texas Toast points and top with pan juices.

Baked Acorn Squash

SERVES 4

2 acorn squash
4 tablespoons butter or substitute
4 teaspoons brown sugar
   salt to taste
   freshly ground black pepper
2 slices bacon, halved

PREPARATION

1. Preheat oven to 350 degrees.
2. Cut squash in half, remove seeds. Cut a thin slice from bottom of squash so squash will sit firmly in pan.
3. Place squash halves in shallow baking pan.
4. Put 1 tablespoon butter and 1 teaspoon brown sugar into each cavity. Sprinkle with salt and pepper. Cover with half slice of bacon.
5. Bake for 35 minutes. Test for tenderness with fork.

Whiskey Custard Pie

SERVES 4 TO 6

1 unbaked pie shell
3/4 cup butter or substitute
1/2 cup sugar
6 eggs, separate yolks and whites
1 cup wild plum preserves (store-bought
   plum will work)
1 ounce bourbon
1/2 cup cream

PREPARATION

1. Preheat oven to 400 degrees.
2. Bake pie shell 15 minutes or until half done.
3. Cream butter and sugar.
4. Beat egg yolks, add to butter and sugar mixture.
5. Stir in plum preserves, bourbon, and cream.
6. Beat egg whites until stiff. Fold into mixture.
7. Fill half-baked pie shell with mixture.
8. Return pie to oven and bake for 45 minutes at 375 degrees. Test for doneness—when lockback blade comes out clean, pie is done.

IV

DUCKS

DUCKS

To a fair weather, sit-under-a-tree dove hunter, or to the quail purist admiring his dog's perfect point, the duck hunter must appear completely mad. There is absolutely nothing easy about duck hunting. In fact, it requires mastering a larger body of knowledge and developing more pure skill than any other type of Texas hunting. But it's worth it, because there is no substitute for the thrill of a flight responding to your call or the rush of wings descending upon your decoys. Duck hunters are seekers of the beautiful. They see beauty in some of nature's most obstreperous moods, in her brilliantly hued birds, in the multi-faceted challenges of the hunt, and in its grand history.

The massive Central Flyway ends in Texas, making our state one of the nation's leading areas for a variety of waterfowl shooting. The High Plains is prime for duck hunting thanks to the millions of acres of grain harvested there. The ponds and stock tanks of the Pineywoods are prime, too. And, just wait until you discover the great hunting along the Gulf Coast, or in the rice fields of Southeast Texas. Texas duck hunters have access to a full spectrum of ducks and duck terrain, more so than in any other state.

If you don't have a lot of experience with waterfowling Texas-style, we urge you to either make friends with an experienced hunter who owns a good, reliable retriever, or hire a professional guide. The latter is a good choice—often the only choice since there just aren't many top duck hunters with a penchant or patience for training greenhorns. In our opinion, the hardest, most dedicated workers in America are duck guides. They're generally willing to share from a lore of knowledge built up over a lifetime. They work like crazy in sometimes impossible conditions and are well worth their reasonable fees.

Duck watching is a sport in itself, with or without a shotgun, and sportsmen can be commended for furnishing a large proportion of the funds which have kept our waterfowl reasonably abundant for all to enjoy. Texans are among the largest contributors to Ducks Unlimited, and this organization's annual fall fund-raising banquets are major social events in the state's metropolitan areas.

Dangers still arise as once common species such as canvasbacks and redheads are on the decline, but good conservation methods do work. In the mid-1950s, for example, the North American wood duck was virtually extinct in the wild. Although still rightfully protected by a high point value, there are more than one million wood ducks in the United States today, and many of these can be found in the eastern third of Texas.

For many years, the U.S. Fish and Wildlife Service has banded ducks to identify flyways and migration patterns, and for other important waterfowl management purposes. If you are fortunate enough to take a banded duck, send the band number to: U.S. Department of the Interior, Laurel, MD 20810. Describe the duck completely, including its condition, such as fat or lean, and how you shot it.

Duck hunters are seekers of the beautiful—
but the search is never easy.

Also note location, date, time, and weather. Some duck hunters keep and wear their bands like merit badges. An indication of the fine quality of Texas duck hunting is the fact that there are more band reports submitted to the U.S. Fish and Wildlife Service from the Texas coast than from any other area in the nation.

Since the type of duck dictates distribution, the following are the species you'll find in Texas. Although ornithologists classify waterfowl into six groups, hunters group ducks as to whether they are puddle or diver ducks. Note that some species may be protected and therefore not huntable in certain years. Always check out duck point values before each season.

Birdwatcher guides often identify puddle ducks as dabblers or dabbling ducks because of the way they feed. They dine in shallow water by the "bottoms-up" method—tail to sky, bill underwater seeking grains, seeds of all kinds, snails, and aquatic plants. Puddle ducks forage in shallow lakes, marshes, fields, and stock tanks, usually close to land, and they'll sometimes feed on land like geese. An at-a-glance reference is the location of their legs, close to center as opposed to the much farther aft configuration of the divers. Puddle ducks take off like helicopters, unlike the divers, which look more like seaplanes building speed before take-off. Some say the

puddlers leap up or spring up, but in reality, like helicopters, they fly up, gaining launch velocity by a powerful down stroke of their wings.

Another quick reference on many of the puddle duck species is the iridescent, prismatic wing window, or speculum, found on the trailing edge of the wing. Some believe this brilliant, light-reflecting speculum serves as a beacon to keep birds together in flight, much like high intensity strobes on aircraft.

You'll find that recognizing ducks in flight has little to do with color, but more often with the shape of the bird, wing action, and especially the size and flight pattern of the flock. Most of the puddle ducks have a flight habit that will test your patience and willpower. They'll often circle the landing area more than once, and if you present your shiny face to the sky, they're gone. If they spot you, their powerful wings can stop them in mid-glide, driving them upward. And, since they are landing into the wind, they not only go up, but also away from your gun. In seconds they're out of range. All this will leave your shot string in the wrong place—under the target.

Puddle ducks have a roost and a feeding area. A normal day would see puddlers leaving the roost early, flying in to feed, returning to the roost at midday, then feeding again in the afternoon before returning to the roost for the night.

Unlike the puddlers, divers prefer open water, coastal bays, and sea coasts. As their common name indicates, they actually dive for food, sometimes to incredible depths. On the bottom, they pick up crustaceans of all sorts: fish, aquatic vegetation, and other marine foods, according to the type of duck.

Where puddlers habitually circle before landing, the divers tend to bore right into decoys low and fast. When they spot something phony, they flare to one side. To take off, most divers accelerate across the water for several yards, feet slapping to build airspeed.

Puddle ducks found in Texas include: wigeon, northern pintail, gadwall, green-winged teal, blue-winged teal, cinnamon teal, northern shoveler, black duck (including mallard-black duck hybrids rare in Texas), mottled duck (Florida duck), and mallard (including Mexican duck intergrade). Two interesting and fully protected whistling ducks are also spotted on the Texas coast and in deep South Texas: the fulvous and black-bellied whistling ducks. The most beautiful of all, the colorful wood duck, is also found where puddle ducks congregate, especially in East Texas.

Texas diver ducks, including even those that perhaps may not be hunted in a given year, include: lesser scaup (bluebill), ring-necked duck, canvasback, redhead, common goldeneye, common and red-breasted mergansers, and bufflehead. Though not technically divers, the stiff-tailed ruddy ducks are grouped with divers because they're almost exclusively aquatic feeders and as good at underwater swimming and diving as any diver.

On rare occasions you may observe some handsome ducks common in the Eastern United States, such as the masked duck, oldsquaw, harlequin, eiders, black scoters, and greater scaup. Hooded mergansers, too, are rare over much of the state, although fairly common in East Texas. Check any quality bird field guide for descriptions of these dandies.

WHERE TO HUNT

Each of the major regions of Texas has its own distinctive duck hunting. While most of the approximately 30 species can be found throughout the state, they are concentrated in specific areas.

PINEYWOODS—Lakes, ponds, rivers, and flooded timber provide great stand-by-the-tree, boat blind, and permanent blind shooting for mallards, gadwalls, wigeons, green-winged teal, and wood ducks. Don't miss out on jump shooting along the rivers.

GULF PRAIRIES AND MARSHES—Bays, marshes, swamps, lagoons, and the inland rice fields offer an incredible variety of ducks and hunting styles, from great puddlers such as pintails and mallards over rice fields, to lesser scaup, redheads, and canvasbacks on the coastal waters, including the extreme southeastern edge of the South Texas Plains.

CROSS TIMBERS AND PRAIRIES, BLACKLAND PRAIRIES, and POST OAKS SAVANNAH—Blue-winged teal and mallards lead a wide variety of great shooting in the lakes, flooded timber, and stock tanks in this area. Lots of good shooting is still possible before going to work in the morning in a metropolitan area.

ROLLING PLAINS—Large impoundments and heavy grain concentration attract mallards, pintails, gadwalls, and wigeons. Late season hunting here can be cold—and tremendously exciting. Hunter density drops because of great distances from major cities.

EDWARDS PLATEAU—Gadwalls are abundant in the stock tanks and lakes of this region. Of course, mallards, wigeons, and pintails thrive, too, and it's here that jump shooting stock tanks has become an art.

SOUTH TEXAS PLAINS (Except for Coast)—Gadwalls are plentiful here too, along with blue-winged teal, greenwings for a while, and wigeons. On the border you may see the protected fulvous and black-bellied whistling ducks and the "Mexican" mallard.

TRANS-PECOS—Where there is water, you'll generally find some shooting, usually on gadwalls, mallards, pintails, and wigeons. An exclusive of this area is the cinnamon teal, which is rare east of the Rockies.

PUDDLE DUCK INSIGHTS

AMERICAN WIGEON   The drake is marked by creamy white forehead and cap, plus stylish green mask running over his eyes and green speculum. His white cap gained him an earlier name not befitting his elegance—baldpate. Large white patches on the forepart of the inner wings are easily seen in flight. The hen has a dove-colored head topped with ecru brown. Her breast and belly are white

Large, white patches on forepart of inner wing identify the American wigeon in flight.

but she lacks the drake's large white wing patch. Wigeons average around 20 inches in length. They are alert, hard to sneak up on, and can be unnervingly loud on take-off with much wing racket and panicky whistling. A flock of wigeons approaches decoys in wide, circling, tight formations resembling teal flights. The wigeon will work to a mallard call. They dine well, in the fashion of geese, out in the middle of an alfalfa, wheat, or barley field.

PINTAIL Mr. Conservative, the hazel-headed drake wears a generous white pinstripe up the neck to the back of the head, originating from his white breast and belly. His bill is blue-gray. He's easy to spot in flight, with his large white undersides, long slender neck, and graceful streamlined wings. Look for his pintail or sprig, the black tail feathers extending far beyond the rest of his tail. The hen wears more of an overall sepia tone. In addition to common puddler feeding habits, they will feed in open grain fields, favoring the rice fields of Southeast Texas. They are also common on stock tanks. One of the longest and heaviest of the puddlers, the pintail drake can exceed 30 inches but usually weighs in at a little less than a mallard. Their flock patterns resemble a flying bow, with a curved leading edge. A fast bird, the pintail maintains a 50-mile-per-hour airspeed, and can hit up to 60. They will come to a mallard call, but most hunters use a pintail whistle to best effect.

A pin-striped, hazel head and blue bill distinctly mark the pintail drake.

GADWALL Compared to his colorful brethren, the gadwall drake is the Willie Loman of the duck world, a dingy, mousy gray with a buff head, brown crown, and a short blue-black bill. He's often called a gray duck. Both sexes have a white breast and belly. Gadwall markings are unusual because, for once, the hen dresses like her mate, with cinnamon upper wings and a head similar to the

A favorite of the Hill Country stock tank hunter is the good-eating gadwall.

drake's in color. Averaging only 20 inches in length, the drake can weigh more than two pounds. In the Hill Country, gadwalls outnumber most other ducks, even the ubiquitous mallard. He frequents stock tanks and lakes. His wings, when landing, appear slimmer than those of the mallard, his body chunkier. Wing strokes are rapid, and gadwalls tend to keep to smaller but looser formations— some are even spotted as loners. He calls and decoys like a mallard, but easier. This grainfed gray duck tastes great; make a place for him on your table.

GREEN-WINGED TEAL The little green-winged teal drake has style. His triple-toned head is chocolate brown and metallic green with a fine stripe of white. He has another distinctive stripe, uncommon among Texas ducks, running up and down just ahead of the wing. The hen is mottled brown on top. She has the smallest bill of all puddlers. A typical greenwing is only 14 inches long and weighs less than a pound. Teal are 50-mile-per-hour birds, capable of acrobatics that produce dove-like agility in flight. Their flight pattern is on the deck like a stealth bomber, hard to spot with a treeline background. Darters and dodgers, they invite some beautiful misses by the unwary, because the combination of small size, swiftness, and erratic flight will make your gun barrel twitch and

The namesake bird for Ducks Unlimited youth organization is the green-winged teal.

your nerves jump. Although they will fly to decoys, they don't respond to standard calls. A gentle "feeding chuckle" and whistle will help bring them in, but go easy. Teal love rice, all other domestic grains, and smartweed, plus insects and small mollusks. Despite these latter sources of protein, greenwings are excellent eating.

BLUE-WINGED TEAL   A white crescent marks the anthracite gray head of the blue-winged teal drake in late fall and spring. He sports a grayish tone on top, and cinnamon underparts. There's a chalk blue patch on his inner wing along with green speculum markings. The hen has a warmer-looking costume, buff on top with creamy feathering underneath. Both drake and hen resemble cinnamon teal in flight. The blue-winged teal leads most other ducks south to Texas, normally arriving in early September. The state usually sets an early season for bluewings and other teal to take advantage of their early migration. Bluewings migrate farther south than most other puddlers, most ending up in South America, some going all the way to Brazil and even Chile. Like other teal, migrating flocks stay bunched and appear to swarm when approaching a stock tank or pocket in flooded timber. They often circle, twist, dip, and swoop up and down in formation before landing. Quiet birds, they aren't easily called, but they come to decoys readily.

A September season is typically set for bluewinged teal since they are early migrants.

CINNAMON TEAL   The drake has a cinnamon-colored head and neck, and the same chalk blue wing patch and green speculum as his close relative the blue-winged teal. This teal is a true Westerner—one of the few ducks found in the Trans-Pecos. Like many Texans, he won't venture east of the Mississippi.

Trans-Pecos hunters are often treated to flights of cinnamon teal.

SHOVELER   Look for a bill that's longer than the head and you've identified the shoveler or "spoonbill." Otherwise, male plumage is very similar to the green-headed mallard drake; however, the shoveler has a green speculum rather than the mallard's bright blue one. The hen also resembles her mallard cousins. The superficial resemblance continues as shovelers average 20 inches in length and are heavy-bodied, although the shoveler's wings are narrower and rake back more. The big bill is the giveaway, and also a giveaway to its eating patterns. The shoveler loves dirty, muddy water and feeds heavily on leeches and crustaceans, as well as snails and aquatic grasses. In other words, grain does not make up a lot of his diet, so he's a better candidate for gumbo than *duck a l'orange*.

BLACK DUCK   The drake is yet another drab dabbler, smudged with black with white wing linings. The hen is more dust-colored, giving an identifiable contrast. The black duck is basically a Yankee, rare in Texas, and we see very few here that are not hybridized. The black mallard hybrid is more common. Black ducks are large, about two

His distinctively long bill gives this drake his name—shoveler.

Mottled ducks closely resemble the rarely seen black duck and more common black mallard hybrid.

is a cleaner brown than that of the black duck. He's a medium-sized duck at 21 inches in length. Mottled ducks are Gulf ducks—called Florida ducks on Florida's Gulf coast. In fact, it's our only resident duck of any sizable population on the Gulf coast; the others are migrants. He feeds heavily on spikerush, rice, bulrush, smartweed, green vegetation, and an occasional fish or snail. Mark him for the gumbo pot.

MALLARD   The drake mallard is the most publicized of all ducks in the world. His iridescent green head and neck, narrow white collar, and reddish brown breast have been celebrated in various art forms in cultures world-wide, from Russia and China to India and Burma, not to mention Luckenbach, Texas. Both sexes have white tails, white underwings, and the brilliant cerulean blue speculum. The hen's top colors are a mottled brown, with the head and breast lighter, tawny shades. Even after migration to Texas, he carries a good average weight of well over two pounds, length averaging two feet. Mallards often fly in a wide chevron formation, and in larger flocks than most other puddle ducks. They cruise at 45 miles per hour, but can accelerate to 60. The mallard decoys well, and callers love him. He doesn't like to land in the open

feet long, and some weigh every bit of three pounds. The black duck is not a picky eater, and will even feed without apparent harm in polluted waters.

MOTTLED DUCK   Both the drake and hen look like the black duck and have white wing linings which show clearly in flight, as do those of mallards. Body coloration

Bird watchers, decoy makers, and water fowlers have voted the mallard number one.

and especially dislikes a chop, so lee shore blinds are in order.

Mallards eat well. They do all the feeding they can on corn, barley, sorghum, oats, and other rich grain fields en route south. In Texas, the heaviest concentrations of mallards can often be found near the peanut fields of North Central Texas, but the birds are hunted successfully throughout most of the state. Just like the fine taste of cornfed beef, our grainfed mallard is excellent fare.

MEXICAN DUCK Often called Mexican mallard, most experts now consider this duck to be an intergrade of the mallard. In any event, the so-called Mexican mallard drakes and hens are similar to the aforementioned hen mallard. Look to the tail for the most reliable difference. The Mexican has brown tail feathers as opposed to the mallard's white ones. The Mexican's speculum is more aquamarine than the violet blue of the mallard. You'll find him only in the Trans-Pecos.

FULVOUS AND BLACK-BELLIED WHISTLING DUCKS Although rare in the hunting season and fully protected, these ducks are worth mentioning since they breed in South Texas. Both ducks have a distinctive berry-brown overall coloration, with a darker top on the fulvous and a

There is no mistaking the colorful wood duck drake.

The protected black-bellied whistling ducks are found in South Texas.

blackish belly on the blackbelly, logically enough. The black-bellied duck has a standout, red-nose bill. Both have long, goose-like legs; the blackbelly is found in the Brush Country and the fulvous is often spotted in the rice fields of the Coastal Plains.

WOOD DUCK The taxidermist's favorite, both the drake and hen wood ducks are striking. The handsome drake has a swept-back crest with iridescent green, nut brown, and heliotrope on the head, blending to Prussian blue on the back. White lines separate the brilliant hues of its headdress. The drake's eyes are red and the stubby bill and chest are a ruddy brown. The hen's shorter crest

A wood duck hen on typical tree roost.

Lesser scaups are better
known in Texas as bluebills.

lacks the flamboyance of the drake, but she has an exotic, tear-dropped white patch around her beguiling eyes. She has an overall brownish top with white underparts. They're small ducks, averaging 18 inches in length. The wood duck is a 10 on the dart-and-dodge scale, capable of 50 miles per hour through the trees. When hunted near wooded ponds and swamps he presents the shooter with all he can handle. His water landings are crash and splash, not at all graceful. And, unlike most other ducks, wood ducks will often land on a tree limb. Although wood ducks don't decoy well, they will sometimes buzz your spread. Look for large heads held high with bills angled down as distinct flight silhouettes. Since feed is mostly vegetarian, with lots of acorns, pecans, hickory, wild grapes, and berries, the wood duck is excellent on the table.

DIVER DUCK INSIGHTS

LESSER SCAUP Nicknamed bluebill for obvious reasons, the lesser scaup can also be identified easily by his dunce cap-shaped head. The drake's head is feathered almost purplish with dark colors down his neck. Look for a bold white stripe on wings in flight. The drake has a salt-and-pepper top, a white breast and belly. The hen is chocolate brown above with a white breast and belly. Bluebills are small targets, about 16 inches long, and they're fast, erratic fliers. Although definitely not grainfed table fare, the bluebill does have a diet high in vegetation. Unfortunately, the rest of the diet consists of crustaceans, insects, snails, and the like. He haunts the coastal brackish bays during hunting season. Bluebills decoy well, make great

shooting, and are okay for highly spiced gumbo. Just ask a Cajun.

RING-NECKED DUCK Though you won't find too many of these in Texas, enough visit to justify identification, since similarities in size, head shape, and coloration make them hard to distinguish, in flight, from the lesser scaup. Up close, you'll notice a distinct white band around the bills of both sexes, but by this time it may be too late. Don't bother to look for ring around the collar, by the way. When present at all, it's too faint to serve as a telltale mark. They are fun to jump shoot and they decoy easily. Ring-necks frequent fresh water, forested ponds, and creeks. They eat more vegetation than other divers, making them fair on the table.

A white band around the bill
distinguishes the ring-neck.

CANVASBACK Look for a long, straight black bill protruding from a reddish-brown, horse-head-shaped neck on the drake, and an equally long bill on the hen. The hen's head and neck color is more tawny than red. The drake has a dark breast and sailcloth white back and belly. The hen is brownish on top with a white belly. Only 21 inches long, they often weigh a hefty three pounds. And they're faster than all other ducks, with a cruising speed of more than 60 miles per hour, reported speeds of 70 miles per hour. Unfortunately, canvasbacks have become increasingly scarce in Texas. They're gun-shy by the time they reach Texas and can be difficult to decoy close enough. When you do see them, they're usually high in the sky in *V*-shaped wedges. They sometimes surprise coastal marsh hunters by flying within range on overcast days, but most often they're going so fast a shot is impossible. Once considered outstanding table fare because they ate so much wild celery, changes in celery availability have changed the duck's diet for the worse.

REDHEAD   Check closely to distinguish the redhead from the canvasback. The best in-flight identification is the redhead's much shorter bill, more pronounced forehead, and generally smaller head. The redhead tends to hold its head up higher than the canvasback. Both drake and hen bills are tipped with black. The neck is squatty, not at all like the graceful, horse-like sweep of the canvasback. Head colors are similar, so look for the redhead's distinct gray stripe running the entire width of the trailing wing edge. The redhead is a smaller, darker bird, averaging about two pounds. Redheads frequent our lower Coastal Plain, favoring open water bays. About 70 percent of the total redhead population winters in the Lower Laguna Madre. You'll sometimes see large rafts of redheads, much like geese on a roost. Redheads will rise a

Redheads are the staple of Texas coast hunters.

few feet then noisily drop back down. They also fly in *U*-formations. A high proportion of their food is aquatic plants supplemented with insects, frogs, and small fish. Like geese, redheads sometimes feed by moonlight. For divers they're above average eating.

COMMON GOLDENEYE   The goldeneye is one of our two fathead ducks, the other being the bufflehead. The drake has an oval-shaped patch on his cheek, a greenish head, zebra-striped upper flanks, and white underparts. The hen has a chocolate brown head, white neck, and white belly. Oh yes, they have golden eyes. They are smaller than average at about 19 inches. While flying, the adult drake's wings create a whistling sound which makes them as captivating to hear as they are to watch. They usually don't decoy well unless driven down on the deck by bad weather. With a diet laden with insects, crabs, mussels, and snails, don't roast 'em.

Glossy black, crested head and zebra-striped breast mark the hooded merganser drake.

BUFFLEHEAD   The bufflehead's head is shaped like the goldeneye's, but the drake's white patch is triangular, not oval, covering most of his oversized head. The drake's head has a purple cast, sometimes revealing a trace of green. The hen's head has a small, more oval patch. Buffleheads look like flying butterballs and are small, 13-inch birds. In flight, drakes display white patches across the wings. If you jump one, the bufflehead makes you think puddle duck rather than diver as he helicopters straight up. They congregate on open water, but tend to fly in small flocks. They'll decoy into typical spreads, often simply splashing in without preamble. Like other divers, their diet is heavy in crustaceans, so don't plan on a succulent supper.

COMMON MERGANSER   For such a handsome fellow, the common merganser gets no respect from Texas hunters, mainly because he's a great fisher and thus almost inedible. A slim-necked duck, the drake features a mallard-green head but distinctive red bill. The hen's head is chestnut brown and sports a bit of a crest. In flight, look for a white patch on half of the inner wing. This merganser frequents the Rolling Plains and Trans-Pecos. He's a large duck averaging about 25 inches, but his size comes from a fish diet so beware of putting him on the table if you're trying to impress company.

RED-BREASTED MERGANSER or SAWBILL This duck goes by a lot of aliases, such as fish duck and sawbill, but he's fairly easy to recognize. His shaggy crest flows behind a green head; the breast is more of a russet than a red. He shows the same wing patch as the common merganser. The drake has a distinctive black wing patch spotted with white. Both drake and hen have dirty white underparts. The hen has a mousy brown head. The merganser's bill is saw-toothed, ideal for feeding on fish, which is their want. They resemble loons in getting airborne, with much walking on water before flight. The hooded merganser is found all along the Texas Gulf Coast and generally left intact by hunters with high standards for table fare.

RUDDY DUCK This is a unique duck. His long, black tail is stiff, often set up like a fan, and he's the only duck found in Texas that dons completely different plumage in summer and winter. The drake puffs up an air sac when showing off to hens during courting season in late spring and early summer, though the duck rarely breeds here. There's a misconception that ruddy ducks are rare. They are just elusive and capable of disappearing beneath the water without even the slightest ripple. Both the drake and hen have oversized blue-gray feet set much farther back than other puddle ducks. The drake that hunters see in fall and winter features a distinct white cheek patch, black cap and mask with a broad blue bill. The body is dark gray on top and gray-brown on bottom. The hen has a smaller, less conspicuous cheek patch, but otherwise at a distance she resembles the drake in winter. These are small ducks with an average length of 14 inches. They decoy readily into standard puddle duck sets.

PREPARATION FOR
THE DUCK HUNT

TEXAS PREFERRED GUN SELECTION If you're serious about Texas duck hunting, your oldest, most beat-up 12-gauge pump with modified barrel is the ideal gun choice. We know guides who clean their pumps with fresh water hoses, use recycled motor oil, and sandpaper the rust away when absolutely necessary. Others take the trouble to sand off varnish and oil the gun stock with lin-seed oil, which protects without glare. For some of us, this might detract from the aesthetics of our hunt. Regardless, the gauge is right and a pump survives most anything—even poling a boat. You'll see a lot of 12-gauge over/under 3-inch mags in the field because they're durable and allow shot size flexibility in variable shooting situations. This gun, shooting the standard 2¾-inch load, is excellent for ducks over decoys. If you elect to use the double, select modified and full chokes for modern loads and steel shot. The type of duck shooting you plan to do most will help you make the best selection.

Shooting over Decoys
We should say shooting over decoys with a halfway accomplished caller in the blind. In ideal conditions, a 20-gauge mag load with a modified or even improved cylinder will do the trick. The 12-gauge is still a better choice, but with decoying ducks you can back off the firepower.

Shooting in Flooded Timber and over Potholes
This is a most popular form of hunting, but often physically demanding. A 12-gauge pump outfitted with a detachable sling is a good choice here. Every ounce you can leave on the bank helps. You're going to be standing until limit time, perhaps leaning against a tree using one hand to call and one foot to splash to simulate ducks feeding.

The 12-gauge, 3-inch mag, modified choke comes in handy, as many shots are farther out than over a decoy set. The three shots of a pump are sometimes welcome. Most importantly, you'll probably be walking in mud with stubs on the bottom and muck sucking down your waders. A walking stick is useful for keeping your balance, testing the water ahead for drop-offs, and breaking ice. Thankfully, we rarely need to break ice in Texas.

Most hunters take a dozen decoys or so on the walk into flooded timber shoots if they're aware of potholes or small clearings surrounded by timber. Again, you're adding weight, so shotgun selection becomes even more important. This is not the place for a 10-gauge.

Jump Shooting
Jump shooting appeals to those who aren't great callers, but who love a challenging hunt. Lots of strategy can be employed, and tension is high as you approach possible duck locales. Again, since a lot of walking needs to be done, weight is a factor to consider. Range is a major element, since long shots are the norm, as is the capacity for numbers of shots. The pump or autoloader, 12-gauge, 3-inch mag in modified or even full choke again gets the nod here. However, we would not suggest a full choke if this is your only gun, since it is limiting. Having an extra barrel is handy. Though some hunters simply haven't mastered a pump shotgun, quality autoloaders have solved this problem. With today's plastic shells, auto-

loader jam is infrequent. The pump is still lighter and nearly fail-safe.

Pass and Field Shooting

Field shooting is most often done for geese and sandhill cranes, discussed in later chapters. The most successful field shooting utilizes decoys, sometimes in a permanent set-up, other times with rags. Although good strategy may have been used in setting up in the field, patience is the byword. The ducks have to want to feed in your area.

Pass shooting entails placing yourself in what you think is a logical place for ducks to cross. A heavy mag load is required and, depending on walking conditions, you might even consider a full-choked 10-gauge.

Your shot size and load is determined by both the type of hunting and the ducks most expected on the scene, plus the pattern of your gun. Each is different.

TEXAS DUCK SHOT SIZE SELECTOR

(All magnum or high velocity load—12-gauge)

	TYPE OF HUNT	LEAD SHOT SIZE	STEEL SHOT SIZE
Mallard, Pintail, Wigeon, Gadwall, Redhead, Canvasback	Over Decoys	6–7½	4
	Pass Shooting	4–5	1
Bluebill, Teal, Bufflehead	Over Decoys	6–7½	4
	Pass Shooting	5	2

Shot Selection

Shooting the high velocity #7½s in a 1¼ load over decoys gives you a shot density advantage out to 40 yards, since you'll have about 440 pellets, around 75 more than the heaviest #6 load. And, it's easier on you. Still, #6s remain an excellent all-round load for any ducks over decoys.

However, if you're in a steel shot area, go immediately to #4s and #2s in the heaviest load you prefer. Although the great controversies about crippling versus lead poisoning seem a thing of the past, misconceptions about steel still exist. These misconceptions may be causing the misses.

Steel makes most of us a better shot out to about 40 yards. It leaves the barrel faster and gets to the target a bit quicker. Steel becomes an ally at short range, since most of us shoot behind by not swinging far enough through, or simply by misjudging the duck's speed. Beyond 40 yards, steel shot slows, and penetration and killing power drop. Leads then become longer and more difficult to judge, and a poor shot results in cripples. Beware of long steel shots; you're far better off not shooting at all.

Steel, by the way, will not damage the barrel of any standard-grade shotgun. Despite all the arguments for open chokes with steel, the fact remains that to kill cleanly past 40 yards, or in other words, in any pass shooting situation, you need all the steel shot on the target possible. Stick with your modified or full chokes in these situations. Under 35 yards, an improved choke is the better choice, as the steel shot pattern tends to be tighter.

Be sure to remove all lead shot from your field equipment and vehicles when in steel shot country. Finding lead shot in such places is *prima facie* evidence of a game law violation.

Carry an oily rag into the field to wipe your gun every so often. A small piece of oily rag tied securely to monofilament line can easily be pulled through the barrel if you're out in the wet for a long time.

DOG SELECTION   Selecting the right retriever is an even more personal decision than selecting the right gun. Your easiest option is to hunt with someone who owns a retriever or, better yet, hunt with a guide whose retriever probably recovers a thousand or so birds a year.

Should you get the urge either to buy a puppy and have it trained, or train it yourself, or to buy a mature, trained retriever, you have some hard thinking to do about the best breed for you. The wrong way to make this selection is by pure emotion. This could easily lead to a double divorce: you and your wife, and you and your dog. Your temperament, family status, and hunting habits all bear heavily on your choice of a retriever. If you are contemplating purchasing a retriever and investing significant sums in training, you may wish to try the following dog compatibility quiz. Don't dwell on the answers. Even if one doesn't apply at all, boldly check the box closest to your beliefs or feelings and move on. Grade your selection in a range of one to five with number one being most like you and number five being least like you.

The waterfowler's most important support system is his retriever.

RETRIEVER COMPATIBILITY TEST

MOST LIKE YOU	1	2	3	4	5	LEAST
1. You are a rugged individualist.	—	—	—	—	—	
2. You are single.	—	—	—	—	—	
3. You're married and your wife doesn't like dogs.	—	—	—	—	—	
4. Your children at home don't like dogs.	—	—	—	—	—	
5. You'd never use the dog for anything but waterfowl hunting.	—	—	—	—	—	
6. Your dog must be as rugged as you, withstanding all weather conditions.	—	—	—	—	—	
7. Your dog need not be even-tempered. You can control him.	—	—	—	—	—	
8. You don't care if the dog is affectionate. He's there to bring back the meat.	—	—	—	—	—	
9. You don't mind dog odor.	—	—	—	—	—	
10. The dog would live in a commercial or professional kennel; never at home.	—	—	—	—	—	
11. The bigger the dog the better.	—	—	—	—	—	
12. Your dog must out-fight, out-swim, and out-fetch any other dog.	—	—	—	—	—	
13. You don't care if your dog looks like a junk-yard dog, as long as he performs.	—	—	—	—	—	
14. You can train even the hardest-headed dog.	—	—	—	—	—	
15. You are intolerant of mistakes and fools.	—	—	—	—	—	
16. You tend to be impatient.	—	—	—	—	—	
17. You think spaniels are for kids, not hunters.	—	—	—	—	—	
18. You have a no-nonsense approach to life rather than a happy-go-lucky one.	—	—	—	—	—	
19. You would be embarrassed if your hunting dog looked like a poodle.	—	—	—	—	—	
20. You would frequently enter the dog in field trials.	—	—	—	—	—	
TOTALS	—	—	—	—	—	
	×1	×2	×3	×4	×5	
GRAND TOTAL	— +	— +	— +	— +	— =	—

The lowest possible score is 20, the highest 100. If you score anywhere from 30 to 70 you should first take a close look at the two most popular retrieving breeds, the Labrador and the golden retriever. If you scored 80 to 100, you might wish to investigate two great but underutilized breeds, the Irish water spaniel and American water span-

iel. If you score 20 to 30, it's a good possibility you'll find an ideal partner in the spectacular performance of the Chesapeake retriever.

Although the quiz is more for fun than anything else, it does have validity. There can be a serious mismatch of your personality and your approach to hunting with that of the dog. For instance, a Chesapeake functions best under stern command, while an American water spaniel won't function at all if yelled at, and there are important degrees in between. Really think about your dog selection because you can enhance your field experience and even your family life by choosing wisely at the outset.

Chesapeake Bay Retriever

The Chesapeake is a good Texas choice only for the waterfowl purist, and best for those who occasionally venture northward out of state to hunt in winter. Working against the Chesapeake in Texas is his double thick oily coat, which can produce an overpowering odor indoors. More importantly, in warmer weather, the dog is too insulated for his own good. Additionally, the Chesapeake does not make a good upland dog for other hunting, such as flushing pheasant and retrieving woodcock. On the positive side, many label the Chesapeake as the toughest, best water-working dog in the world. He's big and durable. This can be an asset in marsh hunting, where we've seen lesser dogs give up after a couple of days of the rough retrieving.

Mature dogs stand 26 inches or more at the shoulder and weigh up to 70 pounds. Some Chessies exhibit a tendency to do battle in the kennel. If this happens, bet on the Chesapeake. He's not a lap dog and generally doesn't exhibit affectionate traits. He becomes loyal to the right master, one who is forceful and decisive. The Chesapeake has a phenomenal memory for marking ducks downed and retrieving them, prioritizing crippled birds and then dead ones. It's as if he thinks through the odds of losing a bird.

Golden Retriever

To many the most handsome of the retrievers, with wavy, gold hair, classic shaped head, and plume-like tail, the golden retriever has a movie star image. He is a strong swimmer, second only to the Chesapeake in endurance and waterfowl-fetching ability. The golden's versatility makes him an excellent flushing dog for pheasant and woodcock, and he has an outstanding scenting capability for downed birds. Goldens are known for their gentleness and are usually great family dogs. A disadvantage is their large size at 70 pounds. And again, in Texas the long hair is a trap for both heat and burrs, making it more difficult to keep the dog comfortable through much of the year.

Labrador Retriever

Labradors come in three colors: licorice-stick black, darkest chocolate, and golden vanilla. Their smooth, rela-

Labs are the most popular retrievers in Texas.

tively short hair keeps them cool and free of burrs. And shedding is less of a problem than with other retrievers. While Labradors are also large dogs, averaging 65 to 70 pounds and a high-stepping 23 inches at the shoulder, they have a calm temperament and can fit into all but the smallest of homes. Contrary to their name, the breed originated in Newfoundland, not Labrador.

The most interesting chapters in the successful history of Labradors in America are just now being written. Labradors are coming into their own as a breed for upland game retrieving and flushing. Sportsmen with a bone deep lazy streak can find joy in the Lab's non-slip ability, waiting still as stone for you to down doves, then on command picking them up while you remain seated in the shade. The Lab can be trained to quarter close to the hunter within gun range, making him an ideal choice for pheasant and woodcock hunting.

Irish Water Spaniel

This retriever could win a poodle look-alike contest. He's a fun-loving, versatile dog with a tight curly coat that comes in but one color: a solid, deep chocolate. He's the largest of the spaniels, averaging about 50 pounds. He's intelligent, learns rapidly, and makes a good house pet.

This dog, retrieving uncounted ducks a day, was the favorite of the old market hunters. He was bred to hunt in the ice-cold, thick cover of Irish marshlands.

American Water Spaniel

If you want a 'coonhound or cougar dog, pass up the American water spaniel, but he'll hunt just about anything else, especially ducks. Weighing in at 30 pounds or so and standing less than 18 inches at the shoulder, he makes a good watchdog, a fine companion, and he's handsome. He has all the spaniel characteristics of friendliness and affection, and he can retrieve. He's only stymied by the weight of an oversized goose. The color of his coat is like that of his Irish cousin, usually a rich chocolate. Use him as a flushing dog on rails, snipe, pheasant, even rabbits. He's a real meat hunter.

Both the Irish and American water spaniels have curly coats, a drawback in Texas unless you like to spend time grooming your dog.

DUCK HUNTING BOATS Many Texans use their bass boats in duck season, and for that reason purchase them in dark green to aid in the camouflaging process. Bass boats provide safe and swift access to large reservoir hunting sites. You can transform a bass boat into a good floating blind by building a tubular frame and draping it with standard military-issue camo netting garnished with local

vegetation cut well away from the hunting area. Make sure the netting is well supported against high winds, because flapping camo netting tends to spoil the illusion and spook the ducks. Chicken wire woven through with indigenous brush or grasses works better for the sides. In fact, a roll of chicken wire prewoven with brush is a good all-round portable blind when not on the boat. Take special care to put a camo cover on the boat motor, even if you're not hunting from the boat.

Another favorite is the spacious aluminum jon boat, again in dark green. This is an excellent choice for shallow water, marsh, and flooded timber. A pushpole is often essential. Floorboards, even if homemade, are a comfort, as water slops in from boots, decoys, etc. Camo netting should be stowed aboard to completely lose the boat after the decoys are set and you're in your blind.

WARDROBE SELECTION Texas duck hunting is unique in that it can take place over a broad range of temperatures, often in the same day. In fact, during one memorable February hunt in West Texas, the temperature switched from a comfy 40 degrees to minus 10 degrees (with a wind chill of minus 40 degrees) within a few hours.

Duck hunters must select garb breathable enough for high-energy walking yet warm enough for keeping still once in place. Modern, membrane-type fabrics allow sweat vapor to permeate out while still repelling rain. In-

sulated vests that open to allow air circulation and lightweight, thin, polypropylene underwear are ideal.

Our favorite item of Texas hunting gear is the three-quarter length, triple-layered parka, which can be left open for air circulation. It repels water well and can be very warm when sealed up. Most importantly, it allows you to sit on a clump of marsh grass without risking diaper rash if you don't happen to be wearing chest high waders.

Headgear varies with the date of hunt. Early on you'll need the lightest-weight water-repellent hat that suits you. Later, the down-filled jobs with earflaps are a comfort and joy should a blue norther get you.

Wader care is essential. After returning to camp during the hunt, either turn them inside out or stuff them loosely with newspapers at night. Back at home, hang them by the feet in a cool, dry area until they're totally dry. Don't dry them in the sun. Store them in an air conditioned area in a plastic garment bag. Under your side of the bed is a good spot. Texas heat is the mortal enemy of waders once they're thoroughly dry, and storage in a garage will cause the waders to deteriorate rapidly. Use the minimum fold you can, preferably none, since creases weaken the fabric.

GEAR SELECTION A dark, durable canvas bag with pockets and a long, wide, comfortable shoulder strap is a must. It needs to be large enough for a thermos, two boxes of shells, several callers, a game strap, a flashlight, and perhaps a bite to eat for the truly dedicated ducker who refuses to return to camp for lunch. Extra gloves and even extra headgear such as a black wool watch cap are good ideas should the weather turn quickly from mild to miserable.

A strap for the shotgun is handy, too, if you have not permanently mounted a detachable one to your gun. If your gear doesn't already provide for it, a lightweight pair of raingear pants should also be tucked in. You'll want game shears and a utility pocket knife for field dressing.

Gloves are a strictly personal choice, as we know some shooters who can't stand to wear any at all. There are light wool gloves with soft leather trigger fingers that work well. For most of us, at least, a waterproof pair for picking up decoys is a must, because we tend to whimper with pain when there's ice on the water. A good tip is to buy these gloves as large as possible, so they'll slip over your shooting gloves.

Your choice of footgear also depends on the time and type of hunting you do. Whatever you choose, don't buy plain uninsulated rubber. You'll die out there. To be fully prepared for Texas, you need insulated chest high waders, essential in flooded timber hunting, and insulated hip or knee boots for blind and boat work.

Wool socks and synthetic wool blends over silk inner socks make a good, lightweight combination. Contrary to some advice, we prefer waders that fit comfortably, not oversized to accommodate lots of socks. Waders that keep pulling off of your feet in muck are one of the world's great abominations.

It's often appropriate to have several duck calls with you, especially with the variety of waterfowl that can be encountered on a typical Texas hunt. Following is a general guide to such calls.

TEXAS DUCK CALL SELECTOR

TYPE	SOUND
Mallard Wood Reed	Should produce a very loud quack, almost a hoarse note. The drake note is lower and reedier. It's important to be repetitive. It can produce the "ticka-ticka-ticka-ticka" feeding call. Have two, both large. You'll want to change out to allow the reed in one to dry.
Rubber Accordian	It will produce a mallard hen quack. When shaken, it imitates a feeding call. Gadwalls, black ducks, wigeons, and shovelers will come to mallard calls. Teal are comforted by feeding calls. Wood ducks will show an interest in decoys where the caller is producing mallard sounds, but usually won't decoy right into the spread.
Pintail Whistle	Produces a perfect imitation of the drake's melodious, soft whistle.
Wigeon Whistle	Easily duplicates the wigeon drake's musical whistle.
Open Water Calls	Since redhead hen's loud quack is similar to the mallard's, any mallard call will do. Commercial "open or big water" calls are available to get more range. The canvasback hen's quack is much higher pitched than the mallard's.

DUCK HUNTER'S CHECKLIST

Hunting license, federal and Texas duck stamps
12-gauge shotgun
Waterproof gun case, camouflaged
Shot shells, by duck and season
Shooting glasses
Duck calls
Decoys (pre-rigged), in mesh bag
Thermos (coffee)
Dark canvas bag with carry strap
Insect repellent for early season
Sunscreen
Camouflaged hats—warm and cold variations
Three-quarter, water-repellent hooded coat in brown or camo
Chamois tan/camo shirts
Insulated vest
Polypropylene or silk underwear
Comfortable khaki slacks with a spare set
Chest high waders/hip boots
Nylon bootie-type waders and shoes
Silk inner socks
Wool/poly blend socks
Game shears
Multi-purpose pocket knife
Self-sealing storage bags
Cooler for game transport
Sweater and lined moccasins for aprés hunt
Water repelling, lubricating aerosol spray
Shotgun cleaning kit with rags
Flashlight
Alarm clock
Game carry strap with multiple loops
Shooting gloves
Waterproof pickup gloves
Blackberry brandy for after the hunt
OPTIONAL:
Blind tool kit with bow saw
Machete
Large hammer
Soft wire
Dark nylon fishing line
10-penny nails
Dog food and equipment

TECHNIQUES THE EXPERTS USE

LOCATING THE DUCKS   Since much Texas duck hunting is done on public access land, reconnoitering and reporting is a most secretive affair; unlike the dove hunting custom, knowledge of hot spots has usually been hard won. This is especially true anywhere close to major metro areas, where hunter pressure and congestion in the hunt area can be intense.

Private duck clubs, notably those in the Pineywoods, are becoming more popular, as groups of duck hunters band together to purchase and improve the waterfowl quality of the land. And jump shooting on private hunting leases has always been fun. The High Plains area offers some hard to get at and sometimes very rugged hunting. Several hours of drive time from any big city thins out the competition.

Guided hunts are an excellent option when you consider that the cost of guide services is the lowest of all the major expenditures usually made before the first duck is down. Guided hunts are numerous in the Galveston Bay marshes, the Katy Prairie rice fields, and the Eagle Lake area. North Texas also provides some guided hunt opportunities. Guides enable you to learn at least the basics of duck hunting for each area of the state, a great asset since there are considerable differences in technique to be found sometimes within just a few miles.

DUCK CALLS   Calling is the most difficult skill to learn, and, fortunately for the ducks, few take time to master it. Duck calling is more effective as game harvest control than the point system used to compute limits: You either get ducks in close for positive identification and kill, or they stay way out of range because you blew a sour note. You can learn the basics in your living room or, better yet, while driving in your car with the excellent training materials that are available on tape cassettes.

DUCK BLINDS   Blind preparation is often another conservation aid. Again, many don't have enough experience in the art of duck blind design and fabrication, especially under primitive field conditions. Puddle duck shooters should take an imaginary helicopter flight over their blind, circling a few times while studying every inch of the ground with 10-power binoculars from 50 feet up. Do you think you could spot an ill-concealed hunter? What if his face were turned up? Could you see his eyes? You bet you could. And, you've just learned the major lesson of puddle duck blind construction: Put a roof, even of netting, on it and never, ever look up.

Blind construction does not require master carpentry skill. You should be working with local vegetation cut from a good distance away, since the fresh cut edges reflect light. If you cut the brush while it's still green it will hold together much better through the season.

A simple tool kit consisting of a small sledge, flat square of hardwood, bow saw, machete, baling wire, large nails, dark nylon line, and a burlap sack or two, along with some camo netting and chicken wire, will usually put you in business quickly.

Before building blinds in public hunting areas, consult Texas Parks and Wildlife Department or federal regulations, since there are always rules as to the what, when,

where, and how-to on construction and removal dates of blinds. Pay special attention to those lakes operated by the U.S. Army Corps of Engineers.

Blind location is key. Since puddle ducks favor close-in locations for shelter and feeding, you'll often have a natural background to work in. Morning sun, obvious flight patterns, prevailing winds, and the bitter Texas north-northwest winds will also shape your blind placement. On final approach, the ducks will be flying into the wind, so your blind-decoy combination must honor this above all factors.

THE ART AND SCIENCE OF DECOYS Decoys represent one of America's oldest continuing forms of folk art. Archeologists working under the sponsorship of the Museum of the American Indian discovered the oldest known decoys at Lovelock Cave, Nevada, in 1924. The only clearly identified species is the canvasback. These decoys, dated at nearly 2,000 years old, were made from tightly woven grasses and painted with native paints.

All 48 species of North American ducks will decoy to one extent or another. Early settlers learned from the Indians how to best attract each species. The Plymouth Colony survived on salted ducks for more than one winter during the early 1600s.

No doubt the decoy's first function was most pragmatic: to lure the bird down to earth. Eventually artistry superseded routine production, and carvers sought to capture the essence of ducks in their facsimiles. The art form has engendered fanatic collectors. Elmer Crowell (1862–1952) of East Harwich, Massachusetts, began carving decoys at age 10, hunting at 12. Later in life, he hunted less and devoted more time to detail carving and decorative painting. Today, it's not unusual for his decoys to sell in the $75,000 range, with prices in excess of $300,000.

Strictly for the purposes of hunting, you must have decoys and an understanding for the fundamentals of deployment. Today, molded plastic decoys, durable and functional, are available at modest cost. Most Texas hunters start their decoy spreads with mallards, often buying oversized ones since they seem to lure better, then adding other varieties to make a more natural combination of mallards and teal or mallards and pintails.

For puddle duck hunting, a good choice is a heron decoy set off to one side. Incoming ducks know that a heron won't stay in a dangerous place. In coastal hunting, goose decoys to one side serve the same purpose. If you're hunting from a permanent blind, try a crow decoy set atop your blind.

Rigging Decoys

Most decoys are sold without lines and weights. Standard lead pyramid-shaped weights are fine for most soft bottoms. Grapple style saltwater weights are excellent for rocky bottoms.

Choosing line is of utmost importance when rigging decoys. The most common mistake is to use a thin string cord. It tangles too easily. Select a heavy, dark nylon line, even up to 1/4-inch thick. You'll pay more per linear foot, but it'll pay off one cold dawn with tangle-free decoy deployment. Pay attention when tying nylon; knots can work loose. The mariner's bowline or standard monofilament fishing knot is recommended. Use a length of line about twice the water depth where you'll hunt. An anchor line at a 45-degree angle to the bottom holds best. For most puddle duck hunting, a good estimation of average depth is less than two feet. For diver ducks things get a lot more complex, since water depths can go to 20 feet or more.

A trick decoy really worth setting up is one that simulates a puddle duck feeding, creating a bottoms-up effect. To make this decoy, attach a screweye to the bill of the decoy. Run 20-pound monofilament line from the eye through another eye you've bolted into a section of scrap angle iron. The line runs into your blind, attached to a stick used as a wind up. When the spirit moves you, yank. Your decoy now feeds and ripples. With the additional aid of your feeding chuckle call, in come the puddlers.

Decoy Placement

Tomes have been written about decoy deployment, so much so that the average hunter is intimidated into thinking too much. We believe there are only two basic rig conformations: one for blinds on the bank and one for blinds set out in water.

The most common situation is a blind on the bank. For this, think fishhook shape. The shank of the fishhook should always point downwind, with each decoy set two or three feet apart. You are fishing for ducks, and they should land inside the barb. The open, decoy-free area inside the bend of the neck's shank should be the natural landing area. Your blind should be as close to this spot as possible; the wind should never be in your face. Otherwise, the ducks will land over you, causing some fancy shotgun gyrations. The best bet is to be placed so you can shoot crosswind into the landing area. The barb of the fishhook should be no more than 45 yards away, your maximum kill distance. Decoys should curve in much closer from the barb to the blind, downwind. They can be strung out loosely along the shank to attract incomers. Again, as a guide, the eye of the hook at the end of the shank should be within extreme shooting distance. Ducks beyond this point should never attract fire, and incomers should be allowed to fly well past this point before you shoot.

When mixing mallards and pintails, set the pintails out farthest, say all the way down the shank toward the hypothetical eye of your fishhook. The white of the pintail decoy is seen at a greater distance. When mixing puddlers, keep the same species together, leaving a little space between the clumps. We suggest you don't mix puddlers and divers in the same spread.

With a water blind, the idea is to surround the blind

with decoys, but use the same general theme to create landing areas near the blind, adjusting the number of decoys according to the type of hunting. Stock tank rigs can need as few as a dozen decoys or less. Rigs in any size water at all need to be at least four or five dozen. Carry the decoys in mesh bags that don't collect water. These can be floated out to ease the hunter's burden.

WATERFOWL WEATHER For duck hunters, fronts are harbingers of good hunting. The huge populations of ducks to the north, placidly gorging on Missouri and Kansas corn, move southward 12 to 24 hours ahead of major storm fronts. Hometown ducks sense the pressure change and begin flying to feed more often. Finally, the winds generally accompanying fronts keep birds on the move.

Of course, right at the heart of a storm is no time to be duck hunting. The ducks will wait it out in the roost. But a drizzle is fine, and overcast is wonderful, since it cuts down on night feeding.

Diver duck and goose hunters get uptight over bluebird weather, as you'd expect, because those waterfowl tend to fly in low earth orbit. But, Texans hunting puddle ducks in flooded timber, stock tanks, and protected ponds often do well on such days, particularly if there's some wind. The brightness helps the ducks see your decoys from greater distances, but they can also see you much better. So, hunt more carefully than ever on such clear, bright days.

DUCKS IN THE SHOT STRING Duck hunters have about the toughest time of all shooters, because their tar-

gets are small, very fast, and erratic, and the conditions are most often terrible. Ever try hitting skeet targets while mired in mud, or from your knees while in a rocking boat, or from a blind restricting your swing? Add high winds, other guns going off, poor visibility, flaring targets, and you begin to wonder how ducks ever became the essence of gumbo.

There are three basic ways to hit: snap shooting, sustained lead, and swinging through. Swinging through is by far the best, since the moving barrel cuts the necessary lead by as much as one half. The sustained lead is often used in pass shooting, and here you need a good idea of the bird's speed. Finally, snap shooting is only effective when you've either surprised a duck, or a duck has surprised you: Fire at a point where you anticipate the duck should be. Good luck. Grouse, woodcock, and quail hunters are usually forced into such shots, but snap shooting at ducks is not recommended.

The hardest thing to accept about ducks in pass shooting is their speed. Even cruising, most species are perking along at 40 miles per hour. When startled, 50 is average, with canvasbacks revving up to 70.

Thinking about how many feet of lead to use ahead of the duck is to ensure a clean miss. Instead, swing through the bird, estimate his length, and at 40 yards hold three times that and pull while continuing to see the target. Add one more bird's length if your tasty puddle ducks seem to be a bit spooked, because they will have gained 10 to 15 miles per hour. If you're hunting the most popular Texas divers—bluebills and redheads—your typical lead is four bird lengths at 40 yards. If divers are really movin' it, add two more bird lengths at 40 yards for a total of six.

The really important numbers are three lengths for puddle, four for divers, more if the birds are obviously moving on or if the birds are farther out. Trying to remember more than this means a sure miss.

FIELD DRESSING DUCKS Just as in quail, we prefer to pluck ducks rather than skin them if the ducks are to be prepared whole. Even if the ducks are destined for gumbo, the skin and fat add flavor to the stock. Ducks should be cleaned as soon as possible by making a cut just below the breast bone and down around the vent and scraping out entrails.

A professional duck-cleaning operation is always an option, but for the more determined, use your game shears to remove wings at the joint nearest the body. Remove legs at the joint above the feet. Next, pull out all the long feathers nearest the wings and tail, and rough pluck the duck. One trick is to melt paraffin in a large pot, preferably over an open mesquite fire at camp. The ratio is about six 12-ounce cakes of paraffin to a dozen or so quarts of water. Don't get the water too hot or the paraffin won't stick. Immerse the birds three or four times to layer them with wax. Then scrape away all the feathers with a pocket knife. You can recycle the paraffin by reheating it and removing the feathers. Skinning, which is acceptable for recipes calling for breast fillets, is much easier.

Pineywoods Menu

Tomato Aspic with Vegetables
Lively Duck and Oyster Gumbo
Minced Scallions and Parsley
Powdered Sassafras Root
Texas Long Grain Rice
Camp Bread Loaves
Indian Pudding

Cypress Valley Zinfandel

YELLOW LADY'S SLIPPER. *Cypripedium calceolus.* Rare and beautiful,
cream-colored to golden yellow. Has one to two flowers at the end of
the stem. Grows to two feet with large, veined, six- to eight-inch
leaves. In wood and bogs. Perennial. April through June.

Tomato Aspic with Vegetables

SERVES 4 TO 6

Tomatoes from the Pineywoods are a very special Texas treat. Many sportsman enjoy using a squeeze juice extractor to make their own tomato juice and sauces.

4 cups homemade tomato juice (canned will
 work)
2 stalks celery, one chopped to yield ¼ cup
1 onion, sliced
1 lemon—2 slices plus 2 teaspoons juice
1 bay leaf
1 teaspoon salt
3 envelopes unflavored gelatin
¼ cup cider vinegar
¼ cup grated carrots
¼ cup chopped cucumber
 bunch of green onions, chopped
 dash of Tabasco
 dash of Worcestershire sauce

PREPARATION

1. Chill one cup of tomato juice.
2. Simmer three cups juice with 1 stalk of celery, 1 sliced onion, lemon slices, bay leaf, and salt for 10 minutes. Strain.
3. Add gelatin to 1 cup chilled juice and ¼ cup vinegar in bowl.
4. When gelatin is softened, stir in hot juice until gelatin dissolves.
5. Refrigerate until it begins to thicken.
6. Add salt, chopped celery, grated carrots, chopped cucumber, and onions into gelatin.
7. Add two teaspoons of lemon juice, dash of Tabasco, and Worcestershire sauce. Pour into individual molds and chill until firm.

Lively Duck & Oyster Gumbo

SERVES 8 OR MORE

This is the all-time favorite sportsman's party entree. The origin is Cajun, but East Texans adopted it and one of our sportsmen friends, Carl Lively, perfected it from an old family recipe. Once you've made the roux, a gumbo can accept most any addition. The last touch is to add the lemon-flavored powder made from finely ground sassafras leaves, called filé. Sassafras has been a favorite for 400 years, the roots often used for teas, and it's said to have curative powers.

6 grainfed ducks, unskinned
2 quarts reserved warm duck stock
1½ cups peanut oil
1½ cups flour
2 onions, chopped—place in bowl near
 roux pan
1 8-ounce can tomato sauce
12 fresh, sliced mushrooms or 1 large can of
 mushrooms
 dash Tabasco sauce
 dash cayenne pepper
 salt to taste
 freshly ground black pepper to taste
1 cup Zinfandel
2 pints fresh oysters
2 ounces brandy
 Texas long-grained rice
 parsley, minced
 green onion tops, minced
 filé powder

PREPARATION

1. Cover ducks with water in large kettle. Bring to boil, reduce heat. Simmer until ducks can be easily deboned. Remove meat from ducks and reserve stock. Keep duck meat warm.
2. Heat peanut oil in large cast-iron skillet.
3. Reduce heat, begin to stir in flour a little at a time. Keep stirring, adding flour like you're making gravy. Smoothness is your first objective. By adjusting heat and stirring, cook this roux mixture until it looks like chocolate and has a consistency of gumbo mud. It will be almost burned when you have it just right. Don't chicken out, but don't let it burn either.
4. When roux is dark brown turn off heat and immediately add chopped onions to cool it down.
5. When roux has cooled add tomato sauce and place mixture in a large pot.
6. Stir in two quarts warm duck stock.
7. Add mushrooms and spices. Go easy on the hot stuff. You can't take it out, but you can add more later. An alternative to hot Louisiana spices is a Bermuda sherry pepper sauce which lends a gourmet touch.

GEESE

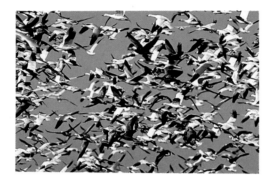

It was a glorious morning for Galveston Bay goose hunting. Following a black night, brisk 20-mile-per-hour winds raised goose bumps beneath our white parka camouflage. Patchy fog shrouded our ghostly quartet as we lay in wait, quiet and still in marsh mud. We were just the right distance from a roost containing more than 2,000 geese. The dawn preflight symphony exhilarated us.

But by 11:15 not one goose had lifted from the roost. Our hunt was over at noon and we were more than a little frustrated, since the roosting geese persisted in cackling at us all morning. We never did figure out what kept the geese on that roost, especially when we heard that other hunting groups had their limits early. However, our morning's hunt ended well in its final minutes.

We spotted four tiny targets on the horizon. Our guide started flagging the geese by flapping a white tablecloth up and down, simulating the action you'll see as snows feed. In a few minutes, the guide began calling them, while exhorting us to keep our heads down. After what seemed an eternity, four magnificent Canadas honked into our spread, flying into the wind. "Take them," came the command, and in an instant all four geese were down. It was a classic execution of the art and science of goose hunting.

Geese are some of the greatest wildlife treasures of the Texas coast. Since most of the great Central Flyway migration starts north of where it's practical to farm the Canadian prairies, populations have been stable at high levels for years. Even if you're not a hunter, the thrill of being smack dab in the middle of 100,000 geese in a Texas rice field is worth the paltry price of admission. Goose hunting is readily available to any Texan and at bargain rates without a guide. Hundreds of thousands of geese—snows, blues, white-fronted or specklebellies, and lesser Canadas along with some Ross' and greater Canada—winter in Texas, primarily in the rice fields south of Houston and on the bays and marshes of the coast. Goose hunting is also good in West Texas, out toward the Panhandle and in the Central Texas flyways.

Geese are hunted by jump shooting, from pit blinds over decoys, from beneath white parkas in a spread of white rags, and from marsh blinds. They are *not* hunted on resting areas or roosts, since this practice drives the geese out of entire areas.

Few thrills in hunting and fishing compare with the sight of geese sailing into the wind, wings cupped above your decoy spread. You know every eye in the flight is riveted on the landing area, so your head is down and you're careful to stay quiet, make no movement, or look directly up. If you must steal a glance at this spectacular sight, do so quickly, under furrowed eyebrows, without actually lifting your face upward. Geese have the sharpest eyes in the waterfowl business. Even with good facial camouflage, a goose will spot the whites of your eyes and flare out of range. When you do look up, if you are looking him in the eye, your goose is within good shooting range. This eye control is an excellent test of both your powers of observation and just plain nerve.

After peeking, firing too soon is the second most common mistake goose hunters can make. Geese are deceptively large, and even the experienced hunter frequently underestimates range to target. Since most goose hunting today is with steel shot, sky busting at more than 50 yards is ineffective. Steel shot does not penetrate well beyond 50 yards, and even well-hit geese may fly on, seemingly not hit at all, only to be crippled or die beyond recoverable range. Despite the knowledge of steel's long-range limitations, we see lots of hunters firing away at 75 to 100 or more yards. If you've never shot steel, as is the case with many first-time goose hunters, we advise shooting at a plywood backstop to compare the penetration of lead to steel shot at 50 yards. You're in for a shock.

Geese rarely fly a straight course, so the long leads also require that you estimate the drift from side to side and the actual direction the goose is flying, particularly on windy days. Geese tend first to fly downwind over your spread. The most productive way to hunt is to let the birds fly over, then call them back so they will fly into the wind, to your spread, wings set. Let the geese get even with you or beyond, then backshoot them. Goose feathers, as well as muscle and bone, are like armor plate from the front; shot penetrates better from the side and rear.

Knowing what to expect on the hunt is vital since weather, equipment, and gun and shell selection can vary widely. Be certain you know whether you're headed for miles of marsh, a short stroll through rice fields, a corn field in the Panhandle, or to a permanent blind. Each form of hunting calls for some specialized gear, and the local weather may make you wish for stuff that would keep you warmer, cooler, or drier.

Most Texas goose hunting is a guided affair, since the finest shooting is concentrated around either federal wildlife refuges or protected, private roost areas. Most guides will not hunt after noon, fearing the pressure may run the geese from a nearby roost, effectively stopping their paychecks until new birds arrive. This puts huntable land at a premium lease fee per acre. Enter the guided hunt to pay for it all. Many rice field hunts are not strictly guided, because hunters are placed in pit blinds and left to their own devices. But hunters are, in effect, guided to preset decoy spreads and locations.

As mentioned in Chapter IV, employing waterfowl guides is among the most rewarding investments you can make. Their efforts often make the hunt. And, like all of us, they respond best to the hunter who recognizes not only their skills, but also the work involved. Practice good hunting etiquette by sharing the load of rags, decoys, and game. This will make the trips in and out more tolerable for all. Your guides will appreciate the help if they are putting out and picking up hundreds of rags and decoys. Volunteer and pitch in. It doesn't take skill, but it does take effort to move through the typical marsh. Leave your

hunting area immaculate. Pick up shells, debris, *everything.*

Goose hunters are apt to come in contact with a host of marsh birds, including the ducks described in Chapter IV. Some of these marsh birds, such as snipe and rails, are huntable, but many others are protected. Some, such as the sandhill crane, have a limited season on some parts of the coastal plain. Check a recent copy of migratory game bird regulations, published each year by the Texas Parks and Wildlife Department, for up-to-date information.

Sandhill cranes are mainly hunted in the Panhandle. However, in recent years there has been an open season in South Texas, though it's much shorter than the goose season in the same region. Given the poor visibility desirable for good waterfowling, very costly misidentifications can occur. An out-of-season sandhill sailing quietly out of the mist is at risk before the gun of an overeager goose hunter, because the trailing legs that distinguish it from a goose might not be readily apparent. If sandhill cranes are in the area, you will usually know them by their distinctive, high-pitched calls.

Other marsh birds, although usually in no danger once they get closer, can momentarily fool the hunter. One long-range identification trick is to watch the wing beat. Egrets, cormorants, herons, roseate spoonbills, and wood ibises have a wing beat that pauses every so often. Geese and ducks keep their wings going constantly until set for landing.

Underhunted snipe and rails offer some of the sportiest shooting in Texas. Both are plentiful and reasonably good eating birds that few hunters seek, partially because it's such hard work.

Most of the nongame waterfowl covered in this chapter are found in the rice fields of the Gulf Prairies and Marshes and in the coastal area of the South Texas Plains.

GOOSE INSIGHTS

The gaggles of geese that blacken Texas skies in late fall and early winter are mainly *V* formations of lesser Canada, whitefronts, and undulating lines of snows and blues. These tourists and their less common cousins, the greater Canada and Ross' goose, are much happier in grain fields than on the water, although all are accomplished divers and generally roost on the water.

Geese are gregarious, as any Texas rice field hunter can tell you. It's not uncommon to see a flight of 25,000 to 50,000 snow geese lift off a roost at the same time. When one of these huge gaggles lifts off, the sound level is overpowering—a combination of wing roar and a wild, cacophonous symphony of honking that will leave you spellbound.

Although we have no scientific proof, it's our guess that the trademark *V* formation of many flying geese is not ac-

A skyful of snows, one of
nature's most exciting shows.

cidental. We think that, just like modern military aircraft, the *V* allows each pilot to maintain safe airspace, and younger, weaker birds may draft at the rear of the formation. The lead birds probably are the strongest fliers with the most experience on the migration flyway. They locate safe roosts and feeding areas.

A whiffling gaggle is one of nature's premier circus shows. Safety lies in getting down fast, so a side-slip maneuver is used, dumping air from the wings, allowing for steep spins and wondrous acrobatics as the birds plummet to safety. Side-slipping to a safe landing is taught early to airplane pilots in mastering a dead stick or no-power landing. Getting down fast is the idea.

Geese land into the wind and check out feeding zones while flying upwind. If you are good enough to jump shoot geese, you'll be amazed to find that their strong wings catapult them straight up like mallards and pintails. Normal takeoffs usually involve a little water walking, however.

Unlike ducks and most other birds, ganders and female geese dress about the same. Unlike human couples, they behave about the same. At age three the pairs mate for life, which is generally from six to eight years. Ganders help build the down-lined ground nests for their young and assist in raising their goslings. It is not uncommon to shoot one of a pair and have the remaining bird return to

find out what happened to its mate. The families fly together, too, with mature geese attempting to keep the younger ones out of trouble. Early season hunters harvest a lot of young birds who won't obey parental warning cries.

CANADA GOOSE Never say Canadian geese, as it will immediately mark you as a greenhorn. Subspecies identification of Canada geese is an expert's game, with 12 currently recognized and many more touted. We Texans make all this simple. There is a big one and a little one. The former is the giant Canada, but you'll see a lot more of the latter, the lesser Canada. We also have the western Canada and interior Canada subspecies, which are slightly larger and darker than the lesser, but otherwise too close to call by most amateurs. The giant Canada (maxima) were thought to be extinct at one time. Today, populations are said to be larger than those during Pilgrim times.

The regal Canada, a common
sight over Texas grainfields.

The Canadas have a black head and neck with a white throat and cheek patch. A white rump band is visible in flight away from the frustrated hunter; wings appear dark with white coverts under the tail.

Texas honkers range in weight from the lesser's 4 to 8 pounds to the giant's 10 to 18 pounds. Confusingly, an old gander of the interior or western subspecies can weigh up to 13 pounds. When they're this large, Texans call them giants. They all cruise at about 30 to 40 miles per hour, but look like they're loafing when actually topping out at 60 miles per hour. The long, slow wing beats fool sky busters into misses measured in yards rather than inches. Watch them serenely overtake flocks of mallards.

You'll not mistake the wild clarion sound of the honker. Canadas tend to keep to themselves and respond to reasonably adept calling, although they are easily spooked with a false note. If you're not sure of your call and the

Canadas have their wings set in descent to your decoys or rag spread, keep very quiet and still.

In Texas, Canadas are gourmands, feeding on corn, maize, or rice, so they make wonderful eating.

LESSER SNOW GOOSE AND BLUE GOOSE These classifications are now generally accepted as different color phases of the same species, the snow; although, this concept will earn you a fight in any Southeast Texas honky-tonk. In the white phase, the wings have black-tipped primaries. The blue goose usually has a white head and dark brown neck and back, but shows mixed white on the underside. Some blue-phase geese will show a lot of white on the chest and belly, so look for dark legs and bills. The legs and feet of the snow and blue geese are dark with a reddish cast. Immature snows are gray on top with tawny, dark legs. Immature blues have a dark head and body with dark legs and feet. The all-white-phase snows are from Siberia.

Their flight patterns sometimes vary from a *V* to a formation that looks like a long diagonal line in the sky. Hunters laugh about waterfowl being on oxygen, but there is one authenticated report of snow geese at 20,000 feet over mountains. Texas rice field hunters know this to be true, and some can't resist seeing if steel shot will climb to 20,000 feet. Snows are somewhat slower than Canadas, capable of 50 miles per hour maximum.

Snows and blues emit a double-note call and respond to calls imitating this sound as well as the traditional Canada honker call. Basically coastal birds, they decoy best to huge rag spreads.

Although snows feed on grain in Texas, they aren't quite as tasty as the Canada or specklebellies; but don't give them away, because this can be overcome with cooking tricks covered later.

WHITE-FRONTED GOOSE Ornithologists named this bird for the white band around the upper mandible or top

Blue geese and lesser snows are different color phases of the same goose.

The white-fronted goose is known to Texans as a specklebelly.

part of its bill. Sportsmen call him a specklebelly. Specklebellies are the only geese in Texas with heads, necks, chests, and upper parts a solid brown, the white front marks the only exception. But the black, splotchy barring on the chest and belly are the quick IDs. Also look for orangey yellow legs and feet. If you don't, the game warden will look for you because limits on specklebellies usually are less than on snows and blues.

In good shooting weather, meaning poor light, immature specklebellies can be mistaken for immature blue geese, or vice versa, because they don't have the adult's distinctive white bill mark and prominent black barring. The younger birds' legs and feet are much duller, too. This could be a costly mistake.

To make matters worse, specklebellies mingle with other geese. They are often alone, however, and have a tendency to cautiously approach decoys, circling lower and lower, testing the patience of all but saints.

Their call mimics laughter and is the most difficult goose call to copy. The solitary flier circling your blind is best left to his inspection without benefit of a concerto from you, since we know of no surefire call except that from the throat of the most experienced guide. However, if the call is properly imitated, they will decoy readily.

Hunters with a keen appreciation for excellent table fare covet the specklebelly for he is, in our opinion, the best eating of the Texas grainfed geese. Don't trade him for a larger snow, whatever you do.

ROSS' GOOSE This is a scaled-down version of the snow goose from the black primaries to similarity in flight speed. Their diminutive size is that of an average mallard. Measuring just two feet in length, the Ross' is the smallest American goose. They are quiet fellows, seldom calling in the air, emitting a bit of a soft cluck while feeding.

MARSH BIRD INSIGHTS

The marsh and coastal goose and duck hunter is, or should be, a birdwatcher if only as a legal defense. Eighty percent of the migratory birds of North America fly through our coastal bend counties each year, and a fair number of these migrants join local residents over the rice fields and coastal marshes. Some of these birds are legally huntable, but by far the majority are not.

Many of our shorebirds are breathtakingly beautiful or so rare as to remind us of our ecological frailty. Some are sporty enough to test our skills, and tasty enough to warrant special effort. Whatever the motivation, we urge you to obtain a good bird guide and study up before your next marsh visit. The rewards are worth it. We have described a few that should be of interest to the Texas sportsman.

LESSER SANDHILL CRANE The best way to hunt

Trailing legs and extended neck
mark the lesser sandhill crane.

this big, imposing gray bird is to get as far from the Texas coast as you can and still be in the state, such as Bailey County in the Panhandle on the New Mexico border. But most hunters, due to hunter density, see their first sandhill over the rice fields of Southeast Texas or out on the coastal marshes. Sometimes this first sighting in bad light has poor consequences for both crane and careless goose hunter.

Slate gray overall, the lesser sandhill features a brick red gimme cap—missing on immature birds—and an off-white throat and neck. This "Little Brown Sandhill Crane," as it's known in many ornithology books, can have a wingspan of six feet. It's fun to watch the wingtips in flight. At the end of each slow, deliberate, and powerful downstroke the primary feathers curl up. Unlike ducks and geese, the sandhill and other cranes will glide from time to time. Look for the trailing legs, a telltale crane feature. Another giveaway is the melodic, purring *kro-oo-oo* flight call. It sounds nothing like a goose or duck and it can be heard for more than a mile on a still morning. Check for the sandhill's extended neck to further distinguish the crane from egrets and herons, whose necks are folded back against their bodies in flight.

Migrating from as far away as Alaska and the Arctic, sandhills head first for the shallow playa lakes and grain fields of the High Plains. In wasted, harvested grain fields, they pose no real problem, but in unharvested fields, sandhills cut through like mini-harvesters. Many landowners welcome hunters for only a day lease fee to save their crops. The landowners don't expect a major sandhill coup, mind you—they know better. But, they do like hunters milling about, like mobile scarecrows, chasing sandhills from the fields.

Sandhills fly out to feed each day from their roosts on the shallow playa lakes. They will feed in the same area until grain is exhausted or they're driven south by weather. Unlike geese, they tend to stay in the fields all day rather than return to protected roost areas at midday. Feeding flights become longer as winter progresses.

During the winter, although usually after the hunting season, the sportsman can be treated to a rare and wonderful sandhill performance: an acrobatic square dance involving 100 or more cranes, leaping, whirling, pirouetting, and preening—all the while emitting their fluting call. The privileged few who've seen the dance of the whooping crane say this sandhill ballet is comparable.

A decoy technique similar to snow geese rag sets is used for sandhills. Gray-tinted rags are substituted for white in order to match the birds coloration. Hunters hide in the 300-plus rag spread under camouflage cloths or tow sacks rough-sewn together. Where available, corn stubble is used in conjunction with rags to completely hide the hunter, since the cranes have excellent eyesight. Some hunters dig shallow trenches for their feet and legs so they can sit rather than lie down—a position that gets old quickly. Stick up decoys can also be employed.

Texas sandhills are grainfed delicacies on the table. They eat a lot of insects, frogs, and aquatic vegetation before migration, but once in the nation's bread basket, and in Texas, they stick to corn, rice, or other tasty grains.

COMMON SNIPE The snipe is the most underutilized and sportiest game resource in Texas. This bird needs an ad campaign. While snipe season is the longest of any Texas hunting season, it takes a lot of hard work, sloshing mile after mile through marshes to get even a shot. Then there's the shot itself, which is as difficult a shot as you can make, especially if you try it when the bird first flushes. Erratic doesn't begin to describe his flight path. When flushed, he explodes from cover. His small size makes him seem faster than he is and farther away. Both factors throw the hunter's synapses into shock. The result is a missed snap shot at a target that is too close, followed by no second shot because the hunter is fooled into thinking the snipe is out of range.

The common snipe is an uncommonly tough hunting challenge.

The snipe is a member of the sandpiper family, though he is stockier with much shorter legs, and the brown on brown stripes on his head are bolder. He thrives in coastal marsh and ricelands. Like the woodcock, a close woodland country cousin, snipe feed by probing the soft earth with their long bills. While woodcock seek worms, snipe also probe for snails, insects, and small crustaceans. They are migratory and are often present in heavy concentrations in season.

It's ironic that "Snipe Hunt" has come to mean a silly, meaningless chase. You may well come home from the marshes feeling meaningless and silly with no snipe, but if you've flushed and shot at them, you'll know the pleasure of some of the most challenging hunting ever.

Snipe are tasty critters despite their crustacean and worm diet. There's more meat on them than on doves, but then again, you won't have near as many in your bag.

AMERICAN WOODCOCK While the best woodcock hunting is on the higher ground of East Texas, some woodcock are found along our marshy coastal area. In spite of his close relation to sandpipers and snipe, Yankees classify the woodcock, properly, as an upland game

The woodcock wingshooter will not overtax his retriever.

bird to be hunted with pointers or setters much in the manner of quail. For matters of dog selection we refer you to Chapter III, for the best woodcock dogs are also the best quail dogs, with one major exception: Many dogs are averse to the woodcock's potent odor. Mature dogs not specifically trained to hunt the bird will often refuse to. But, because woodcock are as well camouflaged as quail and are generally found in denser cover, it's important that your dog be trained to retrieve them.

Woodcock are similar to snipe in overall coloration, with plumage resembling dead leaves and feathers in mottled tones of black, brown, reds, and grays. The woodcock is much stockier than a snipe with a neck like a pro linebacker. Atypical of his sandpiper heritage, the woodcock's legs are much shorter than the 'piper's or snipe's. The eyes are set well back on the head. Some say this enables the bird to spy predators while seeking worms with his long bill stuck into moist earth. Also look for a skullcap barred horizontally on the woodcock.

Woodcock are not heavily hunted in Texas, yet they provide some of our greatest wingshooting. They are present in deep East Texas in good numbers when the migratory birds augment the native population.

Woodcock favor secluded bottom areas with soft, black ground, which crappie fishermen know to be good worming. They stay close to shady, dense cover, but like it fairly open and close to the ground. They feed right on the edges of heavy cover and will fly there whenever possible. You can sometimes spot areas they are using by their numerous little bore holes in soft ground, as well as their whitewash droppings.

When the birds are startled into explosive flight, many hunters mistakenly believe the twirring sound of the woodcock is vocal. In fact, the sound is caused by its primary feathers. Game biologists have proven this by plucking a few of the primaries. The plucked birds rise silently. In any event, the sound of a woodcock's initial burst can unsettle the hunter and cause a premature blast which, if on target, demolishes the bird. Fortunately for all concerned, these quick shots at under 10 yards are often smooth misses. Granted, the woodcock leaves you little time for reaction, but take the extra second to allow the bird to fly out into range and to make sure you are on. Because of the cover, sustained leads are not possible. Use the swing through method; not much lead is necessary since the bird is a lot slower than you think.

We favor a 20-gauge over/under, bored improved cylinder and skeet. Most clear shots are close and it doesn't take a cannon to knock down a bird the size of your fist. Select a #9 shot. Woodcock are unsocial birds and often get up as singles or pairs. A third shot is unlikely. Hitting the second bird of a pair is even more unlikely for most of us.

Since woodcock principally feed on worms supplemented with insects and berries, they are not favored by many at the dinner table, but we consider them a delicacy well worth a proper table presentation. Woodcock hunting goes far back into European history, and aficionados today still hang the birds to heighten their flavor. This works in Texas only if you're sure of no more than 40-degree temperatures. Unlike most upland birds, we generally skin woodcock because the skin and fat impart a stronger flavor than most care for.

RAILS Also lightly hunted in Texas are the solitary, sneaky, and downright difficult rails. Hunting rails is a team effort, because the best technique is to pole a shallow-draft jon boat through marshy areas, gunner forward, at the ready.

The four huntable species of rails are migratory and are

The largest huntable rail is the king, found in the Gulf marshes.

found along the Gulf Coast marshes. They include the king rail, clapper, Virginia rail, and sora. There are also many smaller rails, such as the protected yellow rail and black rail.

The king rail is the largest of the four huntable species, but he is seldom seen. A mottled black with olive streaks, his head is grayish on top and his underparts are cinnamon. The king, clapper, and Virginia rails all have long bills with a slight downcurve. King rails often hybridize with clapper rails, which are similar except smaller and duller in coloration. Clappers usually make up the bulk of the bag on a Texas Gulf Coast hunt.

The Virginia rail is about the size of the clapper but has blue-gray cheeks and often a reddish bill, compared to the olive brown bill of the king and clapper.

The sora is the smallest of the four, with a completely different bill—short, thick, and yellow. He feeds more off vegetation than the snails, fish, and worms eaten by the other three rails.

Most rail hunting is done on the high tide when the marshes are flooded. The birds are not strong fliers and prefer to run away from danger. However, shooting is not as easy as it looks. Most often you'll be shooting from a wobbling boat platform, the bird will not stay up long, and you'll be surrounded by tall marsh grass. Best bet is to stay right on the rail holding a little under to compensate for the fact that he probably is already soaring back down in the time it's taken to mount your gun. We prefer a 20-gauge with #9s—a skeet choke is just right.

As indicated earlier, the sora is the best eating of the bunch, but they all roast up tasty. We like them most in a Cajun gumbo.

COOT This shorebird is a member of the gallinule family. The much-maligned coot is found almost everywhere ducks are. Known in Texas as mudhens, they are also

Pouledux are popular in Cajun
gumbos, but Texans leave coots intact.

called whitebills. Both sexes are mostly black with small
heads, white bills, and gray underbellies. And they're only
about 14 inches long. Coots are comical to watch as they
get into the air, but reasonably speedy when finally airborne, legs trailing behind. They are only slightly more
edible than most diver ducks and look like puddle ducks
when feeding, which is usually on underwater vegetation.
At times you'll see them feeding on the bank. They don't
decoy at all. Cajuns skin them, trim off all fat and pop
pouledux into tasty gumbos. Texans can too, with a little
urging and the right recipe.

COMMON MOORHEN   British ornithologists have won
the battle for naming this bird, known formerly in Texas as
the common gallinule. The moorhen favors freshwater
habitats, shallow marshes, and lake edges. Often mistaken for the ubiquitous coot, the moorhen's easily noted
field mark differences include the rust red bill with a yellow tip, as opposed to the coot's white bill, and a white
streak running the length of the sides just under the
wings. Overall color is blackish gray growing darker on
the top. The common moorhen is usually hunted at the
same time and by the same methods as rails and coots.

PURPLE GALLINULE   With purple head and under-

The common gallinule is now officially
known to bird watchers as the common moorhen.

parts, bright red bill tipped in gold, sky blue forehead
shield, and garish yellow legs, the purple gallinule is the
Dapper Dan of the marsh birds. His back is a bronze
green and he has a white patch under the tail. This is a
spectacular bird to spot in his freshwater marsh home.

The purple gallinule's long toes enable him to walk on
floating plants. Gallinules and coots feed mainly on
aquatic plants and are certainly edible, especially in
gumbo.

Purple gallinules add a special touch
of wild color to Texas freshwater marshes.

ENDANGERED, UNCOMMON,

AND PRETTY

Texas marshes exhibit the richest bird diversity in all North America. Some, like the famous whooping crane, are very rare.

Many endangered and protected birds under Texas regulation frequent the coast or are at least seen there on occasion. These include the endangered brown pelican, bald eagle, Eskimo curlew, interior least tern, peregrine falcon and subspecies American peregrine falcon, and whooping crane.

Uncommon birds sometimes found over the marshes include the reddish egret, white-faced ibis, swallow-tailed kite, osprey, wood stork, and least tern.

Roseate spoonbills lead the beauty parade over the marshes, followed closely by the great blue and little blue herons, plentiful great egrets, white ibis, and tri-colored herons. A common but not-so-pretty marsh dweller is the anhinga. We also see some cormorants, most often the double-crested variety.

Texas lists other birds as endangered or protected and species are added from time to time. All migratory birds are protected by law. We urge every hunter to familiarize himself with this list. Many of these protected species are covered in Chapter X.

WHOOPING CRANE The saltwater marshes of the Aransas National Wildlife Refuge north of Corpus Christi are the wintering grounds for one of the continent's most famous endangered birds. The number of cranes dipped to 15 birds by the start of World War II and now only just tops the 100 mark. Whooping cranes are large birds, four-and-a-half feet tall with seven-foot wing spans. Adults are white overall with black wing tips, a red hat and mask. Black wing primaries are evident in flight. Although a visit to the Aransas National Wildlife Refuge is a great experi-

ence, especially in the fall, the best way to see the cranes is to boat the Intracoastal Waterway through the refuge. The last time we went through we spotted 13 birds, quite a haul, but not uncommon in December through February. The birds begin arriving from Alberta, Canada, and Grays Lake National Refuge in Idaho in mid to late October, and leave Texas by mid-March. All are far north of Texas by mid-April.

One of America's most famous endangered species,
the whooping crane, winters on the Texas coast.

PELICANS Texas pelicans come in two colors—brown and white. The American white pelican is common on our coast, a prodigious soarer with wingspan reaching beyond nine feet who can ride a thermal to great heights. In migration they frequently cross the Rocky Mountains. While feeding in shallow water, white pelicans will often form a conga line rounding up baitfish. They don't dive for their supper like the brown. Hundreds of white pelicans can often be seen nesting on South Bird Island in the Upper Laguna Madre. This island is protected by the National Audubon Society and signs warn visitors not to land.

Texas sightings of brown pelicans dwindled precipitously during the '60s, but they are often seen in the coastal bend, especially in the Port Aransas area. You'll never forget their spectacular feeding dives with great showers of water and menhaden thrown skyward. Gulls can be seen stealing fish right out of the brown pelican's mouth.

WHITE IBIS On a typical marsh hunt you'll see many flights of white ibis. His chestnut cousin, the white-faced ibis, is on the protected list. Young white ibis have white

Brown pelicans fish the intracoastal
waterway near Corpus Christi.

underparts but are dark on top. Mature birds are all white
with black-tipped wings. Their imposing bill is the main
field mark—very long and curved downward like a scythe.

In flight, the scythe-like bill of the
white ibis is a telltale field mark.

ROSEATE SPOONBILL This pink-bodied Texas
beauty often evokes exclamations from those who think
they've spotted a flamingo, a most unlikely occurrence unless one has escaped captivity. With a wingspan of more
than four feet, it's a fairly large bird with a whitish upper
back and neck. The bill, as you'd guess, resembles a large
spoon. Spoonbills feed in a fascinating manner. The birds
swing their partially open bill from side to side in the water, not scooping, but rather sluicing minnows. The bill

Roseate spoonbills entertain
marsh hunters on the Texas coast.

closes when its sensitive nerve endings detect minnows.
Then the bird raises its head and swallows.

You'll often see roseate spoonbills in silent *V* formation
flight or in long lines crossing the marshes. Back in the
'20s, roseate spoonbill wings were the fad in fans, and
market hunters almost wiped them out. Thankfully, the
colorful birds have made a welcome return to our coast.

GREAT BLUE HERON The great blue heron, with his
unmistakable slate color and black cap, is a common visitor to small stock tanks and ponds as well as the marshes
of Texas. When disturbed, he'll utter a disgusted, deep
croak and lift sedately on six foot wings, for all the world
portraying an image of outraged dignity.

Great blue herons are show stoppers wherever
they lift off—from stock tank to coastal marsh.

EGRETS The most beautiful of the Texas egrets is the
great egret, formerly called American egret. He is entirely
white, a yard high with more than a four-foot wingspan. In
flight all egrets pull their heads to their shoulders. While
feeding in shallow water, their lovely, graceful necks are
extended to give them a better view of potential prey, usually small fish. The great egret was the guy the early-day
plume hunters went after, but they've made a strong
comeback. We also have the snowy egret, who should be
called a showy egret in breeding season. The fluffy plumes
on its head, neck, and back curve upward in season, lores
turn bright red, and feet orange. The cattle egret is the
most common, often seen feeding in the fields with livestock where they're probing for insects that have been
kicked up by cattle. You'll even see them riding cattle, but
it's to peck at insects, not as a mode of transportation.

PREPARATION FOR

THE GOOSE HUNT

TEXAS PREFERRED GUN SELECTION We have
covered duck gun selection in Chapter IV, along with rec-
ommendations for guns to hunt rail, snipe, and woodcock; here we will concentrate solely on guns for geese.

The legal limit for geese and all migratory birds is a gun
no larger than 10-gauge with no more than three-shell capacity. If you really want to be consistent with steel shot,

Accidentally imported from Africa, cattle
egret populations are exploding in Texas.

go the limit: Invest in a 10-gauge, 3½-inch mag autoloader.

Some professional guides specializing in hunting near
refuges or manmade roosts say the boom of the 10-gauge
disrupts resting birds. You can tell when 10-gauges are in
action on the marsh or rice field.

If you use a single- or double-barrel 10-gauge, you'll have 80 percent more recoil energy than with your high brass 2¾-inch 12-gauge. We've seen strong men cry after firing "Big Ugly," a particularly obnoxious 3½-inch mag, single-barrel 10-gauge that we used as a sky buster for many years. Full choked, 36-inch "Big Ugly" went along on rice field hunts as a backup to an over/under 3-inch mag 12, and in the days of lead shot could really reach out. But the shooter paid the price. "Big Ugly" could also be used to pole boats and as a pry bar, so it was what you'd call a versatile gun—but not for everybody.

Avoid autoloaders if conditions are going to be really gumbo mucky, with a strong possibility of the hunter taking a pratfall. There is nothing more frustrating than an autoloader action filled with muck when geese cup their wings over you. A 12-gauge pump or double, modified/full, is a better foul-weather gun choice, particularly if you carry a bit of oily rag tied to a piece of monofilament. No matter how muddy, you're still in business.

A gun sling is an absolute must; inexpensive ones are available in nylon, or you can add permanent mounts that allow quick release of the sling.

In terms of shot size, a goose hunter should not shoot less than #2 steel shot. Patterning a goose gun is as important as sighting in your rifle, but only one hunter in a hundred will bother. Steel shot will pattern differently than lead, so make the effort to find out just what your patterns look like at 35 and 50 yards.

Whereas most duck hunters tend to overestimate range to target, it's just the reverse for goose hunting until you've gained experience. Your mind just can't accept the bird's size differential. That's why we recommend the #2s. If you shoot a double-barrel with selective trigger, have a good decoy spread and a good caller present. Dropping back to #4s in the more open barrel will usually give a better pattern density at the 40-yard marker. If geese decoy, the shot can be very effective and result in fewer wounded birds.

Much of the literature on the subject decries the 10-gauge or even mag 12s. But much of this literature was written before steel shot. Ask any busy goose guide how many more cripples he has to wring the necks of now that steel is in.

We suggest using the maximum firepower you can comfortably manage out of the biggest legal gun you can handle. Even then, make sure of a clean kill before swinging to another bird. Too often we see a glider or crippled bird sail on, way out of reach of man or dog. If the hunter had only kept firing at the same bird when it was in range a cripple would've been killed.

A retriever is a must in marsh hunting, but not at all necessary when hunting from pit blinds in a rice field. Refer to Chapter IV for retriever selection tips. If you're planning to do a lot of goose hunting, opt for the larger breeds such as the golden or even the Chessie.

WARDROBE SELECTION Again, the wardrobe used for duck hunting is essentially the same for hunting geese. Select a short boot with rubber bottom and waterproof uppers in a size you can wear over the trout fisherman's booty wader or by itself. For marsh work, we recommend chest high waders that end in a booty, over which you slip on a durable short boot or even canvas running shoes. The latter is a special rig allowing much more freedom of movement across the muck bottoms or marshes than traditional waders. They make great sense when you have to walk a mile or more to good hunting. Having two pairs of the overboot shoes is a good idea, since they tend to get water-logged. Chest-high waders are also a comfort if you have to sit or lie on wet ground.

In the pit blind, you usually don't need waders, but the rubber-bottomed boots come in handy. We have made the mistake of going to a pit blind in a rice field dressed comfortably for a dry hunt, then proceeded to knock a goose down into a decidedly undry adjacent field. When hunting pit blinds in the rain, don the marsh waders.

GEAR SELECTION Geese are very vocal birds, so calling can make a tremendous difference in your hunt. Sitting quietly by a pond just after sundown, we watched and listened as Canada geese on the pond called to incoming flights. Time after time, the flights would reply, cup wings, and whiffle down gracefully until, even to our eyes, the pond became crowded. When the next flight came over, the call from the pond was notably different—a harsher note that conveyed "No room at the inn." The incoming flight flared and continued its journey into the night. Geese do talk to one another, and Canadas use at least 10 distinct calls.

Naturally gifted goose callers use their own vocal cords instead of a commercial call. The rest of us need help. Since geese will respond, take the time to learn their idiom. It's easier than calling ducks, since high-powered duck calling comes from the diaphragm, while goose calls come from the mouth.

Although you can build up a call repertoire, it's comforting to know that the basic highball call for Canada geese is one simple note, similar to that used by football quarterbacks—a "hut" produced with our basic wooden reed call. Snows and blues will answer to this same call, but their typical call is a two-tone "we-honk." Specklebellies usually approach your decoys in silence, so you should be quiet, too. The specklebelly call is a wild one, a loon-like laugh and very difficult to master.

There are also large rubber bellows-type "horsecock" calls, which operate like an accordian and do an adequate job on Canadas, snows, and blues. This call, when shaken, mimics feeding geese. However, it has a distinct disadvantage in that it requires movement at a time when being still is mandatory.

When hunting with guides, it's best to let them call unless you're really good. Even then, courtesy demands that you check with the guide. Most often, all incoming birds need is the sound of one caller, so you run the risk of spooking geese without measurable gain.

GOOSE HUNTER'S CHECKLIST

Hunting license, Texas and federal duck stamps
10-gauge or 12-gauge, 3-inch mag shotgun with
    shoulder strap
Waterproof camouflaged gun case with shoulder
    strap
Steelshot—#4s, #2s and BBs
Shooting glasses
Goose calls, including rubber accordian type
Decoy, shell type
    (often already set in place on guided hunt)
White decoy rags
    (often supplied on guided hunt)
White ¾-length coat—preferably with hood
    (often supplied on guided hunt, check first)
Thermos, camouflaged
Dark canvas bag with carry strap
Insect repellent for early season
Camouflaged hats
Lined, water-repellent, hooded marsh coat in
    brown camouflage
Tan chamois shirts
Insulated vest
Poly or silk underwear
Comfortable khaki slacks and spare pair
Rubber-bottomed boots
Trout stream booty waders
Wool/poly blend socks
Silk inner socks
Multi-purpose pocket knife
Cooler for game transport
Change of apparel for goose lodge
Lubricating aerosol spray
Shotgun cleaning kit
Flashlight
Game carry strap
Shooting gloves
Monofilament line with oily rag
Alarm clock
OPTIONAL:
Dog whistle
Dog food
Camouflage netting to cover pit blind

TECHNIQUES THE EXPERTS USE

LOCATING THE GEESE The best goose hunting is near refuges or manmade roost lakes. For starters, we urge you to try the pit blind hunting leases of the Lissie Prairie and Eagle Lake area, or the marsh hunting out around the Anahuac Refuge. Just check with the Eagle Lake or Wharton chambers of commerce. There are several fine guide services, some of which provide lodges and excellent cuisine to sooth your marsh-abused body.

You can get into some great West Texas goose hunting in public access land, but it's quite a gamble unless you have connections. West Texas is a big place.

CONCEALMENT This is no problem when hunting rice fields or Panhandle playa lakes, where metal pit blinds are provided. The guides usually even have shell goose decoys in place, although we've learned these can be a liability after the novelty has worn off for resident geese. You'll approach a pit blind in pitch dark, so a flashlight comes in handy to locate them. They are generally marked with reflectors. Shine your light down into the pit, taking care not to impale yourself on the reeds used to surround the blind. You're also looking for unwelcome varmints of any sort. We used to partially cover the pit blind with our own camouflage, but if you stay absolutely still and don't crane around this isn't necessary. You may find water in the blind. Your thermos cup now doubles as a bailer, and your rubber bottom boots feel nice. The guide can usually tell you if you'll need waders.

Hunting in a rag spread is entirely different. You are now a decoy, becoming an oversized goose clothed in an aseptic white, mad scientist-type coat. By the end of a typical morning's shoot, it won't be white, but it will blend exceptionally well with the marsh (since you'll be wearing a lot of marsh). You'll be lying in mud, so waders and waterproof jackets are welcome. Look for good stands of three-quarter grass, *scirpus*, that have been chewed on by the geese. The geese love this sweet-tasting sedge grass and will return to it.

When hiding in the middle of a rag spread, it's easy to get yourself into a position where you simply can't get up quickly enough when the geese are all about you. When you do struggle to your feet, you find your parka hood is blocking your vision and you're fumbling for the shotgun safety. Meanwhile the geese fly off, or worse, are shot by your partners. Very embarrassing. As the geese are coming in, stay hunkered down ready to spring up or creak up. Don't sit down. Here's the expert's trick: If right-handed, keep your left hand on your hat, under your parka hood, and your right hand on the gun safety with trigger finger ready. On the caller's signal flip the parka hood back as you stand up, simultaneously bring your gun up and safety off. The rest is up to you. Keep shooting if there's the slightest chance you haven't made a clean kill. We've seen geese fall 50 feet, hit the ground with a thud, then get up and fly off.

Rag spreads are the most common. Gauge the position of the spread according to the daily flight patterns of the geese and the spots where they have obviously been chewing up the marsh. Fresh whitewash completes the proof of recent feeding. This feces has a fluorescent quality that causes it to glow in poor light, enabling geese to find feeding areas and other flocks even at night. Typically, hundreds of rags are draped across every tuft of marsh grass in sight for quite a distance, though today rags are more often replaced by white plastic squares, sometimes with black markings to simulate snow geese primaries. The plastic squares are good because they are durable and don't absorb water. A clear area is left in the middle of the spread, usually at a spot where there are at least some sitable tufts and higher clumps of grass for the hunter's comfort and concealment. Don't make the mistake of hiding away inside a big clump, since your vision and swing will be restricted. If you try to slip up on geese feeding in a field, be aware of the ever-alert sentinels. Not many geese are killed this way unless the hunters are Green Berets. Wind sock decoys are becoming popular, as are balloons and kites.

GOOSE WEATHER When clear weather and a full moon coincide, geese, Canadas in particular, feed all night long like deer. On the morning that follows such a night, you might as well stay in bed. All you'll hear is a gaggle taunting you from the sanctuary of the roost. It pays to check your calendar before making a reservation so that you avoid bright phases of the moon. Also like deer, geese will develop a pattern, flying again and again from the same roost to the same field in a straight line until the grain is gone or shots interfere. They will start at one end of a field and systematically move across it. If there is a weather or wind change, they may abandon a field they've used for days, then return a week later.

Fronts tend to move geese, like all other game, to feed. Light rain and spotty fog are wonderful, especially if they last through the night. Wind is usually helpful since it forces geese to negotiate strong air currents and helps distract them from danger on the ground. It also slows the big birds on final approach to your decoys and can encourage them to fly lower.

Geese won't fly in heavy fog and rain, because they can't see and that fabulous seven-power vision is their best defense. But often, as soon as the fog lifts just a bit, they are off the roost and flying low into the fields, an ideal situation for the hunter. In changeable Texas weather, it's a real advantage to schedule at least three days hunting.

Geese are not necessarily early risers, although you certainly want to be in place before dawn since early feeders are most easily fooled into your decoys. You may hear them on the roost all morning. Many feeding flights don't take off until slugabed times after eight o'clock. Often the birds only feed two or three hours. Then tiring of all this effort, they fly back to the roost just before noon for a siesta. So stay put until the very end of your hunt if you don't have your limit. Invariably, we give up at 11:30, and as we walk out we're strafed by a flight landing right amongst our decoys. One needs an equaniminous personality to survive such moments.

GEESE IN THE SHOT STRING Unlike most duck shooting, with geese you'll often have the opportunity to use a sustained lead technique when pass shooting, because they are so large. We still favor sticking with the swing-through method as a habit. To simplify the lead question, follow the same advice we gave for most ducks. At 40 yards with a 90-degree crossing shot and an unspooked goose, allow three lengths. Add another length for a goosed goose for four total. At 50 yards, our self-imposed limit with steel shot, add another length for all but the giant Canada; a half will do for him.

Remember that a medium-sized goose is almost a yard long, so a sustained three-bird lead at 40 yards is right on nine feet. This is exactly where the mental computer says "no way" and you proceed to shoot way behind. Believe these leads. Override your mental computer and you'll down more geese. Do not stop the gun barrel when you pull the trigger, as this is probably the most prevalent cause of misses.

FIELD DRESSING GEESE Geese, which in Texas are heavy grain eaters, provide some of the finest eating of all waterfowl. Young specklebellies are best, followed by Canadas, then snows and blues. Inasmuch as geese shooting is a team effort, and you may get a choice at day's end, be a good guy and select the smallest, youngest of the specklebellies. Look for wear on nails—less wear equals younger birds—and small wing knobs. Graciously offer the big snows and blues to your friends.

Heat is the enemy of good, sweet taste in all game handling, even geese shot on a cold day. Goose down is a terrific insulator, so there is a possibility your geese could stay too warm. One safeguard is to draw the birds by slicing across the anal area then reaching inside and extracting the entrails. In any event, make sure this is done promptly, even if you are taking the easiest way out and leaving the geese with a professional plucker.

In our chapter on ducks we discussed the time-honored paraffin wax plucking method, which is effective but messy at best. Another method is dry plucking. Start plucking around the neck, forming a complete band first, with the neck of the bird facing you. Press the exposed skin tightly with the thumb of one hand while plucking the feathers out away from you, also pressing hard. You'll feel the sensation of pressing the feathers out of the skin. We keep a disposable propane torch in our truck gear for all-purpose use. It comes in handy to singe off the down and pin feathers left after dry plucking.

If you're going to make gumbo or soup, skinning the geese will do, but we recommend plucking. A plucked goose will taste much better, even in gumbo, because the fat under the skin adds flavor to stock. See the Duck & Oyster Gumbo recipe, p. 90. Geese make a wonderful substitute for ducks if you're feeding the multitudes.

Strong sentiment prevails in favor of breasting geese. It is quick, simple, and diminishes some of the strong flavor. You only lose about five percent of the edible meat, and it's the least edible part. Simply pluck the feathers that are on the center of the breast. With a sharp knife, slice along the bone that runs down the center of the breast until you feel the bony plate that separates the breast from the body cavity. Turn the knife to run along this bone and out to the wing area. Then strip this meat from the skin and feathers. You will end up with a fillet of very usable meat. Repeat the procedure for the other side. With just a little practice you can clean a goose in two minutes. If you insist on saving the marginal meat on the thighs, separate the thigh from the body at the joint. Using your hands, pull the skin from the thigh then cut it at the knee joint.

The same breasting method is effective with ducks, teal, and sandhill cranes. Ducks and geese will have a different taste when cleaned this way, because much of the objectionable odor and taste of fowl comes from the glands and parts of the body cavity, particularly those along the back and ribcage, which are almost impossible to remove or clean. With wildfowl, the best meat is not next to the bone.

Blackland Prairies
Menu
·
Cucumber Soup
Broiled Breast of Goose
Wild Plum Jelly
Calico Corn
Spinach Salad
Lemon Cake
·
Fall Creek Chenin Blanc

PINK EVENING PRIMROSE. *Oenothera speciosa.* Delicately pink, cup-shaped flowers, can also be rose-pink and occasionally white. Low-growing and drought-resistant, it abounds on roadsides and open fields. Perennial, March through July.

Cucumber Soup

SERVES 6

Cucumbers, onions, and radishes are grown in abundance in East Texas. Here's a refreshing use for them.

2 tablespoons butter or substitute
6 green onions, chopped
2 unpeeled cucumbers, diced
1/2 cup raw potato, diced
2 cups chicken broth
1 tablespoon red wine vinegar
1/4 teaspoon dry mustard
1/2 teaspoon dill
   salt to taste
   freshly ground black pepper to taste
1 cup sour cream
   radishes, chopped

PREPARATION

1. Saute chopped white parts of onions in 2 tablespoons butter.
2. Add everything else except green tops of onions, sour cream, and radishes.
3. Simmer for 30 minutes or until potatoes are tender.
4. Puree and strain through cheesecloth for an elegant presentation. A blender is easier.
5. Chill until ready to serve.
6. Just before serving stir in sour cream and garnish with radishes and green tops of onions.

Broiled Breast of Wild Goose

SERVES 4 TO 6

2 boned out breasts of young specklebelly, skinned (reserve other parts for gumbo)
1 cup Pheasant Ridge Chenin Blanc
   freshly ground black pepper
   salt to taste
   pinch dry sage
1 bay leaf
   pinch dry marjoram
1 tablespoon grated onion

PREPARATION

1. Marinate goose breast in all other ingredients overnight.
2. Build mesquite fire, let burn to hot coals.
3. Drain breasts, paper towel dry, and place on grill.
4. Cook medium rare—only 10 minutes or so per side.
5. Slice on the diagonal for serving, and serve with wild plum jelly.

Note: Wild plum jelly recipe is found on p. 287 in Chapter XIII.

Calico Corn

SERVES 6

6 strips bacon
1 green pepper, chopped
2 onions, chopped
10 ears fresh corn (substitute three #10 cans)
2 cups grated longhorn cheese
1 cup light cream
1 small jar pimentos, chopped
   salt to taste
   freshly ground black pepper
3/4 teaspoon powdered ginger

PREPARATION

1. Cook bacon in cast-iron skillet until crisp. Remove and drain.
2. Saute green pepper and onion in bacon drippings until soft. Don't brown.
3. Cut corn kernels from cob, not cutting too deep. Use dull knife to scrape cob, milking it. Add corn to skillet.
4. Add cheese to mixture. Stir constantly and cook for about ten minutes.
5. Add light cream, pimentos, seasoning, and crumbled bacon. Heat until mixture bubbles.

Spinach Salad

SERVES 4 TO 6

6 slices lean bacon—reserve 1/4 cup drippings
1/4 cup wine vinegar
2 tablespoons blue cheese
2 tablespoons sugar
   dash Worcestershire sauce
   salt and freshly ground black pepper to taste

4 cups fresh, washed, and drained spinach, torn
2 hardboiled eggs, diced
2 green onions, sliced

PREPARATION

1. Fry bacon until crisp. Crumble into bits. Reserve drippings.
2. Combine drippings, vinegar, blue cheese, sugar, and condiments.
3. Lightly mix spinach, eggs, and onions in salad bowl.
4. Pour sauce mixture over spinach.
5. Garnish with crumbled bacon bits.

Lemon Cake

SERVES 6 TO 8

1½ cups sugar
½ cup butter
1½ teaspoon grated fresh lemon peel
3 eggs
2½ cups cake flour, sifted
½ teaspoon baking soda
½ cup milk
¼ cup fresh lemon juice
2 cups powdered sugar, sifted
½ teaspoon vanilla
milk

PREPARATION

1. Preheat oven to 350 degrees. Grease 10-inch cast-iron skillet lightly with butter.
2. Cream sugar, butter, and 1 teaspoon lemon peel.
3. Add eggs one at a time, beating well as each is added.
4. Mix flour and baking soda in another bowl.
5. To the sugar mixture add a little milk, then flour, alternating until well blended.
6. Beat in lemon juice.
7. Pour mixture into skillet.
8. Bake for about 25 minutes. Test for doneness with toothpick. Toothpick comes out clean when done.
9. Mix powdered sugar with vanilla and remaining peel, stirring in a little milk (about 2 tablespoons) to make a glaze for spreading on the cooled cake.

VI

TURKEY

TURKEY

Turkeys are the comeback heroes of Texas thanks to East Texas habitat improvement, cooperation of privately funded organizations, and especially the restocking efforts of Texas Parks and Wildlife game biologists. Today, Texas has more wild turkeys than any other state. And turkey hunters can select from two types of wild ones: the eastern turkey and the Rio Grande. A third, the Merriam's, while rare and limited in its Texas range, is common in Arizona, New Mexico, and Colorado.

Turkey hunting has always been of great importance in Texas. In fact, one of the first bird species recorded in the state was a Rio Grande turkey captured by the Long Expedition on its way from Colorado through the Panhandle in 1820. The bird was noted not so much because it was magnificent, a striking sight in the wild, but because of how it tasted over a campfire.

Unlike Rebel turkeys from southeastern states, Texas turkeys were harvested only in the fall, mostly as an adjunct to the ever-popular white-tailed deer, until 1970 when the lone county of Kerr opened a spring hunt. Since then scores of counties have been opened up for spring turkey hunting. Even the Pineywoods opened some counties in 1978. This is significant since the population of eastern turkeys in the Pineywoods area dropped below an estimated 100 birds by 1941.

The principal reason for the eastern turkey's sharp turn-of-the-century decline was changing land use. Pine trees became the cash crop of the growing timber companies, so the turkeys' food-rich oaks, beechnuts, and pecans had to go. While we've heard tales of feral hogs contributing to turkey decimation by vacuuming up turkey food and scarfing up young poults and eggs, research has shown that the feral hog has little effect on turkey populations. Instead, unrestricted hunting completed the near extinction of the eastern turkey.

The Rio Grande turkey, with a habitat not so easily

The titillating stance of a Rio Grande tom also tantalizes spring turkey hunters.

modified by man, hung on, although it too faces habitat loss in developing areas such as the Hill Country.

The spring gobbler hunt is the essence of turkey hunting, as Yankee and southern hunters have known since 1620 or so. It's not only extremely challenging, it's also exciting beyond belief. When you've seen the strut for yourself and heard the gobbler respond to your call, it's literally hair raising.

There is, of course, a wonderful bonus for turkey hunters who must traverse the Hill Country or Pineywoods backroads on their way to the hunt. In a typical year, fields of bluebonnets, cascades of Indian paintbrush, and other colorful wildflowers renew the spirit. About the only thing that can spoil such a hunt is the guy who insists on practicing his calls en route.

Turkey hunting takes some organization, especially in Texas, where the natural complexities of the hunt are compounded by the lack of vast public hunting areas. To hunt in ranch country requires either an all-year deer lease or special arrangements. Bird leases, including turkey hunting, are also available and becoming more popular, as are guided hunts to prime turkey areas around Brownwood in West Central Texas.

The typical feeding range of turkeys is incredibly wide, from three to four square miles a day. This quickly takes turkeys off all but the most spacious leases, since they will feed right off your pastures in no time at all. It helps to have a good roosting area or two on your lease, since in Texas there's a good chance that turkeys will return at sunset to the roost from whence they departed at sunrise, unless that roost has been disturbed.

"Roosting," or finding a turkey roost, is the starting point for a good hunt, fall or spring. But do not shoot turkeys off or near a roost. For one, it's illegal in Texas to shoot turkeys off the roost. You're also liable to get thrown off the lease, and you risk serious bodily harm from fellow turkey hunters. Roosts are hard to come by in most Texas turkey country; that's why turkeys tend to return to the same one come sunset. But wild turkeys aren't dumb; they will find another roost if some fool goes blasting around the original.

Location of the roosting birds enables the hunter to plan an ambush some distance from the roost during the fall hunt, and to plan his blind location for calling in the spring. Again, the blind should be a minimum 200 to 250 yards from the roost. A turkey's idea of a good roost is one with tall, usually deciduous trees such as cottonwood, pecan, sycamore, and hackberry. They normally roost on the flimsy branches, which makes it difficult for a predator to reach them. They also like water close by, preferably at the foot of their fortress of trees. We have seen large flocks of turkeys in the fall return, day after day, to such a roost. You can begin to see that without a roost on your lease turkeys may only appear as sporadically as Halley's comet as they range for feed.

Fall hunting techniques vary widely from the spring for reasons that will become evident as we analyze the bird's habits and patterns. But the difference can be summed up in one word. Sex. In the fall, turkeys tend to flock together according to age and gender. Hens and their young broods stay together. The young toms—called jakes—stay in their own group, and the big, long-bearded gobblers usually flock together. But it's a far different story in the spring when the soap opera's plot thickens and Mr. Tom becomes middle-age crazy, and more than a little promiscuous. At this stage, other mature toms are most definitely not welcome in his majesty's immediate presence. The fall and spring hunts are therefore quite different in character and technique.

TURKEY INSIGHTS

Ben Franklin's proposal that our national bird be the wild turkey rather than the bald eagle probably was discarded because of the other turkey image: that of a dull-witted, pompous-chested bird, incapable of coming in out of the rain, and fit only for the cook's hatchet. Yes, the word turkey is an old synonym for bumbling fool. The wild turkey hunter should never make this assumption. He is dealing with an altogether different entity.

To the casual observer, the three subspecies of turkey in Texas look much alike. However, they are quite different in their ability to survive in their respective habitats.

The Rio Grande turkey ranges throughout most of the state with exceptional populations in the Edwards Plateau, South Texas Plains, Cross Timbers, Rolling Plains, High Plains, and much of the Trans-Pecos. The Merriam's survive only in mountainous areas, as their breeding range is 3,500 to 7,000 feet. Only our Davis, Glass, Chisos, and Guadalupe mountains provide the necessary height. Merriam's are associated with ponderosa pine in these areas, and the ponderosa pine habitat in Texas is quite limited. Just the reverse is true for eastern turkeys that thrive best near sea level, scampering through swamp bottomlands, although records show their range once extended as far west as the Panhandle.

When the eastern turkey neared extinction in the Pineywoods, early attempts at restocking were made with Rio Grande turkeys, but these birds couldn't take the humidity and other swamp conditions. Restocking with Florida turkeys met with limited success. We don't know why they failed. The most successful restocking came with birds from neighboring Louisiana, Oklahoma, and Mississippi. In 1987, 45 eastern birds were released from South Carolina and other southeastern states.

Rio Grande and Merriam's turkeys are about the same size, with toms weighing an average 17 pounds with a wingspan of about four feet. The eastern birds are slightly larger with even longer wings. The three turkeys look much alike with long legs, bare blue heads, iridescent,

Iridescent feathers identify turkeys
in open country; long beard protruding
from breast signifies a trophy.

greenish bronze bodies, and wing feathers barred with eb-ony. The main field marks are tail feather and wing tip coloration. These range by subspecies from the eastern's russet tips to the cinnamon-buff of the Rio Grande and pinkish hue of the Merriam's. The Merriam's has a very distinct buff rump patch which distinguishes it from the other species. Prominent red neck wattles and beards hanging from the breast usually define the tom. Beards lengthen with age, and finding 10-inch beards on mature turkeys is not uncommon. The hen can also have a small tufted black beard, making field identification between jakes and some hens difficult, hence the provision for legal harvest of bearded hens. Hens will often have a lighter overall appearance because of their buff-tipped breast feathers. In the field, the hen's feathers appear grayish, while the gobbler's black-tipped feathers make him look quite dark. White-tipped tail feathers indicate a hybridization from a domestic strain, however, and it's a bad sign if you spot many turkeys marked this way on your range. If interbreeding continues, the wild turkey strain will weaken to the point that future generations will not survive.

The iridescence of the body and wing feathers is important to the fall hunter in header-draw country. Turkeys feeding along a ridge can often be spotted at great distances by a glint of light. Keeping an eye on the ridge lines can pay off in setting up an ambush for the flock.

Spooked hen turkey leaves the scene at 45 mph.

The wild turkey is one of nature's great racewalkers. When spooked he can do four-minute miles, mile after mile if need be, streaking along with head down and extended. The bird's daily range is determined by the availability of juniper fruit, acorns, pecans, beechnuts, dogwood, sumac, grapes, grass seeds, and various insects and beetles unfortunate enough to be in the flock's line of forage.

A popular myth is that turkeys are clumsy fliers, barely able to get by in the air. Forget it. Turkeys look a little ponderous flying up to roost until you realize a 20-pound bird has shot straight up 40 feet or more in the blink of an eye.

Turkeys only fly from danger as a last resort, say, not having good cover in the escape zone. When they do fly, they get up quickly with rapid wing beats, then seem to soar with powerful strokes, hitting 45 miles per hour at full acceleration. Most flights are less than a quarter mile.

10 POINT GUIDE TO KEY TURKEY HABITS

1. Turkeys stick together. They are always gregarious. Scattered flocks stay in a state of panic until they reunite. The phrase "birds of a feather stick together" is apt for wild turkeys.

2. Turkeys are paranoid. They are prey to most every predator, from rattlers to golden eagles. Coyotes, foxes, bobcats, even raccoons and skunks like turkey on the menu. Large hawks and great horned owls find them irresistible. Unlike many other game animals, turkeys think they see danger everywhere.

3. Turkeys see well. They are extremely farsighted, noticing minute movement from great distances, and viewing any movement as impending danger.

4. Turkeys have excellent hearing.

5. Turkeys react quickly to danger, real or supposed. They don't wait around to check you out; they're off like a streak, none of this dumbfounded staring at the hunter. No matter what you are, you're up to no good in the wild turkey's world.

6. The tom is promiscuous in the spring, trying to attract every hen within earshot. He will gobble, strut, and fluff his plumage like he's posing for a Pilgrim Thanksgiving poster. He'll drag his wing tips on the ground, commanding attention of the ladies and warning the competition. The tom's spring gobble is one of the most awesome of wild calls. It is his signal to his harem to come a'running, and a keep-away threat to other gobblers.

7. Turkey tracks are distinctive. A mature turkey track is four to six inches from the heel to the tip of the center toe. The other two toes angle off at about 75 degrees from centerline. This distinguishes the track from a heron's, which has a similar three-toed look. (The heron's left toe is much closer to centerline. Cranes have a much finer toe line.) The turkey track is heavy and coarse from

the weight of the bird and all the mileage he puts in. The mature tom's stride will be about a foot. Turkeys will often leave clear signs scratching for food, especially in the fall.

8. Turkeys love dust baths. In turkey country, look for depressions in dry, sandy soil with a few leftover wing feathers. Large ant beds in Texas often provide a double attraction for the turkey—dusting spas replete with gourmet cuisine.

9. Turkey droppings are sure indicators that a roost is in use. The tom scat can be identified since it's usually three or four inches long with a "j" hook at the end, while hen scat is usually found as small loops and spirals or in small piles.

10. Turkeys are great communicators. They use a number of vocal sounds that are invaluable to the hunter.
    These include:
    a. The lost call. This is described as the "kee-kee-run," which separated turkeys use to reunite the flock. The call is delivered at high decibels with as many as 20 repetitions. This is the call for

fall, used to attract both flocks and individual birds that have been scattered.

b. Food's-on, come-on-in call. This is another call used in conjunction with the "kee-kee-run" in the fall, especially to call in a flock. Purrs, soft yelps, and clucks signal "all's well." A variation is the seductively soft "tree" cluck by the hen, which signals her location to the tom.

c. The spring mating yelp. The all important call for announcing to Mr. Tom that Miss Hen is here, ready, and waiting for his regal attention.

d. The gobble itself is good for locating birds on the roost before the hunt and sometimes for stalking or even calling to other gobblers.

e. The warning calls. A "pit-pit-pit" indicates mild alarm; a sharp "putt-putt" is a panic alarm sending all turkeys within earshot running for cover. We suggest you don't imitate these calls.

PREPARATION FOR
THE TURKEY HUNT

TEXAS PREFERRED GUN SELECTION Once again, the ubiquitous 12-gauge pump, this time full-choked, is the odds-on choice of most turkey hunters. Weight is a big factor since turkey hunting often requires a lot of walking, yet the shotgun needs as much sock as you can carry easily; thus, the 12-gauge pump. The over/under, though tougher to carry, provides a little more choice in shot selection, which can be important.

The fall hunter may well want to consider a light rifle option, such as a scoped (2.5X) .22 magnum, .22 hornet, or even a loaded down .222. Over/under rifle shotgun combinations are available; a good choice for fall is a .222 over the 20-gauge magnum, again with a 2.5X scope of good light-collecting quality. Believe it or not, you can learn to hit skeet targets with the shotgun barrel, despite the scope. However, range masters tend to be nervous until you explain.

Shot size is not what you might expect for such a large bird covered with so many tough feathers. The aiming point on a turkey should be the head, about a three-inch target at the 30- to 40-yard range of a called gobbler. A good overall choice is #4s, in a high velocity load depending on the patterning of your gun. BBs or #2s may not pattern densely enough to be consistent this close, especially considering the head will be moving. For an excellent option plan, #4s can be used in a modified barrel with an over/under, #2s in a full. The #2 mag load barrel is selected for a turkey that just won't come closer and is effective out to 50 yards.

The typical turkey shot is more like a rifle than a shotgun, aimed rather than a pointing swing. Shots on flying turkeys are very rare and usually shouldn't be taken at all. Even if you hit the bird you most likely will cripple and lose him.

Although it looks like sin, we usually take the trouble to wrap camo tape around the gun barrel, especially for the spring hunt, and we sand off any varnish sheen on the stock. Usually the first thing turkeys spot is a glint off the gun barrel as you move it into position. Then they're gone.

WARDROBE SELECTION Since the fall turkey hunt requirements are nearly identical to those for deer hunting, we'll concentrate on your spring fashions. No question that olive green camo is in order for everything, including your T-shirt. This is Texas though, so light, cool cotton is nice. Perhaps a camo vest to combat pre-dawn shivers. Light rain gear for drizzly mornings is good to have along on any spring hunt.

Most good spring hunting will not be in the rock strewn, terrible Chihuahuan desert, so heavy duty boots are not appropriate. Lightweight nylon or quail boots are good choices.

Your wool waterfowl gloves will drive you batty in the spring, but gloves are very important—not for warmth, but for camouflage. With all but the mouth calls, your hands will be in motion frequently, and remember that in-

Properly camouflaged hunter blends into background even without a blind.

credible turkey eyesight. Our choice is lightweight, black skeet range-style shooting gloves, even if they do look a bit odd. By the time turkey hunters apply makeup, they look funny anyway, so you might as well go all the way because you'll kill more birds.

The camo gimme hat used for early season doves is a good bet for the spring hunt. When used with a face net it's close to ideal. But don't try to look western, since you'll do a lot of brush busting getting to your blinds. You might even resort to still hunting, and we've discovered cowboy hats have an affinity for mesquite trees.

GEAR SELECTION First, to complete the camouflage illusion, you'll need makeup in shades of dark green and brown, or at least some lampblack. Don't be concerned about how you look in your war paint. Just try not to be seen by normal folk.

Another essential is a sling for your shotgun, especially when you're carrying out a 20-pound bird. Make sure the sling is detachable—slip-on nylon types are available—since a sling left on the gun in the blind will surely snag in brush while you swing on to the turkey.

A prepacked backpack is great. Pack it with your hunting license, a small plastic container of water, the smallest practical flashlight, folding knife, compass, watch, rain jacket, extra shells, cigarette lighter or waterproof matches, first aid kit including snakebite kit, wrap bandages and small adhesive bandages, camo netting, a whistle, and a light lunch. The whistle should be on a lanyard to wear around your neck. We consider the whistle a must because turkey hunting is most definitely a solo proposition, and it's easy in Texas terrain to turn an ankle badly enough that you have difficulty walking.

TURKEY HUNTER'S CHECKLIST
  Hunting license
  Whistle on lanyard
  12-gauge shotgun
  Camo tape for shotgun barrel
  Shot shells—#4s/#2s
  Rifle ammo for fall hunt
  Shooting glasses
  Insect repellent
  Sunscreen
  Backpack—dark green
  Small water container—like hikers and bikers
    use
  Lightweight camo trousers
  Cotton camo T-shirt
  Dark cotton socks
  Small flashlight
  Camo netting
  Net face mask
  Camo makeup and makeup remover
  Lightweight nylon or quail boots
  Lightweight rain gear—dark green
  Lightweight camo vest
  Folding knife
  Large cooler with ice
  Turkey calls
  Compass
  First aid kit
  Watch in dark, non-reflective case
  Cigarette lighter or waterproof matches
  Alarm clock

TECHNIQUES THE EXPERTS USE

The consistently successful spring gobbler hunter is a consistent reconnaissance man. This is the essence of the hunt, since proximity to toms is the *sine qua non*.

Carry your call with you for recon work. It's hard to beat the box call since it so easily duplicates the gobble and a seductive yelp. An extra expert's touch is an owl call, since roosting toms will gobble at the hoot of an owl just before dawn and again just after sunset.

Your gobble call is best used during an afternoon scouting expedition, right up till dark. Still hunt through the turkey range, gobbling every so often, and then wait patiently for a challenge response. The mating yelp is best for scouting in the morning after the toms are off the roost. Even if you don't locate the roost on the first try, keep still hunting, stopping to yelp throughout the morning. Gobblers in the vicinity will respond, and at least you'll narrow the hunt area. While still hunting, particularly in the Pineywoods, keep a lookout for scratching and tracks in bottoms, and for depressions where turkeys have been dusting.

If you're in big country, a handy item is a topographical map from the U.S. Department of the Interior Geological Survey. You can not only note turkey locations, but also find your way back to camp. The topo map is very useful when you're in unfamiliar country. You can usually spot likely roost locations by seeking out bottoms and water sources. Turkeys try always to roost in the highest tree near water, so these areas should be your first scouting priority. During the day, it's safe to approach a possible roost since the turkeys will be out to lunch. Unlike other game, the turkey's sense of smell is not acute, so your scent will not pollute the roost (no offense meant). Look for droppings, feathers, scratchings; the more sign, the better potential for an opening day stakeout. Don't stop with just one roost, especially in public hunt areas, since you may have opening morning competition from hunters and other predators like bobcats, which like turkey for breakfast. Locate as many high-potential roost areas as possible and make sure you can find them in pitch dark.

After you've found the birds, carefully select blind positions. Your first priority is height, because toms are more confident coming uphill to the hen. Another is natural cover into which you can disappear. A third consideration is a reasonable field of fire within shotgun range. Pay attention to what's behind your blind, too, since a favorite tom trick is to circle the caller's location, coming in from the side or back. When this happens, about the most you can do is sweat. You could increase your odds at a clean shot by knowing the terrain. For instance, a turkey will not run into thick brush, so there may be a natural path he'll follow where you could get a shot. Just remember, you have to be able to find your preferred blind location in pre-dawn darkness.

Fall hunts also profit greatly from locating the roost. In much of the Rio Grande turkey's range, scouting can be carried on in conjunction with still hunting for deer. Again, pay attention to the glints emanating as tiny black specks from distant ridgelines.

If you know the roost location and have spotted flocks out feeding, set up an ambush. Turkeys hate to cross fence lines, but they will follow them for some distance if they lead back to the roost. Though they really prefer to find a place to pass under a fence, when they have to cross over one they often post a sentinel, then the flock queues up and jumps over one at a time. They jump straight up and over the fence, so they're exposed only momentarily. Where possible, this maneuver is carried out in a protected area, say where a fence line goes through a grove of pin oak. By knowing all this you can position yourself to intercept the flock.

Calling flocks in the fall is difficult, a talent reserved for true virtuosos. Not even experts can consistently call flocks, particularly mature toms. A more successful fall technique is to deliberately scatter the flock. You can even run right at them. Remember that turkeys are gregarious and panic when separated. Scattered turkeys will reply to the lost turkey call augmented with soft clucks and rapid high-pitched yelps. Don't be shy with your fall calls. Lots of lost turkey soft clucks and yelp calls breed confidence in the regrouping flock.

When hunting scattered flocks it's important to set up a makeshift blind quickly and as close as possible to where the birds separated. Cedar bushes are ideal. Camo netting carried in your backpack usually can be thrown up fast, giving you good cover in seconds.

THE SPRING HUNT Why take advantage of a sex-crazed gobbler in the spring? If you think it's not only unethical, but also poor game management, you're wrong on both counts. The spring hunt requires learning skills and mastery of woodsmanship beyond that of all other upland bird hunting. And the harvest of gobblers in the spring usually is done without harm to turkey reproduction. A single gobbler can mate with several hens, and the gobblers taken are usually surplus. Hens are protected, left in peace to nest and hatch their young. Approximately 45 percent of the adult population is male.

The first thing to remember is to chigger-proof your precious hide during spring hunting. You are going to be snuggling up to lots of chiggers, ticks, spiders, and other assorted tiny varmints, so be prepared. As dumb as it looks, tuck your pants legs into your boots or slip on elastic bands like bikers use. Tuck in your long sleeved shirt and spray yourself liberally with insect repellent, concentrating on your waist, pants cuffs, and neck. Keep your hat on.

Let's now imagine that you've scouted effectively and are within a couple of hundred yards of a likely roost. You are well camouflaged, set up in a blind that covers minute movement, and it's just before dawn on a clear, still day in spring gobbler season—typically April in Texas. There is only one thing left to do—call the tom to you.

This is where many otherwise hunt-skilled Texans back off too quickly. There is a broadly held belief that calling turkeys is a big deal, too difficult for the average person to learn. Wrong. Spring turkey calling is far easier than waterfowl calling. In the first place, there is only one tom turkey, while there are many varieties of ducks and geese that require a wide range of calls and techniques.

There's really no excuse for not learning at least the fundamental turkey calls, since there are many excellent self-teaching records and cassette tapes on the market. Even hunters with tin ears can use calls that rely on mechanically produced sound rather than vocal chords.

The best turkey call is the diaphragm mouth call, which leaves your hands free while you use it. It can exactly replicate all turkey sounds except the gobble, and there are some callers who can even accomplish this feat. Non-musical types have a hard time with this call and the other common suction type yelper, which mimics the ancient turkey wing bone call.

A modest investment in an array of calls is in order if you are serious about Mr. Tom. Your biggest investment will be in a box call, which you'll need in any event. Give the diaphragm call your best effort before deciding you can't handle it.

A ROUNDUP OF TURKEY CALLS

Box Call

This is highly recommended for the amateur. It is easily mastered, and with just a few minutes of self-instruction you can call turkeys. Ownership of such a call makes you an instant expert. The box call's sounds are created by striking a pivoting lid on one of the sides of the box. One side usually produces the high-pitched yelp that is the mating call of the hen; the other side produces a tom yelp. Either side can make soft, inviting clucks. When shaken, the box lid strikes both sides rapidly, producing a most realistic gobble. Be loose in learning to use the box call. Try to develop a rhythm rather than stiff, evenly spaced strokes.

Peg and Slate Call

This is a favorite of old-time hunters. In fact, it probably dates back to Plymouth Colony times. Slate calls are now made where the slate itself is set in a wooden frame. This is good for the beginner since it eliminates one variable. This is also an easy call to learn and is one of the best producers of the turkey cluck and soft whine. A variation on this call is the striker box call, used in much the same way.

Mouth Calls

These include the suction, wingbones, mouth diaphragm, and tube types. The latter is difficult to learn by yourself; you need a master music teacher at your side to perfect it. The mouth diaphragm also takes time to learn. When buying one, make sure it fits the roof of your mouth, because there's a risk of inhaling and choking on these small

Turkey hunters have a wide choice of calls but the easiest to master is the big box.

calls. After much practice, the diaphragm calls sound the most realistic of all, especially if you have an ear for musical pitch. They can be operated without using your hands, so you can concentrate on canvassing for the first tom appearance. However, a little too much is made of this feature, since the odds are strongly in your favor that you can gently put down a box or slate and peg call and pick up your gun before the tom shows. The last of the mouth calls is the wingbone type, which also takes a lot of train-

ing. Experienced guides can produce masterful, soft tree yelps as well as mating yelps on wingbone calls.

Most of the spring hunting action occurs from just before first light to around eight o'clock or so. The mating yelp is the most important call of all, and fortunately the easiest to master.

Don't yelp until you're sure the tom is off the roost. If you can reproduce the soft tree clucks, do so, because it helps the gobbler locate you. Otherwise, wait until the big bird hits the ground.

How many yelps to use? Try three or four fast, eager-sounding yelps to start. Remember, you are now telling the tom you're available, ready for love, and prefer a rendezvous at your place. Bear in mind that most hens go to the gobbler, so you've got to be more than coy. We're talking heavy-duty propositioning.

But don't overdo. No female wants to sound desperate. Time yourself deliberately, leaving five minutes between each yelp series. Also, if you are actually working the bird and know he's talking turkey to you, get the sound level down. The louder and more frequently you call, the more chance you run of hitting a false note, causing the gobbler to leave his phone off the hook and seek companionship elsewhere. If a gobbler is obviously a long way off, you can yelp at him harder and faster. This is no time for whispered promises.

The simplest call to use, and one that is useful spring and fall, is the cluck. Softly executed, two to six clucks before first light tell the gobbler that all is well and a good woman is around. This will prime him for the mating yelps to follow. It's a little like flirting. The cluck call struck with more authority signals "Where are you? I'm here." This is not the same as the lost turkey call, which is more of a yelp usually delivered in a lengthy series, rising in intensity then backing off.

DECOYS   There is no doubt that a hen decoy will help. We've used ours, "Goldie," for many years with much success. She's quite a femme fatale. A combination of the right mating yelps and spotting "Goldie" has caused many a tom to run straight at her in wild abandon. Decoys offer a major advantage in that they will often draw the turkey into a clear area for a good shot.

It's at the very end of the calling process that the over-eager hunter blows it. Don't make that mistake. Instead, when the tom, whom you know has come closer and closer, suddenly shuts up, you should also shut up and stay perfectly still for at least a half hour, moving only your eyeballs trying to spot him. It is right here that we've lost many a turkey, having convinced ourselves that he's spotted something fishy and sneaked off. More often, the tom is to one side or behind you, carefully casing the joint before moving in for the tryst. He's used to his women coming at his beck and call, so he'll remain a bit wary of your coy act.

Sometimes toms won't gobble, although you know they are in the area. One reason for this is that the mating drive has abated. If so, they just won't gobble. A positive scenario is that the tom has a veritable harem of hens roosting with him or nearby. Betting on the latter, mount an afternoon hunt where you emit weak gobbles interspersed with hen yelps and clucks. You may just challenge a mature tom and have him come a'running. Late afternoon gobbling, as we noted earlier, is a way to locate another roost for the next morning's hunt, too. When using this technique, stay in place for at least 45 minutes before moving on. Again, patience is a big factor. You are often more successful than you know.

Finally, after your shot drops the turkey and he's flopping about, resist the urge to shoot again. If you've made a good head and upper neck shot, the follow-up at a flopping bird will just ruin meat. Reload and walk swiftly to the downed bird. Don't run. If need be, shoot again at the head. If the turkey ran away at your shot, odds are you'll never see him again. But do check it out. There is always the possibility of the fabled Golden Pellet.

WEATHER Turkeys can be hunted well in the rain, and rain usually makes it easier for you to move in the woods without sounding like a truck. Lots of wind is one thing you don't want because it lessens the effectiveness of your call, masking the sounds of turkeys' response and/or their movement toward you. Like other big-game animals, the turkey is more cautious in high wind since it deprives him of one of his major senses, hearing. Even his eyesight is confused by brush and leaves whipping about. If you must hunt in the wind, call more loudly than usual, wait longer for a response, and set up where you have maximum field of fire.

FIELD DRESSING The first time you clean a turkey is likely to be an intimidating experience. Remember two things: Turkeys are, without question, the best eating of any bird, wild or domestic, and it's just a matter of size. As you begin cleaning, try to think of the turkey as a giant quail. The anatomy is the same, and the job ahead will seem much more manageable.

Here's how to go at it. Place the turkey on his back and pluck feathers away from a large area around the vent. Cut a thin slice horizontally across and just above the vent, wide enough to easily reach inside and remove the innards. Reach up into the body cavity and break through the diaphragm to remove the heart and lungs. Save the heart as well as the liver and gizzard. Put these in your ever-present zip-type plastic bag. Peel away and discard the gizzard's rough wrinkled skin covering. Slice the gall bladder from the liver without puncturing the bladder. This is important since the contents of the bladder will taint the liver.

Next, remove the crop from the neck area. This is very important because the food within will spoil rapidly. A little slit along the neck allows you to pull it free. Do this carefully if you plan to mount the bird.

If you don't dry pluck the feathers in the field and allow the bird to cool down, then the best bet is to immerse it in boiling water before plucking. Be sure to get all feathers, especially the pin feathers. Although there is not much fat on a wild turkey, it really is worth it to pluck rather than skin, which admittedly is a lot easier. If you intend to smoke the turkey, leaving the skin on the bird will make it a lot more moist and flavorful.

Warm weather is the deadly enemy of turkey meat as it is with all game. Carefully wash out the carcass and keep it cool to preserve flavor. If the outside temperature is 40 degrees, you could hang the turkey in a game bag; otherwise, store it on ice.

Post Oak Savannah
Menu

·

Pickled Black-Eyed Peas
Mesquite Smoked Wild Turkey
Cornbread Dressing
Brandied Sweet Potatoes
Pumpkin Pie

·

Oberhellmann Cabernet Sauvignon

INDIAN PAINTBRUSH. *Castilleja indivisa*. Slender cream-colored
flowers surrounded by showy, red-orange bracts on a three- to five-
inch spike. Plant grows to two feet tall along roadsides
and fields with well-draining soils. Annual, March through May.

Pickled Black-Eyed Peas

SERVES 6 TO 8

2 pounds canned black-eyed peas
1 onion, thinly sliced
2 cloves garlic, mashed
   dash Worcestershire sauce
   salt to taste
½ cup olive oil
1 bay leaf
¼ cup wine vinegar
   freshly ground black pepper

PREPARATION

1. Put peas and onion slices in canning jars.
2. Combine other ingredients and bring to boil.
3. Pour over peas and chill overnight.

Mesquite Smoked Wild Turkey

We suggest using a water pan charcoal cooker, or as an alternative a 55-gallon oil drum cooking grill with the fire at one end, water pan in the middle, and wild turkey at opposite end in disposable roasting pan. In this latter case, keep the turkey covered in foil for first 3 hours or so, then uncover to brown. Wild turkey dries out very easily.

1 wild turkey—skin should be kept on
   butter or substitute
1 tablespoon Tabasco sauce
2 tablespoons Galliano
   seasoning salt
   Greek seasoning or lemon pepper
2 onions, quartered
   celery stalk
   dry white wine
   thyme

PREPARATION

1. Start mesquite fire.
2. Rub turkey skin with butter or substitute.
3. Mix Galliano and Tabasco. Smear on skin of turkey.
4. Dust skin with seasoning salt.
5. Coat inside with butter, rub with thyme and Greek seasoning or lemon pepper.
6. Place stalk of celery and quartered onions in cavity.
7. Place turkey on grill above water pan or away from fire in roasting pan if using an oil drum cooker.
8. Add water and white wine to water pan to fill.
9. Chunks of mesquite, soaked in water, may be added to fire to create more aromatic smoke.
10. Cook until legs pull away easily. We usually let it cook all day, allowing the fire to gradually burn down.

Cornbread Dressing

Cornbread:
1½ cups yellow corn meal
1½ cups all purpose flour
  1 teaspoon salt
  1 teaspoon baking soda
  1 tablespoon sugar
  2 teaspoons baking powder
1½ cups buttermilk
  2 tablespoons peanut oil
  1 egg, beaten
Dressing:
  1 cup chopped celery and leaves
  1 cup chopped onion
  2 cups chicken broth
  2 eggs, beaten
  1 teaspoon poultry seasoning

PREPARATION

1. Preheat oven to 425 degrees.
2. Mix dry ingredients. Stir in buttermilk, peanut oil, and 1 beaten egg. Mix well.
3. Pour batter into greased 9-inch cast-iron skillet and bake for 20 minutes.
4. After cornbread has cooled, crumble enough to fill six cups.
5. Cook chopped celery and onion in broth for five minutes. Stir in the 2 beaten eggs, seasoning, and cornbread. Mix lightly but well.
6. Bake in cast-iron skillet at 325 degrees for 30 minutes.

Note: When cooking a turkey in a covered grill we recommend that you don't stuff it with dressing; you need to allow the heat and the aromatic smoke to enter the cavity.

Brandied Sweet Potatoes

SERVES 4 TO 6

2 large sweet potatoes
½ cup butter or substitute
1 cup sugar
2 eggs, well beaten
1 tablespoon milk
  grated lemon rind (½ of lemon)
1 shot brandy
½ teaspoon nutmeg
½ teaspoon cinnamon
  salt to taste

PREPARATION

1. Preheat oven to 350 degrees.
2. Skin and boil sweet potatoes. Mash.
3. Mix butter, sugar, eggs, milk, and lemon rind.
4. Blend in brandy and spices.
5. Add mashed sweet potatoes.
6. Bake in greased cast-iron skillet for 45 minutes.

Pumpkin Pie

SERVES 4 TO 6

Pumpkins were a reliable crop for the early settlers, a natural go-with for the abundant supply of wild turkeys.

1 unbaked pie shell
1 small pumpkin or 1 16-ounce can of
    pumpkin
    salt to taste
4 ounces butter or substitute
¼ teaspoon cinnamon
½ teaspoon nutmeg
½ teaspoon allspice
3 eggs, lightly beaten
1 cup evaporated milk
1 cup sugar
½ pint heavy cream
    pecans

PREPARATION

1. If using whole pumpkin, cut into chunks. Steam until tender.
2. Preheat oven to 400 degrees.
3. Brush pie shell with egg white. Place in pie pan or cast-iron skillet.
4. Mash pumpkin with butter and spices. Blend in eggs, milk, and sugar. Pour into pie shell.
5. Bake for 45 minutes. Test for doneness with toothpick.
6. Let pie cool.
7. Whip cream and spread over cooled pie.
8. Sprinkle pecan bits over top, or decorate with pecan halves.

VII

PHEASANT

PHEASANT

Maxim's de Paris features *Pheasant a la Souvarovv,* a gourmand's delight. The bird is stuffed with black truffles and *pâté de fois gras,* then basted and glazed with expensive brandies and cordials. Purchase of this entree at Maxim's could conceivably damage the U.S. balance of payments and is, therefore, highly unpatriotic. Why not prepare this yourself? All you need are high brass #6s.

Pheasants are top ranked as fine cuisine and are accorded the respect commensurate with their table quality in the world's finest restaurants. But it took a considerable effort for pheasant to reach Texas tables via Texas grain fields.

At the outset, many Texas naturalists objected to pheasant release programs. In the epilogue, we will have much to say about the risks inherent in exotic game introduction to the Lone Star State. Our native game can be and is threatened by exotic imports, and it's difficult to dispute the fact that pheasants are an exotic import.

But, in fact, these magnificently plumaged birds quietly introduced themselves to Texas as World War II occupied other theaters. They strolled into Baja, Oklahoma, by way of the High Plains ecological area. They've thrived over the intervening decades, finding the Panhandle's swing from ranching to grain crops and irrigation much to their liking.

Ring-necked pheasants found their own way to the Texas Panhandle in the 1940s.

Pheasants have been around a long time; by some estimates their ancestors can be traced back more than 25,000 years. The pheasant's native home ranged from the eastern shore of the Black Sea to China. The bird the Greeks identified as *Phasianus Avis* in literature as early as 500 B.C. had successfully made the whole of Asia its habitat.

Early American writings, including mention of George Washington's attempt at stocking, contain many references to pheasant imports even prior to 1776. These early tries failed for lack of proper habitat.

The breakthrough came in 1881, near Corvallis, Oregon, with the introduction of Chinese ring-necks to the Williamette Valley by Judge Owen Denny, then the consul-general at Shanghai. Ten years later, 50,000 pheasants were harvested in the valley during the first hunt. Today, American hunters claim 10 million pheasants annually. Pheasants do not seem to have harmed the native bird populations, and while some claim they have intruded upon the prairie chicken's habitat, they occupy a niche that is basically uncompetitive with native birds for food and range. And, pheasants don't interbreed with other species.

Among the TPWD's ring-necked pheasant stocking programs is one begun in 1964 along the Texas Gulf Coast. This program involved experiments with hybrids to make the birds more adaptable to the coastal environment, more water resistant. Since 1977, huntable populations have been extant in selected Gulf Coast counties.

A measure of the success of the Texas coastal stock-and-release programs came in 1978–79, when pheasants were traded with Louisiana for eastern-strain wild turkeys to rebuild our decimated population of those native birds. In this case an exotic helped a native.

Release programs that began in 1974 in Carson and Gray counties are the reason for pheasant populations in these areas. The Canadian River break country had blocked southward range expansion, so TPWD's releases south of the breaks helped bridge the 40-mile-wide barrier.

Ring-necked pheasants have become increasingly important to Texas bird shooters. Since the '40s, our High Plains area has become a giant producer of irrigated grain crops such as corn, wheat, and sorghum, and some farmers have instituted practices suggested by TPWD that provide roost and other cover as well as feed. These efforts have paid off for farmers, since pheasant hunting has become another cash crop.

Although adverse conditions such as drought or disease can motivate landowners to request reduced bag limits from the traditional two per day, four in possession, one of the great fallacies regarding pheasant and quail is that we can increase populations by decreasing hunter harvest. Pheasant and quail, like most wildfowl, have short lifespans, and experts estimate an annual death rate of 60 to 80 percent regardless of regulated hunting pressure. The 20 percent of pheasants and upland game birds that survive under both good and bad conditions reproduce and replenish the population. In actuality, spring and summer rains, nesting habitat, and winter cover are the major determinants of fall populations in the Panhandle.

Today, pheasant season has become the Mardi Gras of the Panhandle as thousands of sportsmen flock there in mid-December. Estimates place the opening day harvest at up to 90 percent of the total for the typical two-week season. There are two explanations for this: hunter density and unwary young birds. Pheasants learn quickly what hunters are all about.

The Panhandle crossed by the Long Expedition in 1820 en route from Pike's Peak was criticized by Edwin James in his chronicle, *Account of an Expedition from Pittsburgh to the Rocky Mountains.* "I do not hesitate in giving the opinion that it is almost wholly unfit for civilization and of course uninhabitable by a people depending upon agriculture for their subsistence . . . the scarcity of wood and water, almost uniformly prevalent will prove an insuperable obstacle in the way of settling the country." From James' accounts came the sobriquet "Great American Desert," a misnomer for our Southwest.

In contrast to the surly mien of the Panhandle in 1820, replete with cranky Bad Heart Indians (Kiowa Apache), the inhabitants today are among the world's most hospitable folk. In fact, the welcome accorded hunters in most of Texas is somewhat unusual compared to other states. Noteworthy is the courtesy that is reciprocated, even during a hunter invasion by thousands spending millions. Sportsmanship is the rule, not the exception.

Hunt breakfasts in churches, fraternal lodges, and other community centers are the norm, and no one's a stranger. Everyone receives a hearty welcome and send-off for the pheasant hunt.

In pheasant hunting, the law insists upon sex discrimination. Hunters are only allowed to take cocks. Look for the long tail and the white ring around the collar, and don't shoot unless you are 100 percent certain it's a cock. You can't be certain just by looking for long tail feathers. Hens can also have long tail feathers, but they never wear a pearl necklace. Always look at the head and lead in relation to the head or you'll run two major risks: shooting a hen or harmlessly peppering 20 inches of colorful cock tail. It's quite difficult to judge sex on a straightaway shot, and poor light will make that ring hard to spot. Don't be tempted to rationalize that it's got to be a rooster. See the ring first. Cock pheasants can also be identified by their cackle when flushed. Also be aware that the pheasant's speed, equal to that of a dove in full flight, will limit your judgment time.

PHEASANT INSIGHTS

The pheasant rooster is the original cock of the walk, Beau Brummell personified. If he could wear gold chains and a Rolex he would. The really puzzling thing is how such a flashy, yard-long bird can disappear right beneath your feet in virtually no cover.

His head should show up like lights on a game warden's

Neophyte pheasant hunters often wonder how gaudy cocks vanish into sparse cover.

truck. How can he hide wearing an iridescent green and heliotrope cap and glossy ear tufts over his bright carmine masked yellow eyes? And beneath his jeweled crown plumage he wears a bright white pearl choker. (A note of caution—the white band is sometimes missing.) The cock's equally regal cloak is feathered with iridescent copper, hash-marked with black, bronze, and white. Beyond his short, rounded wings he brandishes a long, pointed tail with russet undertones and brief, black horizontal stripes.

The hen, while smaller and less gaudily garbed, may also have a long tail, making the long quill not in itself a fail-safe field mark for the shooter. The female pheasant's sedate dress is more delicately scaled over a buff brown. She lacks the bright head plumage and never has a white neck band, so these are sure field marks in flight when light and angle are adequate. Custom calls for the first hunters spotting a flushed hen to immediately yell "hen," thus keeping safeties on across the firing line.

The hen never has a white band and blends beautifully with grain field or brushy habitat.

Pheasants are grain-belt dwellers, thriving where they have access to sorghum and corn. But they also need cover—brushy fence rows, grown up pastures, tall grass and weeds, windbreaks, ungrazed playas, and marshy areas. This roost and loafing cover is often missing, especially where mega-agriculture is the norm.

Although some pheasant experts talk of roosting in trees, this is not the case in Texas, since our Panhandle is not exactly Sherwood Forest. Our pheasants roost on the ground in heavy grass or weeds, with watch duty assignments to guard against coyotes and 'coons.

At dawn, pheasants usually move out of their roost to feed, making a pit stop for gizzard gravel at a nearby road. In typical weather they'll feed until midday, then return to the roost or to close light cover where they lie low, dust, and loaf until late afternoon. The last hour of shooting time will often find them back in the grain field. Dark sends them to roost again.

Pheasants are smart and very sensitive to hunters marching about and the shock waves from their shotgun barrages. They will quickly change their daily cycle, and hunting becomes, if not more difficult, more strategic as the season wears on.

Pheasants will rarely fly more than a mile. Most often they will sail down within a quarter mile, tail spread as an air break. The cock usually emits a loud, hoarse, chicken-like cackle when flushed, while hens tend to be quieter. Though not as startling as quail, pheasant wing-whir will definitely get your attention.

The average lifespan of a cock in the wild is actually less than that of a dove, though it's hard to imagine when you contrast the size and perceived hardiness of the pheasant. Most birds shot in Texas are hatched in June. TPWD field crews take a census each September. The census is expressed in bird sightings per square mile on a scale of five to one. A five indicates a banner year, with 3.0 being average. The census can be misleading due to factors such as unusually heavy cover that makes birds more difficult to see, but it's a good barometer of the December hunt.

If you are in the position to check a fairly large number of harvested pheasant cocks on opening weekend, enough for statistical validity, you can play wildlife biologist by inspecting the spurs of the birds' featherless legs. Birds of the current year will have soft, gray, thimble-shaped spurs of less than 3/4 inch. Older birds wear longer spurs with a harder, polished appearance. If 80 percent of the bagged roosters are youngsters you've had a normal hatch in that area. Another important reason for aging your own birds is to determine the best method of cooking. However, hunters that aren't trophy or mounting fanatics have been known to trade a larger bird for someone's small one, making sure the spurs are less than 3/4-inch and conical.

Another misconception regarding pheasants deals with taking cocks only, which is the law. An unbalanced sex ratio is not a problem for pheasant propagation, unlike some other wildlife. Game biologists tell us that the ability of the cock to mate successfully with 10 or more hens each spring has, in fact, almost always assured us of a huntable number of cocks. Hens are a potential resource, but this idea is not yet popular.

Pheasant cocks are polygamous and territorial. This is where the spurs come into play, fending off other suitors. The brightly hued tail, wattle, and ear tufts are used to attract the opposite sex. A typical cock will bow, bob, strut, crow, and tail spread his way into the heart of up to 10 hens within his domain. The hens will establish nesting areas within this territory and lay from 8 to 12 eggs, which hatch in about three weeks. In two more weeks the chicks can fly. Their worst enemies include coyotes, raccoons, feral cats, owls, skunks, and hawks.

In the Panhandle, at least average spring-summer precipitation is important for chick survival because the best cover is created by rain. Freezing weather and heavy snow can have a devastating effect on the overwintering population. A mild Panhandle winter followed by a wetter-than-average spring and summer produces the best fall hunting in this part of Texas.

PRAIRIE CHICKEN INSIGHTS

Texas has two prairie chickens: the rare, endangered, and protected Attwater's and the less rare, but huntable, lesser prairie chicken. Both are related to the more common grouse of the Northern Great Plains. The small population of Attwater's is concentrated in the Coastal Bend, including the Attwater's Prairie Chicken Refuge near Eagle Lake.

Attwater's almost suffered the same fate as the passenger pigeon. Tales of wagonload shoots and "flights obscuring the sun" were common. Early settlers had no trouble bagging plenty for the pot, since they were easy to hunt. Market and competitive shooters killed off a popu-

This endangered Attwater's prairie chicken rooster has his own refuge in the Texas coastal bend.

lation of half a million or more by 1900. Habitat eradication almost completed the kill.

Old Texas Game, Fish, and Oyster Commission records show there were upward of two million lesser prairie chickens in the Panhandle in the late 1800s. But with the Dust Bowl of the '30s and clean farming taking out the native grasslands, populations dwindled to unhuntable numbers by 1937, when the season was closed. The chemical control of shinnery oak and wide use of herbicides also lessened the lessers considerably.

A two-day lesser prairie chicken season was opened in 1967, mainly on private lands along the Oklahoma and New Mexico borders. The two-day season in October has been maintained in most years since. October was selected because most of the birds have not yet begun to depend upon domestic grain and are still feeding on insects and green vegetation. A later season could result in overkill, since birds are concentrated in the sorghum and wheat fields.

Prairie chickens at 16 to 17 inches in length look a little like mega-meadowlarks. Males and females look alike. The lesser is a reduced, overexposed version of the Attwater's—smaller and paler. Both have short, blunted

Lesser prairie chickens are native to the High Plains and their populations are now growing.

tails. Their overall coloration is brownish buff with dark brown barring, with less pronounced chevrons on the lesser. Roosters display inflated neck sacs during courtship; the Attwater's is golden and the lesser's is a warm orangey-red. Elongated neck feathers called pinnae erect to show the bloated sacs. These quill-like pinnae features are the source of another name for the prairie chicken—pinnated grouse.

Lesser prairie chickens have established booming grounds to which they return year after year in very early

A successful High Plains
lesser prairie chicken hunter.

The South Texas wild chicken takes
his name from his song *cha-cha-lac*.

spring. Booming grounds are flattened areas where the males stomp and whirl, boasting with their inflated air sacs and "booming," a resonant sound much like that achieved by blowing across the mouth of a soft drink bottle. Kiowa Apaches were said to have modeled some of their famous sun dance rituals after the whirling dervish of amorous prairie chicken roosters.

Like doves, prairie chickens have a habitual flight pattern from roost to grain at first light. Hunters hiding in the grain fields or lurking about fence lines in cover that breaks their outline hope for a flight to cross within pass shooting range. For this reason, the usual gun selection is a 12-gauge, full or modified, with at least high brass #6s. Again, like dove hunting, prairie chicken hunting can be a social event, since having widespread hunter coverage on grain fields is a good strategy. (The pheasant sweep strategy discussed later is no good because the prairie chickens will flush wild, well out of range.) Some use dogs to hunt the roost pastures after the morning flight. To obtain a two-bird limit in the two-day season takes a good pass shooter with gambler's luck.

CHACHALACA INSIGHTS

This Texas wild chicken is even harder to come by than the prairie chicken. If you're a South Texas Brush Country hunter, you may run across a gray-brown bird that looks like a cross between a turkey and a pheasant belting out "cha-cha-lac." It's the chachalaca, or Mexican pheasant.

A big bird, the chachalaca is army olive drab on top with a lighter olive coloration underneath. His long, glossy, dark green tail is tipped with white.

Although plentiful in Mexico, the chachalaca's range in Texas is confined to the Rio Grande areas in the impenetrable thorn brush and willow thickets. They roost as high as they can, often in flocks where they will harmonize loudly like a barbershop quartet—a sound you'll never forget. Some sportsmen say these musical birds will come to the sound of Mexican *conjunto* music played loudly on a portable radio. Some wildlife management areas offer permit-only hunts for chachalaca. Both the chachalaca and prairie chicken provide excellent table fare for the fortunate few who bag them.

PREPARATION FOR

THE PHEASANT HUNT

Lightweight but effective firepower is the choice on pheasant. The typical hunt requires lots of walking and little shooting, often with shots at up to 45 yards at a tough bird well protected by feathers, especially on the frequently taken going-away angle. All this adds up to a pump or autoloader 12-gauge, modified choke, with high velocity #6s—a good selection for opening weekend. Later in the season, high velocity #4s are recommended because shots will be longer on the remaining cocks.

Pheasants flush almost vertically off powerful legs, usually soaring 10 to 15 feet. A shot taken during liftoff will invariably be under the fast-rising bird. The hunter must wait for rotation—the moment when the cock tilts over to a more horizontal flight angle—then swing in front of the clearly identified head.

Don't shoot too soon. If the bird flushes close, the wing noise and imposing size of the bird spooks the uninitiated into a snap shot. By the time you recover from this error, the bird is in level flight going straight away from you at around 50 miles per hour, making a sure-kill second shot very difficult. The quick trigger finger might also bag you a hen.

Visualize a Lear jet and a 747 taking off. They both reach approximately the same ground speed, roughly 150 miles per hour, before liftoff. But, unless you observe the aircraft taking off at the same time on parallel runways, you'd swear the smaller jet is going much faster just as it's airborne. Conversely, the 747 appears to be stalling out. Think of doves as Lear jets and pheasants as 747s.

Crossing and quartering shots are common on pheasants, especially as hunters to either side of you manage to miss. The crossing shot on a pheasant gives you a dove-speed target that seems like a 747 suspended almost motionless in midair. Keep swinging through the target, which is the head, not the whole bird, as if you were dove hunting; that rooster is not stalling.

Going-away shots are the hardest, not just because of the bird's escape velocity, but also because of the armor plating provided by 20 inches of rooster tail. Even high brass #6s may not be enough at the outer limits of your range, and many hunters make it a practice to load #4s as second or third shots to give more penetration. The longer straightaway shots produce an unfortunately large number of lost cripples, since wing-damaged birds can easily elude even dog-supported hunters. Unless the bird absolutely crumples in midair, go ahead and shoot again on a wounded bird. Don't worry about quail field etiquette. Be sure rather than sorry, because the wounded pheasant on the ground is hard to retrieve. This may well go for a bird peppered by a fellow hunter on your flank. Often the best option is for you to shoot as well, to be sure the bird is stone dead in the air. Of course, you'll present the bird to the first shooter. He may well reciprocate later in the hunt.

DOG SELECTION   A good flushing dog or retriever can add immeasurably to a pheasant hunt, especially a hunt conducted solo or with a small group. However, you seldom see a dog on a typical Texas hunt. The main reason is that the large sweeping group approach favored in the grain fields of the Panhandle sets up a situation in which most dogs would be unwelcome, unless they can comport themselves literally at their master's heel until a bird is definitely down and needs retrieving. Such dogs are hard to find and even harder to train just for pheasant season.

We would discourage using your quail-trained pointer since you run the risk of frustrating fellow hunters and the dog himself. Any of the retrievers described in the chapter on ducks, notably the Labs and goldens, make excellent retrievers for pheasants. In other states, these dogs are accustomed to such double duty.

Two breeds not mentioned earlier should be given strong consideration if you have the time, money, and inclination to develop a pheasant specialist: the English springer spaniel and the lovable cocker spaniel.

American Cocker Spaniel
It takes a cocksure hunter to show up on a Panhandle cock shoot with a cocker spaniel. The key is in obtaining your cocker pup from hunting stock bloodlines going back at least four generations. There is a great deal of difference in the lap dog, bench-bred cocker and the working variety, so be certain of your source. Surprisingly, the field cocker has a better temperament than his show-off cousin, making the breed even better suited as a pet around the home. As you'd expect, the cocker responds best to even-tempered training in contrast to the get-tough tactics required for many breeds.

The cocker was named after the woodcock, *ergo* he's good on the same. Cockers are also handy as stock tank duck retrievers and for cottontail hunting.

English Springer Spaniel
Most dog authorities rank the English springer as the premier pheasant dog, and he is, indeed, fun to hunt behind, especially when you're alone. A well-trained springer will work close, quartering just ahead of the hunter. He usually has a better nose than the Lab or golden. When his docked tail hits high rpms, he's on a pheasant and the hunter needs to be close by. At the flush the trained springer will instantly sit, expecting his trained hunter not to miss. Sitting still, head up, gives him a good marking angle as he awaits his master's command to fetch.

The English springer does a respectable job on duck retrieval and is particularly good at marking doubles and triples if his master can get the shooting done. He'll give you good sport on rabbits, woodcock, and quail unless you're a real purist.

More crippled pheasants are lost per bird bagged than any other upland game bird. Long shots and the pheasant's deceptive speed, its size, heavy feathers, and ability to run and hide on the ground add up to many lost cripples. A good retriever cuts way down on lost birds, and more sportsmen should consider adding this dimension to their pheasant hunts.

WARDROBE SELECTION   Meteorologists usually identify the coldest spot in Texas as Dalhart, a key city in Panhandle pheasant hunting. This area gets all of our blue northers and most of our snow. Underfoot, when the ground is thawed, it's black, gumbo mud of the slickest and stickiest consistency. Yet the Panhandle can seem warm on a clear, windless mid-December day. You'll probably have to fly there, so being prepared takes as much strategy as any Texas hunting.

Though you haven't much packing space if you plan to hunt several days in the winter Panhandle, we suggest an extra pair of worn-in boots. Like a misfiring gun, soaked, unusable boots will stop a hunt cold. We favor lightweight, waterproof quail boots for dryer hunts, the rubber-bottomed, leather top variety for wet hunts. Wear the quail boots on the plane to save space. Smooth soles are best in muddy stubble fields, minimizing the pick up.

Extra socks are a blessing. Light, poly socks under wool are excellent. Carry at least two pair of each per day of hunting. If you plan to stay out all day, keep an extra pair with you; an ounce of prevention's worth a ton of hunting comfort.

Insist on lightweight gear in all your pheasant hunting. A pound of foot gear equals more than ten carried. As mud builds up, even on smooth soled boots, you'll be wearing out your leg strength against a much higher load factor. Don't compound the problem with heavy clothing. Begin by wearing light, polythermal underwear instead of the heavy cotton sort.

To cope with weather extremes, wear your hunting coat on the plane and pack a commodious game vest. The game vest can be worn over a shirt or light down jacket to keep you comfy in warmish weather, and under a rain jacket if necessary. The hunting coat, again equipped with oversized game pouches, and a thermal turtleneck shirt should add enough protection for anything you'll face. A ski mask prepares you for the worst. Brush pants, two pair, complete the wardrobe. They shed underbrush and dew better than jeans.

Carry a gimme hat for bluebird days and one with ear flaps for the more likely weather you'll encounter. You may wish to have the hats in international orange if you're going to hunt with strangers. This makes your head look less like a bush.

Gloves are an aggravation to most hunters but usually a necessity on pheasant fields. We use a full wool glove on our forearm hand, and for the trigger hand we wear a glove with the fingertips cut out. As a precaution, carry the mate to the full glove.

There's no need to overload on shells. This is not a dove or duck hunt. Your shots are going to be few, your limit small.

Thirst can be a problem if your hunt takes you up and down enough grain fields and there's no snow to eat. A plastic backpacker's water bottle is a good solution.

Since feet are so important to this hunting, a small first-aid kit of antiseptic ointment and blister bandages in your pocket is a good idea in the field.

Your favorite folding knife, game shears, and zip-type plastic bags complete essential field gear.

PHEASANT HUNTER'S CHECKLIST
  Hunting license
  Lightweight 12-gauge shotgun, because of all
    the walking
  Backup shotgun
  Hard gun case for airline travel
  Tape for gun case

Shot shells—high velocity #6s and #4s (Arrange
    to buy on location.)
Lightweight field boots
Rubber-bottom/leather top boots
Two pair poly socks per day
Two pair wool socks per day
Moisturizer for face and hands
Sunscreen
Lightweight hat (orange option)
Ear flap hat (orange option)
Ski mask
Rain suit
Polypropylene thermal underwear (extra pair)
Regular underwear
Game vest
Hunting coat with game pockets
Down or insulated vest
Chamois shirts
Brush pants (one pair per day)
Turtleneck sweater (polypropylene)
Down jacket
Folding knife
Game shears
Sealed hand towels
Zip-type plastic bags
Cooler for game transport
Lined moccasins for aprés hunt
Shotgun cleaning kit
Lubricating aerosol spray
Wool shooting gloves
Wool half gloves
Alarm clock
First aid equipment (antibiotic ointment, blister
    bandages)
OPTIONS:
Dog food, treats, water bowl

TECHNIQUES THE

EXPERTS USE

LOCATING PHEASANT For most Texas hunters, remote as they are from prime hunting areas, the preseason scouting techniques used in other states are impossibilities, since pheasant hunting often requires a round trip of a thousand miles or more.

Uninitiated airline security personnel stationed along the major routes to pheasant-hunting areas display an understandable nervousness when they are inundated with gun cases. Thoughts of Texas secession must cross their minds. Airlines prohibit ammunition on board so you should make arrangements for a supply at your destination. Identify your gun case well; you'll be surprised how many look alike. If you plan to tape your case shut—a good idea—leave it open before boarding because the check-in personnel may wish to inspect it. You will have to sign a form stating the gun is unloaded. Keep reinforced packing tape inside the case ready for use. Most cases hold two guns, and, even if you're sure of the faithfulness of "Ol' Betsy," use the space.

If you're planning your first hunt and don't have access to veteran Texas pheasant hunters or Panhandle landowners, TPWD is a good reference, as are civic organizations such as the Dumas and Dalhart 4-H clubs, Morse and Hart Lions clubs, and chambers of commerce in Stratford, Plainview, Hereford, Pleasant Grove, Muleshoe, and other Panhandle cities. Allocate extra time on your first trip to drive around to other areas asking locals about the quality of hunting, number of birds taken, and the whereabouts of other good local sources. Again, Panhandle residents take pheasant hunting seriously and are usually very cooperative in helping you make contact.

In urban areas, the newspaper's outdoor writer is often a good source of contacts. Begin your checking in the early fall with TPWD, since they will have completed their annual September bird census and can begin to give you some idea of the quality of the hunt ahead.

Because the most satisfactory way to pheasant hunt is with a group of friends, efforts to recruit a compatible group are worthwhile. Don't wait until Pearl Harbor Day to do this, since other hunters may book the best hunting.

Pheasant hunting is very much like the end game in chess. The strategy in chess is to design a checkmate that anticipates all escape routes. This holds true in pheasant hunting. The objective of any pheasant hunt, whether by one person or 10, is to maneuver cocks into a trap where they will flush within your gun's range. Pheasants will run away from hunters and stay on the ground until all cover is exhausted or until they reach an even greater threat.

In a normal day's cycle, pheasants will move at first light from their ground roosts in thick cover of grass or weeds into the harvested grain fields. A drive is organized with most of the hunters spread out across a stubble field at distances of about 25 yards apart, less if only a narrow strip is to be covered, with the remaining two or three hunters acting as blockers at the end of the field. There do not have to be as many blockers since their very presence creates a threat and barrier to the advancing pheasants.

In group hunting, don't just form a straight line. Have the hunters at both ends of the line start first. The objective is to gradually form a *U* much like a fisherman's net, in an attempt to force pheasants near the ends into the center of the shallow *U*.

An infantry-like advance is not only tiring and less fun, but also less productive. A slow advance, even using a programmed stall for a moment or two—especially near the blocker end of the field—will almost invariably make the pheasants nervous. Often the sudden cessation of noise may make them flush within range of the blocker or line.

Panhandle grain fields are usually best hunted by groups.

Be sure to set up such tactics in advance so your line stays intact.

The larger the group the more important it becomes to have a hunt master. Safety is the first priority, starting with careful and considerate drive-hunter placement, blocker stations, and clear instructions as to when it's safe and sporting to take a shot.

If you're hunting with a leaderless group of strangers, albeit friendly, someone needs to find out the group's hunting mindset. Most will agree that the person nearest the cock when he flushes has the first shot. But, if missed, anybody else in range of a safe shot can have it. Most Texans have no trouble with shooting a wounded bird on the ground, as this is a humane and sensible approach, but there are those whose upland game training may say nay.

Usually the choice of a hunt leader is informal, tending toward someone with good local knowledge and obvious hunting experience generally conveyed by dress and demeanor. Normally blocker assignments will rotate as various members of the team need a bit of rest; children and older hunters may need a little extra blocker duty.

A word of warning: Your informal leader can misdirect the hunt because he may lack the perceptions of a true pheasant strategist. We've seen hunters plow up and down Panhandle maize fields all day long, while birds that fed all night under a full moon rested comfortably in roost cover. The leader kept doggedly on the grain field sweep tactic because "they were here last year." Avoid this by learning pheasant habits yourself.

Smaller hunting groups can be more effective when birds are judged to be in loafing cover or still in roost areas. This is especially true of working fence line cover, irrigation ditches, or small draws. Always set up a blocker, then thoroughly work all cover to the end of each such trap opportunity. You'll often be surprised at how tight the birds will hold, almost to the point of stepping on them. They know the cover won't allow them to run unprotected to either side of the advancing hunters.

Hunting pheasants alone is usually not much fun, but if you want a few solitary hours strolling after pheasant on your own, make skinny strip cover your priority and try to hunt where other parties haven't been, for they will have vacuumed the landscape. To hunt wider cover, zig zag until close to the end, then stop and try to unnerve the pheasant into flushing. Sometimes you'll come across marshy playa lake areas with heavy cover which may be worked solo with some hope of success.

As in dove hunting, a team approach to marking downed birds reduces cripple loss. Triangulation always helps. Unless cocks are flushing everywhere, which can happen but seldom does, all nearby hunters should carefully watch the bird that's been shot at, and continue to watch it out of sight. Many pheasants fly on apparently untouched, only to drop suddenly quite a distance from the hunter. A sharp eye might detect a dropped leg after the shot and this bird should be marked well. When he does come down, it's likely he'll be close because he may be unable to run.

Move with dispatch to the downed bird no matter how hard you thought he was hit. Pheasants are durable and many birds are long gone before the ambling hunter makes the scene. In fact, most pheasants are still alive when picked up by the hunter. One of our hunters once carried around a pheasant in the game bag of his jacket all morning. When the hunter got in his vehicle and took off his jacket the pheasant leapt out to perch on top of the spare tire.

A humane way of killing the bird is to put pressure on his heart by firmly grasping across the small of the back. Hold as much pressure as you can until the bird's head has dropped, then hold a few seconds longer. This technique is much more professional than chicken style neck wringing and better preserves trophies for mounting.

WEATHER FACTORS Heavy rains and high winds will stop most pheasant hunts. First, in the Panhandle heavy rain usually means impassable roads—really impassable—since even access roads can't be negotiated with four-wheel-drive, let alone the fields on foot.

High winds make an already nervous bird positively paranoid. Like deer, pheasant rely heavily on their acute hearing to avoid danger. They'll run even without hunter provocation. Of course, high winds put dogs out of shape too, as do heavy rains. If you must hunt in high wind, hunt silently into it because the pheasants won't hear you as soon. Look for sheltered cover. Though it's hard to come by in West Texas, the little there is may hold birds avoiding the wind noise. Roosters with the advantage of a high wind on their tails are awesomely fast, so in addition to masking your sound, hunting into the wind may help slow down the bird.

Panhandle snow provides a rare opportunity for tracking pheasants. Cocks are often identifiable by size of track and length of tail marks. The track is from 2½ to 3 inches long and shows three evenly spaced big toes and a much smaller toe at the heel. Snow is particularly revealing when trying to determine the likelihood of birds in dense cover. Just patrol the perimeter looking for tracks leading in. Fresh snow in blue norther cold will often cause the birds to stay tight in roost or loafing cover.

Pheasants will feed on bright nights and thus may delay their normal morning advance to grain fields. So roost and cover hunting at first light might pay off better than forming ranks for the charge across the grain.

FIELD DRESSING To preserve game flavor, hunters often take advantage of hunt rest periods to gut birds. This is particularly important in warm weather. Carry sealed hand cleansers for quick clean up.

Plucked pheasants taste better, make a better table presentation in some recipes, and are essential for the classic roast. It only takes a moment to rough pluck the bird in the field while he's still warm. Use game shears to clip off the head and one leg, open the crop, and trim off wings. Then pluck away. Place the bird in a zip-type plastic bag and go after another. As spurs identify the male pheasant, state law requires that a single foot remain attached to the carcass until reaching its final destination.

Once home you may wish to skin the pheasant. Use your folding knife to open the skin from vent to neck. Use your game shears to snip off the remaining leg at the joint. Roll the skin down and off each drumstick, then pull the skin away from the breast, all the way to the wing joints. Use your game shears to clip these joints and the joint where the back attaches to the breast. Now simply pull the breast and legs away from the back. If all you want are pheasant pieces, you can then slice the breast away from the breastbone and slice off the drumsticks.

Pheasant freezes well. Be sure to mark the date and indication of age. Since the meat is drier than domestic fowl, don't leave pheasant in your freezer for more than a few months.

High Plains Menu

·

Celery Soup
Skillet Prairie Chicken
Corn Pudding
Glazed Carrots and Onions
Deep Dish Wild Plum Pie

·

Pheasant Ridge Sauvignon Blanc

TAHOKA DAISY. *Machaeranthera tanacetifolia*. Numerous red-violet to purple flowers on a low sprawling plant with fernlike leaves. Grows four to 16 inches tall on plains or hillsides with sandy soils. Annual, May through October.

Celery Soup

SERVES 4

1½ cups chicken stock
1 cup milk
2 tablespoons butter
6 tablespoons flour
  dash garlic powder
  salt to taste
  freshly ground black pepper
½ cup finely chopped, cooked celery

PREPARATION

1. Warm chicken stock and milk in saucepan.
2. Melt butter in another saucepan. Mix in flour slowly to creamy consistency. Don't brown.
3. Gradually add warmed stock and milk mixture.
4. Stir over medium heat until soup mixture comes to a boil.
5. Add seasonings and cooked celery and cook for one more minute.

Skillet Prairie Chicken

SERVES 4

  flour
  salt to taste
  freshly ground black pepper
1 prairie chicken, cut in serving pieces
2 tablespoons peanut oil
2 onions, sliced
1 cup water
¾ cup milk
  paprika

PREPARATION

1. Place flour, salt, and pepper in paper sack. Add fowl pieces and shake well.
2. Heat peanut oil in cast-iron skillet.
3. Brown meat. Add onion slices and water. Cover.
4. Cook over low heat for 60 minutes. Remove fowl and keep warm.
5. Add water if necessary to approximate 1 cup of liquid in the skillet.
6. Blend in milk, 2 tablespoons flour, salt, and pepper and stir into pan juices. Cook 2 or 3 minutes more.
7. Sprinkle paprika on fowl and serve with pan gravy.

Corn Pudding

SERVES 4 TO 6

2 tablespoons butter or substitute
1 16-ounce can creamed corn
2 tablespoons sugar
1 teaspoon flour
  salt and freshly ground pepper to taste
2 eggs
1 5.33-ounce can evaporated milk

PREPARATION

1. Preheat oven to 350 degrees.
2. Melt butter in cast-iron skillet.
3. Pour creamed corn into skillet. Add sugar, flour, and salt and pepper.
4. Add eggs and milk, stirring to blend well.
5. Bake for 60–70 minutes, or until toothpick inserted in center comes out clean.

Glazed Carrots and Onions

SERVES 4 TO 6

These go well with many game recipes, especially venison.

1 pound small white onions, peeled
2 dozen small carrots, scraped
⅓ cup plus 2 tablespoons butter
½ teaspoon sugar plus sugar to taste
⅓ cup beef bouillon
  water
  salt
  white pepper

PREPARATION

1. Melt 2 tablespoons butter in cast-iron skillet.
2. Add peeled onions. Sprinkle with salt and sugar to taste.
3. Saute onions until golden.
4. Add bouillon and simmer until bouillon evaporates.
5. Place carrots in saucepan.
6. Add water, ⅓ cup butter, ½ teaspoon sugar, and salt and pepper to taste.
7. Bring to boil, reduce heat. Cook uncovered until carrots are tender and liquid has evaporated.
8. Serve onions and carrots on same platter.

Deep Dish Wild Plum Pie

SERVES 4 TO 6

5 cups pitted fresh plums (about 2 pounds)

3/4 cup brown sugar

2 teaspoons tapioca

1/4 teaspoon ground cinnamon

    dash nutmeg

    salt to taste

1 tablespoon butter

9-inch pastry crust

2 cups flour

1 teaspoon salt

2/3 cup vegetable shortening

    cold water

PREPARATION

1. Preheat oven to 375 degrees.
2. Combine plums, brown sugar, tapioca, cinnamon, nutmeg, and salt. Set aside for 20 minutes.
3. Pour mixture into 9-inch cast-iron skillet and dot with butter.
4. Mix 2 cups flour and 1 teaspoon salt. Cut in shortening until all pieces are the size of #00 buckshot.
5. Sprinkle a little cold water a bit at a time over the buckshot pieces until all are moistened.
6. To make pastry crust, form flour mixture into a ball, flatten on floured surface. Roll from the center until 1/8-inch thick. (In camp a chilled longneck beer bottle will substitute for a rolling pin.)
7. Place crust over filling, trim, seal edges, and cut slits in crust.
8. Bake for 45 minutes.

VIII

DEER

DEER

Deer hunting is the state's leading outdoor participation sport, garnering more than half a million hunters. When you include family involvement, upward of a million people migrate to deer country each fall.

One of the reasons for the enthusiasm is the incredible hunter success ratio. In areas such as the Edwards Plateau, eight out of 10 hunters annually kill at least one whitetail. This contrasts sharply with the national average of one deer for every 10 hunters afield.

Elusive quarry for more than half a million Texas white-tailed deer hunters.

Actually, the Texas deer herd is seriously overpopulated in many areas and is attempting to survive on land that is grazed beyond its carrying capacity. Hunters have not kept pace with the incremental annual gain in the deer herd and the subsequent increase in deer density per acre. Consequently, more deer die from natural causes than at the hands of hunters.

In most counties, more deer *should* be harvested by hunters. More hunter pressure will ultimately lead to larger deer, larger antlers, more productivity, and higher resistance to attrition by natural causes such as starvation and predators. Of course, livestock also must be kept within the carrying capacity of the range. This responsibility falls under the rancher's domain. When landowners allow twice the acceptable number of domestic livestock and deer to fight it out for available grazing, it can lead to deer disaster, especially in drought years.

The landowner-controlled system has created a Catch 22 by allowing this deer density while discouraging hunters with expensive lease fees. The hunting lease business alone brings in several hundred million dollars annually and provides a substantial part of ranch revenues. And more than 250,000 hunters each year are unable to find a lease. TPWD has established a Deer Hunting Lease Registry designed to match hunter and rancher.

Spanish grants and the immense ranch holdings acquired by the earliest settlers set the precedent for private ownership of almost all Texas lands. Private land is still

protected by tough trespass laws. Heavy fines are common, followed by jail sentences for second offenders. Laws provide for confiscation of firearms, other equipment, and loss of hunting license, so don't cross a fence line unless you have permission.

Deer were nearly wiped out in most of the nation by 1900. The situation was serious enough in Texas for the legislature to pass a law establishing the first deer season in 1881. Nineteen years later, the U.S. Congress passed the Lacey Act, prohibiting interstate traffic in wild game taken in violation of state law. This slowed down market hunters enough to let whitetail rebound almost everywhere. The deer were quick to adapt to a new environment that included millions of human inhabitants. One whitetail we know lived for years in a downtown Dallas park area.

Members of the Texas white-tailed deer subspecies, *Odocoileus virginianus texanus*, have smaller bodies than deer of eastern and midwestern ranges, and they're even smaller in the Llano Basin, where field-dressed weights average only 60 pounds. The national field-dressed average weight is 110 pounds. Conversely, poorly formed racks and spikes are common in the Llano Basin. In Llano County, where we've hunted for 20 years, about 12,000 deer are killed annually by some 14,000 hunters. This is more than the entire deer population in some states, let alone the harvest. This doesn't apply presently to all of Texas, but the same threat exists. Hunters in the Llano Basin have shot off nearly all the quality bucks, possibly creating a drain on the genetic pool, and landowners

Texas has more than 4 million white-tailed deer and more than its share of trophy racks such as these.

have taxed the land's grazing capacity with overabundant livestock.

It isn't surprising that the first permits for harvesting antlerless deer—does—were issued in selected Llano Basin areas in 1953. What is surprising is how long it took for both hunters and ranchers to accept the necessity for taking does, until you consider the powerful bias present in the thinking of both groups.

First, the ranchers' viewpoint: The more cows, the more calves. The more does, the more fawns. The more deer, the more income to be derived from lease fees.

The hunters' stance: We no longer have the need for meat, but we still have the passion for the hunt. We are hunting because of something in our spirit and part of that something is best expressed in a big rack. The bigger the rack, the greater the excitement. Does don't have racks.

While the TPWD has done a tremendous job of educating both interest groups, we are still far from attaining the one-to-one herd balance some game biologists strive for. Roughly three-fourths of the deer killed each season are bucks. Most hunters are passing the buck mentally and abdicating their individual responsibility for game management.

Learn to leave the four-, six- and small eight-point deer

that will produce the better racks of tomorrow by rebuilding the genetic pool. We try to take a doe or older spike before we go after Godzilla. It never worked when we promised ourselves to take a doe at the end of the season.

The exchange value of a deer hide a century ago was known as a "buck," a prophetic euphemism for the big-buck financial impact of deer hunting in Texas. Newcomers to Texas, many of whom are accustomed to more public hunting lands, sometimes resent this. There is some public land in Texas however, especially in the Pineywoods of East Texas where there are national forests and timber company land open to public hunting. The TPWD manages some areas you can hunt by permit. Applications, always for a specific area, are obtainable from TPWD, 4200 School Smith Road, Austin, TX 78744. Some of the wildlife management areas where you can make deer hunting applications are: Gus Engeling, East Texas; Gene Howe, Panhandle; Kerr, Hill Country; Chaparral, South Texas; and Sierra Diablo, West Texas. (See Chapter I for a complete WMA list.) Applications are usually accepted in August. Permits are issued on a drawing basis on the more popular WMAs, especially for deer hunts.

There are other WMA hunts during the year for feral hogs, javelina, ducks, dove, quail, squirrels, and even spring turkeys. Deadlines for applications and drawing procedures vary from year to year, so we suggest calling the Texas Parks and Wildlife toll-free telephone number before September: 1-800-792-1112. WMAs where hunting is allowed are listed in their respective ecological areas in Chapter I.

The Texas Parks and Wildlife WMAs are model research centers for the study of ecological relationships unique to Texas. Grazing is one of the big issues with specific attention to the coexistence of domestic livestock, deer, and, in some cases, escaped exotics on the same land. Much has been learned on WMAs about improving wildlife quality, and controlled situations have produced bigger, healthier deer with better racks.

Hunters on wildlife management areas are required to wear hunter orange as a safety measure. Like most western state hunting regulations, the rule requires that 400 square inches of daylight fluorescent orange be worn, with at least one square foot—144 square inches—worn on both your chest and back. We keep several plastic "dayglo" vests in camp. These come in handy for guests and for our spring rabbit hunts with young hunters. This practice is an excellent safety precaution that deer generally don't notice. (The deer's visual capacity will be discussed later in this chapter.)

The dedicated deer hunter will eventually dig a little deeper into his pockets and lease his hunting rights. A typical lease contains from 1,000 to 1,500 acres. Day leases are readily available, but we feel long-term leases shared with friends are the most rewarding.

In selecting an area to establish a lease or day hunt, you should know that Texas has almost every variation of deer hunting found in America, excluding deep snow tracking, though you may encounter blue northers and even some snow and ice. Texas offers hunting in swamps, tall-timber forests, second-growth forests, heavy brush, desert mountains, scrub oak and cedar breaks, marshes, and breathtaking canyons.

Chambers of commerce are fertile sources of lease information, as are numerous hunting periodicals published in the state. TPWD also provides a hunting lease locator service; call the toll-free number.

Fully enjoying your deer lease depends upon two things: a compatible group of hunters who like and respect one another, agreeing to a set of written rules, and secondly, an excellent relationship with the rancher, with whom you should also have a written agreement.

The ideal lease arrangement is year-round, since this assures frequent outdoor sorties every bit as rewarding as the hunt itself. Though most deer leases are seasonal, many offer other fall hunting in season such as dove, duck, quail, and turkey. Still other leases have stock tanks full of bass, crappie, and catfish. South and West Texas leases may also have feral hogs, javelina, and blue quail. Even with seasonal leases, most ranchers allow access to prepare stands, set up base camp, and to place and service feeders. Sportsmen derive a great deal of pleasure from the pre-season strategy discussions on stand placement, whether to feed or not, condition of the herd, predictions of the hunt, and set up of lease work parties.

You should be familiar with terrain features, stand placement, individual hunter peccadillos, and adjacent lease habits. For example, some like to still hunt, perhaps the most enjoyable way to pursue whitetail. Others may like the more sedentary stand hunt. Still other situations might call for a deliberate drive hunt involving full group cooperation. Knowing all of these details can help in organizing the hunt and increase the odds in the hunters' favor. Some common sense and practical agreements we've reached include making sure that stand hunters stay on the stand till a certain hour. Still hunters know exactly where they can and can't walk. And everyone knows where everybody else is. Even the choice of hunting spots is a function of the group's interactions. We like to draw cards, high card getting first choice.

Rancher relations should be a required course for all deer hunters in Texas. In truth, a lot of mistrust and misunderstanding have built up between ranchers and hunters. Many hunters make the mistake of approaching the rancher on an adversarial basis. And many ranchers are wary of hunters, for good reason, since they have suffered many, many abuses.

A rancher wronged is worse than a woman scorned. Hunter-rancher problems usually develop from oversights and carelessness with disregard for basic hunting ethics. While you are on a rancher's property, you are in his home, and the strictest etiquette is required, not to mention common sense. Always leave gates the way you found them. It's a mistake to leave a gate open for even a short period. You better believe a prize bull will magically appear and slip through to another pasture, immediately impregnating a prize heifer. It seems that if anything goes wrong with the livestock, it's always prize, a synonym for very costly.

A rancher knows his land like you know your living room. Know his rules and abide by them. One way of assuring understanding is to write the rules down as part of your lease agreement and give copies to all members. In fact, most intelligent hunters will have even stricter rules than the typical rancher in the interest of both the safety and aesthetics of the hunt. By codifying and adhering to these rules you begin the journey to mutual respect. It goes without saying that these rules include a strict adherence to both the spirit and the letter of the laws governing hunting and trespass, as well as to the self-imposed law of fair chase.

Common courtesy, too, often appears uncommon. It surprises us that few hunters think to bring the rancher's wife a small gift at least once a season. And what's wrong with inviting the rancher's family to a special Saturday evening dinner in your camp, perhaps during a preseason work party? Above all, know that good relations stem from a mutual respect for land and game. Rare is the rancher who will not share your philosophy.

Too few hunters think "family" in connection with the hunt experience, thus many camps miss the civilizing woman's touch. Granted, certain hunting conditions can make the atmosphere inappropriate for a family outing, but there are other opportunities. For instance, years ago, we instituted a Darling Does weekend when our spouses are invited to the camp—to hunt or just soak up nature. The men do all the cooking and cleaning, and they provide guide service. Wives are instructed to relax and enjoy. Of course, the rancher's wife loves to come to these events, and we've formed close ties over the years.

Like dove hunting, the deer hunt is usually a social event, especially the time spent in camp. We celebrate our hunting with fine evening meals and accompany them with good wines and spirits in moderation, which brings up a most important aspect of hunting and lease etiquette. Liquor is taboo while hunting. We have a long-standing rule we firmly believe every hunter should abide by: *If you take a drink during the day, you're through hunting for the day*. State wildlife management areas specifically prohibit the presence of alcoholic beverages in hunt areas. Violations call for forfeiture of permits and violators are expelled, as well they should be.

Texas' four million whitetail and mule deer are distributed unevenly through the state, with a sprinkling of Carmen Mountain whitetails in West Texas. Humongous whitetails lurk in the heavy thickets and dense brush of the Pineywoods and the Cross Timbers and Prairies, but these areas are extremely hard to hunt. A productive hunting area for whitetails is the South Texas Plains, incorporating the Brush Country's fabled Boone and Crockett racked deer. But in terms of sheer number of deer and deer kills, the Edwards Plateau is the premier whitetail area.

The Hill Country's special beauty, easy-to-negotiate open live oak, oak scrub, and mesquite offers an ambiance suitable to the enjoyment of any whitetail hunter. Heading out into the Trans-Pecos, entering the Chihuahuan Desert, you encounter a different face of nature. An Apache Indian legend tells of God at the moment of Creation throwing all the world's leftover rocks into West Texas. This vast, arid terrain has its own haunting beauty, but nary a shade tree for our sportsmen.

In the Glass, Davis, Chinati, Van Horn, and Sierra Blanca Mountains, as well as some other mountains of the Trans-Pecos, you're into desert mule deer range. Al-

The mountains of the Trans-Pecos hold excellent populations of desert mule deer.

though smaller than the Rocky Mountain mulies of New Mexico and Colorado, Texas mule deer offer challenging, physically demanding hunting. Our mule deer are found just on the eastern edge of the species' range.

Mule deer hunting differs from whitetail hunting in that it requires more walking, climbing, and spotting activities in wide open, rugged country. The lunar astronauts practiced in our mule deer range in an area known as Hell's Half Acre. You can find every known variety of geological formation in the Trans-Pecos. All we can say is, wear the best boots you can buy and carry water.

Mule deer and whitetails overlap in Brewster County. True to form, whitetails stay down in the draws and brush areas, while mulies like open, high ground. Don't think this makes them easy to spot. Their coloration blends perfectly into the desert mountains, so unless they're moving, you won't see them without patient glassing.

Perhaps because of their inaccessibility and the fact that as a consequence they are less familiar with *Homo sapiens*, mule deer appear less wily than whitetails. Though they have the same detection gear—eyesight, hearing, and smell—they often have a fatal flaw. Unlike the cautious whitetail, they'll panic and run in the open from danger, often stopping to look around to see what caused the commotion.

The Trans-Pecos is home to the Carmen Mountain whitetails. These are found in the Chisos, Rosillos, Christ-

A Carmen Mountain whitetail rack looks much like that of a very small whitetail.

mas, and Chinati Mountains and in the Sierra del Carmen of South Central Brewster County on both sides of the Rio Grande. The Sierra del Carmen forms the eastern border of Big Bend National Park, so few of these unusual whitetail subspecies are harvested by hunters. The antlers of Carmen Mountain whitetails have even forks reminiscent of very small whitetail deer. Carmen whitetails are often mistaken for the better known diminutive Coues whitetail subspecies. Coues are found in southeastern Arizona and often called Arizona whitetail. They're also hunted in southwestern New Mexico, west of the Rio Grande, and in northern Mexico.

Pronghorn antelope are found in huntable numbers in the High Plains, Rolling Plains, and Trans-Pecos, a tribute to the landowners of those areas since the antelope was nearly extinct in the '20s and further decimated by the drought of 1964–65. At one time, some two million pronghorn antelope roamed Texas as far east as the Cross Timbers and Prairies.

TPWD issues pronghorn permits to landowners who are well aware of their value. The Alpine and Marfa chambers of commerce are excellent sources for contacting

ranchers possessing these permits. After that, it takes money and an accurate, flat-shooting rifle. Hunter success ratios approach 90 percent.

Elk are native to the Trans-Pecos. Sparse, free-ranging herds exist on private land in the Eagle Mountains, and larger herds can be found in the Glass and Guadalupe Mountains. In 1988, Texas swapped Rio Grande turkeys with Oregon for elk to be released in the Wylie and Davis Mountains. Herds on private land are found in other parts of the state, including eastern Texas. *Eh-kahg-tchick-kah*, as the Indians call them, are rare and rarely hunted, and then by special permit only. Another name for this mag-

Elk range free in the Glass Mountains of Texas, and there is a large protected herd in the Guadalupes.

nificent animal, which often weighs more than 700 pounds, is *wapiti*.

The original elk in Texas were the long extinct Merriam's. The ones we sometimes see today are transplanted Rocky Mountain elk. The Trans-Pecos is good elk range, so our herds are building and hunting permits are issued occasionally. But elk in Texas are mainly to be admired and revered, as they once were hundreds of years ago by Indians, who credited *Eh-kahg-tchick-kah* with creating the earth and accorded him the stature and omnipotence of a god.

AVERAGE ANNUAL DEER HARVEST

ECOLOGICAL AREA	DENSITY PER SQ. MI.	HERD ESTIMATE (000)	AVERAGE HARVEST (000)
Edwards Plateau	(40)	1,400	167
South Texas Plains	(17)	450	66
Pineywoods	not available		29
Post Oak Savannah	(27)	338	27
Cross Timbers and Prairies	(22)	205	22
Gulf Prairies and Marshes	(50)	130	8
Rolling Plains	(10)	52	5
Trans-Pecos	(9)	24	2
Blackland Prairies	(8)	7	0.4
High Plains	not available		0.2

The chart shows at a glance that two of the best places to have a lease or arrange a fee hunt would be in the South Texas Plains and Edwards Plateau. The ratio of harvest to herd size in the Gulf Prairies and Marshes and Blackland Prairies show these areas to be the toughest in which to find a deer. What's interesting to note is that the Gulf Prairies has a lot of deer, more than 130,000, with the highest density per square mile, but the hunting is made rough by the swamp thickets, heavy underbrush, and cover of its low-lying geography.

WHITETAIL INSIGHTS

By hunting season in November, Texas whitetails have normally shed their reddish summer coats for grayish brown. The whitetail, mulie, and Carmens all have white bellies and inner legs, and a white patch typically covers their chins and upper throats. The tip of the nose will be blackish, turning white farther up the nose then blending into the overall coloration. The whitetail is named for the white of the undertail, seen by millions of clumsy hunters who've unwittingly jumped their quarry. This is the origin of the age-old phrase "high-tailed it" to describe a hasty exit.

Also by hunting season, buck deer have fully developed antlers. In Texas, whitetail antlers begin growing in mid-March. Male fawns will only develop a button, known to biologists as the pedicel. The first set of antlers develop in the spring and summer a year after birth and start as two single beams (spikes). If the antlers do not branch into other points, these deer, called spikes, are considered genetically deficient and should be harvested.

A yearling on poor, overgrazed range may develop spikes instead of a beam with points. It's possible for a healthy yearling to have up to 10 points. Sportsmen count a point as being at least one inch long, or capable of hold-ing an Aggie's class ring. The measure in the Boone and Crockett Club's *Records of North American Big Game* is one inch, too. Size is mainly a function of nutrition. Antlers get larger each succeeding year, bringing a larger rack, until a deer's prime, 4½ to 5½ years of age. Deer are aged in fractions because they are born in June or July and harvested in November or December.

Deer have a gestation period of about 200 days and seldom live past the age of 10. Eight years is considered old. The condition of a deer's teeth is a good indication of its age. Game biologists with microscopes can view cross sections of cementum layers of teeth and establish an age estimate. One cementum layer equals one year of life. Laymen must check the deer's mouth after the kill, looking for dark dentine on the jaw teeth near its tongue. As deer age, the enamel of these six jaw teeth wears down, exposing more dentine each year.

The deer's permanent premolars, found ahead of the molars on the lower jaw, have fully erupted by 19 months and obviously would show no wear at that age. After that they grind off about one millimeter per year. By 10 years or so, the teeth are ground down to the gum line and the deer can no longer feed.

But let's get back to what sportsmen really care about, the racks. The growing antler bone is covered with a soft, hairy skin called velvet. The growing bone is soft and injury-prone, and many malformed racks are made during this stage as the bucks whack against unyielding surfaces. The antlers keep growing through August into September, when the bone finally hardens and the velvet is rubbed off.

Outstanding racks start with good genes and good nu-

Great racks are inherited but proper nutrition is critical for full development.

The hunter knows the rut is about
to begin when he finds a buck scrape.

This antler rub has been marked with
a rutting buck's personal scent.

trition. In other words, antler conformation is a function of heredity and diet. This constitutes the principal difference between the deer of the Hill Country and those of the Brush Country. Brush Country ranchers work hard at maintaining deer with good genetic backgrounds, and many require that deer killed have a point count often as high as 10 points and a 20-inch beam. Conversely, as we've noted, the typical Hill Country deer are not as well fed and are hunted with much less discrimination; consequently, the typical Hill Country hunter has less splendid racks to choose from.

Spring and early summer rains are critical to good antler development, even when there are good genetics. Texas range land in the South Central Plains, Edwards Plateau, and Trans-Pecos, when it is grazed within normal carrying capacity, is incredibly nutritious and mineral-rich, conducive to good antler development. That's why our trophy deer racks, when compared to Yankee deer, are disproportionately large to overall body weight. In Texas, *muy grande* refers to racks, not body size or weight.

Antler growth is closely associated with testosterone levels, which in turn are closely related to the sex life of a buck and the mating season, the rut. As the hormone level rises, antlers reach their peak and bucks begin rubbing and polishing their horns. Just prior to the rut, bucks will create scrapes or lairs for future liaisons by marking or scenting the areas, which are usually about two feet square. This is accomplished in several ways. Special scent glands in the buck's forehead allow the buck to rub or mark trees with his personal musk while he's polishing his antlers and browsing on leaves and twigs. He will also paw the ground in his scrape and urinate on the loosened earth. The final touch of perfume comes when the buck rubs the inner surfaces of his hind legs together, releasing a musky scent from his tarsal glands. Bucks will make several "scrapes" and revisit these areas, which stake out his realm. Hunters have a high success ratio when hunting near scrapes.

Estrus is the downfall of many a buck. In Texas, the rut can stretch out for several weeks through November into December, so it's somewhat difficult to predict. The rut tends more toward early December in the Brush Country and Trans-Pecos, later than the rest of the state. This has important implications for the hunter. Regardless of timing, when does go into heat, hunting bucks is considerably easier, since, like humans, they are driven by their hormones. With male deer, necks swell, gonads enlarge, and caution dwindles.

A rutting buck in pursuit of a doe will typically have his tail out, head down, and mouth open. He's smelling the pheromones in the urine of a doe in estrus. The doe's tail will usually be raised away from her body, indicating she's ready for mating. Often the doe will circle, leading the buck on a merry-go-round chase. A buck in rut has a strong proprietary interest in his does and will readily fight other bucks to drive them from his territory, which can also be advantageous to the hunter.

By late December or early January when the rut is over, antlers begin falling off as the supply of testosterone decreases. We have known this to happen earlier in Texas, especially in the Edwards Plateau. When it does, you're out of luck on a buck hunt. We believe this is attributable mainly to overgrazed range, since bucks in good condition appear to keep their antlers longer.

Speed. Smell. Sight. Sound. The four S's of whitetail preservation. These senses are immensely well developed in comparison with their human counterparts. So when matching woodsmanship with an animal that has much keener senses and can magically bound away at 40 miles per hour, you've got to exercise brainpower as well as firepower.

Deer are often credited with telescopic vision. Not true. If you stand perfectly still they won't notice you. But they can see the slightest movement and discern minute gray scale variations. Conventional wisdom says that deer can't see color, but recent biological studies challenge this theory. The whitetail's range is restricted: in the Trans-Pecos, within a square mile or 640 acres; in the Hill Country, within 300 acres. In his range, a whitetail will know the right look of everything. Although the deer may not be able to see color per se, a fluorescent orange vest can stand out distinctly as a light patch against darker background. This contrast is what the deer will notice, even if the object is motionless.

We believe deer can discern color in bright daylight, so it makes sense to stay still. Still hunt with great patience. Watch the deer's tail. If it twitches, his head will come up to look around. Don't attempt to slip behind a tree or drop to the ground when a deer looks in your direction, because he'll be gone at the movement. Instead, freeze. If you blend relatively well and you're standing downwind, you might not spook him.

Deer find human odors highly offensive. They use their sense of smell to identify other deer, to forage for food,

This whitetail got a whiff of man,
much to its displeasure.

and even to scent the trail of pheromones secreted by the interdigital glands between the toes of other deer. Deer can also distinguish between some 600 varieties of edibles. So arrange your hunt to have the wind in your face. Don't smoke and don't wear cologne or aftershave. Don't relieve yourself near a stand you plan to stay in for long. Deer can easily scent where you've been. If you rest for a spell under an oak tree, the next deer who comes along will know it. In other words, don't smell any worse than you have to. Even on a calm, windless day, your odor will waft in ever-widening circles like ripples on a pebbled pond. On such a day, consider moving your stand from time to time if you aren't still hunting. A steady breeze will carry your scent a long way, even hundreds of yards, to the sensitive proboscis of a whitetail.

Deer also have remarkably sharp hearing and often spook to natural sounds such as a quail flushing, a javelina rooting, even a gust of wind. Even more surprising, they often won't spook to things you'd expect, like a distant shot or a nearby pickup engine. They will spook and quickly depart from out-of-place sounds such as two-legged animals clomping through woods, or the snap of twigs breaking, or the crack of a carelessly shut bolt. They will often stop at a shrill whistle, particularly if they haven't actually seen or smelled the hunter. Motorcycles drive them batty, but they'll ignore semi's on the highway.

Our observation is that a deer has stored in his memory bank the implications of everything he sees, hears, and smells. Any variance or disturbance to his normal life will give the hunter an unwelcome view of the whitetail flag. If he spots you upwind, but you're motionless, he may stay put; but a faint whiff of you or a slight sound will mean adios.

Deer must have water—sometimes hard to come by in Texas—food, shelter, comfortable bedding, an escape route, and sex in season. Like most animals, deer are creatures of habit and, unless disturbed, they routinely use the same bedding areas and take the same routes to forage and water. They prefer routes with ample cover, such as draws and creek beds. Whitetail predators attack mainly from the ground, so the deer tend to keep their eyes on the ground rather than looking up, a bad habit exploited by hunters.

Deer feeding habits vary in each ecological area according to the type and availability of food. In the heavily populated Edwards Plateau, acorns and other masts are preferred treats, although forbs (small, leafy plants) and browse (the tender tips of tree and shrub branches) are important. Hackberry, Spanish oak, scrub oak, blackjack, post oak, and live oak are four-star restaurants to whitetails in the Hill Country. Heavy acorn years can mean difficult hunting, because deer don't have to roam far to dine well. Cactus, browse, and forbs are the fast-food stops for the big deer of the Brush Country.

Sportsmen must know the difference between supplemental feeding and baiting. Deer feeders spewing out

corn—one of the worst foods a deer can eat—are a common sight on ranches during hunting season. This constitutes baiting, not supplemental feeding. It's amazing how many of these benign feeding programs terminate the day after deer season closes, and it's equally amazing how many stands overlook feeders. No true sportsman would consider shooting over any baited area. By contrast, supplemental feeding furnishes key nutrients when needed to preserve the deer herd, in or out of the hunting season.

The key to healthy deer and good antler development is a diet rich in protein—at least 16 percent of total consumption. Corn meets less than half of this requirement, thus cornfed deer can be inferior and develop stunted racks. And, for the record, deer starve on hay.

Other studies show that precise percentages of minerals such as calcium and phosphorus are vital. These two minerals should be present in ratios of 1:1 to 1:2. The optimum diet contains 0.64 percent calcium and 0.56 percent phosphorus. Deer pellets containing the correct protein and mineral mix are commercially available at most reputable feed dealers. A good feed store won't sell you pellets containing urea, because deer cannot digest this protein. Only crude proteins should be used.

A supplemental feeding program may be useless on your lease. If you have poor range populated beyond its carrying capacity with deer and livestock, it is doubtful you can help by feeding. You need a new lease. TPWD biologists are available to ranchers to assist in determining range carrying capacity and recommending harvest quotas.

Texas celebrates spring with wildflowers and spotted fawns.

Sex and season determine the special food needs of deer. Does require good nutrition almost all year, during the fall and winter to assure reproductive success and in the early spring during the stress of gestation and lactation when fawns are really soaking up the milk. Fawns usually double their weight in two weeks and begin browsing after a few weeks; supplemental feeding can be important to the fawn crop if a summer drought is blistering your range. Bucks need top nutrition during antler development in winter and spring. Note that the times of year calling for supplemental feeding, if practical at all, are usually *not* during hunting season.

For sportsmen unable to maintain free choice game feeders, which require almost daily trips, there are many durable electric-eye and time-controlled feeders on the market. Experience has taught us to rely more on timers. These feeders are usually mounted high up on tripods to allow feed to scatter. A convenient design allows the feeder drum to be lowered by crank so that one person can easily fill the drum by himself. The spinner mechanism which scatters the feed requires a pellet cube size of $^3/_{16}$ inch, otherwise it will jam. Surround the feeder with a low fence pen to keep cattle out. The barbed wire fence should have a smooth wire on top and give the deer plenty of landing room inside so they will feel confident about jumping in.

If you've been given bad advice and have been feeding corn, it's a good idea to mix some corn in at first to help the deer become accustomed to the new feed's scent and taste.

Often you can negotiate with your rancher to plant food plots of oats, winter wheat, or peanuts. We have an arrangement for a special oat patch planting and we consider this as important a part of our lease agreement as length of lease, fees, number of hunters, and game that may be taken. There is a *quid pro quo* in that the rancher's livestock will ultimately graze the field.

TPWD provides a helpful booklet, *Supplemental Feeding*. We suggest this as required reading for all sportsmen, because misconceptions about feeding are common and often perpetuated by those wishing to sell you lots of corn.

Sportsmen can also be much more proactive in gathering the information needed for really professional deer herd management. Harvest records should be expanded to note field-dressed weights (keep scales available at camp), antler measurements, and age. Perceptive sportsmen can learn, with assistance from TPWD, how to estimate deer density, buck-to-doe ratios, percent of fawn crop, and percent of spikes to bucks. The lease members can make an effort to shoot all spikes 2½ years and older from the herd; it's helpful to thin spikes in the yearling class if you're certain that it's genetics, not poor nutrition. Utilizing this information is impossible without rancher assistance, and frustrating without game-proof fencing or the cooperation of all surrounding ranches. But, this should not deter you from learning the basics of game management and applying what you can when you can.

To the uninitiated, even the supposedly distinctive tracks of the whitetail can be misread, often confused with domestic sheep. A more common error is to mistake domestic sheep and goat droppings for those of deer. This can be a bad mistake when checking out a lease for the first time. As you will see from the track comparison illustrations that follow, it is very difficult to tell the whitetail track from the mule deer, but luckily, the need to do so is rare. However, mule deer and pronghorn sometimes occupy the same range, and this comparison is tricky, too. A running track will reveal that pronghorn lack dewclaws and that mule deer bounce with all four hooves hitting the ground at once, back feet together behind front, with all four close together.

DESERT MULE DEER INSIGHTS

Foot-long ears, a small tail, double-forked antler beams, and a white rump patch distinguish the mule deer from the whitetail, even though both wear the same coat. The mulie's pendant-shaped tail is smaller and never flags. When he bounds away, he tucks his tail in. The main beam of the mature mulie's antlers forks twice into points straighter than those of the typical whitetail.

Mule deer bounce away in pogo stick fashion when spooked.

Texas desert mule deer favor the slopes of headers in the mountains of the Trans-Pecos. Mule deer generally don't receive the hunter pressure of whitetails, and their habitat is wide open. Their basic defense is to hide, then

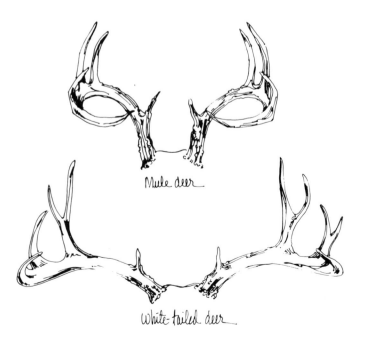

exit, often without undue haste. Pressured enough, they sidle off to the farthest point from civilization they can reach.

Mule deer will bed down with minimal cover, almost completely in the open, usually in a high place where they can survey the terrain. When the north wind is blowing, look for them on the lee slopes in a sunny location. On warmer, early December hunts, seek them in the cool, shaded sides of ridges. It takes patient glassing to pick them out. You should carefully scan every small shrub, rock, and depression.

Mule deer are also more gregarious than whitetails, sometimes congregating in herds of 30 or more. They seem more at home and less spooky than whitetails. A curious whitetail is a nervous critter, soon gone. Mulies will stand and study anomalies in their environment, investigating strange things. The whitetail hunter often mistakes these traits for stupidity—we don't.

Typical mule deer habitat is open, rocky terrain, but they still can be hard to spot.

The mule deer's habitat is usually much testier than the whitetail's. No tower stands here, but rather towering headers. The usual mule deer hunting routine is to glass, spot the deer, and begin climbing your legs off. The real fun begins after a successful kill. Often there's a long, rough return to camp, perhaps requiring horses or backpacking to bring the meat out.

PRONGHORN ANTELOPE INSIGHTS

When you're scoping out a trophy pronghorn buck, you're looking at virtually the same animal that prehis-

toric predators coveted millions of years ago. After surviving the icy Armageddon at the end of the Pleistocene Age, the pronghorn has no near relatives on earth, but, like the white-tailed deer, he's barely survived contemporary man. By 1920, 99.9 percent of the pronghorns on this planet were dead: shot, chewed, starved, and fenced out of existence. Early settlers were good at slaughtering these beautiful animals, especially when they were herded by blue northers and driven into net wire fence corners. A pronghorn can crawl under a barbed wire fence, but is trapped by net wire.

The pronghorn is close in size to the Texas whitetail, at 100 to 110 pounds live weight, and 34 to 36 inches at the shoulder. Texas pronghorns are lighter colored than those on more northern ranges, with a tawny upper body, and cream belly and lower brisket. The white dickey of the upper neck is supported by a pale chest shield. The cheeks and lower jaw are also white. A black streak runs beneath the jawline of bucks, who almost always wear a dark brown highwayman's mask to the tip of their black noses.

Pronghorns favor wide open prairie where their incredible eyesight is their main defense.

Bucks and does both have large white rump patches which serve as fire alarms. Unique in all the animal kingdom, the erectile hairs of the patch blossom out to signal danger. When other members of the herd see it, they're gone.

Yet another solo act by our pronghorn is the annual horn shed. Not to be confused with deer and elk that shed antlers, pronghorns actually shed horns from a bony core. The pronghorn is the only hooved animal that does this. The bone core, covered by a velvet skin, grows larger each year for about five years. The horny outer sheath pops open and falls off soon after the rut in October and November. The pronghorn, much like the deer, then rubs off the furry velvet.

Bucks and does both have horns, but doe horns are small, *sans* prongs. The buck's horns resemble the musical lyre and should be well above the ears for a trophy. Estimate the length of the horns against the length of the head and muzzle. If the horns are longer, shoot; they are probably in the exceptional 12- to 14-inch category. The prong itself is sharkfin shaped, projecting from the main horn. Imagine the curved tip of fins pointing upward. Prongs are defensive weapons used for deflecting the incoming horns of rivals.

Telescopic eyesight is the pronghorn's main line of defense. You'll put your binoculars on a promising pronghorn several hundred yards out only to find him looking right back at you. That's why they favor wide open spaces. You'll not find pronghorn in a mesquite thicket. In fact, the march northward of mesquite in the first half of this century eliminated huge chunks of pronghorn range, not to mention rancher patience. We can thank the Spanish for this incredibly tough plant competitor—especially good for cooking fires and dove roosts—as it was not indigenous to the Americas.

The pronghorn's eyeballs bulge, adding 360-degree peripheral vision to his telescopic sight. (And we thought only mothers and linebackers could see behind themselves.) They also have excellent hearing, comparable to the whitetail, as well as a good sense of smell for foraging and sniffing out stalking hunters.

Pronghorn bucks are the real randies of the animal world, so it's no wonder they survive. In early fall, bucks begin rounding up their harems, invariably gathering

A large doe harem hangs in the balance.

more than they can handle. Harems of more than 30 does have been noted, but 10 to 20 is more common. The trouble starts as Mr. Pronghorn tries to keep his doe herd intact until each is ready for him. He spends most of October chasing does, trying to keep them in line.

With an eight-month gestation period, most fawns are literally dropped in June, since birthing occurs with the doe standing. The doe likes to leave the herd to give birth. She wants privacy and a hidey hole good for at least five days. On day five, the fawn can outrun a coyote—an important factor in West Texas.

TPWD studies have clearly demonstrated the impact of coyotes on pronghorn fawn production. It's dramatic in uncontrolled coyote country. Still, the pronghorn herd in Texas, averaging 15,000 to 20,000, now seems stable, and we have been able to hunt them by limited permit since 1955. This is remarkable, because 30 years earlier there were virtually no pronghorn in the state.

Catalysts for rebuilding the herd were the closing of the season in 1903, coyote control, transplanting activities by wildlife protection agencies, and enforcement of game laws. Enforcement during the Depression was carried out more by ranchers than the TPWD's staff, which was miniscule at the time.

Permits are issued to landowners, who, in turn, issue them to hunters in exchange for fees. This eminently successful system has the same drawback as the white-tailed deer lease system—money. Trophy hunting tends to imbalance the buck-to-doe ratio, especially when the hunter must have deep pockets to hunt.

Most pronghorns are found in the Trans-Pecos, with some herds in the High Plains as you near the New Mexico border. There are a rare few in the Rolling Plains.

It is customary in Texas to patrol ranch roads by vehicle until a herd is spotted, then you begin a stalk. This is best handled by flatbellies. We prefer simply to get out before dawn near a water hole, or on the edge of a draw, and spend the day still hunting. The pit ambush is a favorite of many. Chasing down the animals from a vehicle is not acceptable. This is not only unsporting, it's illegal. Also unacceptable to sportsmen are incredibly long, running shots where the chances of a clean kill are non-existent.

AOUDAD AND DESERT

BIGHORN INSIGHTS

The aoudad is our state's only nonnative animal given big game status. For centuries he prowled the rugged Atlas Mountains overlooking the Barbary Coast of northwest Africa, putting all would-be hunters to quite a test. Aoudads were introduced to Texas in the late '50s, and they have since thrived. Our stock came from a New Mexico game ranch and they were let loose in spectacularly scenic Palo Duro Canyon, which, as you'd expect, is at almost the same latitude as the Atlas Mountain range, 32 degrees north, and possesses the same climatic conditions. The south slopes of the Atlas Mountains overlook the Sahara.

Aoudads are hefty animals; rams average about 180 pounds and stand 36 inches or so at the shoulder. They

Aoudads are the only nonnative animals accorded official game status in Texas.

record books if they were not outside their native range by some 6,000 miles. World-recognized game trophy records for Africa and Asia are maintained by Rowland Ward's and are necessarily strict on such matters. There are other record keepers, living off hunter egos, which record nonnative species including Burkett and Thompson B. Temple. (See Epilogue for exotic insights.) The aoudad is now a naturalized citizen of Texas and has lost the opprobrium of exotic. Sportsmen generally agree with this, while at the same time applauding the state for its aggressive and successful stocking effort. World record or not, aoudad hunting will test you.

The desert bighorn sheep, another prehistoric settler of Texas, has not adapted with such ease. TPWD first made a heroic effort to re-establish this wild sheep in the Black Gap Wildlife Management Area south of Marathon. Bighorn restoration efforts have also been made at the Sierra Diablo and Elephant Mountain WMAs, and on the Chillicote Ranch near Presidio, a private ranch under contract with the TPWD for bighorn work. The first ram hunting permit was issued in 1988, for a hunt in the Sierra Diablo WMA.

The bighorn's curl is what motivates a hunter to subject his body to the wild sheep's habitat, which is most inhospitable to man. The more remote, rocky, and inaccessible, the better sheep like it. That's why hunters who claim North America's Grand Slam—Rocky Mountain bighorn,

are an overall buff color, blending well with several thousand square miles of West Texas. They can last several days without water, sustaining themselves by browsing on cactus, yucca, century plants, mesquite, and most vegetation with the audacity to grow west of the 100th meridian.

Aoudads are considered game animals only in Armstrong, Briscoe, Donley, Floyd, Hall, Morley, Randall, and Swisher counties of the High Plains. Elsewhere they are considered domestic animals. Aoudads range freely in other areas, and we have admired them along the 5,000-foot-plus headers of the Glass Mountains.

Many believe the aoudads of Texas would dominate

Desert bighorn sheep have been the subject of extensive restoration efforts in Texas.

desert bighorn, Dall, and stone sheep—count much coup.

A sportsman may not have access to many bighorns in Texas for years to come, but he should know how to estimate curl, since most regulations in other states call for at least three-quarter curl to be legal. Viewing the sheep in profile, imagine a line drawn from the base of the horns straight through the eye. This line must intersect the tip of the horn to be three-quarter. The legendary full curl is when the tip of the horn comes past the eye, completing a full circle.

Edwards Plateau hunters will stumble across an exotic sheep that has done a lot of escaping from the so-called game proof spreads. This is the mouflon, rarely as genetically pure as relatives found in his native Sardinia and in the islands of Corsica. He crosses frequently and easily with domestic sheep, including the Barbados. When this happens, he is downgraded from mouflon to just plain Corsican. If you're disposed to pay a fancy fee to shoot a mouflon, be sure you know the difference.

Mouflon-Corsicans cross fence lines more easily than experts give them credit for, thus their spread into adjacent ranges. Many of these crossbreeds roam the Edwards Plateau. We find them quite easy to slip up on, and we would no more shoot them than a domestic sheep. Any comparison between this animal and wild sheep, except for horn size, is a charade.

THE BIG THREE TEXAS EXOTICS

The big three exotics are blackbuck antelope, fallow deer, and axis deer. Blackbuck antelope are native to India and

There are more blackbuck antelope in Texas than in their native ranges in Pakistan and India.

Pakistan and weigh up to 90 pounds. Their horns are spiral, and those measuring 20 inches from base to tip are considered mountable. Today, there are more blackbucks in Texas than in Pakistan and India.

Fallow deer have palmated antlers like a moose, but not on such a grand scale. Still, the antlers are impressive to a whitetail hunter. By whitetail standards these deer are also big bodied, up to 175 pounds. They have several color phases, including pure black and pure white.

A fallow deer will average twice the body weight of a typical whitetail.

Axis deer are also native to India. Weighing up to 175 pounds, a base-to-tip main beam measurement of 30 inches classifies them as mountable to some. Their coats are a lovely mottling of brown and white.

A late '80s survey found approximately 400 exotic game

Towering racks make axis deer a favorite target of exotic *bowhanas*.

ranches in the state with a total of more than 100,000 animals. Twenty-five percent of these animals ranged at will in pastures without high, well-maintained game fences. TPWD conducts a "spotlight" deer census each year, and in recent years the census takers saw more exotics in Kerr and Real counties than native whitetails. Kerr and neighboring Real County have almost 40 percent of Texas exotic big game. The pioneer ranch for exotics is the King, which introduced them more than 50 years ago. The King Ranch wildlife specialists are top drawer. The premier ranch for accessible exotic hunting, provided you have the cash, is the YO, outside of Mountain Home in Kerr County. The YO has a superb game fence, completely enclosing its extensive pastures, and does a most professional job of management.

PREPARATION FOR

THE BIG GAME HUNT

TEXAS PREFERRED GUN SELECTION In the first place, mule deer and aoudad are about as big as Texas big-game hunting gets. We are not, after all, talking about Alaska brown bear, so keep your 300 H&H magnum sheathed. What we are talking about is a one-shot Texas hunt where the kill is clean and no meat is wasted. In Texas, this hunt can take place over incredibly varied habitat, which quickly narrows rifle choices.

If the rifle selected can also be used on other North American game, so much the better. But, most Alaska brown bear guides won't hunt with you unless you're packing at least a .300 Winchester magnum, a rifle that only a macho greenhorn would show up with on a Hill Country lease.

We have also seen old-timers harvest deer after deer with a .222 Remington, said deer always being shot in the ear or some such. Again, please don't make your Texas deer lease debut with such a caliber.

Between the two there are at least 25 very popular calibers, any one of which will certainly do the job in the hands of a decent rifleman with minimal buck fever at reasonable ranges. This selection should be a carefully thought out, personal decision. For what it's worth, short of a barroom brawl, we do have some mildly controversial opinions.

The Winchester .243 and the 6mm Remington, beloved by many a Hill Country stand shooter, have too great a potential for wounding and losing game in other parts of Texas. The hunter who uses a .243 in the Brush Country, under most conditions, is ill-advised. Anything less is a crime against nature. This is an excellent choice for children—little recoil and great trajectory ballistics, but not for the *muy grande* hunting of the South Texas brush.

An excellent compromise is the .25–06 Remington, which, with a 120-grain bullet, delivers a full 300 pounds per foot more energy than the heaviest factory .243 load, and yet has a most acceptable recoil. The .25–06 is a wonderful all-purpose rifle, flat as a cheap pancake and hard-hitting.

Any .30–06 owner who starts an argument with you about his choice will win in Texas hunting. At least a dozen bullet types and weights, including the varmint-getting "accelerator," are at his beck and call, so he wins the adaptability award *nolo contendere* by other caliber defenders. It's not an especially flat shooting rifle, but it gets the job done at 300 yards. Depending upon your bullet weight selection, it certainly packs the mail in foot-pounds of energy. It travels well to other western states too, as does its close counterpart, the popular .308.

The Texas sportsman is most often found clutching a much-used .270, however. The popular bullet weight is 130 grains. In a soft point, this load delivers 100 pounds per foot more energy at 300 yards than a 150 grain out of the .30–06. The .270 has a much flatter trajectory, and it doesn't kick as much. The .270 is available in some light-weight beauties that make mule deer and pronghorn hunting a mite easier.

Of the remaining 20 or so possibilities, the only one given serious court, mostly by trophy hunters of the South Texas brush, is the 7mm magnum. This caliber should only be considered by hefty types in good physical condition, because if you can't cope with its recoil, it's not for you. Although it's still on the heavy side for Hill Country whitetails, it sure is a sweet shooter for long-range work, delivering 300 foot-pounds more than the equivalent .30–06 at 300 yards, and on a much flatter line. If you plan to hunt out-of-state for mountain mulies and elk, the 7mm mag becomes a good choice.

The big debate seems to come from devotees of small calibers who claim the .30–06, .308, .270, and 7mm mag waste meat. This is simply not true, because meat can be wasted with any caliber bullet that is misplaced. Sportsmen most often go for the lung shot, which rarely wastes more than a few ounces of rib meat yet is the surest of kills under all but coop-shoot conditions, since it gives the hunter a one-square-foot target. On such a shot, the high foot-pounds of energy of the larger calibers will anchor the deer, preventing a cripple lost in heavy brush. The smaller calibers simply do not drop deer on lung shots at Trans-Pecos distances, and one lost deer equals a lot of rib meat. Many small caliber hits allow the mortally wounded deer to run, which is not humane.

Perhaps more commonly, the small caliber shooter will aim for the neck, knowing the knock-down limitations of his rifle but having a steady hold at medium ranges. This can waste more meat and, unless the neck is broken, the wounded deer may escape.

Meat is made less tasty, if not ruined completely, when a deer is spooked and/or wounded and runs for quite a distance. The deer builds up an astronomical metabolic rate flooding the muscles—ham steak, for instance—with blood and adrenalin. At the same time, oxygen is burned out of the muscles, increasing the amount of waste residues such as lactic acid. What we're saying is that a deer that runs very far before or after your shot tastes a heck of a lot gamier than the instant kill we advocate.

Terrible things happen when you gut-shoot a deer or attempt a straight-away shot. A shot under the tail must hit a grapefruit-sized opening in the pelvic girdle to allow the bullet to pass through the deer's gut to strike a vital area. At best, you have an awful mess to field dress. At worst, you will wound the deer in a ham and probably lose him.

Scopes are a must for the Texas hunter, even in the Hill Country. In the first place, scopes make for a safer hunt. They also make for clean kills, even in the typically poor light of early dawn or near dusk. We recommend the variable 2½x7 or 3x9 for hunting flexibility. Leave the scope on the lowest setting, cranking up the power only as necessary to compensate for distance.

The following sketches pinpoint the optimum shots for each of four basic shooting angles: side, front and rear

quartering, and front. To repeat, we almost always go for the lung shot. If you are tempted by a trophy deer facing completely away, the only shot is to the neck.

If the deer is a good distance out and either well above or well below the hunter, hold a little lower than for a normal trajectory. With the rifles we've recommended, this is not a big factor at ranges less than 200 yards. It gets to be critical the farther out and more acute the angle. Many a hunter has missed trophy animals learning this lesson the hard way.

Keep in mind that the size of the whitetail is deceiving. This is particularly true when the deer is sporting a large rack. The fact is, even a mature Texas buck is not likely to stand more than 32 inches at the shoulder; the average is more like 30 inches. The back of a Texas whitetail will come just about up to your waistline.

The smaller than expected size throws off our range perception and also explains why even a large buck can slip out of danger, belly-crawling away in the skimpiest of cover. If you can make a reasonable estimate of range, knowing shoulder height allows you to accurately gauge how high to hold on long shots. Simply measure the distance of the shoulder height on the vertical reticle of your scope; that distance is equal to 30 inches. A shot distant enough for an eight-inch-high trajectory would require a hold one quarter the perceived length on the reticle.

Another deer measurement worth remembering is that there are 12 to 13 inches between the tips of the ears, so antlers reaching beyond the ears are in the good to excellent category. Racks spreading a good way past the ears can mean Boone and Crockett. It's helpful to learn the bits-and-pieces philosophy of deer spotting, starting with the ears and ending with the rear legs that angle like a dog's, which is one of the deer's more unusual natural features. Also odd are the various white patches on the whitetail's inside legs, muzzle, and belly. A whitetail can be very difficult to spot when he's immobile and bedded. Look for the slightest flick of an ear or twitch of a tail.

Unless the rack has completely dominated your decision to shoot, here are some other considerations:

—Learn to judge deer body size. If you can't, don't shoot until you are able.

—Select a fat deer. Hunt early in the season. Take a doe. Look very closely at the hams; they should be round not flat.

—Age doesn't have as much to do with tenderness or taste as many people think. That is, unless the deer is so old—say 7 or 8—or so ill that it can no longer get enough to eat.

—Even though they are easier to hunt, bucks in rut are not good table fare due to activity and stress levels.

AFTER THE SHOT Many deer are crippled and lost each season by those who simply don't believe their bullet has hit, especially with smaller calibers. A running deer may only flap its ears and go right on out of sight. After you shoot, keep watching the deer carefully. If he rears straight up you've probably hit him hard in the lung-heart area, although a shot through the neck that doesn't break the spinal cord will cause the same reaction. A tucked in tail is almost always a sure sign of a wounded deer; maybe you'll see the deer weave just a bit, another telltale sign. A hit on the head, spinal cord, or antlers will drop the deer immediately. Even if the deer is in plain sight, wait a few minutes with your sight on his upper neck. A deer hit in the antlers will soon jump right up. If the deer humps its back, bad news—you've gut shot. But even if you see no sign of a hit whatsoever, follow this routine:

1. Set landmarks, carefully marking both the spot you last saw the deer and the spot where you may have hit him.
2. Reload if necessary as silently as you can.
3. Wait 30 minutes to allow the deer to weaken and your adrenalin to subside. Don't push the deer. He will often bed down within 200 yards if wounded, but not spooked.
4. Go to the spot where you think your bullet hit the deer and search for blood, hair, and tracks. Look for blood sign between that spot and the landmark where you last saw the deer.
5. Blood sign will give you a clue as to where you hit the deer and where he is.
   - Dark blood increasing as you trail—Heart—within 75 yards.
   - Dark blood decreasing—Leg—look for a cripple you may never find.
   - Bright red, foamy blood—Lung—within 100 yards.
   - Bright red, ample—Neck—up to 300 or 400 yards.
   - Little blood mixed with unmistakable innard—Stomach—within one mile.
   - Little blood and saliva—Jaw—may never find.
6. When you're fairly certain of the gut shot deer, take even more time before you move at all, an hour or so. If you get him up while trailing, stop and wait, don't push him.

Carry a little roll of surveyor's tape with you and mark the last blood sign if the trail becomes hard to follow. Zig zag forward from this mark patiently and slowly until you find another drop of blood. Examine the ground rock by rock, leaf by leaf. Then mark again and repeat the zig zag search, cutting wide arcs across the line the deer was on. The tape comes in handy to mark the deer when you find it, particularly if you can't drag him out yourself. It's also useful to mark your trail to find your way back to the deer, especially at the point where you hit a ranch road.

Don't clomp down the middle of a blood trail because your feet will demolish the very sign you need most. Trail to one side. Look up and around frequently for two rea-sons: You may spot your wounded deer, or you may find blood sign above ground level. You may even have to get on your hands and knees from time to time. Be patient. Many deer have been lost because a hunter didn't take the time to thoroughly check for blood sign.

If you're on a blood trail at dusk, it's usually better to mark it and return in the morning; however, in some parts of the state coyotes will eat the deer by morning. So, if the trail is clear and you have a gas lantern in camp, you'll be amazed at how little drops of blood stand out in the closeup glare of such a light source. Leave your gun in camp, for legal reasons. You may find the deer if it has died from loss of blood.

Even if you're 100-percent sure of a clean kill, approach the downed deer cautiously, rifle at the ready. This is doubly important when your deer has run off and you finally track him down. A wounded deer can seriously injure or even kill with its hooves.

If the deer crosses a fenceline into another rancher's pasture, you're in a heap of trouble in Texas if you haven't worked out the trespass problem in advance. Our best advice in this instance is to mark the fence crossing well, and seek out the landowner. Texas trespass laws give little leeway for the ethics of this situation, or the fact that you are required by law to make every reasonable effort to recover wounded game. Stay out of this pickle by talking it over with your neighbors before opening day.

Driving at night in deer country can be dangerous—many deer are killed and many vehicles damaged. Drive with care on back roads, slowly enough to pull off the road and turn off your headlights if a deer is blinded near the pavement. If you hit a deer, you are required to report the incident to a game warden or the highway patrol. If the wounded deer runs off, carefully note the exact location by landmarks such as a creek, highway signs, or a distinctive gate. Note your odometer reading before driving on, so that you will know the exact mileage from where you placed your call to the authorities.

OFF-ROAD VEHICLES Texas roads are covered with sporty four-wheel-drive off-road vehicles, almost none of which ever encounter a mesquite thorn. What's worse, owners of these vehicles have the mistaken opinion they are impervious to the hazards of icy or rain-slick roads. In truth, 4WDs are almost totally unnecessary in Texas hunting except for the Trans-Pecos.

A pickup truck, preferably with wide tracks so it won't cut the rancher's roads, is usually a much better choice. It's handy for hauling gear, moving blinds or sacks of high protein feed, or for recovering field-dressed deer. In the Trans-Pecos, consider a vehicle with high road clearance.

There are gumbo mud situations where 4WDs pay off, but if you're on a lease, don't tear up the pastures. Before he tosses you, the rancher will point out that your tracks will be there forever, and he's right. Truthfully, we have gotten in far more trouble with our 4WDs than we have gotten out of.

Speaking of getting into trouble, one of the fastest ways we know is to acquire an all terrain vehicle (ATV), especially if a young sportsman is let loose on it. Except for the rare professional situation, such as rescue or game warden patrols, the ATV is an abomination that has despoiled much wilderness and seriously injured many sportsmen. Particularly dangerous have been the three-wheel models in the hands of the young or inexperienced, because they have a tendency to rear up and over. ATV manufacturers have withdrawn three-wheel models and agreed to provide free safety training to buyers, but we suggest a "no ATV" policy for sportsmen. Many riders compound the ATV risk by ignoring safety devices and protective clothing such as helmets, goggles, gloves, and boots.

In much of Texas, the topsoil layer is thin and easily broken, leaving tracks for an eternity. Our barrier island beach dunes are incredibly fragile. One should take care even walking upon them, let alone ripping asunder their tender ecology.

ATVs used indiscriminately during nesting and birthing periods disturb wildlife, and we have observed that the higher pitch of a two-cycle engine drives deer batty at unbelievable distances. You won't see a welcome mat for ATVs at our lease.

There are many leases in the more rugged areas of the Edwards Plateau, South Texas Plains, and Trans-Pecos where the intrepid sportsman will find comfort in a 4WD. If Texas terrain is bad enough for a 4WD, it's *bad*. Be prepared:

1. Don't stint on tire quality, ply, or size. Consider inner tubes with puncture-resistant sealant for the Brush Country. Have at least one good spare.
2. Carry an air hose that fits into the sparkplug hole or a portable air compressor that runs off 12 volts or a small scuba tank. Add an air gauge.
3. Also carry the following: A set of basic tools that includes socket wrenches, ax, and shovel.
4. Extra fan belts and water hoses.
5. Extra fuel tanks. It's often worth it to have these permanently installed, since many leases are far from gasoline pumps.
6. Big jack. There are models available that would tilt a pyramid. These are probably responsible for more rescues than any other piece of equipment besides air hoses. With this jack and your spare tire as a base or pothole stopper, you can work your way out of a heap of trouble.
7. Big planks. Two 2x12s about four feet long are wonderful aids.
8. "Come-along." This is especially important if you have not invested in a bumper winch. The mechanical advantage of this device is enough to pull you out of deep mud or a pothole.
9. Long, heavy-duty chain. Also add as much rope as you can afford and store.
10. Jug of water and paper towels.
11. First aid kit that can be left on board permanently.
12. Flashlight committed to the vehicle.
13. Portable CB unit. Consider having another portable unit left in camp so that emergency communications can be set up.
14. Most important of all, duct tape—the all-time leader in offroad repair work.

When breaking themselves into 4WDs, many people fail to remember that the vehicle itself should be made to do most of the work. Pull large trees out of the way with the vehicle, not your back. Use the vehicle to help you pull big deer up a steep slope. Let air out of the tires when driving in sand, down to 12 pounds or so, to creep through the sand. And, most importantly, don't overestimate the vehicle's ability to get through. The feeling of power that overcomes you with your first 4WD is soon dissipated when you bury it in unrelenting gumbo mud.

We like to tow our 4WD, so we've rigged it with a towbar. A trailer is usually the best rig, saving wear on the 4WD and perhaps the inconvenience of disconnecting the drive shaft. The tow allows for sportsmen themselves to be transported in comfort with all the grubby gear stuffed into the 4WD. Coming out, the 4WD carries not only game, but usually a supply of mesquite firewood for the homestead.

In some prime South Texas brush hunting and in other parts of the state, the rancher will not allow the hunter to operate his 4WD on the ranch; instead, hunters are transported by guides. Call before you manhandle your 4WD 300 miles.

WARDROBE SELECTION Most deer hunters wear what comes naturally to Texans: cowboy hat, jeans, and work boots. Add a flannel shirt and a down-filled vest and you're set for 90 percent of our hunting. It's the other 10 percent that can tear you up.

Hunters have a system that copes with the vagaries of Texas weather. The system starts with the aforementioned uniform. Then, starting from bottom up and skin out, we go for the best, most comfortable boots we can afford. Not cowboy boots, but good, all-terrain stuff. Waterproof them with mink oil until they glisten. Break these in before season if they're new. Next, you need pairs of thin silk socks and thick wool ones. For bitter cold you'll want longjohns. Select lightweight, machine-washable poly blends that wick away moisture. The old cotton stuff is awful when wet, and silk is overrated except for sexiness. Go for two-piece, since you may wish to whip the top off while climbing after a mulie.

In colder weather, portly hunters go for insulated coveralls to keep their backsides covered. A down vest and/or down jacket are superb choices since they will crunch up to nothing for carrying and feel mighty good on a stand once you're there. Get the down jacket with a carrying pouch you can hang on your belt.

For rain, a ¾-length poncho with hood is our choice. It allows for freedom of movement and sheds rain well. An alternate is a lightweight, two-piece rain suit which can be stuffed in a day pack for extended hunts in dicey weather. Most often, however, you'll know what you face as you head out of camp.

Another flexible item of clothing is a wool turtleneck sweater worn under your hunting jacket. It will provide all the warmth you need for even the most bitter Texas winter. And late-season Texas hunters would do well to stuff a pair of wool gloves, the kind that allow fingertip feel, into their field kit.

Comfort-seeking sportsmen also find room for a dark wool ski mask. This rig is a secret weapon for staying on a stand during a blue norther, and it eliminates face shine, a major deer spooker. Headnets are a good idea for stalkers.

For open-country hunting headgear, we have found nothing better than a dark, well-used felt or beaver cowboy hat. A good cowboy hat will shed rain, seal in warmth, shade your face, pillow your head, and cushion your seat. Your cowboy hat also works as a good utensil for carrying water, swatting flies, chasing cattle, deflecting brush, and signaling hunters, plus it makes a good rifle rest. Last, but certainly not least, a cowboy hat makes you look taller and identifies you with the heroic image of the western cowboy.

GEAR SELECTION Most sportsmen we know are suckers for the newest gadget hawked by their favorite outfitter. A safe bet at our lease would be that at least one new knife will show up each opening weekend along with a new-fangled knife sharpener, the owner of which will start bragging before the grub is stowed.

The fact is, if you're going to hunt all over Texas, the list of gear needed for first-class effectiveness, not to mention comfort, is astonishingly long. This is especially true if your camp is ill-provisioned with certain standard equipment such as that used to skin and butcher deer. But avoid dangling shiny new gear from every belt, loop, and orifice of the body. To a deer, such a creature will sound much like an oncoming Panzer division, hard to miss and very scary as it clanks its way through the thickets.

The wilder and longer your hunt, and the bigger the country, the more gear you'll need. In the Hill Country, a folding knife and small flashlight is about all you need. In the Trans-Pecos, an all-day hunt requires a bit more.

Knife selection should be made with care and a liberal budget since your choice should be highly functional, last a lifetime, and assure your hunting partners that you aren't a damn fool. One way to convince them you're a bit daffy is to select a bayonet-length weapon and carry it into the field like a crusader.

The vastly preferred Texas knife is the folding belt knife with a durable lock blade. When carried in its leather sheath on the belt it's quite unobtrusive, yet locks out to several inches for serious field dressing operations. You will see most of these in the classic clip-point blade shape, mainly because most of us think this shape is what a real knife should look like. The clip point is, in fact, adequate, but a drop point is better because the back of the blade helps hold the skin away from the belly sheath.

With reasonable care your folding knife is all you really need, but we'll suggest a handy little knife for the newcomer that will help you field dress like a seasoned pro from deer one. This knife, called the Wyoming big game knife, is shaped like a fish gutter with two surgical steel replacement blades. Slip the hooked end under the skin and you can zip the hide open like you're taking off a coat. This knife is great for skinning, too.

Knives take a beating on a hunt so a quality sharpener is a must. Consider a V-type ceramic crock stick. These are small, portable, safe to use, and they ensure a proper edge angle. A large honing stone and oil should also be standard camp gear. A small sharpening steel with a chisel edge is excellent for field touch-ups and makes quick work of splitting the pelvic girdle. A small chef's meat saw is another camp must, for it greatly simplifies skinning and butchering.

Carry a length of nylon parachute cord with you for a variety of applications, from hoisting your rifle up a tree to tying the legs of a deer carcass to ease transport.

Most hunts call for a flashlight, perhaps to find your way to and up a tree before dawn, or to signal a pick up after dark. Go the professional route; select a small, black, anodized, aluminum light. With a little care it's good for a lifetime of hunting. It costs too much to lose, so rig a secure loop for it on your belt.

If you're hunting on a large, unfamiliar ranch, we recommend two more pieces of gear: a compass and a geodetic survey map or map supplied by the rancher. The map is used not to keep from getting lost—a rarity on a Texas lease—but rather to pinpoint likely deer crossing and bedding areas, and to plan the hunt from the standpoint of hunter location. We also use the map to pencil in locations of turkey, blue quail, and javelina for pursuit once the venison is aging.

On that extremely rare occasion when they've moved the camp on you (you're never lost, of course)—remember two things: First, stay on any road you come to. Your buddies will eventually come for you. This is where your flashlight is a comfort. Second, don't cross any fences.

For day-long hunts, sportsmen favor fannypacks complete with an integral belt, since this rig doesn't restrict movement and rides well on a long trek. A small plastic canteen will hold all the water you'll need, especially if you favor apples for a midday snack. Also stick in the bright orange surveyor tape mentioned earlier, and, in your hip pocket, the ever-ready wad of toilet paper.

Since we like to skin a deer upside down, we always have a couple of gambrels in camp—spreaders with hooks to hang the deer by the hocks of the rear legs. These can be rigged to pulleys to facilitate hoisting. Block and tackles are not necessary for Texas deer. Deer bags and a large ice chest complete with block ice are essential, especially in early season, because heat and flies ruin meat quickly.

DEER HUNTER'S CHECKLIST
  Hunting license
  Ties and pen for tags
  Scoped rifle and sling
  Gun case
  Bullets—correct caliber
  12-gauge shotgun
  Shotshell variety—#8s to #4s
  Old cowboy hat
  Dark wool ski mask
  Shooters' gloves
  Turtleneck sweater
  Two-piece thermal underwear
  Down vest or jacket
  Three-quarter length raincoat with hood
    or lightweight, two-piece rain gear
  Two pairs of worn-in boots
  Two pairs of wool socks
  Silk inner liner socks
  Jeans or twill pants
  Dark chamois shirt
  Insect repellent
  Aerosol insecticide
  Plastic canteen
  Lock blade, drop point knife with sheath
  Sharpening steel with chisel edge with sheath
  Small, black police-type flashlight with belt loop
  Nylon parachute cord
  Gambrel
  Pulley with nylon line
  Small meat saw
  Knife for gutting and skinning
  Game bags
  Wide belt
  Rattling horns
  Rock sling
  Large ice chest
  Block ice
  Garbage sacks
  Zip-type plastic bags
  Compass
  Lease maps
  Belt fannypack
  Moccasins for camp
  Sleeping bag
  Lubricating aerosol spray
  Rifle and shotgun cleaning kit
  Toilet paper
  Alarm clock
  Stand tool kit: hammer, ten-penny nails, 2x4s,
    bow saw, pruning saw, and hatchet
  First aid kit

TECHNIQUES THE EXPERTS USE

LOCATING DEER AND ANTELOPE The Texas lease system puts you in the general area of whitetail and mule deer. The antelope permit system serves the same function. But trophies and a consistent supply of meat will go to the hunter who takes the time for reconnaissance. Preseason, simply stake out likely areas and patiently glass an area for several hours a day. If you don't already know the deer patterns of your hunt area you may want to do a little scouting: Look for tracks, crossings, bedding areas, and fresh droppings, which, if they're moist and shiny, have been deposited within 24 hours. Look for whitetail magnets such as oat fields and oak trees. Crawl through thick beebrush patches or other good bed cover looking for flattened grass and scuffed earth. As noted earlier, rubs and scrapes are good omens.

Binoculars, essential on mulies, are also important for Texas whitetail hunting, especially for trophies. Slow motion is the way to go; the bigger the country, the more deliberate the glassing. If you haven't had much experience using binoculars, a little practice in your backyard will help a lot. You'll be surprised how hard it is to find an object at first, and how easy it becomes with practice. Move the glasses up-down-up-down without haste until you can locate an object instantly. Remember that quick, jerky movements are easily spotted by deer.

Even at relatively short ranges, binoculars are important in Texas, particularly when judging trophies in bad light, which always seems to be the case when you're looking for trophy racks. Light gathering capacity is what you pay for in quality binoculars, so don't buy them for less important reasons.

Scoping with your rifle scope to seek out deer is another greenhorn trick, not recommended. You should be prepared to shoot anything your gun is pointed at, and this may well include another hunter if you're scoping with your rifle. You'll soon have no hunting friends if they see you up to this foolish bush trick.

Spotlighting deer is taboo in Texas. If you have a powerful light and gun in your vehicle or on your person it's *prima facie* evidence of poaching. A light in the woods at night—gun or no gun—is sure to beckon a game warden or angry rancher.

A trophy seeker's library should have the Boone and Crockett Club's *Records of North American Big Game*. These records list the top whitetail in Texas by "locality killed." Many of the top 100 white-tailed deer listed come from counties throughout the South Texas Plains Brush Country. There are listings from counties throughout Texas, but most are from this area. In addition, several counties in the Trans-Pecos are listed as sites of trophy antelope kills.

TEXAS HUNTING STYLES To hunt the Brush Country takes the biggest lease budget in the state. Hunting is most often done from stands overlooking lanes cut through the brush, called *senderos*, through which all manner of game tend to run, including coyotes, javelina, feral hogs, turkey, bobcats, and big deer. You can find leases or package hunts with terrain suitable for still hunting, but the tall towers are most common. Trucks rigged with spotting platforms are often used to locate trophy deer, because these rigs give visibility above the dense brush.

The Edwards Plateau and Trans-Pecos are particularly suited to the joys of deer stalking and still hunting. What Texans call header-draw country enables the sneaky hunter to slip along ridgelines with good concealment and excellent visibility. This is also good country to learn just how good deer early warning systems are. You gain an education by watching an overeager still hunter spook a deer at 500 yards.

The still hunter pursuing deer in likely terrain, but without a sighting at the outset, needs to move very slowly, stopping often. The deer you seek may be just on the other side of a mesquite thicket or bedded down just over a ridgeline. If you see a deer, watch his tail carefully.

Again, if it twitches, the head is about to come up. Freeze until the deer resumes feeding. Clothing that blends well with the terrain is essential. Gloves and face netting are good since you will be moving at the deer's eye level.

Always hunt into the wind. Many city hunters overestimate their ability to still hunt, somehow convincing themselves they have innate Indian-like qualities. These Indian hunters push many deer into the range of more cautious still or stand hunters. Not many Texas hunters use masking scents, but if you plan to still hunt in thick cover, now is the time to start. Masking odors range from skunk and deer urine to apples and acorns. There are many unscented soaps available, which, if used just prior to a hunt, greatly reduce body odor. Be sure to wash your hair thoroughly. Odor neutralizers are also available, and they're very effective, especially when used after showering with unscented soap.

Still hunters and stalkers often add two Texas tricks to their deer hunting repertoire: rattling and slingshotting. If the rut is definitely on, two good-sized antlers rattled smartly against one another to simulate bucks at war can work wonders if you've invaded a buck's territory or attracted an interloper from an adjacent stakeout. The rut can be an on-again, off-again deal, so it pays to scout the situation before spending a lot of time rattling.

Best odds call for rattling early in the day, working an area for only 30 minutes or so, rattling intermittently from a well-concealed spot. Yes, bucks will charge the rattler, but far more often they will cautiously slip up to the

Rattling is a dramatic way to locate trophy bucks during the rut.

sound, so keep a careful watch. Watching while rattling will bruise a knuckle or two, but if a buck does come to you it's one of the great thrills in hunting.

Slingshotting consists of using a thong sling to heave chunks of rock into draws. This sometimes causes irritated whitetails to come unglued, rise from their beds and break into the open. The drawback is that it may only present a long running shot, though sometimes it's makeable. In any event, it's fun and makes a good midday activity in canyon country. And you may locate big bucks for a later stalk.

On rare occasions, drives may be set up. A more frequent practice is a couple of hunting buddies agreeing "You go thataway, I'll go thisaway, and we'll surround him." In header-draw country, this informal plan can produce results.

Stand hunting from tall towers or tree stands is most common in the Hill Country, the Brush Country, and the Pineywoods. On the typical lease, stand placement is a major topic of discussion and a good test of hunter observation, skills, and experience. It is equally important from a safety point of view, because each stand's field of fire must not include another stand. This sounds reasonable, but you'd be surprised how many stands are built right on top of one another. This often happens on fence lines of adjacent ranches and can create a very dangerous situation. When this occurs, don't start a war; just don't hunt your stand, and remove it when you have the chance. Better yet, don't build a stand near a common fence line.

Elevated stand hunting is a common way of hunting on most Texas deer leases.

Most leases have spots for elevated tree stands, towers, and ground blinds. Ground blinds are less expensive and more portable, and they can be elevated by placement on rock outcroppings or slopes above well-traveled areas.

Oak trees covering much of the Edwards Plateau offer many easy-to-build tree stand opportunities. Stout steps are a must for safety's sake. Small chain saws and pruning saws simplify the job of gaining visibility.

The most popular stands are towers, and there are several good commercial types available at reasonable cost. These also offer greater portability than the homemade tower, and costs come out about the same unless one of your partners owns a lumber yard.

Once the stand is in your expertly chosen position, check it for field of fire. Often a little chain sawing will greatly improve the view.

Stand hunters are well advised to check out stands the day before the season opens. Be prepared to fend off yellow jackets and wasps with aerosol spray. Owls, raccoons, and other assorted varmints have been known to take up residence in unused stands. A little cleanup is usually in order.

Sound is your worst enemy when stand hunting. We use old carpet samples to muffle sound and to cushion our rifles. If your sling comes off easily, remove it to curtail accidental noise. Although whitetails don't often look up, they can and do at the wrong moment. Take care not to silhouette yourself in stand openings. Keep your face in the shade and don't wave your rifle barrel out the window.

Be sure to equip your tower stand with comfortable, cushioned chairs. We always keep a lookout for used secretarial chairs which swivel silently—they're ideal. Small, folding stadium seats with cushions are a treasure in a tree stand, greatly extending your time aloft. So is a plastic bottle for urine if you're serious about remaining in that particular stand. In any event, stand hunting is a game of patience, and all that you can do to make yourself comfortable will increase your odds.

Wait out impatient hunting partners. Be sure you're the last to leave your stand, since a spooked deer will often run right under you. Be on your stand well before sunrise and right until last legal light. Those 15 minutes at the beginning and end of a day are the most productive by far. Don't overlook midday, especially if other hunters are making for the chowline on routes that may push deer to you. Always walk upwind to your stand, and walk as quietly as possible to minimize the spook factor.

Everything of significance in deer hunting comes down to a respect for the animal's senses and a knowledge of its patterns of feeding, watering, bedding, and escaping. Deer react pretty much the same to either a warning from or loss of one or more of their senses. If they can't hear well because of driving rain or high wind, they'll behave the same as if they heard something slightly awry. They'll become skittish, suspicious, and harder to hunt, or they'll simply stay in their beds, safely hidden from sight.

Let's see how this works in practice. It's a cold and windy night. Rain pours, hiding the moon. Food is scarce. Will the deer move in the morning? Yes, especially if the wind dies and the rain turns to drizzle. Stay out there still hunting or on a stand. If there are deer in the area they will get up. Use the wind; hunt into it. It will mask your scent. Along with the wet turf underfoot, the wind will cover most noises you make. Every deer hunt can be analyzed on the basis of weather conditions, food availability, and sex situation.

Let's take another example. It's a bright, Comanche moon night, calm and still. There's a tremendous acorn mast this year. It's early season and there's lots of ground cover. The rut has not begun. If you're trying to fill a buck tag you've got a day's work ahead. Stand hunters are going to get very bored. The buck will likely not move at all until just at last light, because he ate all night and, if he needs a snack, all he has to do is vacuum a few acorns without leaving his bed, which is safely covered by thick, early season brush. Make the last five minutes of such a day count. That's all the real buck hunting time you've got.

Most deer hunting falls between these examples. The best advice we can give is to think like a deer.

The Texas Agricultural Extension Service estimates that approximately 11 million pounds of boneless deer meat are harvested annually. Some tastes good, some doesn't. After your one, accurate, clean kill shot there's much to be done. Here are the first steps you'll need to take:

1. Make sure the deer is dead. Open eyes indicate this. Closed eyes or rolling eyes mean the deer is still alive. Ditto for breathing. If you're uncertain, as an absolute last resort shoot again high on the neck.
2. Completely fill out a tag with your name, ranch, and county. Mark or cut out the correct date and affix the tag to an antler or foreleg.

DEER TAGS Tagging regulations are spelled out clearly in the TPWD hunting guide each season. The big mistake made by 99 percent of all hunters is to not tag their deer "immediately upon kill." The regulations do not specify where to tag except that it be "on any part of the carcass so that it is not disturbed, damaged, defaced or lost . . . ." On a buck, the antlers are easiest. On a doe, the foreleg is the usual place for attaching tags and completed permits if required. The second most common mistake is to forget to complete the tag correctly. Marking the date and month is almost impossible without reading glasses for hunters past the age of 40, so remember your glasses.

If you give any portion of a deer—or turkey or antelope—to another hunter for transporting, he must have a "legible hunter's document" from you. This do-it-yourself document must bear your signature, complete name and address, date of kill, name of ranch and county where the kill was made, your hunting license number, and special permit number if applicable. If the entire animal is transported by another person, just leave all the original tags and permits in place.

FIELD DRESSING There are two old wives' tales taught to hunters with regard to field dressing. We will dispel them here:

1. Don't bother cutting the jugular. This messes up a trophy. Field dressing will remove the blood if the bullet hasn't.
2. Don't bother cutting off the tarsal gland, because during the rut you may transfer a foul scent to the meat while field dressing.

Of course, you will be told 17 times back at camp that you should have removed the tarsal glands immediately. A way to avoid this unfounded ridicule is to wait until you've completely finished field dressing. Then carefully cut off the glands to reveal the membrane through which you'll tie the deer's legs for transport and for hanging from a gambrel in camp. This way you won't insult anyone and you'll make handling the deer easier. Don't tell anybody you waited to do this. They'll never know.

The field dressing procedure is the same for whitetail, mule deer, pronghorn, aoudad, and elk. All that's necessary is a drop point, lock back knife with at least a 3½-inch blade.

Many expert texts on the subject recommend splitting the deer from stem to stern in the field. This isn't necessary in most Texas situations, nor desirable. Splitting the pelvic arch and completely opening the chest cavity is better done in camp for two reasons. You will protect the meat from contamination and the job will be easier in camp where you'll have better tools and facilities for hanging.

STEP 1. It's amazing how often we forget to take off our watches and roll up our sleeves until our hands are already bloodied.

STEP 2. Prop the deer with its legs in the air, head uphill. Use stones or tree limbs to raise the hips and shoulders.

STEP 3. Remove genitalia.

STEP 4. Starting at a point just under the brisket, pinch the skin and gently insert the knife blade, making a two-inch cut. Slip two fingers into this cut, lifting the hide away from belly muscles, and slowly pull the hide away, exposing the belly muscle sheath. Cut down and around the genital area. As you gain experience this can be combined with STEP 5, but taking a moment to do this on your first few deer will build your confidence. The whole idea is to make the cut without puncturing the paunch and intestines. Take our word for it; you don't want to puncture any innards.

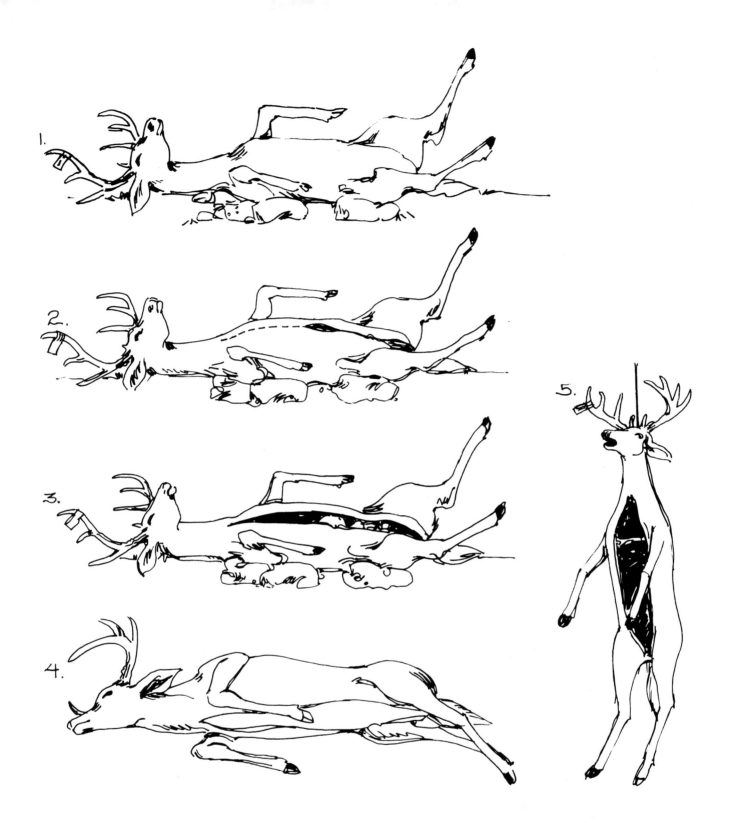

STEP 5. Now, using the same two-fingered guide, carefully cut open the thin layer of belly muscle from brisket to pelvis. The intestines will begin to bulge outward.

STEP 6. Slice the diaphragm away from the chest wall, then reach up into the neck area as far as possible and cut the windpipe free. Pull outward releasing the esophagus, heart, lungs, and liver. You may have to snip some connecting tissue here or there.

STEP 7. Slice down between the hams to the pelvic girdle, then cut a two inch circle around the anus. Carefully core the pelvic canal, remembering that the bladder is inside. Core away all connecting tissue. Next, coming from the abdominal side, core around the bladder itself until you've connected with your other cuts. Now you'll be able to remove the entire excretory tract. This step is by far the most difficult and delicate. Some hunters have simplified the process by using a chisel edged sharpening steel. This chisel, when nudged by a rock, will easily cut through the seam of the pelvic girdle, making it easier to remove the bladder and excretory tract. A tough steel knife in the hands of an expert will do a job on this seam, but knife points are at risk. If transport is near, an even easier trick is to have a meat saw on board.

STEP 8. Roll the deer on its side and pull away all the innards. Save the heart and liver in a plastic bag.

STEP 9. If you're not going to drag the deer in and must wait for pick up, tie the deer up by its neck to whatever you can find in order to facilitate draining. Prop open the chest to allow for air circulation. An alternate method would be to drape the deer belly down over a rock or on clean grass.

NOTE: When skinning a deer for mounting, start well behind the shoulder and neck to leave ample hide for the taxidermist to work with.

GETTING THE DEER BACK TO CAMP There are four basic scenarios in Texas deer hunting:

1. Shoot the deer where you can drive the jeep right up to it. This is especially useful in doe hunting, where a doe on the road is worth two in the brush.

2. Shoot the deer where you have only a short drag over reasonably level ground. Tie the front legs to the antlers, if possible, and tie the back legs together. Break off an 18-inch stick. Tie your rope to the deer's rack, then to the stick. Grasp the stick with both hands behind your back and start for the road.

3. A deer shot in swampy terrain or very rocky terrain may require teamwork and two stout poles, saplings, or pusher rods. Tie the deer, legs up, between the two poles and bring him out as on a stretcher. This beats the heck out of tying the deer to a single pole, where it will swing back and forth like a heavy pendulum, demolishing your shoulder blades. A good alternative, if available, is a packhorse or mule trained to handle carcasses.

4. A deer shot in extremely inaccessible terrain can be brought out on pack sacks after quartering the animal. Unless you're an Olympic athlete, this is a job for two if there's any climbing involved. If there's any chance at all that other hunters may mistake you for a live deer, be sure to add a lot of international orange to the pack.

SKINNING THE DEER The easiest way to skin and butcher a deer is to proceed rapidly to the nearest processing house and let George do it. But skinning is not all that difficult, and usually it's easier and more convenient to do it yourself, not to mention cheaper.

Skinning a freshly killed deer is a five-minute job. It takes much longer to skin out a cold deer. We suggest that Texas hunters skin their deer as soon as they get back to camp. Rarely are there hard freeze conditions which would make it desirable to leave the skin on. Temperatures above 40 degrees are more common. Heat destroys meat quality and the hide retains body heat. All transport-ing should be done with the deer nicely quartered inside an ice chest.

Head up or down? We've skinned hundreds of deer both ways, and by far the easiest method is "hog dressing," the hind legs split by a gambrel with the hooks inserted between the tendon and bone of the upper rear legs, head down.

STEP 1. Girdle the skin around the leg below the Achilles' tendon. Don't cut the tendon. Slit the skin on the inside of the legs up the hams to the pelvic area. Saw off the lower legs. Pull the skin away from the hocks to expose the tendon area.

STEP 2. Insert the spread gambrel hooks between the tendon and the bone, then hoist the deer high enough for the rack to easily clear the ground. We use a pulley rig.

STEP 3. Begin pulling and slicing tissue where necessary. Use short flat strokes to avoid slicing hide or meat. When you've pulled the skin down to the tail, skin around it; then, pulling the tail firmly, cut it off at the base and continue skinning.

STEP 4. From here on down your weight is the best tool. A warm hide will peel right off, requiring only a persuasive slice with the knife now and then.

STEP 5. When you reach the front legs, slice the skin inside the leg down to and around the joint. Saw off the lower front legs and start pulling again.

STEP 6. The neck is the toughest area to skin and will require more pulling and slicing, but it will give way readily when the deer is warm. Pull the skin all the way down over the head.

STEP 7. Cut through the meat right behind the jaw all around the neck. Saw off the head.

STEP 8. Trim off bloodshot areas and rinse the carcass with water, wiping off any hair. Pat dry.

STEP 9. Protect the carcass by covering it with a cheesecloth deer bag tied off at the top and bottom to keep out flies and dirt. Commercially available cheesecloth bags let air circulate to dry the meat. The deer should be hung in shade.

STEP 10. Allow the deer to hang as long as weather permits. If the ambient temperature is over 45 degrees and is expected to remain that way, you should quarter the deer within a few hours. If it's more than 50 degrees, quarter the animal immediately.

Aging. The sportsmen we know have consumed hundreds of deer with minimal aging and average hang time of a day or so in cool weather. We haven't eaten better venison anywhere in the world, though we know some people swear by weeks of aging. If you use a professional meat locker, it can't hurt to let the deer age for a week or so.

QUARTERING   Since most Texas deer need to be on ice for transport, sportsmen should learn to quarter their deer from the upside down hang.

STEP 1. The tenderloins are inside the deer; you'll spot them along the backbone. They're only connected by tissue. Gently lift them out and slip a thin-bladed boning knife behind them to peel them out.

STEP 2. Pull the shoulders out from the body. They're only connected by tissue at the scapula or shoulder bone. Cut the tissue free behind the scapula and remove.

STEP 3. Cut around the hams starting at the root of the tail and cutting down around the ham. Don't remove the hams yet. You have a much more important task—the backstrap. Cut down either side of the backbone all the way to the neck with an extra sharp boning knife. Then, starting at the hams, run the flat of your knife along the ribcage, slowly working across each rib with the knife point against the backbone. The backstrap will gradually pull away. Go slow. This is the best part of the deer, with the tenders, and you'll be severely chastised by fellow sportsmen if you waste the merest morsel. Keep working all the way down to the neck. When finished, you'll have two long succulent strips of meat; one from each side of the backbone.

STEP 4. Continue cutting one of the hams down to the pelvic girdle until you reach the ball and socket. Slip your thin bladed knife point into the ball and socket and cut out the tissue. A twist should now release the ham. If not, reach for your meat saw.

STEP 5. Ask a friend to hold the carcass while you repeat this step with the other ham. Otherwise, the carcass will fall to the ground.

STEP 6. You may wish to saw off the neck and take the time to bone out the rib meat. However, go no further in camp or you will be violating game laws. Under Texas law, sausage making and fancy cut butchering must be done at home. It makes it difficult for a game warden to judge the sex and number of deer being transported if all he sees is a pile of sausage. You may legally discard the boned-out neck and ribcage, most often burying them. Be sure to abide by your rancher's rules on this. Carcass disposal can be a sensitive subject.

Primitive Weapons and Handgun Hunting

Black powder and bow hunting, especially for white-tailed deer, has become increasingly popular in Texas. Hunters find they need enhanced skills as stalkers and stand hunters to be successful, as well as a great deal of practice with the weapons of choice. The following information is designed as a starter for those interested in primitive weapons or handgun hunting.

MUZZLELOADING   Texans have accepted the muzzle-load mystique lock, stock, and barrel and are having a lot of fun smoking up the deer lease with black powder. Newly designed frontloaders are amazingly accurate at reasonable field ranges, and .50 caliber bullets such as the popular mini-ball deliver adequate knock-down power out to 100 yards and beyond. A comparison with the classic .30–30 Winchester ballistics is instructive. A 170 grain .30–30 leaves the barrel at 2,200 feet per second with muzzle energy of around 1,800 foot-pounds. A common .50 caliber 175 grain black powder projectile can develop muzzle velocity of more than 2,100 feet per second and

Black powder firearms have a large following in Texas.

energy of just under 1,800 foot-pounds. In other words, a .50 caliber black powder rifle qualifies as a deerslayer in the hands of a practiced sportsman.

But practice it will take. The variables of patch and ball combinations, powder loads, sight alignment, and your black powder rifle's eccentricities make for complexities far beyond those of the breach-loaded centerfire rifle.

Even though Roger Bacon accurately listed the directions for making gun powder in 1242 (and we know that his formulation with potassium nitrate [saltpeter], sulphur, and charcoal remains about the same today), history does not record the date that firearms were invented. Bacon knew that compressed gunpowder would explode and could propel a projectile, but, as with many of his other projects, he didn't follow through. In the early 1300s, handheld cannons were developed; they were fired by a burning rope touched to a powder trail leading to the end of a barrel stuffed with more powder and whatever heavy junk was handy. The result was not too accurate, but could discourage an opponent at close range, provided he stayed still.

Inefficient firearms such as matchlocks and wheel locks followed, and by the early 1600s a flintlock, utilizing a one-piece frizzen and ignition pan, was developed in France. The frizzen is the piece the flint-edged hammer strikes when it falls forward. The downward movement of the flint across the frizzen produces sparks and also opens the top of the pan. The sparks fall into the priming powder, and maybe the thing fires.

Pioneer Americans became adept at getting these cantankerous weapons to fire and take wild game. Europeans, particularly the German Junkers and their Jaegers, were also refining their ability to shoot flintlocks with great accuracy, perhaps even more skillfully than Americans, but at targets and during programmed hunts. The Europeans loaded flintlocks by forcing a lead ball of exactly the same diameter as the bore down through the barrel's rifling. This aided accuracy because spin was imparted.

The American wilderness required something more of its settlers—silent, speedy reloading. A whitetail wouldn't sit around long for the loud, lengthy pounding it took to seat a bullet in the traditional European style. Indians got downright impatient. In the 1740s American marksmen switched to a greased patch. The diameter of the ball was reduced slightly to compensate for the patch, which then allowed the bullet to slip silently into the barrel and sit on top of the powder load. The patch also cleaned the barrel, sealed gas-leak gaps around the bullet, and gave the rifling a grip on it. Spin was thus imparted, helping the bullet fly as true as the European version.

All this might have become a piece of world history trivia if not for the Boston Tea Party and the subsequent shootout at Yorktown. While the red coats were noisily loading we were shooting. The world's oldest written constitution followed, and with it a guarantee found in Article II of the 10 original amendments proclaiming our right to keep and bear arms.

"A well regulated militia being necessary to the security of a free State, the right of the people to keep and bear arms shall not be infringed."

This history is cherished today by muzzleloaders who frequently gather at events called rendezvous to reenact battles that commemorate U.S. historical events. Participants take great care in the rifle they tote and the way they dress. It would not do to show up with an anachronistic muzzleloader or hat.

Although a few states specify that only flintlocks may be used for hunting, Texas is not one of them, nor do we have a special black powder season. By far the most popular muzzleloader for hunting in Texas is the percussion. This muzzleloader relies on an ignition system that makes use of an explosive cap that fits over the cone of a nipple which allows fire to pass through a hole into the powder charge. Fulminate of mercury is the usual primer.

If a sportsman is not conversant with muzzleloading, a lot of research, study, and practice lies ahead. The first step is to decide your most likely objective—target shooting, squirrel hunting, or deer hunting. Muzzleloaders are usually single-purpose firearms, so select one with care.

For the deer hunter, a short, 26-inch barrel, half-stock percussion muzzleloader in .50 or .54 caliber that fires a conical hunting projectile is a very practical and highly efficient weapon. Such firearms will also handle the traditional patched lead ball and are relatively inexpensive. After lots of target and varmint hunting experience, the new muzzleloader will find this a handy piece to use from a Texas deer blind. Many move on to custom guns, kits, and even flintlocks as they get more involved in this fascinating sport, but we urge beginning with something you can master. Under no circumstance should you pick up your great, great granddad's Civil War gun and try to fire it—the thing will probably blow up. It belongs over the mantel.

Black powder comes in several grades, from coarse (Fg) to fine (FFFFg). The grade typically used for hunting is the fast-burning FFFg. Black powder messes up a barrel, and you'll see muzzleloaders cleaning their weapons with hot, soapy water.

In Chapter X we discuss the "Ten Commandments of Shooting Safety" suggested in the Texas Hunter Education Program. Muzzleloader hunters need to learn and obey these same rules in addition to a whole different set. The Hunter Education Program's "Ten Commandments of Muzzleloading" point out some of the things you'll have to master before you can consider yourself a safe Daniel Boone. More information may be obtained by contacting TPWD in Austin.

1. Muzzleloading firearms are not toys. Treat them with the same respect due any firearm.
2. Use only black powder of the proper granulation in

Safe muzzle loaders not only keep their powder dry, they measure up.

8. Do not load directly from a powder horn flask. Use a separate measure. A lingering spark in the barrel can ignite the incoming charge, causing the horn or flask to explode in your hand.

9. The half-cock notch is the safety notch on a muzzleloader. Always be sure that it is functioning properly. If your lock or trigger seems to be functioning improperly, take your firearm to a competent gunsmith for checking and correction of the problem.

10. The nature of a muzzleloading firearm requires that you exercise caution and skill. Make sure that you know the proper steps for care, loading, and use.

Black powder enthusiasts often move into muzzleloading shotguns and handguns. Shotgunning with a muzzleloader is great fun and efficient for upland game such as quail. However, pass shooting on geese could require the absorption of more recoil than most sportsmen are accustomed to.

The muzzleloader sportsman will need to add various items to his deer hunt checklist. Perhaps the most important addition is a measure to assure a consistent powder charge. Something to carry powder in and keep it dry is necessary, and various flasks and horns are available for this. A ball starter is essential to work the ball and patch into the barrel. Once slightly below the muzzle crown, a patch knife is used to trim excess patch. Patches can also be precut and pre-lubricated. After a further assist into the barrel from the ball starter, the ramrod is used to seat the ball over the powder charge. A capper makes loading a percussion gun easier—a number of caps are held in a square tube ready for placement over the nipple. A loading block makes field reloads faster, often an important factor when hunting. All of this and usually more is stuffed into a purse-like carryall, which muzzleloaders call a "possibles" bag.

The black powder shooter will find that in some states outside Texas he can extend his hunting opportunities through participation in special muzzleloading seasons.

HANDGUN HUNTING Most sportsmen are not big on handgun hunts for deer, although pistols and revolvers are excellent choices for some varmint hunting, small game, and even hogs.

The principal objection to the handgun hunt for deer is lack of knockdown power, because even the big blaster .44 magnum barely breaks the 1,000 foot-pound barrier at the muzzle, and at the grand distance of 50 yards, factory loads drop off to around 750 foot-pounds. This is about the same energy that a 170 grain .30–30 bullet has left at 300 yards. A .30–30 shooter would not think of attempting such a shot. Not many can handle the .44 magnum, so they drop down to a .41 magnum or .357 magnum, the other major big game gun choices. The .357 delivers less than 500 foot-pounds at 50 yards, the

your muzzleloader. These firearms are not designed to withstand the higher pressures developed by modern powders.

3. Never fire a muzzleloader unless the ball or short charge is firmly seated against the powder charge. An air space between the powder and the projectile will cause the barrel to be ringed or bulged, thus ruined for accurate shooting. In some cases, this may cause the barrel to rupture, with possible injury to shooter and bystanders.

4. Do not exceed the manufacturer's recommended maximum load or try to use multiple projectile loads. When in doubt, see information concerning loads from an authoritative source.

5. When loading your muzzleloading firearm, do not expose your body to the muzzle. Grasp the ramrod only a short distance above the place where it protrudes from the barrel. Push it down in short strokes rather than grasping it at the outer end. If the rod breaks, you could hurt your arm on the splintered end of the broken rod.

6. Always make sure that your downrange area is a safe impact area for your projectiles. Round balls may carry as far as 800 yards.

7. Never smoke while loading, shooting, or handling black powder.

.41 only a bit more than 600, depending upon barrel length.

Handguns are also difficult to shoot with accuracy at moving targets in field conditions. Factor in buck fever, and the odds climb toward a probable cripple, the anathema of sportsmen.

Now, having covered all these negative things, the well-trained, thoroughly practiced sportsman can upgrade his firepower with 6-inch or longer barrels or even use a break type pistol in calibers up to the .30–30. He can train himself to fire from dead-steady rests (never allowing a hard part of the firearm to touch wood), from modern stances such as the Weaver, discussed later, or by using a cheat stick. Most important of all, the sportsman will be a hunter with the patience to wait out the ideal stand shot, or the woodsmanship to execute a superb stalk. Finally, he knows shot placement and will only take those shots that promise a clean kill.

Although some big game handgun pros may try to discourage new shooters from starting out with .22s, sportsmen generally recommend it. The argument against the .22 is that its light recoil makes practice unrealistic and that upgrading to heavy recoil and noise is more difficult. There is some truth to this, and the shooter wishing to gain skills with big bore handguns should not dally overlong with the .22 before touching off some heavy stuff. But, the .22 itself becomes a valued small game hunting handgun, and you should select a long barreled model with hunting in mind. It is inexpensive enough to pour hundreds of rounds through and will serve for practicing the fundamentals.

If you are completely unfamiliar with handguns, by all means seek expert training. Be leary of the expert friend. Like all other hand-eye skill sports, bad habits are quickly learned and tough to eliminate. If at all possible, seek training from a police-sponsored organization. Handgun techniques have been considerably improved in recent years, but many range training programs remain stuck in the past. Major metro area police must keep up with deadly force. Another bonus of police level training is that the skills acquired lean toward hunting versus match competition.

Many older sportsmen learned basic shooting in the armed forces, where the style for handguns was to have both arms extended and locked. Modern police training favors the stance developed by California police officer Jack Weaver. The Weaver stance has you rotate your torso a quarter turn away from the target toward the gunhand side. You then fully extend the gunhand across your chest. Next, overlap grip the gunhand with the weaker hand. The weak arm is bent. *Pull* towards yourself with the weak hand. *Push* away with the gunhand, equalizing the isometric pressure. When shooting off a rest such as a tree limb or fence post, lay the back of the weak hand against the hard surface—instant Weaver stance. It's a good idea to have your hat under the braced hand. In this

stance, recoil from heavy caliber guns is channeled straight back, although you'd better believe a .44 mag will jump up some. Therefore, in addition to picking up steadiness, you're better prepared for a follow-up shot if necessary.

Misses are caused by one or all of three common errors, each of which can be minimized by lots of dry firing practice and .22 work.

1. Sight alignment—either of front to rear or with target.
2. Jerking the trigger—flinch.
3. Lack of follow-through.

It may be hard to figure out why you missed; trigger jerk could be disguised by recoil. All heck breaks loose when you touch off a .44 mag, and you may well have your eyes closed on the second round, hand atremble.

An instructor will help you determine master eye, or you can do it yourself. (See Chapter X.) If at all possible, you should learn to handgun hunt with both eyes open. This enables you to better judge range (through depth perception) and follow moving game before and after your shot. Practice dry firing at a one-inch black circle inked in against a white paper background. Stick this target up about 20 feet away. The one-inch black spot should be resting like a pumpkin on a post above your front sight, which has been carefully aligned in the rear sight. Squeeze only when you have a good sight picture. Stop when you weave off alignment, but hold the trigger slack you've gained. Squeeze more as you come back in alignment. Do this a lot—10 minutes or so a day before going to a range. You can even do this while watching TV during commercials. Not even "Make my day" handgunners can hold absolutely still—we all wobble. That's another reason why hunters always try to fire off a rest of some sort, even a stick carried with them and stuck in the ground for the sitting or kneeling shot. Remember to use the Weaver stance. And, take care not to place your hand in front of a revolver cylinder to steady it; powder burn is painful.

A major difference between handguns and shotguns is that in shotgunning you never consciously see the front sight, only the target. With handguns, even if the target is a little fuzzy, you must be able to see the front sight clearly. For younger shooters this is usually easy; grizzled sportsmen find it more difficult. Scopes with long eye relief optics that resolve this problem are available for handguns. The long eye relief assures that you will not place your eye too close to the handgun and its kick back.

A good rule of thumb with handguns is that you should be competent enough to put six-shot groups within a grapefruit-sized target from whatever position you care to use at whatever range. The only caveat is if you are good enough to group this well beyond the effective killing range of your handgun, please don't shoot a deer. For most of us, this grapefruit grouping rule will ensure being well within clean kill range. Try it at 50 yards.

The deer hunter's option excludes automatic pistols because they won't handle the magnum loads. Either the break action, single shot, large caliber pistols or the big revolvers should be selected. For the record, pistols chamber cartridges directly into the barrel, while revolvers have *revolving* cylinders which are both magazine and chamber.

Pistols and revolvers cause more nervousness around deer camps than rattlesnakes, and they're far more deadly. They are so easy to point unthinkingly in a dangerous direction and so easy to unthinkingly carry fully loaded into camp. Sportsmen tend to view handguns as unnecessary accoutrements to the deer hunt. Macho caliber handguns holstered Billy the Kid style usually mark a dangerous greenhorn. But hunters do respect the skilled shooter who makes clean kills with handguns, as they do those equally skilled hunters who are successful with arrows and black powder.

Handgun hunts are appropriate for feral hogs, javelinas, alligators, coyotes, and other varmints. The thick brush in a typical hog hunt and the often tiring chase make the handgun a reasonable and convenient choice. Besides, it gives a 400-pound boar a sporting chance to turn the tables, which always adds a little dash to the hunt.

There is a "traveling" exception for carrying a handgun on a long trip, and no permit is necessary. It is illegal to carry handguns in the passenger compartment of a vehicle or on your person, concealed or not. You may carry a shotgun or rifle of legal length in the passenger compartment, or even on your person. Just don't walk into a bar.

BOWHUNTING Bowhunting is a complex subject in its own right, beyond the scope of this basic sportsman's guide, but a good place to practice the sport is in predator hunting, since game can often be called within bow range. A predator-trained bowhunter is much more likely to be safe and effective on deer and other big game.

If you are motivated to try your hand at bowhunting, seek expert guidance and start modestly until you are confident you can handle a bow. Many a sportsman, initially enamored of the concept of Indian hunting, has some used bow equipment piled in a closet. Others have wounded and lost deer through inexperience, deer that might have been cleanly killed if the hunter had mastered predator hunting. Remember, an archery stamp is required if you plan to graduate from varmints to deer or turkey.

Sportsmen whose muscle tone may be less than perfect, perhaps from too much city life, need first to be concerned with draw weight. The legal minimum for any game animal is 40 pounds, and you'll be surprised at how difficult even this light draw is until you learn the technique.

The basic bow types start with the classic longbow. Aes-

Texas sportsmen who have mastered the bow
have more opportunities than most to hunt.

thetically pleasing, the longbow is also inexpensive and simple to handle. But it takes strength to use, and even a heavy bow will not boost an arrow anywhere near the 200-feet-per-second velocity preferred by hunters. The bow is also long and, therefore, not handy on a hunt.

The other types—recurve, various compound bows, and overdraw bows—produce more velocity. Modern bow hunters select compound bows—including the now standard round wheel design—to yield flat trajectories and good velocities. A major advantage of compound bows is what archers call draw-weight let off, which makes a 60-pound draw feel more like 30 to 40 pounds at full draw, a tremendous advantage in holding on game. Many compound bows allow for an adjustable draw-weight so that you can tune the bow to be comfortable for you. These bows are more compact, an average four feet from tip to tip, and may be constructed with advanced fiberglass materials which are durable and easy to care for. Bow technology is constantly improving, with designs such as the compound-cam and overdraw capable of velocities approaching 250 feet per second. These velocities are for pros only; for most hunting situations, lower arrow velocities are recommended because amateur hunters will achieve better shot placement.

Your personal draw length is critical in purchasing a bow. This is the distance measured from your throat to the end of your fingers when stretched out in front of you, parallel to the ground. And, just as in firearms, you need to determine your master eye.

Crossbows are specifically prohibited in TPWD regulations, as is any other device that propels the arrow with anything other than energy stored by the drawn bow. Compound bows are legal in that the bow string is not locked at full or partial draw.

The would-be bow hunter is going to find the situation even more complicated when he gets into arrow selection. The most popular hunting arrow shaft material is aluminum, also the most expensive. Shaft length must be computed from your draw length plus a little for clearance. Shaft diameter and arrow weight go up with draw-weight.

There is a wide consensus on using hunting broadheads of no less than 7/8-inch in width; state law specifi-

Texas bow hunters must use razor sharp broadheads of no less than 7/8-inch width when hunting deer.

cally prohibits anything less, or use of target or field points on big game. Arrows used in hunting must be marked permanently with the name and address of the hunter. This can be etched or done with non-water-soluble ink. Incidentally, it is legal to have a shotgun and shells no larger than #4s with you in archery season, but don't shoot at deer or turkey.

Broadhead arrows have incredible killing power, especially with a heart-lung shot. Since so much internal damage is done, the blood flow to the brain is instantly stopped. The broadhead will often pass through the chest cavity of predators, even deer. This seems to indicate great energy as expressed in foot pounds, an incorrect impression—the energy of the arrow when it leaves the bow is much less than that of a .22 short. In case you are tempted to add to your arrow's killing power, state law prohibits poisons, drugs, and explosives.

The list of bowhunting accessories is mind boggling, but a basic is a shooting glove to protect fingers. In addition, most use an armguard as the bowstring will deliver a smart slap. You'll also need a quiver and, again, the choices are wide. Many archers use a camouflaged hip quiver to protect themselves and the broadhead edges. There are even bow sights and range finders available. (Comanches never used these, though.)

Trans-Pecos Menu

Jalapeño Quail
Venison Fajitas
Guacamole
Pico de Gallo
Roasted Sweet Peppers
Sopaipillas
with Wild Black Bee Honey

Cerveza Superior

CLARET CUP CACTUS. *Echinocereus triglochidiatus*. Bright orange-red flowers bloom out of the tops of the stems of a low-growing, cylindrical plant. Clumps grow three to four feet across. From Del Rio throughout the Trans-Pecos. Perennial, April through May.

Jalapeno Quail

SERVES 8 AS AN APPETIZER

8 quail, rinsed and dried
1½ cups softened butter or margarine
1 lime
   salt and pepper to taste
2 mild jalapeno peppers, cut into 4 strips
    each
8 thick slices of bacon

PREPARATION

1. Rub birds with softened butter.
2. Sprinkle with salt and pepper, squeeze on lime juice.
3. Insert strip of jalapeno in each cavity.
4. Wrap with thick slices of bacon.
5. Broil, turning, until tender and a crisp brown, about 35 minutes.

This spicy appetizer disappears about as fast as a covey. If dinner will be awhile, add some Tex-Mex appetizers to soften the blow.

Venison Fajitas

SERVES 6 TO 8

"Fajita" means "little girdle" and describes the thin girdle of meat at the bottom of a steer's rib cage. With beef, the traditional fajitas are cut from skirt steak, but with venison, it's best to use a better cut, even from a ham. We slice off ½-inch-thick pieces from a boned-out ham as a starting place when using venison.

1½ pounds venison ham—sliced ½-inch
   thick in six-inch strips
6 limes
2 garlic cloves, minced
2 green chile peppers, minced
1 onion, thinly sliced
  fresh cilantro, remove stems and chop
    leaves (dried oregano may be
    substituted)
  salt to taste
  freshly ground black pepper
2 cans beer

PREPARATION

1. Place one layer of venison slices in deep glass baking dish.
2. Cover slices with lime juice, some garlic, onion, cilantro, peppers, and pepper.
3. Add second layer of meat, and again add garlic, peppers, onion, pepper, and cilantro.
4. Add your favorite beer to almost fill pan. Cover and marinate meat overnight. Toss meat every so often so that all surfaces are marinated.

5. Cook over hot mesquite fire, turning only once. Do not overcook.
6. Salt to taste.
7. Cut on the diagonal into very thin strips.

Wrap fajita-style in flour tortillas with guacamole, sour cream, pico de gallo, shredded cheese, and refried beans.

Guacamole

YIELDS 3 CUPS

2 ripe avocados, peeled and pitted
1 small lime
2 ripe tomatoes, peeled and chopped
1 small white onion, finely chopped
  salt to taste

PREPARATION

1. Use dinner fork to mash avocados into lumpy texture.
2. Squeeze juice of lime into mashed avocados.
3. Add tomatoes, onions, and salt to taste.

Pico de Gallo

SERVES 6 TO 8

"Gallo" is rooster in Spanish, so pico de gallo means, roughly, "peck of the rooster." Aficionados ladle it on fajitas, chalupas, or anything else that needs a spicy peck of flavor.

2 small yellow chile peppers
8 green chile peppers
1 white onion, finely chopped
6 green onions with tops, chopped
6 tomatoes, peeled and chopped
  pinch of fresh cilantro leaves
2 tablespoons peanut oil
1 tablespoon red wine vinegar
  salt to taste

PREPARATION

1. Roast yellow and green chiles over open flame until blackened.
2. Peel, remove seeds, and devein and chop finely.
3. Combine peppers with other ingredients and chill.

Sopaipillas with Wild Black Bee Honey

SERVES 6 TO 8

The small, wild black bees of the Big Bend are famous for the sweetness of their honey. We have prowled the caves of Pulliam Ridge in search of this honey, a risky business since these bees are much more aggressive than domesticated honeybees. Today, they have become very hard to find. They would seem to have some of the fearsome characteristics of the killer bees which now threaten our state's crops. Many have been smoked out to make room for the more tractable honeybees. The wild black bees' nectar sources include whitebush, catclaw, and mesquite. The small, white flowers of the whitebush have a fragrance reminiscent of vanilla, and this can be detected in the honey. One of the world's finest dessert treats is a sopaipilla laden with this honey, which can usually be purchased while you're obtaining camp stores.

4 cups flour
3 teaspoons baking powder
4 tablespoons sugar
1½ teaspoons salt
3 tablespoons vegetable shortening
1 egg, slightly beaten
1½ cups milk
   peanut oil
   wild black bee honey

PREPARATION

1. Mix dry ingredients. Cut in vegetable shortening.
2. Add egg and milk a little at a time. Stir to form soft dough, firm enough to roll.
3. Cover dough and let rise for 30 minutes.
4. Roll dough ⅛-inch thick on floured board. Cut into 3-inch triangles.
5. Heat peanut oil at least 1 inch deep in cast-iron skillet.
6. When peanut oil reaches at least 350 degrees cook triangles in oil a few at a time. Turn them quickly so they will puff on both sides, then turn again to brown. Remove from oil and drain on paper toweling.
7. Serve with honey.

IX

HOGS

HOGS

Many have been regaled with tales of fearsome 500-pound Russian boars running amok, killing hapless *vaqueros* on the King Ranch. As for the ferocious javelina, doesn't the name itself connect with javelin-like tusks? Have you heard of the scary javelina traveling in packs of 50, gutting mule deer hunters unfortunate enough to be caught at dusk in the draws of the Trans-Pecos? Edge closer to the fire and clutch your .400 magnum. Danger lurks in the cold and dark.

> "Beware the Jabberwock, my son!
> The jaws that bite, the claws that catch!
> . . . The Jabberwock, with eyes of flame,
> Came whiffling through the tulgey wood,
> And burbled as it came!"

Feral hog folklore and javelina jabber have long been popular topics around Texas hunt campfires, spreading myths that bewilder even the most stalwart sportsman. Like Lewis Carroll's nonsensical poem, most of it is jabberwocky.

Feral hog folklore enlivens many a Texas hunting campfire.

Ignore the myth that javelina are inedible, the feral hog not too far behind. In fact, feral hogs are wonderful table fare, considered tastier than domestic pork by some. Properly dressed and prepared, the javelina, too, holds its own at the barbecue pit or sausage smoker.

Most sportsmen harvest feral hogs as an adjunct to deer hunting. Exciting hunts for feral hogs can be arranged in the off season, while a planned javelina hunt is an excellent alternative for the hunter who has already bagged his deer. And though many nationally recognized game-guide authors insist that these two animals never occupy the same range, in the South Texas Plains you'll find feral hogs and javelina commonly crossing the same *sendero*.

FERAL HOG INSIGHTS

There is some evidence that North America had its own *Sus scrofa*. Carbon-14 dating of fossils found in northwestern Arkansas identifed a swine which could easily have found its way down to East Texas millenia ago. Feral hog genealogy is thus quite complex. Similar to what's happened in America since Ellis Island, the hog's family tree has many branches and offshoots. Feral hogs are all descended from domestic hogs, but many have also crossbred with descendants of European wild hogs.

The hogs which 19th-century Thicket settlers brought to the area were the root stock of the feral hogs that abound in the Pineywoods today. These hogs were an essential part of pioneer life and are a major reason why bears are extinct in East Texas. Black bears and settlers shared a preference for pork; the settlers had no intention of losing this food chain battle.

In the early 1900s, when other game such as bear, deer, turkey, and passenger pigeons was nearly or completely extirpated from Texas, feral hogs were being hunted by subsistence hunters. While game laws and transplant activities were bringing back the deer and turkey that had nearly succumbed to the inexorable presence of man, unprotected feral hogs were hunted even harder. Today, they're still unprotected except by their own intelligence and craftiness, and they are still thriving. Hunt them with respect.

Not recognized with an official hunting season or bag limit, feral hogs are not awarded game animal status in Texas. But the premeditated feral hog hunt is the roughest meat hunt in the state, and bringing home the bacon in feral hog form usually takes a fair amount of hunting skill and endurance.

Most hunters have no idea how difficult it is to hunt the feral hog. He's a wily, intelligent foe with almost extrasensory ability to detect danger. And, he's got a toughness worthy of Jack Dempsey. When the feral hog makes a stand, the more dogs you have the better. Armed hunters must get to the action quickly or there will be fewer dogs. A wounded feral hog is a dangerous adversary, capable of killing dogs and goring men.

It's estimated that more than 3,000 feral hogs are harvested annually in Texas. That's undoubtedly on the low side. With no enforced season or limit, many kills go unreported. The hogs are frequently shot by landowners, both in defense of crops and fences and for the quantity and quality of good eating they provide.

Feral hogs have a surprisingly wide range in Texas. We have taken them in river bottoms of the Edwards Plateau, from *senderos* in the South Texas Plains and, as you'd expect, from Pineywoods bottomlands and Gulf Prairies and Marshes.

The same Brush Country ranches that feature trophy deer hunts are also good bets for winter feral hog hunts.

Although not recognized as game animals in Texas, feral hogs can give the hunter all the challenge he needs.

There will be a fee, but much less than for deer, with twice the action and four times the good eating.

One of the best and most popular public hunts for feral hogs in Texas is on the Engeling Wildlife Management Area in Anderson County. Apply in late November to TPWD for a permit. These hunts are usually scheduled in February. There are often far more applicants than can be accommodated, yet far fewer hogs are taken than would be preferred by wildlife biologists, proving once again the craftiness of the wild hogs.

The feral hog's coat, or pelage, is the key to his survival. Without it he couldn't withstand the environment. Hogs have no sweat glands, and domestic hogs with their hairless skins can alter their internal heat production only slightly. Feral hogs have a much greater tolerance for both heat and cold, but their movements still can be predicted by temperature extremes. In the heat of summer, they will be more nocturnal, seeking cool beds near water during the day. On winter days, when not pursued by hunters, they are far more active, especially at dawn and twilight, engaged in what's called diurnal and crepuscular activity. If you're going to run hounds in winter, let them out near feeding areas just before dawn, since the feral hogs will be up and about.

Feral hogs are thinner and more agile than domestic hogs, for obvious reasons. They are not as pure a strain as wild European hogs nor are they as streamlined, but, compared with domestic hogs, they are much more so—you'll not find the round, pink fatness common to the barnyard. Habitat and available food creates a wide disparity in weight and physiological characteristics. Boars can weigh up to 400 pounds. The feral hog can move at almost the speed of a deer, at least 25 miles per hour or more. They can easily cover 20 miles a day. In areas where food is scarce, they'll cover twice this distance. If you're a hunter following hounds you'll get in your aerobics. This is not a recommended sport for desk-bound sportsmen.

Whitetail hunters in hog country have often been fooled by feral hog tracks, because the difference between the two is subtle. The hog track is rounder, and where dewclaw prints are seen they are more pointed and extend farther out to the side than the whitetail's, but not as far back. The track of a feral hog is on more of a straight line than that of a domestic pig, and, unlike domestics, feral hogs can and do jump over logs and run up steep banks.

A sure sign of hogs is torn up turf and wallow. He's not called a Pineywoods rooter for nothing. Feral hogs mark trees by rubbing and gouging them with their tusks, and their bristly hair is often left in evidence.

Feral hogs are one of nature's archetypal survivors. They can sniff out tubers and even water two feet or more below the earth's surface. The food they won't eat has not yet been discovered; they are omnivorous. During fall and winter a typical feral hog's food supply comes from acorns, but they'll consume anything in their paths. When there are more hogs than the range can handle, they can eat other wildlife out of house and home, and even eat the wildlife. Competition for mast, such as acorns, makes them a serious threat to deer, turkey, and squirrel; they also damage turkey populations through nest predation.

Despite reports of up to 50 hogs in a herd, the average herd size is eight, with no more than three adults per group. Boars usually go their own way until breeding time rolls around. When it does, there's a lot of action, as several boars will root around a single sow in estrus at the same time, with breeding going on day and night. During this time feral boars are apt to charge other suitors head on, then circle and slash, circle and slash, like switchblade muggers. Like humans, feral hogs are polyestrous, physiologically capable of breeding all year. There are two farrowing peaks in July and February. Since gestation is 112 to 114 days, this means that breeding peaks are in March and October. Breeding peaks vary greatly with habitat, food, and weather conditions. Litter size averages five.

JAVELINA INSIGHTS

Hunters who think of javelina, sometimes called Mexican hogs, as pigs are mistaken. Though distantly related over millions of years, feral hogs and javelina are not in the same family. The javelina's single dewclaw and two functional teats knock it out of the swine family. Javelina are native to this hemisphere, migrating from South America, while feral hogs descended from domestic European hogs gone wild.

Game biologists insist upon calling javelinas *collared peccaries*, after the light-colored band circling the neck. This collar is often missing on our Trans-Pecos variety, which is usually dark brown or black with salt and pepper coloring.

Some national outdoor writers claim the name javelina came from the Spanish word for spear or javelin because of the animal's "long, lean shape and spearlike tusks." Does a stubby-legged, pig-like animal nearly a yard long and 20 inches high, weighing perhaps 50 pounds, with two-inch tusks look like a javelin to you?

The better folklore etymology is that javelina is a derivative of the Spanish word for wild boar, *jabali*. In truth, a javelina does look like a diminutive wild boar and makes a most ferocious mount, dorsal bristles flared and tusks protruding rudely. The sight of a good javelina head on the wall is fearsome indeed, and naturally the owner will make a case for his courage as he tells the inevitable charge story.

And charged he may have been. Texas javelina travel in packs of 16 or more. We've counted close to 50 in a band. It can get pretty nerve-racking when you're in the presence of such a herd and they're all popping their teeth, gnashing their tusks, chomping, chewing, and snorting. When something scatters such a herd, most likely your sound or scent, the herd will start milling around, bris-

The official name for javelina is collared peccary, the collar referring to a white band just behind the neck.

Prickly pear cacti are a principal source of water for javelinas.

tling, grunting, and will suddenly begin running in all directions, including yours.

Actually, javelina are not aggressive. In fact, they're social animals with a wide range of vocal communications and even reciprocal grooming. Javelina will stand side to side, head to tail, and rub their heads against flanks, rump, and scent glands. The scent gland, located in the center of the back eight inches or so forward of the tail,

secretes a skunk-like musk. You'll have no trouble recognizing it. This gland works full blast when the javelina is frightened. Wildlife biologists believe this communicates alarm to the herd. This scent can also give away the locale or recent location of a javelina herd.

Javelina are game animals with seasons and limits that vary by county. Although not many Texans hunt javelina with dogs, those who do will tell you that a javelina can be provoked by dogs. Some authorities attribute this to a natural fear of coyotes, which have become the major natural predator of javelina. Take special precaution to keep your quail dogs away from javelina, since there have been many reports of injuries.

Javelina are found in Texas across the South Texas Plains, the Edwards Plateau, and Trans-Pecos. Much of this terrain is arid, an environment with which the javelina are well prepared to cope. They can go just under a week without water, because they can reduce evaporative water loss by two thirds and urinary water loss by more than 90 percent. In fact, they don't seem to need free water for drinking because they can quench most if not all of their thirst from prickly pear cactus. Many observers have flatly stated that prickly pears are the javelina's favorite food. Actually, the cactus is their favorite beverage. Javelina prefer more nutritious forbs, agave, mesquite beans, pinyon nuts, seeds, and grass. However, in the absence of all other foods, the javelina will use prickly pear cactus as emergency rations.

Javelina roam up to 6,000 or more feet, but retreat to lower elevations before really cold weather begins. They need dense brush habitat to thrive. As it does with many other game animals, the human commitment to land clearing reduces the population more than any other factor. About the only damage javelina would seem to do to range, viewed in human terms, is to spread the growth of prickly pear cactus, which is not really that bad, as many a South Texas rancher will tell you. Burning off prickly pear spines to allow cattle to "drink" prickly pears is a time-honored way to save a herd during a Brush Country drought.

Myth has it that, like feral hogs, javelina are omnivorous, but it's seldom if ever that they eat meat. Biologists describe them as generalist herbivores, which translates to an ability to eat almost any plant, cactus spines notwithstanding.

Like the feral hog, javelina sows are also capable of breeding all year, but they tend to concentrate breeding activity in late fall and winter. Gestation is about 145 days and piglet twins are the norm. Sometimes you'll hear of aggressive interaction between boars near sows in estrus, but, unlike feral hogs, disputes are uncommon among javelina.

The javelina is the smallest cloven-hooved animal in the state. Their tracks resemble those of the feral hog, only smaller. They can easily be confused in the shared range of the South Texas Plains. Their tracks also can be mistaken for those of fawns. Javelina will kill a snake by jumping up and down, stomping it with all four feet, much as feral hogs, deer, and pronghorns will do. Even rattlers are dispatched in this fashion.

Javelina are becoming an important game species in Texas, with season harvests in the 25,000 range. Much of this harvest is wasted because many think that javelina are varmints unfit for eating. The bad rap comes from hunters who are put off by the appearance, difficult field dressing, and most of all, the malodorous secretion of the scent gland above the hams. These hunters claim they are improving the range by shooting off the javelina. Others are simply after ferocious wall mounts and can't be bothered by dressing out the meat.

PREPARATION FOR THE HUNT

TEXAS PREFERRED GUN SELECTION Your scoped deer rifle is the easiest choice for javelina hunting. Deer hunters often spot javelina en route to and from stands or while still hunting. Javelina usually have a small range, depending mainly on food availability. After locating the herd, hunting with a flat-shooting, scoped rifle becomes less than fair chase and many sportsmen go to pistols, black powder, or bow. The latter is very sporting in that the javelina's keen sense of smell and hearing will test your Indian-style prowess.

It's quite a different story with feral hogs, except for those hunted from tower stands overlooking Brush Country *senderos*. A scope could get you gored, and your favorite bolt action just might not throw lead fast enough in the heat of battle. Before you grab your .30–30 lever action, consider that the feral hog may weigh in at 300 pounds and be moving toward you at 25 miles per hour, giving him a high kinetic energy level. You would not want all this energy suddenly released on your tender body, so perhaps a heavier caliber is in order.

Provided it has open sights and is preferably slide action or semi-automatic, a .30–06 with at least a 150 grain bullet would be a good choice for the Pineywoods and other bottomland hunts. Many have hunted feral hogs with 12-gauge pumps or autoloaders loaded with 00 buck or rifled slugs, a most effective load, but one that will obviously handicap you on the longer shots you sometimes get even in the Pineywoods.

Again, we've seen intrepid hunters go afield with .44 mags and .357 mags, both of which provide a world of sport. These handguns will definitely do the job if your hand isn't shaking too much. Just don't wound a feral hog charging at close range because he'll keep coming.

HOUNDS FOR FERAL HOGS Many varieties of hounds can be trained to hunt feral hogs. If you ever encounter hound hunters, such as those who hang out in Dog Alley at Canton on the first Monday of each month, ask them about "hog dogs." There are two adjectives to describe a hog dog which survives more than one trip: tough and beat up. Don't send an amateur dog on the trail of a big feral hog. In the best hog habitat—thick Pineywoods bottoms—hounds are by far the most productive way to hunt. Cover is essential for feral hogs and Texas bottomlands provide plenty.

The premier dog for feral hogs is the short-eared Plott hound, faster in pursuit and a better fighter than his cousin the long-eared Plott. The long-eared Plott gets the nod on two characteristics beloved of dedicated hog hunters: a more melodious voice and good cold trailing ability. But the serious meat hunter will elect the short-eared breed, bad voice and all, because he gets the job done.

As hounds go, Plotts aren't gigantic. Their standard weight is 60 pounds. Most colorations are brindle, a beautiful coat to behold. The original Plott lineage goes back to European boar hounds introduced to America by a German immigrant, Jonathon Plott, who brought the dogs to North Carolina.

WARDROBE SELECTION For the most part, Texas hog hunters will also be deer hunters, so we refer you to the wardrobe section in that chapter. Popular times for feral hog hunts are late winter and early spring, which calls for the same basic wardrobe as the deer hunter who prefers still hunting and stalking.

GEAR SELECTION No special equipment is required for hunting javelina, but it's a far different situation with feral hogs. You are not dealing with a cottontail here, but rather 200 pounds plus, requiring complex processing. There is no doubt that a guide is worth every *sou* when it comes to debristling and field dressing hogs.

If you must do the job yourself, you'll need a great deal of specialized equipment, and there are no short cuts. First, you need some way of getting the hog to camp quickly. A vehicle is best, but an old fashioned hog pole will suffice if you and your partner have the strength. It's difficult to rig a stretcher for hogs because of the weight involved. Shoulder pads for protecting you from the poles will be welcome on your way back to camp.

In camp, you need a large capacity butane burner complete with a large pot, because you're going to have to heat 30 gallons of water to 150 degrees Fahrenheit. Get a thermometer so you can be exact. Next, you'll need a 55-gallon drum or its equivalent, a stout block and tackle, and a gambrel like that used for deer. Remember, you may be dealing with a couple of hundred pounds of dead weight. You'll find a long-bladed boning knife a comfort along with a large meat saw; the amateur version used for deer will prove inadequate.

Next on your list come a bell scraper, a wire brush, and lots of clean, coarse cloth. You need a work table of some sort large enough to accommodate the entire carcass. Finally, you need some method of chilling the carcass if you're far from town. Your hog is obviously beyond the reach of your picnic cooler.

FERAL HOG HUNTER'S CHECKLIST
- No license is required
- Rifle with open sights in dense cover
- Gun case
- Ammunition
- Hog pole
- 3/8-inch line
- Shoulder pads for pole
- Folding skinning knife
- Waterproof boots
- Flashlight
- Butane burner
- Butane tank
- Wrenches to connect tank to burner
- Long-bladed boning knife
- Large meat saw
- Large-capacity pot
- Clean 55-gallon drum
- Heavy-duty block and tackle
- Gambrel
- Bell scraper
- Wire brush
- Clean, coarse cloth
- String for tying off organs
- Plastic bags
- Large ice chest
- Alarm clock
- (Select wardrobe form Deer Hunter checklist)

TECHNIQUES THE EXPERTS USE

A lone feral hog hunter without hounds has his work cut out for him. This should not be a solitary hunt. Even with several hunters and a pack of hounds, this is Texas' toughest hunt, from location of game to table delivery. Intimate local knowledge is the key, plus access to enough land where you can prowl lots of creek and river bottoms until you find the telltale torn up earth. Careful inspection of the soft bottomland will give you an idea of the freshness of sign and the direction in which the herd was moving as it fed. Knowledge of feeding preferences, especially acorns in the fall, may enable you to set up an ambush.

Feral hogs are incredibly difficult to sneak up on. If their sense of smell is so keen they can find a truffle two feet beneath the earth, how do you suppose you smell to them? Nature compensated for their poor eyesight by endowing them with especially acute hearing.

One of the most successful ways to hunt feral hogs is to arrange a paid hunt in the Brush Country, selecting a tower stand overlooking a *sendero* leading through bottomland. As with deer, your scent is diffused by being airborne.

Bringing home the bacon is no easy task.

If the weather turns hot, your troubles are multiplied, since feral hogs will seek the densest cover available and stay put until dark.

Shot placement is very important, because a quick kill ensures higher-quality meat. We prefer a shot at the neckline since it preserves the makings for souse and headcheese. These delicacies are wonderful, especially when prepared by someone else, since the work requires expert processing. Shots to the shoulder mess up far too much meat, and a gamble on heart placement may accomplish the unthinkable, a gut shot.

If you're a smart feral hog hunter you won't go for the oldest, baddest, biggest boar around. For eating purposes, you want a medium-sized hog weighing 100 pounds or less. This size is a lot easier to haul out of the woods and field dress, no easy chore for the amateur.

FERAL HOG FIELD DRESSING Whenever possible, take the whole hog, innards and all, to your local butcher. However, if you can't get your kill to town, you may wish to try this original Pineywoods procedure, though you might wish you hadn't. (Most modern hunters would start on STEP 7 below.)

STEP 1. Before putting any more holes in the hide, scald the whole hog to aid debristling. Fill a 55-gallon drum with 30 gallons of water. It's critical that you heat the water to 150 degrees Fahrenheit. Use a thermometer to check the temperature. If the water's any hotter, you'll set the bristle and never get it out, and if the water's too cool you're just wasting time. The drum should be positioned under a stout pole rigged with a heavy duty block and tackle, from which you've suspended a gambrel.

STEP 2. Separate the ligaments at the joint of each hind leg, insert the gambrel, and hoist the hog over the drum.

STEP 3. Dunk the hog into the 150-degree water. Monitor the water, since the temperature will drop quickly in cold weather. It's a good idea to set up a reserve hot water supply on a nearby butane burner so you can add more hot water to the drum and keep the temperature constant. A 100-pound hog should be submerged three to five minutes; six minutes for a larger hog. Keep the hog moving, bobbing up and down a bit. After three or four minutes pull him out far enough to see if the bristle is ready to work loose. When the bristle starts to pull away, gently hoist the hog out of the drum and manhandle him to a nearby work table. You can leave the gambrel in place, attached to the rear legs.

STEP 4. Now comes the fun part. You'll need a partner or two because speed is essential in scraping off the bristle. Use bell scrapers and a clean, coarse, burlap, tote-sack-type cloth to rub the hide with a circular motion. Keep at it. If he cools, the bristle won't come out. If you're really serious, singe the hide with a blowtorch and finish scraping with a wire brush. If it's pigskin gloves you're after, you'll need to shave the skin with an ultra-sharp knife to prepare the hide properly.

STEP 5. Carefully clean your boning knife, skinning knife, and meat saw.

STEP 6. Rehoist your squeaking clean hog, moving the drum out of your way and replacing it with a bucket. First, to remove the head, start your cut at the back of the neck at the first joint of the backbone. Continue all the way across the back. Sever the esophagus and windpipe and the head will drop. Continue the cut around the front to just behind the jawbone. The head will now come free, leaving the jowls on the carcass.

(NOTE: At this point an accomplished butcher would cleanse the head and trim it out after removing the tongue and brain, saving the head to make headcheese or souse.)

STEP 7. Now you can "field" dress the hog in the sense of handling a deer. Make a shallow scoring incision between the hams. As with a deer, don't puncture the membrane that encloses the abdominal organs. Cut upward from the neck along the breastbone, stopping before you penetrate the abdominal cavity. Return to the point between the hams. Carefully insert your skinning knife, blade away from the intestines, and slice down through the membrane to join the chest cut you've already made. The intestines will tend to fall forward, but tissue will hold them.

STEP 8. Cut down between the hams to the aitchbone. Use the meat saw to carefully split this bone, remembering that the bladder is underneath. Cut around the anal area to loosen the rectum, and tie it off. Pull the intestine down and out, snipping connecting tissues as needed. Now you are ready to remove all the entrails, pulling them out while carefully slicing the connecting tissue until you get to the diaphragm. Cut through the diaphragm to the backbone and around both sides to access the heart and lung area. After snipping the esophagus, all should fall free into your pre-placed bucket. Remove the tail close to the base. Rinse the body clean with cold water.

(NOTE: A professional butcher would take much care to preserve the edible organs, especially the heart and liver. The small intestines are used for authentic sausages. Real aficionados carefully clean the large intestines and stomach to make chitlins or chitterlings.)

STEP 9. While the carcass is still warm, use your meat saw to split the carcass lengthways.

STEP 10. Again, while the body is still warm, skin the hams. This will aid in chilling the meat and in creating a grocery store appearance.

STEP 11. Rush to a meat locker, if possible, and chill the center of the ham to below 35 degrees, since warm meat is difficult to butcher cleanly. If you're in an inaccessible camp in warm weather, your only alternative may be to rough quarter the carcass enough to fit the meat into an ice chest. Usually three sections per side will reduce the carcass to manageable size.

A. Cut right behind the shoulder blade to remove the forequarter.

B. Cut around inside the hams to take off the hindquarter.

C. You may wish to split up the remaining midsection, depending on space requirements.

JAVELINA FIELD DRESSING Field dressing and skinning procedures for javelina are similar to those for deer. It's quite important to proceed rapidly to ensure the edibility of your meat. First of all, the hide is easy to remove when the body is warm, and fleas and ticks that seek body heat will remain attached to the javelina's hide—not yours. You also need to hurry because the animal's scent gland can quickly taint the meat. In addition, the usually warm temperatures of Southwest Texas javelina seasons can cause meat to spoil.

Javelina myth has it that you must slice out the scent gland on the back as soon as the animal is down. This runs the same risk as removing the tarsal glands from the legs of a deer in rut—contaminating the knife, ergo, tainting the meat while field dressing. The scent gland is entirely contained within the skin, so by skinning according to STEP 6 below, you remove the gland with no fuss or muss. If you plan to mount the head, read STEP 5 first.

STEP 1. With the animal on its back, start at the diaphragm, four or five inches behind the front legs, and make a shallow cut down and around the reproductive organs and anus, lifting the skin away from the intestines.

STEP 2. Cut away the reproductive organs and pull the anus area out and away from the skin. Now cut through the pelvic bone and break it apart. Pull out all intestines.

STEP 3. Slice away the diaphragm muscle from the abdominal area, and grab the esophagus and windpipe as high up as possible and cut them out. Now, pull out all organs including the heart, lungs, liver, and stomach. You'll see the kidneys connected to the ribcage. Cut these away and discard. We don't save javelina organs.

STEP 4. Cut off all four feet at each knee joint.

STEP 5. Skin the javelina. Many hunters will want mounts, so first make a cut that encircles the body starting at the point where you made your first incision, at the back of the forelegs.

STEP 6. Strip the hide downward and off the legs. You may have to make a shallow cut here or there to free connecting tissues, but while the carcass is warm this is an easy chore. This step automatically removes the offending scent gland. Don't touch this gland or allow it to touch any meat.

STEP 7. Pull the hide up and over the head like you'd take off a T-shirt. Depending upon your patience, skill, and distance from a taxidermist, you may just want to sever the head and transport the iced-down remains straight to town; if not, you can proceed as follows:

STEP 8. When you reach the ears, using a very sharp knife cut the ear cartilage away from the skull. Eyelids, nostrils, and lips are handled with the same surgical precision.

STEP 9. Heavily salt the entire hide and take it to a taxidermist or glove maker. Javelina hide gloves are finer and more supple than pigskin or deerskin.

As for your meat, whether it be feral hog or javelina, remember that pork spoils rapidly, so don't take any chances. An optional chilling method for use in mild weather is to fill a tub with cold water, blocks of ice, and three pounds of salt. Insert rough cuts to chill them quickly.

Be sure to cook your meat thoroughly to avoid the often forgotten but potential problem of trichinosis.

South Texas Plains Menu

Cerviche
Border Tamales
Mexican Bean Soup
Basic Salsa
Rio Grande Arroz Verde

Cerveza Mas Fina

DRUMMOND PHLOX. *Phlox drummondii.* Brilliant rose-red with deep
red, sometimes violet eyes. Color varies to violet, pink, and white.
Blooms in clusters on stems eight to 20 inches tall along roadsides
and uncultivated fields. Perennial, May through October.

Ceviche

SERVES 6 to 8

This is best made with fresh caught fish. Freshwater bass or crappie are excellent, as well as flounder, red snapper, speckled trout, sea scallops, and shrimp.

2 pounds fish, cut into ½-inch cubes
1 cup lime juice (can be bottled)
1 onion, chopped
3 jalapeno peppers, seeded and finely
   chopped
1 small can green chiles, chopped
½ cup tomato sauce or stewed tomatoes
⅓ cup olive oil
¼ cup stuffed green olives, chopped
1 tomato, peeled and chopped
1 clove garlic, minced
   pinch of thyme
1 tablespoon fresh, finely chopped cilantro
1 tablespoon finely chopped parsley

PREPARATION

1. Place cubed fish in covered glass baking dish or plastic container. Cover with lime juice. Let stand overnight on ice or in refrigerator. (Lime juice actually "cooks" fish.)
2. Drain off lime juice—press cubes gently with paper towels.
3. Combine all other ingredients and pour over fish.
4. Let stand for several more hours in refrigerator or ice chest until flavors are blended.

Basic Salsa

YIELDS 1+ CUPS

2 ripe tomatoes, one finely chopped. Hold
   the other in reserve.
½ white onion, finely chopped
   cilantro leaves
3 hot green chiles, finely chopped
   salt to taste

PREPARATION

1. Blend all ingredients. Add salt to taste.
2. Add freshly squeezed tomato juice of reserved tomato if salsa is too thick.

This is to be served with all Tex-Mex dishes, or just with store-bought tostados as camp munchies.

Rio Grande Arroz Verde

SERVES 4 TO 6

2 cups cooked white rice
4 tablespoons stick butter or substitute
1 green bell pepper, finely chopped
3 Poblano peppers, finely chopped
1 onion, minced
1 cup sour cream
½ pound Monterey Jack cheese, grated

PREPARATION

1. Preheat oven to 350 degrees.
2. Cook rice or reheat precooked.
3. Melt butter in cast-iron skillet. Saute peppers and onion until soft.
4. Mash softened peppers and onion to a pulpy mixture.
5. Place half of the rice in a cast-iron pot or 2-quart casserole dish. Add a layer of part of the pepper mixture, then a layer of grated cheese; add sour cream. Repeat layering.
6. Bake, uncovered, until cheese melts.

Mexican Bean Soup

SERVES 8 OR MORE

1 pound pinto beans
2 bottles beer
3 quarts water
1 cup chopped onion
1 clove garlic, minced
1 chunk salt pork or ham bone
1 tablespoon chili powder
½ teaspoon oregano
4 fresh green chile peppers or 1 4-ounce can
   of green chiles
   salt to taste

PREPARATION

1. Cull beans. Wash, then soak in beer overnight.
2. Drain beans, rinse, and place in large cast-iron pot.
3. Add enough water to cover amply.
4. Add onion, garlic, salt pork, chili powder, oregano, and chile peppers.
5. Simmer for several hours adding water as necessary. Add salt only to taste at the end.

Border Tamales

YIELDS 6 DOZEN

Tamales go back to pre-Columbian times, and the making of them can transcend even the evanescent joy of having created a great dish. Making tamales can be a party, a reunion, a social affair.

Corn was the staff of life for early civilization below the Rio Grande, and then the making of tamales had religious significance. Today, many Mexican traditionalists make and eat tamales as part of their Christmas festivities.

The sportsmen in our group have often gathered for what we call the "tamale factory." Our goal is always to make 1,000 tamales in one day. The goal has never quite been attained, with some blaming the constant quality control testing procedure for the short count. But, everyone has good fun, good food, and a supply of tamales for the upcoming deer season. Tamales freeze well and are easy to steam for a quick midday meal or pre-dinner appetizer. When making a huge batch it's advisable to have a source for premixed *masa* and corn husks by the hundreds. Most major Texas cities have a *barrio* where the fixings can be obtained, but call well ahead to order large quantities. In the meantime, the following recipe will introduce you to the art and science of tamale making.

6 dozen corn husks
4 cups vegetable shortening
16 cups masa harina
6 cups warm (not hot) chicken broth
4 tablespoons baking powder
2 teaspoons chili powder
2 tablespoons salt

4–5 pounds feral hog shoulder (lean,
    domestic pork will substitute)
2 medium onions, chopped
8 tablespoons chili powder
3 jalapeno peppers, seeded and finely
    chopped
1 teaspoon freshly ground black pepper
2 teaspoons ground cumin
1 teaspoon cayenne powder
6 cloves garlic, minced
    dash of Tabasco sauce
2 teaspoons oregano
    salt to taste

PREPARATION

1. Soak corn husks in cold water to cover. We use an ice chest.
2. Simmer feral hog shoulder in water to cover until tender. Fork stuck in shoulder should come out easily.
3. Beat shortening in large metal bowl until fluffy. (Takes 5 minutes with heavy-duty electric mixer, longer by hand.)
4. Add masa harina to shortening a little at a time, splashing in warm chicken broth as you go. Dough will separate if broth is too hot. Add broth sparingly. Don't let the mixture become runny.
5. Stir in baking powder, chili powder, and salt.
6. Work the masa until it forms a thick paste and doesn't stick to your hands.
7. Remove feral hog from pot and shred meat into small pieces.
8. Saute chopped onions in large cast-iron skillet.
9. Add shredded pork to onions and brown.
10. While browning meat add chili powder, jalapenos, black pepper, cumin, cayenne, garlic, Tabasco, oregano, and salt.
11. Simmer meat mixture until ingredients are thoroughly mixed. This is the filling.
12. Drain corn husks and pat dry between toweling.
13. Using wide-bladed knife spread masa dough lengthways on wider half of each husk. The width of the spread masa should be no more than enough to allow the dough to just overlap when the corn husk is rolled.
14. Dribble meat filling down the center of the dough.
15. Fold in on long sides, then fold over narrow end to make a neat little packet open on one end. (If you have helpers remind them that neatness counts.)
16. Place a small amount of water in bottom of steamer. A cast-iron dutch oven with a trivet on the bottom is perfect.
17. Arrange tamales upright. They should not touch the water. Cover them with a dish towel, then cover the pot and steam the tamales for up to four hours.

A secret is to have your *amigos* assigned to various tasks. We reserve masa preparation for the greenhorns since it's the most work. Preparing the feral hog filling is obviously a job for the most experienced; it's easy and you get to taste. Even the helpless can handle corn husk drying. Masa spreading and tamale folding is a job that requires a fine touch. Don't assign a klutz. Administrative supervision is for the person who can't do anything.

Another suggestion is to make extra filling and use it in tacos or chalupas to reduce tamale loss and to keep your factory workers happy. Mucho cervesa assists too.

X

SMALL

GAME

SMALL GAME

Many sportsmen believe that happiness is the look of wonderment reflected in the eyes of a youngster first introduced to the wilderness experience by hunting small game. Yet, small game hunting has not gained the popularity it deserves in Texas and has been underutilized as a learning ground and rite of passage for boys and girls. It is a valuable, if not absolutely necessary, step in becoming first a conservationist, then a competent big game hunter, then a dedicated conservationist.

The still hunter who can fill a pot with haunch of squirrel can surely do it with one of venison. Squirrel hunting is one of the most challenging and satisfying experiences available to sportsmen. The eastern half of Texas is replete with the eastern gray squirrel, also known as the cat squirrel. Fox squirrels inhabit this same range but extend much farther west, giving us squirrel hunting over much of the state.

Rabbits are our most populous small game, but they are largely ignored in Texas. This mystifies us for several reasons. First of all, rabbit hunting provides good shooting and an ideal venue for teaching shooting skills to youngsters. Second, cottontails taste great. Third, Texas has millions of cottontails, jackrabbits, and swamp or marsh rabbits. And finally, in some pastures, proliferating rabbits can actually eat enough grass to make a difference in food available for livestock.

The tasty cottontail is an underutilized game resource in Texas.

Raccoon, opossum, and the unofficial Lone Star symbol, the nine-banded armadillo, are considered table fare, but you're required to have a trapper's license to hunt raccoon and 'possum if you plan to use them for food or their fur. The trapper's license also covers all the other protected fur-bearing animals, including beaver, otter, mink, ring-tailed cat, badger, muskrat, skunk, civet cats (spotted skunk), fox, weasel, and nutria. We don't think of armadillos as game animals, but they do taste good. With adult supervision, the young naturalist can learn much from live-trapping certain of these animals in humane box traps that capture the animal without injury.

Bobcats and coyotes are also considered small game in other states, but Texans think of them first as predators. They will be treated in the following chapter.

County laws for Texas squirrel hunting vary, and in the prime habitats of East Texas there is often a spring hunt as well as the traditional fall/winter hunt. The typical bag limit, where one exists, is 10 with 20 in possession. But, be sure to verify this in the hunting regulations at the start of each season. For many counties, you will find the notation, "No closed season; no bag limit." Don't get too excited. Some of these counties have small populations of fox squirrels, and be assured you'll have a day's work cut out for you to come up with 10 squirrels.

You'll not find rabbits or armadillos featured in the TPWD regulations, but a hunting license is required to hunt them. Most often your rancher will welcome a rabbit hunt, as hunter control saves grass for his cattle. Armadillos can also pose a mild threat to cattle by their diggings. As you'll discover, armadillos are difficult to clean, but sportsmen who have eaten armadillos have relished every bite.

Raccoon hunting in East Texas is often done with hounds, a sport with limited access to outsiders. There's a virtual cult of 'coon hunters in this area. If you can wrangle an invite you'll have a night to remember.

'Coon hunters, with or without dogs, often take opossum as an accidental byproduct. Both the raccoon and opossum make reasonably good eating, although most of us don't deliberately hunt them for the table.

Throughout much of the state, 'coon hunting offers potential for a winter hunt after deer season. Such a hunt had best be made with explicit permission from the rancher or landowner. And, it's a smart move to notify the local game warden of your intended hunt area, because to be effective without dogs you'll be using powerful spotlights to find the 'coons in the trees. The nocturnal critters seldom come out during the day. 'Coons will respond at night to predator calls such as those discussed later in Chapter XI.

Often, 'coon skins have a good market value, and the conservation-minded sportsman will learn to skin the animal carefully. For this reason, as well as potential conflict with deer season, we discourage 'coon hunting until very cold weather sets in. It's a shame to take a scruffy, molting raccoon in warmer weather, unless you're starving or your camp is under full siege.

Trapping for Texas furbearing animals is a highly specialized, often commercially oriented endeavor. A surprisingly large number of Texans supplement their incomes through trapping, and our state has its fair share of furbearers. Fur value to Texas trappers and fur hunters has ranged from $6 million to $26 million annually, depending upon harvest and fur prices. Trapping for food and fur was once essential to prehistoric hunters and many of the Indian tribes that ranged Texas. It is still a vital tool of TPWD's wildlife management activities, necessary to obtain specimens for naturalist studies or to control the spread of diseases.

The most efficient trapping method utilizes the steel leg-holding trap, which has been in use in America for more than 200 years. It's this trap that gets the anti-trapping folks stirred up. Most sportsmen hunt in areas where the use of such traps would endanger other wildlife and livestock, so they are best left to the professional making a living from furs, conducting wildlife research, or controlling wildlife populations and disease.

But there is a place for live trapping for the dedicated sportsman, because it takes a high level of outdoor skill and knowledge of wildlife habits. The young naturalist can learn from firsthand observation, and the sportsman can gain a new skill helpful in the control of skunks, raccoons, squirrels, pets, and other small animals making a nuisance of themselves around the homestead.

SMALL GAME INSIGHTS

SQUIRREL TPWD regulations identify two of the eight species of squirrel found in Texas as game animals: the eastern gray squirrel, or cat squirrel, and the fox squirrel.

Of the nongame squirrels, three are fairly common. The thirteen-lined ground squirrel, so named for the alternating rows of spots and lines on its back, is seen in daylight in the Cross Timbers and Prairies, Rolling Plains, and High Plains ecological areas. The Mexican ground squirrel, also diurnal, is marked by nine rows of squared white spots on its back and is found in the Trans-Pecos, Edwards Plateau, and South Texas Plains. East Pineywoods sportsmen may catch a glimpse of eastern flying squirrels soaring from treetop to treetop just at sundown. These small, nocturnal squirrels live in Spanish moss country and river bottoms.

The eastern gray squirrel, found throughout the Pineywoods, is anything but small game when you talk numbers and dollars. More than 40 million gray squirrels are har-

Heaviest concentration of gray squirrels is in the eastern half of Texas.

vested nationally, and conservative hunter expenditure estimates are at the quarter-billion-dollar level. The gray squirrel fur is actually more of a salt and pepper blend. Texas gray squirrels are riverbottom dwellers known to frequent live oak hammocks. They adapt readily to urban sprawl if the right trees and foods are available. Their favorite diet consists of pin, red, blackjack, overcup and white oaks, elm, pecan, black gum, hackberry seeds, and even bark and insects. Calcium needs are met by gnawing on shed deer antlers, bones, and turtle shells. Gray squirrels will migrate if mast foods run low. Eighteenth-century accounts tell of migrations of these animals by the millions.

The fox squirrel in Texas often has a reddish black cast, although there are many color variations. The fox is larger than the gray, but both are similar in behavior, disposition, and shape. The fox squirrel ranges all the way across the state to about the 100th meridian, beyond which arid conditions limit suitable habitat. Fox squirrels are less picky than grays when it comes to food. Dietary flexibility explains their wider range in the state.

Fox squirrels are found over much of the state.

The principal breeding season for both fox and gray squirrels is very late in the year. Some game biologists suggest that the short days of late December trigger the process. Texas wildlife management experts have noted that gray squirrels breed throughout the year, with a peak in July and August in addition to the more typical winter solstice peak. Fox squirrels also have a second breeding peak as females come in estrus in June as well as December/January. The gestation period for both is about 45 days. Surprisingly, it takes the naked, newborn squirrels up to five weeks to open their eyes, and they're not weaned for eight or nine weeks.

Squirrels have a keen sense of smell, which is just as well, for they cannot remember for more than a few minutes where they've cached acorns. But they can sniff out a buried acorn even through a light layer of snow. The squirrel's short-term attention span is a good fact to file away in your long-term hunting memory.

When spooked, the gray squirrel's most common response is a mad dash through the tree canopies. He'll also flatten and freeze to the trunk or limb. Although the gray will play hide and seek, the fox squirrel is more apt to scamper around behind the trunk. Squirrels will sometimes miss a limb and fall. Like cats, they right themselves in mid-air, landing on their paws, and are seldom hurt in a fall.

The best times to hunt, as with most game animals, are early and late in the day. Overcast days will extend the hunting time.

RABBIT   No other state has the variety and number of rabbits Texas does, yet rabbit hunting is accorded no status whatsoever. Rabbits are not even classified or considered game animals in Texas, and few will admit to hunting them. However, there are a discernible number of sportsmen who know what great sport rabbit hunting holds, especially challenging with rifle or pistol. And we are acquainted with others who have surreptitiously sampled cottontail stew and found it enjoyable.

Texas has five distinct species of hare and rabbit: California jackrabbit, also known as black-tailed jackrabbit; Davis Mountains cottontail; Audubon cottontail, found throughout the western half of the state; swamp rabbit, found only in East Texas; and the ubiquitous cottontail, found everywhere but the upper reaches of the Trans-Pecos.

The difference between a hare and a rabbit is that hares are born with hair while rabbits are born naked. Jackrabbits are hares, with the typical large ears and feet. They prefer green vegetation and forbs when available, but exist nicely on range grasses, cactus, sagebrush, and mesquite. Jackrabbits prefer to dine in the open, relying on both their sense of hearing and speed for safety. This *al fresco* habit tends to concentrate them in pastures that have been overgrazed by livestock, so large numbers of jackrabbits are a tip-off to ranchers to move livestock off an overworked pasture.

Texas wildlife biologists estimate that a little more than 100 jackrabbits will eat as much range grass as a small cow, or as much grass as a half dozen sheep. Jackrabbits do their most serious damage to crops, even cotton. Needless to say, sorghum, wheat, and maize are choice for their ample appetites.

Jackrabbits usually feed early in the morning and late in the afternoon. On moonlit evenings, they'll often wait until midnight to begin feeding and continue till dawn. They don't like a lot of wind because of their reliance on hearing to detect danger. Rain slows their feeding. Dry,

Uncontrolled populations of jackrabbits can do major damage to Texas crops.

calm days are their favorites. Their extra-long ears pop up like radar antennae and rotate to focus on any threatening sound. If the fix is close they often hunker down dead still, ears pasted to their bodies; if distant, they'll sneak away. When pushed, jackrabbits will bound away at 40 miles per hour.

The infectious disease tularemia is a real and ever-present danger in handling all types of rabbits. Sportsmen are advised to wear rubber gloves while cleaning and skinning. The danger is not as great as once believed. The viral disease is now controlled by modern antibiotics and only rarely do people die from the infection. A rabbit with tularemia is usually sluggish. When cleaning, check the liver for yellowish spots, though often you can't tell. Tularemia is contracted most frequently through direct blood contact, notably when hands are scuffed up with nicks and open cuts. The usual symptoms are high fever with swollen lymph glands. When eating rabbit, cooking the meat to well-done eliminates any tularemia risk.

Hunting rabbits after a few heavy frosts greatly reduces the incidence of tularemia, because infected animals die and the insect carriers go into hibernation. That's why sportsmen in Texas prefer winter hunts after the regular deer season.

Jackrabbit mating behavior is similar to that observed in singles bars. It's a year-round affair exhibiting lots of chases, jumping up and down, and fighting between the sexes. Wildlife biologists tell us the purpose of the pursuit is to excite the female. The gestation period averages 40 days, with a typical Texas-sized litter of 14. We could be covered over with jackrabbits in no time at all.

In contrast, the cottontail and his cousin, the swamp rabbit, are neither as frenetic nor as prolific as the jackrabbit, though they too are year-round breeders in Texas. These less promiscuous cottontail cousins have litters averaging four after a shorter gestation period of just 26 to 27 days. Four litters a year is typical. Hares and rabbits are induced ovulators, meaning that ovulation occurs after copulation. This explains why they are available as a principal food source for virtually every carnivore.

Cottontails are more likely than jackrabbits to be up and around in the daytime, and they will often feed into mid-morning. The second major feeding period is from sunset to an hour or so after, longer on dark nights, in contrast to the jackrabbit habit. Cottontails prefer brushy cover, especially in cold weather months when their diet switches to woody plants. They are much slower than jackrabbits, and their ears and feet are also much shorter. The most distinctive field mark is apparent with their name; otherwise the body is grayish-brown on top, whitish on bottom

The swamp rabbit averages twice the weight of a cottontail, reaching six pounds, and has a much denser fur which comes in handy in his damper environment. Texans call swamp rabbits "canecutters," because cane is a favorite coastal habitat.

Injured rabbits emit a high-pitched squeal which predator hunters imitate in calls. The penetrating squeal, which some liken to a baby wailing, is repeated over and over and can be heard at long distances when the air is calm.

RACCOON   "That 'coon tugged the attic stair pull chain up after him, so we couldn't get the stairs down to go after the rascal," lamented the frustrated wife of a sportsman we know. She was experiencing what every outdoorsman eventually learns; 'coons test out well on the animal I.Q. scale, right under the higher primates.

A glance at a raccoon forepaw track tells the tale. The long, thin, human-looking fingers are somewhat opposed, like a thumb. Although the 'coon lacks a true thumb, the

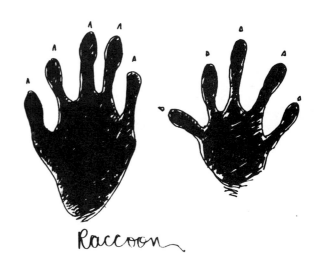

Raccoon

flexibility of the opposing fingers gives him all the dexterity of Fagin. The raccoon's tactile and discriminatory ability approaches that of man. They can actually snare flying insects. This means they have no problem opening latches or prying off garbage lids, which they learn to do rapidly. They use their extraordinary sense of touch to feel out food, both on land and under water.

Raccoons are everywhere in Texas, but are rarer in the Trans-Pecos where their cousin, the ringtail, holds forth.

Raccoons are capable of eating most anything, but they need to be close to water.

Every schoolchild can recognize a raccoon; its black mask over a whitish face has appeared in innumerable cartoons. The coat is bushy, ranging from gray to black on top. Every viewer of the old Davy Crockett TV series knows about the ringed tail, although the four to seven rings can be hard to see.

Raccoons have excellent hearing and night vision. The red eyeshine known to spotlighters comes from an iridescent membrane behind the eye. A similar membrane creates the luminosity noted in the eyes of many animals, such as cats and deer, although deer and most other animal eyes reflect green.

Raccoons are nocturnal, so these youngsters have been caught out after bedtime.

Many zoo visitors have come to the conclusion that raccoons always wash their food before eating. In truth, cleanliness is not an issue with the 'coon; his concern is inspecting and identifying the food by touching it carefully.

One thing is sure. The typical 'coon eats a lot of whatever he finds, poses a threat to crops, and is a nuisance to city dwellers who find their garbage spread across the lawn each morning. Thirty-pound 'coons are not uncommon in Texas, although the average is closer to 20 pounds; 'coons over 60 pounds have been taken.

The Texas breeding season is in February, gestation lasting from two months to an extreme of 70 days, with litters ranging from one to eight. Newborn 'coons arrive complete with 'coonskin coats, but it takes eight to 12 weeks before they're ready to leave the den, which is often a hollow tree.

Although males are polygamous, pair bonding does oc-

cur, and it's not unusual for a couple to hole up for the winter and the gestation period in the same den. Raccoons don't really hibernate, they just cuddle up until the weather is more to their liking.

The male raccoon's downcurved baculum (penis bone) enables him to maintain copulation for an hour or more. The baculum is found in all carnivores and primates except man.

It should be noted that raccoons can carry the rabies virus and, like dogs, can and do communicate the disease to man. Raccoons infected with rabies are unusually lethargic, so care should be taken in approaching a tired looking 'coon. Possums carry rabies, too, but the natural incidence is low.

RINGTAIL   Where the raccoon prefers dens in trees, his cousin the ringtail prefers rocky areas, cliffs, and stone walls. Their trim bodies make them much more agile than raccoons, as well as stronger climbers and jumpers. Ringtails are also nocturnal, like raccoons.

Ringtails are commonly found in the Trans-Pecos and Edwards Plateau.

The ringtail is easily identified by a tail as long as the rest of his body. The striking tail is usually black banded up to seven or nine times over white, and always ends in a bushy black tip. Another giveaway is a decidedly catlike face, with big eyes that appear even larger since they are outlined in white. Ringtails are much smaller and skinnier than 'coons, and they don't have quite the range of raccoons. Although they are scattered through Central Texas into the Pineywoods, they are concentrated in the Edwards Plateau and the Trans-Pecos.

If you're prowling about in South Texas and see a yellowish brown raccoon with a long, skinny tail and a snout that reminds you of an anteater, you've spotted a coatimundi. Coati favor wet lowlands and are relatively rare. They are great climbers and favor caves, because tree nests are hard to come by in their range. Like raccoons, they eat what they find. However, unlike their nocturnal cousins, the coati are active in daylight hours. The mating season is later, too, coming in April. The older, solitary males are excommunicated from bands of females and youngsters except during the mating period, when they get the Amazon treatment from the dominant females. They are usually on the endangered list, so don't hunt them.

OPOSSUM A pointy, white-cheeked face capped with leathery ears and a squat, gray body followed by a long, scaly tail make the opossum easy to identify, especially when he's hanging by his tail. Their five-toed tracks are even more strange, and the hind foot big toe often slants backwards. A big male 'possum can go to 10 pounds. The female has the kangaroo pouch of other marsupials.

Opossum

Thirteen days after mating, 13 tiny newborn 'possums try to grab ahold of one of 13 teats hidden in the marsupial pouch of the mother. Those that strike milk will pop out again in about 60 days ready to be weaned. At birth, the entire litter, which may run over 13, can fit comfortably in a tablespoon.

Female 'possums are tough ladies. A mamma 'possum can take a full jolt from a pit viper such as a rattlesnake and seemingly never even acknowledge it. If pressed, she'll play 'possum, feigning death with a catatonic trance. Experts now believe she is alert during this state. Long thought to be among the dumbest of animals, 'possums are grudgingly being accorded some credit in the I.Q. department.

Further confusing the folklorists, these cute little animals that date back about 11,000 years can and do kill

The main ingredient of a classic East Texas recipe for roast opossum and sweet 'taters.

one another over females in a fight complete with vicious slashing and biting. But, the female had better be in estrus or the victor may still be in trouble; female 'possums have been known to kill suitors if they weren't in the mood for love. A dominance dance usually precedes mating.

Roast 'possum and sweet 'taters is a time-honored dinner in East Texas. The main course is usually harvested at night as a byproduct of 'coon hunting.

ARMADILLO The real armadillo paradox is that this South American invader has been enthusiastically embraced by Texans as an unofficial state symbol. Texans are not wont to heap honors upon non-natives.

Armadillos are fighters that chase, kick, and jump at each other, but, like well-padded, helmeted football players, little comes of the aggressiveness. They are the shape of a football but twice the size and covered with a bony carapace, a dark brown shell.

The most important thing ignorant critics need to learn about armadillos is that the light pink meat is delicious. It tastes somewhat like pork only better, more tender, juicy, and nutritious.

Yes, there have been a few instances of leprosy in Lone Star armadillos, but not enough to spread panic. The leprosy bacterium found in armadillos is very similar to that which can infect humans, but don't be alarmed—medical

The unofficial state mascot roots
for his invertebrate dinner.

research has not shown that leprosy is transmitted by contact with armadillos.

Armadillos like to eat bugs, so their habitat must have soft, deep, moist earth suitable for nurturing insects. This diet limits their range in Texas to non-arid areas. And, since armadillos are not furbearers, they can't take cold weather, which can cause armadillo die-offs in the northern portions of their range.

As to the armadillo's impact on the natural ecosystem, the jury's still out. They do root up lots of invertebrates such as ants, termites, centipedes, roaches, and beetles, some of which are harmful to crops. But in the process they dig lots of burrows, which, in turn, have been known to trip livestock, causing injuries.

Another strike against these critters is that armadillos aren't considered an important food source, perhaps because cleaning one takes almost as long as dressing out a deer, and they yield much less meat.

A popular myth about armadillo breeding is that the female must be rolled over on her back. This is simply not true since, like most mammals, armadillos mate with the male mounting from the rear. Texas armadillos breed in the fall. Newborn armadillos look identical to their parents after 150 days of gestation. The typical litter size is four. All of the young in the litter are the same sex because they develop from a single fertilized egg that splits four ways early in development.

Cold weather keeps armadillos up and about during the day; otherwise they prefer the cool of a Texas night. Their eyesight is awful, hearing is average, but their sense of smell is superb. Like hogs, they can identify and sniff out tasty morsels well below the earth's surface.

Armadillos are natural scuba divers, capable of crossing a small stream by walking across the bottom. This may be another reason why people think of them as mini-tanks.

This unique little animal is the subject of intensive biomedical research to discover how they cope with high levels of carbon dioxide (CO_2) without fainting.

BEAVER Another natural scuba diver is the beaver, who can submerge himself for 15 minutes without benefit of compressed air or especially large lungs. The beaver's secret is his slow utilization of oxygen. Beavers fold their front paws against their chest when swimming, kicking with the webbed paws of their hindlegs and steering with their broad, flat tail. The tail can also serve as added propulsion, but the beaver prefers to paddle along.

Once seriously threatened, the beaver has made an amazing revival throughout North America and most of Texas. In fact, he's invaded some suburban Dallas areas and poses a threat to trees throughout North Central Texas.

An aquatic rodent—the largest rat—the beaver must have a water source. These furry engineers are capable of managing the water resources of their environment to an incredible degree. Texas beavers are cavemen, often burrowing into stream banks to create housing for their colonies, rather than building the typical stick lodge of the north. Beavers are monogamous and usually mate for life.

Beavers can get big—the record is more than 100

Beavers are a threat to
many urban areas in Texas.

pounds—and so pose a problem for the amateur trapper. Though their fur generally has a lower value in Texas than in northern states, beavers are sought by professional, properly licensed trappers.

RIVER OTTER Otters are often spotted by fishermen in the rivers and lakes of the Pineywoods and Gulf Prairies and Marshes. Cartoonists have caught the specific characteristics: bulb nose, cat-like whiskers, cylindrical body with short legs, and webbed feet followed by a long, fat, pointed tail.

Like beavers, otters make good parents and devote much time to training their offspring. As you'd guess, this is a sign of extraordinary intelligence. Otter mothers teach their young to hunt, fish, and swim.

Man has been able to take advantage of the otter's native intelligence and abilities. Since otters can stay underwater for three to four minutes, Europeans and Asians have used them for centuries in commercial fishing.

In addition to being smart, otters are well equipped with highly refined senses. Their whiskers help them zero in on fish vibrations to make them effective murky-water fishermen. Their sense of smell enables them to use scent markings to identify one another as well as locate certain foods. Their tactile ability is incredible, enabling them to handle tiny objects, even under water. Their hearing is acute, and they employ a wide range of communication sounds. About the only sense not top flight is their sight, although they see movement readily. As for mobility, they can easily overtake a bass.

River otters often entertain East Texas bass fishermen with their playful antics.

Sportsmen not big on steel leghold traps much prefer the otter as entertainment. Otters appear to love play, though some of this may be training for their young. Anyone who's watched the frolics of an otter family belly mudsliding over and over again into the water knows what we mean. Like circus seals, they'll bounce objects off their bulbous noses and play follow the leader.

MINK Every woman knows the lovely chocolate brown color of wild mink. White spots are located on the chin, throat, chest, and belly, and the trained eye can distinguish one mink from another by the fur pattern.

Minks are tabby cat-sized but weasel-like in appearance, with a long, sleek neck and furry tail. They are found throughout the eastern half of the state, but heaviest concentrations are in the Pineywoods, where they provide occasional excitement for trappers. Mink favor swampy terrain and are found near creeks and rivers.

All the jokes about a mink's sex life are true. Both the male and female are polygamous. The female often battles the male during mating, and, at best, it's a struggle for the male mink. If the female is not receptive, watch out, it's war. But, once they do manage, copulation can go on for hours.

Carnivores, mink will capture and kill anything within their capabilities and, as trappers know, they will feed on carrion.

When injured or threatened, mink stink up the atmosphere from anal gland emissions. Some find the aroma worse than a skunk's, but fortunately mink can't spray the vile discharge.

BADGER A fat, flat weasel, grizzled golden topaz on top with white cheeks, striped forehead and nose, and black triangular patches ahead of his ears, the badger confidently prowls the prairies and deserts of western Texas. He's the "foe that comes with fearless eyes" to all manner of rodents, and he wouldn't back down to a Sherman tank.

Keep your dog away from this squat fellow. His loose skin won't allow the dog's teeth to engage meat, but his razor sharp teeth and powerful jaws certainly will. This 15- to 20-pound animal can keep a pack of dogs at bay should they be foolish enough to get between him and his den.

Badgers are den animals, and all the important things of a badger's life center around his home, from birth of

Badgers prowl much of West Texas and are known for their daunting ferocity.

young, to food storage, to hunt headquarters. The typical badger will work from six or seven den sites as he hunts an area. Dens can be legbreakers to livestock, which places the badger on the Texas rancher's hit parade.

Badgers are world-class diggers, and in soft soil it takes a backhoe to stay with them. Most dens are scooped out as a badger goes after a ground squirrel in its small burrow. The larger burrow thus created is used every so often as an outpost for a future hunt. That's why only one in six dens is occupied.

Badgers nap during the day and hunt at night with the help of their keen sense of smell. Badgers are found throughout West Texas and the South Texas plains all the way to the coast.

MUSKRAT Contrary to the melodic promises of "Muskrat Love," these overblown field mice can get downright nasty when provoked. All five pounds of furry fury can surprise a sportsman. Their long, razor-keen incisors make a switchblade seem tame.

A broad head, rusty brown coat, flat sided rattail, and webbed hind feet identify the muskrat. They really do ramble, sidling slowly about the marsh, usually at night when they're easy prey for predators and trappers. But, thanks again to muskrat love, they have a high reproduction rate. Given proper habitat, they are one of our better demonstrations of a renewable resource.

Their soft, velvety fur and the ease with which they're trapped make the muskrat the premier furbearing animal in North America, with market values of pelts in the $25 million range annually. Neighboring Louisiana is the top muskrat pelt-producing state, although better quality furs are obtained in northern climates.

Creeks and rivers, marshes and ditches provide ideal habitat, so muskrats are found from the Canadian River all along the Red River down the Gulf Coast to the Trinity River. Muskrats will build domed lodges about two feet high or occupy dens set in river banks. If times get tough in the dead of winter, they'll eat their home, the marsh vegetation they used to construct their lodge.

Like armadillos and beavers, muskrats are natural scuba divers capable of 15-minute dives. A high tolerance to carbon dioxide makes this possible, along with the ability to quickly pump a surplus of oxygen back into the system upon reaching the surface.

The musk in the name comes from the musky odor produced by both sexes during breeding season. Natural musk oil was an important fixative in perfumery, serving the same purpose for humans as for muskrats—sexual attraction. We get the full name from the Indian word "musquash."

SKUNK Texas is blessed with an abundance of skunks in at least six fragrances: striped, Eastern and Western spotted, hooded, hog-nosed, and Gulf Coast hog-nosed.

To the sportsman, the most significant skunk charac-teristic has to do with its vile smelling musk and how to avoid being sprayed by same.

Technically, the musk is a potent chemical compound, butylmercaptan, which if chugalugged would knock you out. It can cause a painful burning sensation if sprayed into the eyes, but will not cause permanent damage. As you would treat any chemical contamination, flush affected eyes with water ASAP.

Skunk musk is stored in two scent glands surrounded by the sphincter muscles of the anus. The skunk can compress the sphincter to fire the contents of one or both glands out to 15 feet or more from nipples that protrude from the anus. The skunk can aim by changing the direction of the nipples and so can spray to the side and even to the front, and across an arc of up to 45 degrees. All this adds up to a sure hit within 15 feet or so.

The atomized spray permeates the area, and if you pass through it even at some distance downwind, the taint will impregnate your clothes. It's so potent skunks even avoid getting it on themselves. Spraying can be prevented by pressing the tail firmly against the anus. However, we don't recommend this maneuver for the amateur naturalist.

Skunks can neither see nor hear particularly well, but have little to fear from other animals or humans. Ever so often, one will not sneak away at your approach, which can lead to a confrontation that you will lose unless you

Trappers would avoid this skunk because of the wide white stripe. You should too, for other reasons.

take immediate evasive action. If the skunk starts growling and stamping stiffened front legs, leave. Leave more rapidly if the skunk turns its rear toward you, arches its back, and raises its tail. The spray follows very quickly.

If you do get sprayed, scrub your skin with tomato juice before bathing and bury your clothes in soft earth for at least 24 hours. It's best to forget where you buried your skunk rags.

Striped skunks are the most common and are found in every Texas county. Trappers rate the pelts on the lack of white. A pelt with no white except for around the neck and head area is judged #1. A wide, white stripe is undesirable.

The spotted skunks are distributed as their names indicate—Western spotted are in the western part of the state, and Eastern spotted in the eastern portion. These are smaller than the striped skunk and much more agile. The spotted skunk often does a handstand when threatened and can walk for some distance on his forelegs, ready to spray. The Western gets his fair share of cottontails in the winter, and all skunks are good ratters. As a whole, skunks are beneficial in that they help control insects that are potentially harmful to crops. However, they do raid quail nests and can be rabies carriers, as can all carnivores. Spotted skunks are often called civet cats in many parts of Texas.

The hooded skunk looks a lot like the striped but is trimmer and has an exceptionally long tail. Also, from a respectful distance, look for a ruff of longer hairs that forms his hood. He's found only in the Trans-Pecos.

The hog-nosed skunk typically has a wide, white band of fur down its back, spreading onto the tail. He's found across the southern portions of the state from the Trans-Pecos to the southern Pineywoods. A close relative, the Gulf Coast hog-nosed, or Eastern hog-nosed, is found where you'd expect, and he is the largest skunk on the continent. His white stripe is narrower than that of the hog-nosed.

Contrary to popular observation, skunks are not socializers, although winter dens can shelter a number of skunks. Males just don't like other males.

FOX Texas has four foxes: the red, gray, swift, and desert, also known as the kit fox.

The gray fox is found in almost every county with the exception of the northern tier of the Panhandle above the Canadian break. The swift fox inhabits these northerly counties as well as the majority of the High Plains ecological area.

The red fox is most populous in northeastern counties

The red fox, which ranges over most of northeastern and central Texas, is one of our most beautiful wild animals.

The gray fox, found through most of
the state, often surprises the sportsman
with his talent for climbing.

and is found throughout the Cross Timbers and Prairies, Rolling Plains, and High Plains. The desert or kit fox is found just in the Trans-Pecos. He has extraordinarily large ears and is much smaller than the red and gray foxes. The kit fox is more naive than the other foxes and is easily reduced in number during any predator control campaigns. Uniquely adapted for desert life, he has developed hair under his feet that enables him to scoot over soft sand. His speed and agility enable him to run down the desert rodents which are his major food source.

Most biologists believe the red fox was introduced for hunting, primarily in the southern U.S. and in Eastern and Central Texas. He is a favorite of trappers since his pelt is usually in demand.

Foxes make good parents, staying with their pups until they are ready to hunt on their own, usually in October of their first year. The vixen will return to her den periodically to nurse her pups while the male continues to hunt, bringing prey back to the den or safely stowing it nearby.

Foxes are territorial and mark boundaries with scent, not only to warn off competition but also as a guide to the home range. They should be viewed as beneficial by ranchers and farmers, because they control populations of rabbits and rodents and their pelts are a valuable resource.

Look for gray fox dens in brush piles, rocky areas, even hollow trees. Red foxes tend to dig their dens, and also take over those dug by badgers. Sometimes more than one fox family will inhabit the same den. A great treat for the young naturalist is to observe foxes at play near a den. Apparently foxes even play as adults, a rarity in the survival-oriented animal world. Foxes are intelligent and have earned their reputation for craftiness by maneuvers to throw off pursuing hounds, for example, taking to water to hide their scent.

WEASEL Texas has only one type of weasel, and, unfortunately, it's not the one everybody loves, *M. ermines*, better known to the female of our species as ermine. In true Texas tradition, we hold title to the big one, the long-tailed weasel, largest of the North American species at 13 to 14 inches in length. A smallish head, elongated neck, and long tail are supported by short legs.

Lone Star weasels stay a mousy brown with yellowish underparts all year, in contrast to Yankee long-tailed weasels which turn a lovely white. Look for a spot between the eyes and a band on each side of the head between ear and eye.

Weasels are fantastic ratters. Their body design equips them to track pocket gophers and ground squirrels in their tunnels or burrows. They are courageous street fighters, very quick and aggressive when cornered. They fear no enemy and can whip much larger prey. Coyotes and foxes can usually defeat a weasel and will bite off its head and leave the carcass uneaten, apparently acknowledging the weasel's competition for prey. Other animals with far fewer skills are accorded plaudits in proverbs, but not the weasel, who takes a bad rap: "weasel words," "weasel-faced," "weasel it out of him."

NUTRIA Nutria in Texas should serve as a warning to those who see no danger in introducing exotics to a natural ecosystem. Although fur farms in Louisiana make money from an annual harvest of some one million nutria hides, nutria are pests in Texas. They damage crops and

Nutria have invaded Texas from Louisiana and
pose a threat to earthen stock tank dams.

are a constant threat to the earthen dams of stock tanks that provide life-giving water not only to livestock, but to all game in times of drought. To worsen the situation, feral nutria pelts have a limited value in the fur market.

The nutria resembles a large, fat rat with a long, scaly tail. They have webbed hind feet since they are basically aquatic mammals. Their guard hair fur is long and coarse. Only belly hair is used in the fur trade.

Con artists played a major role in introducing nutria to the United States during the '30s, touting them as the original weed eater. In fact, large numbers of nutria can eat a lot of plants, creating problems when they munch crops instead of weeds. Nutria are effectively controlled by cold weather in northern states, but not in Texas.

In their native Argentina, nutria are controlled by caymens, relatives to alligators, but not many Texas stock tanks have native populations of alligators. Nutria usually dig large burrows up to 10 inches in diameter, about four feet into earthen dams. Enough of these holes and the dam begins to leak or erode.

Nutria have spread to the edge of the Edwards Plateau and Rolling Plains. In their prime habitat of marsh lands, they drive out the much more desirable muskrat.

PORCUPINE Porcupines were almost omitted from the *Sportsman's Guide* for lack of a place to logically insert them. Most wouldn't consider them a small game animal, and who ever heard of trapping for a porcupine coat? Since they are vegetarians it wouldn't be accurate to classify them with the predators, although many a predator has been bested by the porcupine's famous quills. So, we've stuck them here, hidden away after the lowly nutria. This is a bit unfair, since they are very interesting animals ranging throughout most of West Texas. They are adaptable to a wide range of habitats and should be reckoned with carefully.

The porcupine is the second largest of the rodents in America, a butterball weighing up to 20 pounds. In Texas, he's lighter in color than porcupines not exposed to so much sun and he may actually appear golden from a distance. He turns a slightly darker brown in winter.

Porcupine quills make the animal unique to our continent and also provide him with the best self defense of small mammals. The quills start from in front of the eyes and extend almost to tail tip. When another animal is foolish enough to lay siege, he can erect all quills simultaneously thanks to a muscle layer over his entire back.

These quills have tiny barbs that not only hold them in the attacker's body once stuck, but also function to work the quill deeper as the victim's muscles twitch. No wonder these vegetarians are held responsible for a lot of kills on coyotes, bobcats, dogs, even cougars and cattle. They won't kill you, but with a hide full of quills you may wish you were dead. Contrary to popular myth, porcupines cannot aim and fire their quills like missiles.

Porcupines can't see well, but they don't really have to.

Porcupine quills can disable
a hunting dog or even the hunter.

Their sense of smell is acute and their hearing is not bad. When threatened, you'll often see them rear up on their hind legs looking for all the world like a miniature bear. When they really get mad and feel trapped, they'll turn their tail to the idiot attacker and begin thrashing. This ensures that quills are driven well into the offender's hide. They are nearly impossible to extract without a surgeon's help. We don't know of many vets accomplished at quill removal, so keep your quail dogs away.

PREPARATION FOR

THE SMALL GAME HUNT

Unless you're on a trapping expedition, preparing for a small game hunt is blissfully easy. A scope-sighted .22 rifle or small gauge shotgun, sharp pocket knife, and game vest will do the trick. Since the .22 is often used by youngsters, we prefer a bolt action with a 1–3 power variable scope for squirrels or iron sights. Don't buy a cheap .22 scope; go ahead and invest in decent optics. Also, install a strap for carrying and steadying the offhand shot.

For squirrel hunting, .22 hollow point shorts are ideal. They will kill cleanly, mess up less meat and make minimal racket.

For rabbit hunting, most elect a .410 or other small gauge shotgun. Hunting rabbits with a .22 rifle or pistol adds greatly to the sport and has developed many an outstanding big game hunter.

For 'coon and 'possum hunting, either an open sighted, single shot .22 or single barrel .410 is a good choice. Both are light to carry, durable, safe, and effective for taking treed game.

DOG SELECTION

"He hauled out the bleached skeletons of two grown coons and dropped them at the feet of his friend. After he had descended, he said, 'I'll still admit that coons won't take up a dead tree, but this tree was not dead and them coons weren't dead neither when they clumb it. I told you Bowie and Bonham were the best cold-nosed hounds that ever worked a cold trail.'"

Jeff Porter, *THE COLD-NOSED HOUNDS*
Quoted by J. Frank Dobie in *TALES OF OLD TIME TEXAS*

Porter was typical of the dedicated 'coonhound runner—a passionate exponent of his dogs' treeing ability and melodious voice, and of the breed that produced them. A sure way to get into a wrangle is to claim superiority for one breed over another. But, as a practical matter, any of the six mainline hound breeds, and a lot of others, produce great hunters.

The only American Kennel Club recognized breed is the black and tan. The redbone, bluetick, English, treeing Walker, and Plott are classified as types rather than true breeds, even though they may be purebred in the sense of having a canine family tree going back several generations.

Black and Tan 'Coonhound

The black and tan is to small game hunting what the black Lab is to waterfowling. A strong performer in the woods, relentless on the trail, agile, fast, and aggressive in pursuit, his booming, mellifluous voice is thrilling to hear when he's chop-barking "treed." Yet, at home, like the Lab, the black and tan is a sweetheart, a gentle and lovable companion.

The black in his name comes from the glossy ebony head and saddle blanket set off by the buttery tan coloration of feet, legs, and underparts. He's a 50- to 60-pound dog with short hair ideal for Texas thickets; he's not overlarge.

The black and tan is an excellent choice for squirrel hunting and can be trained to tree squirrels in the day and 'coons and 'possums at night without getting confused. For those so inclined, the black and tan is a fine hound for cougars and bobcats, feral hogs, even black bear.

Black and tans were originally introduced by Virginia fox hunters from English strains for fox hounds. The black and tans that produced the separate American

The black and tan 'coonhound is a favorite of East Texas hunters.

breed were thought to have been rejects, not good enough for the elite sport of fox hunting. Subsistence hunters soon found these so-called rejects worth their weight in gold for finding good eating, and from there the selective breeding started to produce a hound with excellent treeing capability. Bloodhound blood was introduced to increase the black and tan's trailing qualities, so by the early 1900s a great hound emerged but, of course, no greater than *your* favorite bluetick, Walker, redbone, or Heinz 57.

Beagle and Basset Hounds

These two hounds are top choices for rabbit hunters. Both dogs make great pets, affectionate and good natured. The basset, though close to the ground, can weigh up to 70 pounds. The smaller beagle only stands from 13 to 15 inches tall at the shoulder. The beagle is also used for some pheasant hunting and, with training, he can be developed into an effective squirrel dog.

But it's chasing rabbits that's made the beagle the most popular hound in the U.S. The beagle's relative lack of speed is an asset in rabbit hunting. The rabbit tends to keep moving ahead of the dog and to circle within its known and limited range, giving the hunter a good chance to ambush the circling rabbit.

The beagle is easy to train, making him a wonderful choice for children. He's almost ready to hunt on instinct alone and will respond readily and willingly to any instruction that comes his way.

Beagles are the premier dog for cottontail hunting.

WARDROBE AND GEAR SELECTION Rabbit hunters will want to focus on the type of gear favored by quail hunters, since terrain and late season weather conditions are the same and lots of walking is called for.

Squirrel hunters spend a lot of time on stand and need to consider the additional warmth requirements of staying absolutely still as well as camouflaged.

Raccoon hunters have the additional concern of busting through brush in the dark, so durable clothing becomes a major issue, as does footgear. Hunting boots with rubber soles are good choices in 'coon country.

SMALL GAME HUNTER'S CHECKLIST
Hunting license
Furbearer trappers' licenses
.22 rifle—scoped with sling
.22 ammunition
.410 shotgun—full or modified
.410 shells—high velocity #6s
Game bag/vest
Sunscreen
Hat—camouflaged
Head net (squirrel)
Chamois shirts—camo
Insulated vest—camo
Brush pants
Rubber-bottomed boots (raccoons and squirrels)
Regular upland game boots (rabbit)
Silk inner socks
Wool socks
Game shears
Pocket knife
Zip-type plastic bags
Rubber gloves for cleaning rabbits
Rain gear
Squirrel calls
Alarm clock
OPTIONAL:
Dog whistle
Dog food/water/pan
Spotlight for night hunts

TECHNIQUES THE
EXPERTS USE

SQUIRREL HUNTING TIPS The bag usually fills up faster if the hunt permits scouting time. The hunter can set up a stand near a nut-bearing tree and often harvest several squirrels from one well-hidden location. This is where the .22 shorts come in handy, since they won't disturb other squirrels working the nuts for very long. After a well-placed shot, stay still; mentally mark where the squirrels fall and pick them up after you're satisfied the area is devoid of stew meat.

When scouting, look for nut scraps littering the ground during early fall. In winter, switch emphasis to looking for den trees. Good binoculars are helpful in determining if a den is in use, because you can spot signs of use around the entrance. Use a call in scouting, either a mouth call or bellows that imitate a squirrel bark. Your objective is to get the squirrel to answer back so you can pinpoint his location. Don't try to call him to you like a turkey or varmint.

Many squirrel hunters combine a still hunt with a scouting expedition. Still hunting requires good woodsmanship, because the rascals can spot movement or pick up the sound of a snapped twig at quite a distance. Exercise patience, stopping frequently to observe and call. Mark good nut tree locations for follow-up on the next hunt. Don't go plowing through on this hunt if you can return here before dawn the following day.

A majority of still-hunting squirrel hunters selects a .410 no matter how qualified they might be as good Indian hunters. You're going to scare a few squirrels across the tree limbs, setting up shots that will test your wing-shooting ability.

Hunting squirrels with a dog can be a lot of fun, whether you use a hound bred to tree game or a breed such as the beagle who learns the hard way. A dog barking treed will immobilize a squirrel; the hunter's chore is to spot the quarry, not always an easy task.

Texas has a split squirrel season: one in the month of May and another in early fall lasting into mid-winter. Being in the Texas woods in May or October has to be one of the sportsman's most enjoyable experiences.

RABBIT HUNTING TIPS Cottontails and jackrabbits can give the serious rifle shooter all he needs to perfect his sport, and the former will fulfill the gourmand. Jackrabbits can be eaten, and many have found their way into stews, but the tender cottontail is the much preferred table fare.

Rabbits and hares also like brushy habitats and edges. A cottontail will readily utilize burrows, but this is rare for a jackrabbit. Jacks prefer forms, body-sized shallow depressions dug under cover. Jackrabbits are comfortable in the wide open since, like antelope, they have good eyesight and great speed.

Cottontails are more secretive and more apt to have figured out an escape route than jackrabbits. Jacks bound away when startled, seldom pausing. In contrast, you'll often see a cottontail stop to evaluate the situation, unless beagles are on to him. When he stops, the cottontail may well have an escape route in mind, since he is very territorial and very well acquainted with that territory.

Since rabbits tend to be late sleepers, after staying up most of the night, "kicking 'em up" is a time-honored method of rabbit hunting, well suited for the stamina of youth. Kicking them up with the help of healthy beagles or basset hounds is a lot more productive for the senior sportsman. In Texas, when landowners and game wardens are in accord, spotlighting rabbits at night provides good hunt training for youngsters. Of course, spotlighting with any firearm is strictly against the law during deer season.

The dog hunter needs to find a bit of cover and wait out the circling rabbit. The rabbit will often turn at the outer limit of his known world and attempt to lose the hound by doubling back. If the hunter has an option, it's smart to get above the brush or otherwise attempt to establish a reasonable field of fire from a stand.

The hunter more interested in a limit than in perfecting rifle skills should select a shotgun, the lighter the better. Shots are at close range and a 10-gauge is not necessary. Field loads of #6s out of any shotgun are fine.

RACCOON HUNTING TIPS Lone Star 'coon hunters fall into three main categories: those with dogs, those without, and those defending property. There is a surprisingly large contingent of 'coonhound hunters in Texas, concentrated in the Pineywoods. Canton's First Monday market—held the first weekend in any month—is as good a place as any to make contact. Down on Dog Alley, you'll find all manner of 'coon dogs to admire and you'll hear a wealth of tales about their prowess. This is a sport rich in tradition, mostly centered on the hounds.

Most serious 'coon hunting happens at night. For hunters following the hounds at night, important equipment includes a headlight, brush-resistant clothes, and rubber-bottom boots. It's going to get wet and scratchy before it's all over.

In other parts of Texas, the tradition is to spotlight the 'coons, beaming a powerful light into suitable trees hoping to pick up the den tree filled with bright red eyes. Another tactic, more fully explored in Chapter XI, is to call raccoons. This is especially effective in more open terrain.

In all parts of the state, including heavily populated areas, raccoons can challenge man's domain, turning attics into 'coon dens and garbage cans into messy dining rooms. In more remote areas, 'coons wage constant war against camps and camp equipment. Hunters with deer feeders will also find raccoons a problem. Low fences that keep livestock from deer feed will only amuse raccoons.

In good 'coon country, the hound-running sportsman needs to seek out the lowest, marshiest terrain, because sometime during the night the 'coons will go to water. Often this will not happen till past midnight.

Although late summer 'coon hunting is best in terms of concentrated populations, the hunter or trapper interested in skins should plan hunts during the December and January fur season, when the fur is at its finest, and times don't conflict with deer season. Fur season usually ends January 31.

Opossums are often bagged during 'coon hunts, and many Pineywoods residents have been known to capture the critters for pen fattening on corn.

TRAPPING The art and science of the professional trapper is beyond the ken and scope of typical sportsmen, but the expert outdoorsman should have a basic understanding.

First, for animals designated by TPWD as furbearers, licenses are required up the chain of distribution from the trapper to wholesale and retail fur dealers. Landowners or their agents are specifically exempted from the law if depredation or nuisance can be proved. F. Lee Bailey would've loved these cases. Not many landowners are hauled into court by complaining furbearers, so the point is moot. The landowner is not supposed to *retain* the pelt of a furbearer during the open season unless he has a trapper's license.

A separate license is required for individuals selling live furbearing animals. This furbearing animal propagation license can be used only for sales made to properly licensed or permitted buyers. *Never* try to keep a wild animal as a pet.

There are other detailed rules, and changes are possible year to year, so we urge consultation with TPWD before setting out to make your fortune as a Texas trapper or fur hunter.

TPWD sets forth a few conditions in favor of the furbearers, such as prohibiting the shooting of an otter or any furbearer from a boat or hunting with the use of explosives. The most important law requires that all traps be checked at least every 36 hours; more frequent checking is recommended.

The professional trapper avoids setting traps where domestic animals roam, and TPWD speaks up for kids by making it illegal to trap within 400 yards of schools. There are also specific provisions to allow for the unlicensed transport of suspected diseased furbearing animals to public health facilities. All sportsmen are urged to report any suspected diseased animal to TPWD.

Live trapping can come in handy even in metro areas. Often the local animal control office will have a variety of commercial box traps available for no charge, except for a refundable deposit. If you have a choice, take the oldest trap because the shine of a new one may spook game.

Following are a few bait ideas for live trapping:

1. Fish is the all-time favorite, attracting otters, raccoons, armadillos, skunks, mink, and weasels.
2. Sweet corn, honey, watermelon, and fried bacon are raccoon favorites.
3. Fresh vegetables, such as lettuce, cabbage or apples, work for rabbits, opossum, and muskrat.

4. Fresh peanuts, cereals, grains, and peanut butter with molasses will attract squirrels and gophers.
5. Chicken entrails appeal to a variety, including skunks, mink, 'possum, turtles, and weasels.
6. Cantaloupe and really ripe bananas turn on nutria.
7. Would you believe cheese for mice and rats?

FIELD DRESSING

Squirrel

Game shears and a sharp folding knife make this a snap:

1. Make an incision across the squirrel just under the tail. Clip off all four lower legs with the shears.
2. Put your foot on the tail and pull steadily until the hide comes over the head and off the front legs.
3. Peel off the hide on haunches. Clip off the head.
4. Remove entrails and wash thoroughly.

The game shears make it that much faster, but your field knife will easily do the whole job.

Rabbit

A thin skin makes rabbits even easier to clean. We advise wearing rubber gloves. Make a shallow cut across the center of the back, grasp the loose skin, and pull in opposite directions. Cut off the head and legs, remove entrails, and wash.

Raccoon

If your 'coonhound hasn't chomped the hide you may wish to case skin your raccoon. This method works for all the Texas furbearers except beaver and badger. It also works for bobcats and coyotes. Case skinning works best when the animal is still warm and is the preferred technique for obtaining a quality hide.

CASE SKINNING

1. Dry the pelt if necessary. Rubbing it with an old towel speeds the process.
2. Using a parachute cord, tie the 'coon's hind legs to your deer pole at a height that allows you to work it easily. Slit the skin around each leg, then down the inside of the legs and in front of the sex organs.
3. Pull the tail up and start cuts about ¾-inch up from the vent on the underside of the tail. These cuts encircle the vent and join the first cuts. On many furbearers, especially and including mink, there are vile smelling glands just above the anus. Don't cut into these or your olfactory glands will be highly offended.
4. Start pulling the skin casing off the carcass. The tailbone may take a little persuading, but it will work loose. Cut off the front feet and work the skin off the legs.

5. When the hide is down around the head take it slowly. With an extra sharp knife cut off the ear cartilage close to the head, and be careful not to cut the lips and ears.

6. Slip the skin casing over a board, flesh side out. It makes the job easier to let the fat harden. Allow the skin to sit for a while in a cool place. Scrape away all the fat. This is not an easy task with a Texas fat cat raccoon. A spoon or butter knife works well. This is called fleshing.

7. Let the skin dry fur side out by tacking it to an improvised stretching board until it's completely dry, perhaps a week. Remove and continue to dry in an airy place.

8. Hide stretching boards obviously need to be of different dimensions. A raccoon board is about a yard long, 2 x 10. Consult a professional skinner for other board size suggestions and for techniques beyond the normal scope of the sportsman. Consultation with a professional skinner or fur buyer is especially recommended if you plan to sell a legally taken pelt and want to ensure highest quality and value of the pelt.

After skinning, proceed to gut the raccoon much as you would a deer.

Hunter Safety for Youngsters

TEXAS HUNTER

EDUCATION PROGRAM

The Sportsman's Guide to Texas contains a wealth of background information for the young person about to enter the state's mandatory Hunter Education Program. The following material focuses on firearm training, but the course will cover many other topics, including wildlife identification, hunter responsibility, and conservation issues. The student familiar with the material in this guide will be well primed for the formal course, but it should be noted that this is not a substitute for the textbook work and hands-on training of the state's Hunter Education Program.

If you are developing a young sportsman, you should make sure the youth is enrolled in the mandatory Texas Hunter Education Program. Hunting instruction programs are located throughout the state, and you can easily locate a class convenient for you. Even if you have already taken the basic course, we recommend you take it again with your son or daughter because the shared learning experience is most rewarding and is something the youngster will remember for the rest of his or her life.

The course does a great job in helping instill hunter ethics and firearm responsibility, including instruction in gun handling, safe hunting methods, survival, and basic first aid. The young sportsman will come away with an enhanced sense of conservation, game management, and courtesy. Some of the courses offer expanded material on Texas game animals, poisonous plants, snakes and insects, and even live firing on a nearby range. Other state-sponsored programs include muzzleloading and archery basics.

Each successful student 12 years of age or older is issued a TPWD hunter education identification card, honored in other states which require hunter education prior to issuing a hunting license.

To locate a Texas Hunter Education Program instructor, contact your local game warden or call the TPWD Hunter Education Section toll free at 1-800-792-1112.

The Texas Game Warden Association sponsors many special hunts for orphaned youngsters each year. This outstanding continuing effort to teach young people gun safety and outdoor skills was pioneered in 1960 by Gene Ashby, who died in 1978. Gene was a TPWD game warden who understood that orphans would benefit from the outdoor experience, and that Hill Country herds overpopulated with does could be thinned out in the hunting instruction process.

His idea was embraced by sensitive ranchers who first opened their gates to the orphans and their volunteer guides. Operation Orphans, Inc., is now headquartered at Camp Gene Ashby in the Edwards Plateau county of Mason on the Llano River. It has bunkhouse facilities and extensive land of its own and is one of Texas' finest TPWD/rancher/hunter cooperative ventures.

Any sportsman with access to small game hunting can do for their own or other children what's being done at Camp Gene Ashby on a smaller, but no less rewarding scale.

Although every young sportsman needs to take the Hunter Education Program, you can begin to teach the basics of safe and responsible firearm handling. This will reinforce the learning process and build the youth's self confidence.

It's best to seek the TPWD professional to train your child if you are not an accomplished shot, fully confident of your gun skills. For most, this is especially good advice in teaching the use of a shotgun, since bad habits can quickly be developed. But, if you've been well trained and you hit where you aim, it's really fun and rewarding to teach the use of the rifle.

Safe firearm handling is the obvious key. Start by teaching the importance of controlling muzzle direction, that loaded guns demand respect, and that the hunter must be absolutely sure of the target and what is around and beyond it.

We find it helpful to begin with an unloaded airgun, in a model that has an action that can be left open. Start with the action open and safety on. Again, emphasize safe barrel direction. Show the various ways to carry a firearm safely—cradle, double hand, trail, shoulder, elbow, and with a sling. For instance, demonstrate why you would not use a shoulder carry with someone behind you. If *you* don't know the benefits and dangers of these carrying styles, you need the Hunter Education course yourself. Point out that the firearm must always be unloaded in a vehicle.

The air gun will allow you to teach a child how to keep the finger off the trigger and the safety on until ready to fire. It also allows you to reinforce the importance of having the action open when the gun is handed over to someone else, and to emphasize respect for the firearm.

Most sportsmen discourage their children from using toy guns because they tend to create precisely the wrong attitude toward firearms. Unfortunately, modern electronics have led to a proliferation of laser type, star wars games for children that even award points for "killing" opponents. And violent television programs don't help.

STEP ONE Obtain copies of the "Ten Commandments of Shooting Safety" from a local game warden or directly from TPWD. Give one to each student for his very own. Encourage your trainees to learn the commandments by heart. At their age, they're used to homework assignments.

Ten Commandments of Shooting Safety

I. Treat every gun with the respect due a loaded gun. This is the cardinal rule of gun safety.

II. Guns carried into camp or home must always be unloaded, taken down, and have actions open; guns should always be encased until reaching the shooting area.

III. Always be sure barrel and action are clear of obstruction.

IV. Always carry your gun so that you can control the direction of the muzzle, even if you stumble. Keep the safety on until you are ready to shoot.

V. Be sure of your target before you pull the trigger.

VI. Never point a gun at anything you do not want to shoot.

VII. Unattended guns should be unloaded; guns and ammunition should be stored safely beyond reach of children and careless adults.

VIII. Never climb a tree or fence with a loaded gun.

IX. Never shoot at a flat, hard surface or the surface of water.

X. Do not mix gunpowder and alcohol.

Review the commandments point by point, amplifying where you think it's appropriate. Here are some suggested comments you might add to each rule.

I. The first commandment, "Treat every gun with the respect due a loaded gun," covers all others. Keep the gun on safety until you're ready to shoot, though the safety does not take the place of responsible gun handling.

II. Stress that no one, including adults, is allowed to enter camp unless the action is open, gun unloaded. An open action is synonymous with courteous behavior. Actions should be open and guns unloaded in vehicles. The more respect you show for safety, the more you will be accepted and respected in camp.

III. Before going to the range or to hunt, check the barrel from the breech end, model allowing. (Never look into the barrel, but do observe from the side if there is any chance that the barrel may be clogged.) Check the action. Double check proper ammunition. Teach how to identify the caliber on the barrel and on the base of a cartridge. Even a partial obstruction, like a gun patch, may make the gun explode.

IV. While afield, point your barrel away from other hunters. Always have the safety on.

V. Be sure of a totally safe zone of fire around and

beyond any target before deliberately aiming, taking the gun off safe, and firing. Always be aware of other people, dogs under low-flying birds, buildings, telephone wires, water—anything you do not intend to shoot.

VI. This commandment, "Never point a gun at anything you do not want to shoot," is another cardinal point. Don't use the scope on a gun to spot game—you could be pointing at another person, and this practice brands you as unsafe, unreliable, and discourteous.

VII. Unattended, loaded guns are unsafe. Form the habit of unloading and leaving the action open.

VIII. Deliberately unload guns before crossing fences or ditches so you're definitely safe. If alone, place the gun flat on the ground and slip it carefully under a fence when crossing. Avoid sliding the gun on dirt or mud that will clog the barrel and/or action. With a partner, hand over safe guns one at a time, barrels pointed up.

IX. Flat, hard surfaces, water surfaces, and rocks are unsafe backgrounds because bullets may ricochet wildly.

X. Drunks and drug abusers are deadly, oblivious to what's safe or unsafe. They are unwelcome in our camps and should never be allowed near firearms.

The commandments, perhaps in a slightly different wording, are widely disseminated with every gun purchased and we've heard them all our lives. But, you'll win money every time if you bet experienced gun handlers to recite them, or even paraphrase. We just don't keep such long lists in our minds. We've noticed that the best way to ingrain safe gun handling is repeated review with each new firing range or camp experience, stressing what's important in the context of the moment—"We're approaching camp, let's unload, open action." The statement you can make over and over again is . . . *"Always point the muzzle in a safe direction."*

STEP TWO Before proceeding with this step you need to determine your young shooter's master eye.

Check for master eye control by having the student form a circle between index fingers and thumbs of both hands. Select a small but visually distinct object a few yards away. Have the student keep both eyes open, form the circle, then face the target head on and swing the finger circle up to point at the object you selected. Tell him to carefully sight with both eyes still open through the circle. Now have him close the left eye. A right-handed student should see no difference in alignment of circle and object. Try closing the right eye. The right-handed student should not be able to see the chosen object through the finger circle using his left eye. This indicates a right master eye.

If a student is right handed and has a left master eye, he may have to learn to shoot a shotgun left handed or undergo some extensive training beyond the scope of an amateur instructor. Reverse this for left-handed students with right master eyes. For now, though, just learning to shoot a rifle that is *aimed*, not pointed as with a shotgun, it may suffice to simply tape over a lens of the student's shooting glasses. A right-handed, left-master-eye student would have his left lens taped. Remember, this is only a stopgap, because a hunter must be able to shoot both a rifle and a shotgun *with both eyes open*. A one-eyed person is incapable of correct depth perception, which is vital to a hunter. Mismatch of hand and master eye may suggest a visit to an ophthalmologist.

Upon ascertaining correct master eye, it's time to spend a few hours with a sightless BB gun. If it's established that a safe background exists and the youngster is a safe shooter, he or she can practice this method. First, tape up a series of small bore targets across a heavy cardboard background, such as a packing case. Have him place his index finger down the side of the barrel and just point his finger at the target over and over for a while. Swing up, point finger, say "bang," and repeat. He will shoot where his finger points.

Then have the young shooter, BB gun off the shoulder, safety on, prepare to shoot at one of the targets at your command: "right, middle, left." Be within easy range of the targets. Have the student keep both eyes open, bring the gun up quickly, release the safety, and fire where he thinks he's pointing. He should do this without deliberately aiming. This is often difficult at first, because the untrained eyes will tend to see two barrels. Keep it up until all he consciously sees is the black bull's-eye of the distant target. Remember, you have removed the sights from the gun. There's just a bare barrel. He will soon be plopping BBs in or near the bull's eyes.

It's important that you don't let your student take aim deliberately. As soon as he can see the target he must fire without thinking. Point—pull. Point—pull, over and over. As your student progresses, toss out two or three ping pong balls on the ground and have him shoot the balls, following the same pattern as before.

Have your student practice these procedures on a daily basis for at least a week, preferably longer. The more BBs fired the better. He should be hitting closer and closer to where he points. If not, you'll need to give additional coaching. The most common error at this point is to not have the head in the correct position; the cheek should be tight against the stock.

Lots of BBs help develop confidence and better shooting skills in young shooters. Think of it. How many rounds do you fire on a range each year before hunting season?

STEP THREE We are great believers in on-the-job training when it comes to teaching youngsters from scratch. After some necessary preliminaries, safety can be effectively stressed in field training in a way youngsters understand and appreciate.

Each participant must understand that the simple safety rules are very serious and that the privilege of using firearms and hunting involves truly adult responsibility. Don't take Step Three—going to the gun range—unless you are sure of thorough comprehension.

The magic firearm for creating a sportsman is a quality manufacturer's bolt action .22 rimfire, single shot rifle with open sights. We favor starting on the range with high velocity .22 shorts because they are less expensive but still accurate. The students might be interested in knowing that the .22 is more than 100 years old, and that original .22 rimfire ammunition has not changed much in a century. The .22 is so named for the diameter of the lead bullet, $^{22}/_{100}$ths of an inch. This shotgun pellet size was readily available to the French inventors of the .22 in the mid-1800s.

The trainees in your course must be persuaded that the diminutive .22 carries a wallop and will travel quite a distance. The wallop is proved by shooting a can filled with water. The one mile distance warning printed on all .22 packages just has to be accepted and drilled into the

The bolt action .22 rimfire rifle is still the premier training firearm.

young mind, because it is true. In fact, in discussing this point you can briefly introduce the basic concept of trajectory. The youngster can expect his high velocity .22 short, zeroed in to hit the bull's-eye precisely in the middle at 50 yards, to drop about eight inches at 100 yards. The more powerful .22 long rifle will drop only about six inches at 100 yards. With these basic facts, you begin teaching the Kentucky windage concept so necessary to hunters. Kentucky windage is the art of holding your sights above, below, to the left or right of a target to compensate for wind or distance variables. It is only learned through experience. Leading a moving target and other sophisticated techniques should be left for later. Keep it simple.

Brief your young trainees on the local range procedures. There is usually a range officer whose specific commands are to be obeyed immediately. Rules include standing away from the shooting stations until an all-clear signal is sounded. The signals may vary, but safety procedures remain standard throughout the country. One bell may signal "stop shooting, clear gun, leave action open, and stand behind stations." Often you are required to place the cleared gun in a rack behind the station. Two bells usually mean it's safe to go down range to the targets. A third bell may indicate that it's okay to return to stations and commence firing. Only after the range has been cleared for firing may students approach their stations to set up sandbags, cartridges, spotting scopes, rifle, and other paraphernalia; otherwise there will be loud remonstrations.

The formality of the range is good for a first outing, since youths see adults carefully minding the range officer and routines. They observe the safe conduct which prevents accidents. Safe gun handling is serious business, and Texas has stricter gun laws than many other states. The sportsman should be aware of gun control issues. Good sources of information include the National Rifle Association, the Texas State Rifle Association, and the Texas Sportsman and Gun Owners Association.

If you do not own an accurate .22 bolt action for range use, rent one for training. Although single shots are preferred, your bolt action repeater can be made safe by loading only one round at a time. Confidence is, after safety and range etiquette, the second big lesson to be learned at the range. We have yet to find a youngster who couldn't learn to shoot with reasonable confidence-building instruction.

Both eye and hearing protection are musts for all range shooting exercises. It's a good idea to start the habit of hearing and eye protection from the outset. You'd be amazed to learn how widespread hearing loss is among 40- to 60-year-old shooters. Older sportsmen, particularly those from rural areas, didn't pay attention to ear protection. Use ear protection—it would be a shame to miss hearing your grandchildren say, "Good shot, grandpa!"

A good understanding of the iron sight picture is essential. The top of the front sight should be aligned with the top edge of the rear sight. The bull's-eye should rest perfectly on the top of the front sight.

You should align the sights yourself and shoot a tight, three-shot bull's-eye group to prove that each rifle is shooting where it should. If any sights are off, this gives you the opportunity to teach how to sight in, carefully firing three-shot groups until the rifle is zeroed in on the 10X ring. If the rifle is already sighted in, save this lesson for another trip—your students are ready to shoot.

Our instincts are pretty good given very little help. Observe natural trigger finger placement. If it's not on the pad of the first joint gently suggest that it should be. Watch for correct breath control. Most of us instinctively hold our breath while attempting a delicate manual job; the mistake is usually not in holding the breath, but in holding it too long, producing strain and trembling. Coach taking a breath when the sights are well aligned on the bull's-eye. Help the shooter relax if his muscles are tensed. Suggest he expel a little breath, hold it, and gently *squeeze* when the sight picture is perfect. Stop squeezing if the sight picture is not right. If you hold your breath more than a few seconds, the rifle will begin to move as your heart rate increases.

Again, not having the cheek tight against the stock is a major oversight, even with experienced shooters. Overcome a tendency to look up by teaching the spot weld of cheek to stock.

Teach your trainee to hold the sight picture after the shot. If he moves the barrel after pulling the trigger it's possible to affect bullet placement. Follow through is important. Begin the habit of having him call the shot, telling you where the bullet hit relative to the bull's-eye.

Although it's virtually impossible to see a .22 bullet in flight, urge the trainee to try to "see" it all the way to the target, then call out the hit location. The object is to get the student to concentrate. Concentration minimizes trigger jerk, flinch, and movement immediately after trigger pull, and it also begins to teach good hunting practices.

STEP FOUR   The long awaited field trip.

Since there is often a gap between range work and the first field trip, start the field trip with exercises that simulate safe hunting. Use a quarter as a target at about 75 feet. Tape the coin to a safe backstop that will show misses. A piece of cardboard tacked to a tree with a hill beyond works well. Hit the quarter first yourself. (Quarters are made of a soft metal that won't cause bullets to ricochet.) This lets all shooters see that you know what you're doing. (If necessary, fudge by using your scoped .22 from a bench rest, but hit the coin.) Then, set up another quarter and state that whoever hits it first in fair rotation wins it. Allow all to have a chance at winning, which might cost a few quarters. Students love to find and keep the dented quarters as tokens of their marksmanship. Encourage offhand shooting and begin to teach some of the basic positions, especially sitting, since it's a practical hunting position. Prone is seldom useful in the field. Also teach using a rest where possible when hunting. The standing offhand shot is the most difficult. Although you'll want to practice this, don't overdo; mastery is best left to advanced training, because you do not want to destroy confidence.

One at a time, let each shooter single fire until familiar with the iron-sighted .22 and until each demonstrates good safety habits. Be alert to unsafe handling and gently remind any offender of the summary rule: *Always point the muzzle in a safe direction.*

Now for the first hunt.

Hunting for rabbits is perfect for a small group, whereas hunting for squirrels would be discouragingly difficult. We take only one single shot training firearm on the first hunt, except for our backup revolver in case we must dispatch a wounded rabbit. We like to have one young hunter stalk ahead of the rest of the nimrods with a .22 short in the rifle, gun on safety. Make sure each student is well behind the shooter's zone of fire. Be certain the one shooter keeps his gun on safe until brought to the shoulder and aimed at a rabbit.

Each shooter gets to shoot at just one rabbit. If the rabbit escapes, the student goes to the back of the pack. This produces good concentration and, depending upon the abundance of game and number of hunters, is a practical way for a sportsman to start out. Any wounded rabbits are dispatched quickly by the trainer with the constant reminder that this is a very important part of becoming a good hunter. The successful hunter carries his prize and after the hunt the trainer will help each with cleaning, and, ideally, cooking and eating. Young sportsmen should learn never to waste game. Varmint and trophy hunting can be taught later. Explain that under no circumstances do you shoot songbirds or other nongame creatures.

We have concentrated on the .22 rifle because we believe it's the best firearm for beginning hunters and the best choice for most small game situations. Shotgun training is a little more difficult, but not as much so for youngsters as you might think. Again, our instinctive hand-eye coordination is a wondrous thing, as instinct-shooting experts have proven with thousands of shotgunners. Two things mess up neophyte shotgunners: not using the master eye and thinking too much. The latter also messes up a fair number of more seasoned sportsmen.

The fit of a shotgun is very important. You should be able to comfortably reach the trigger of a shotgun with its butt in the crook of your elbow. Then snap the shotgun to your shoulder with both eyes open. Your eyes should be lined up with the sights and point of aim. Stance is like that of a fighter: feet apart, weight a little out front. If you're right handed, your left leg will be advanced. Don't allow your stance to block your swing. Your lead foot should be pointing ahead of your anticipated target in ideal situations.

The fundamental to learn in shotgunning is to swing through the target and keep swinging. Tell your youngsters to imagine the shotgun barrel as a garden hose. They're to "soak" the target by spraying it in flight. The ideal will be to swing the stream of water out ahead of the target and let the target and water run together. This is exactly what happens to a shot pattern in flight. It's spread out because the gun barrel is moving. It's obvious that if the garden hose stops or the gun barrel stops, there is but a single stream of water or shot, no elongated spray. Youngsters must learn this most important technique from day one. If you're the example, you should certainly be qualified to hit a reasonable number of clay pigeons on a skeet or trap range and make it look easy.

An economical alternative to going out to the range is to purchase an inexpensive mechanical trap or even less costly hand thrower. In a way, these are even better than fixed ranges, because you can vary your throws and positions.

It should be reiterated that the foregoing is not intended as a substitute for the Texas Hunter Education Program, but rather as an introduction and reinforcement. The student who is guided through all of these steps with love and patience and who studies his "Ten Commandments of Shooting Safety" has received good training in conjunction with the Texas Hunter Education Program.

Edwards Plateau
Menu
.
Lentil Soup
Hassenpfeffer
Bee Cave Squirrel
Potato dumplings
Red Cabbage with Apples
Dutch Peach Pie
.
Fall Creek Carnelian

TEXAS BLUEBONNET. *Lupinus texensis.* Striking blue flowers on a pointed, white-tipped spike. Blooms throughout Texas (and only Texas) in the early spring. The most common of the five species in the state, it grows in a variety of poor, well-drained soils. Annual, March through May.

Lentil Soup

SERVES 6 TO 8

Dried lentils were a staple of the working-class German. The beans kept well and made a delicious soup or even a filling midday meal with the addition of sausages. It's a meal by itself with cornbread and tomato slices.

2 cups dried lentils
2 quarts water
½ cup diced salt pork
1 cup chopped onion
1 carrot, scraped and chopped
1 celery stalk, chopped
2 cloves garlic, minced
1 ham bone
1 bay leaf
2 whole cloves
2 tablespoons cider vinegar
   dash Tabasco sauce
1 teaspoon salt
   freshly ground black pepper to taste

PREPARATION

1. Start water heating in cast-iron pot.
2. Thoroughly rinse lentils in cold water. Throw into pot.
3. Saute diced salt pork. Add onion, carrot, celery, and garlic and cook ten minutes.
4. Add ham bone. Tie bay leaf and cloves in cheese cloth and add to mixture.
5. Add vinegar, Tabasco, salt, and pepper and bring to boil.
6. Reduce heat and simmer for two hours. Add more water as needed.
7. Discard spice sack when ready to serve.

Hasenpfeffer

SERVES 6 TO 8

6 slices lean bacon
3 cottontails, cut into serving pieces
   salt to taste
   flour
1 onion, minced
1 clove garlic, minced
1 cup Fall Creek Carnelian
1 cup chicken stock
2 tablespoons brandy
1 teaspoon red currant jelly
1 bay leaf
   pinch rosemary
   pinch thyme
   juice of 1 lemon
   freshly ground black pepper

PREPARATION

1. Cook bacon until crisp in 5-quart cast-iron pot. Set bacon aside to drain. Keep grease hot.
2. Shake rabbit pieces in paper bag filled with salt and pepper and flour.
3. Brown rabbit pieces in hot grease, set aside to drain.
4. Pour off extra grease and cook ½ cup minced onion and garlic until onions are transparent.
5. Add wine and chicken stock. Bring to boil.
6. Stir in brandy and jelly. Add bay leaf and pinches of rosemary and thyme.
7. Add bacon, crumbled into bits.
8. Cover and simmer for two hours. Check for tenderness. Rabbit pieces should be tender, but not fall apart. Usually cottontails will take another 30 minutes of simmering.
9. Stir in lemon juice and add freshly ground pepper to taste.

Bee Cave Squirrel

SERVES 4

Hunting bees was as important to early settlers as bagging deer and turkey, and often took more skill. Honey was a staple of the frontier, particularly in the Edwards Plateau with its many limestone caves and oaks. Some of the bee caves were probably in use for more than 1,000 years or more before they were destroyed by the settlers. Honey was often smeared on venison, used in cooking, and ladled onto biscuits.

2 whole, dressed squirrels
1 cup honey
2 cups apple cider
2 bay leaves
1 tablespoon cornstarch
2 tablespoons cool water
2 tablespoons butter, melted

PREPARATION

1. Start mesquite fire. Preheat oven to 350 degrees.
2. Smear honey over squirrels.
3. Broil squirrels over mesquite fire until browned, about 5 to 10 minutes.
4. Turn squirrels, coat with more honey. Broil until completely brown, about 5 more minutes.
5. Place squirrels in baking dish. Add cider and bay leaves.
6. Place in preheated oven and cook for 60 minutes.
7. Strain meat juices into a saucepan.
8. Mix cornstarch and water. Add cornstarch paste and butter to meat juices and thicken over medium heat.

Potato Dumplings

SERVES 8

8 medium potatoes
3 egg yolks
3 tablespoons cornstarch
1 cup bread crumbs
   salt and pepper to taste
   flour

PREPARATION

1. Peel potatoes and boil in salted water until tender.
2. Drain potatoes and mash.
3. Blend in egg yolks, cornstarch, bread crumbs, salt, and pepper.
4. Add a little flour for consistency and shape into dumplings.
5. Roll each dumpling in flour and drop into boiling water.
6. Cook, covered, 15 to 20 minutes.

Westphalian Green Beans and Carrots

SERVES 4 TO 6

1 cup chopped carrots
1 cup cut green beans
2 slices bacon
1 onion, sliced
1 apple, peeled, cored, and sliced
   vinegar
   sugar
2 tablespoons butter
   salt to taste

PREPARATION

1. Cook chopped carrots in a little salted boiling water for 10 minutes in covered pot.
2. Add cut green beans and cover. Cook until tender, then drain.
3. Cook bacon in cast-iron skillet, remove, and drain, reserving 1 tablespoon of drippings in the skillet.
4. Cook sliced onion in bacon drippings until tender. Do not brown.
5. Add sliced apple, vinegar, sugar, butter, and salt. Cover and cook another 5 minutes.
6. Add back the vegetables and heat.
7. Sprinkle with crumbled bacon.

Red Cabbage with Apples

SERVES 4 TO 6

2 pounds red cabbage
⅔ cup red wine vinegar
2 teaspoons salt
2 tablespoons sugar
2 tablespoons bacon fat or substitute
2 medium apples, cored and cut into thin
   wedges
2 onions, mince ½ cupful, peel the other
   and leave whole
4 whole cloves
1 bay leaf
1 cup boiling water plus additional as
   needed
¼ cup dry red wine

PREPARATION

1. Cut cabbage into quarters. Discard core.
2. Shred cabbage. Place in mixing bowl.
3. Add vinegar, salt, and sugar and mix.
4. Melt bacon fat in 5-quart cast-iron pot.
5. Add apple wedges and ½ cup minced onion. Cook until apples brown slightly.
6. Add cabbage mixture, 1 whole onion studded with cloves, and bay leaf.
7. Add 1 cup boiling water.
8. Bring mixture to boil, stirring. Reduce heat and simmer 2 hours.
9. Add more boiling water if necessary.
10. Before serving, remove studded onion and add red wine.

Dutch Peach Pie

SERVES 4 TO 6

This recipe is from Stonewall in the heart of Texas peach country.

1 unbaked pie shell
1 dozen ripe peaches
1 egg, lightly beaten
1 cup sour cream
¾ cup sugar
¼ teaspoon salt
2 tablespoons flour
½ teaspoon cinnamon
½ teaspoon nutmeg
Topping:
¼ cup brown sugar
3 tablespoons flour
2 tablespoons butter
½ cup chopped pecans

PREPARATION

1. Preheat oven 350 degrees.
2. Peel peaches. Slice thinly. Arrange in unbaked pie shell.
3. Mix egg with sour cream, sugar, salt, flour, cinnamon, and nutmeg, and pour over peaches.
4. Bake for 20 minutes.
6. Mix topping ingredients and dust over pie.
7. Bake for 15 minutes more.

XI

THE

WILD

ONES

THE
WILD
ONES

"Oh, Wilderness were Paradise enow!" declared Omar Khayyam in his *Rubaiyat*. This sentiment was not necessarily true for pioneer Texans and the ranchers who followed, poisoning, trapping, shooting, and otherwise subduing any creature deemed a predator, depleting a once numerous population of large carnivores, raptors, and reptiles. Later, there were those who employed light aircraft to strafe golden eagles from the skies. It wasn't unusual for just one airborne shotgunner to down 400 eagles a year, quietly gathering them up by the pickup load and burying them to hide the illegality. Naturalists refer to this practice as the SSS theory: Shoot. Shovel. Shut up. Each year thousands of acres of Texas animal habitat is "improved" to exclude wildlife.

Hindsight has led naturalists to the conclusion that predators help maintain the ecological balance necessary for the existence of all living things in a healthy state. This outlook is still hard to accept by a developer who would like nothing better than to gobble up another chunk of wild real estate or by a rancher whose livestock has been harassed by a pack of coyotes.

Texas Parks and Wildlife Department views itself smack in the middle of industrial/developer needs to convert prime habitat for human use, and the needs of wildlife. It's not an easy place to be, because to take the position that a major new industry will endanger a few mangy coyotes may not be totally defensible in modern Texas. "You have to appreciate the fine line these folks (TPWD staffers) must walk," explains David Baxter. "If they go too far in the direction of wildlife they are seen as preservationists, insensitive to jobs and human needs, more interested in

Texas is still rich in the wild ones,
symbolized by this majestic golden eagle.

Many Texas sportsmen would like to see the bobcat given official game status.

bunnies than people. Lean too far the other way and they are perceived as selling out to big business."

Yet the stakes are higher still than just maintaining the balance of nature. The wild ones are as necessary to the human spirit as music, art, and literature. Something in the soul flies up at the sight of a soaring eagle, or the presence of a cougar.

Our state is still rich in the wild ones and thanks to the habitat protection programs of the TPWD and the Texas Nature Conservancy, we achieved some notable success in the final decades of the 20th century, particularly with rare and unusual birds such as the Attwater's prairie chicken, whooping cranes, bald eagles, and peregrine falcons. The TPWD nongame and endangered species program extends to a startling 8,000-plus vertebrate species. Hunters can provide much needed support to these programs by purchasing a Texas nongame stamp or the beautiful nongame art prints issued annually.

Although cougars are holding their own, many sportsmen would support establishing game species classification with strict seasons and bag limits. And many would like to see bobcats and coyotes given at least furbearer sanction, as opposed to the "Let's shoot one" predator status. At least the bobcat's pelt has to be tagged before sale, albeit offering small comfort to the particular bobcat involved.

Treeing Walker hounds are not a welcome sight to this Texas cougar.

Texas alligators have made a dramatic comeback in Southeast Texas. The importance of the alligator in maintaining the fragile ecology of marshlands has been affirmed, and this once-endangered species is no longer excluded from Texas hunting regulations.

Gray wolves, probably even red wolves, didn't make it in our state. And the legendary Texas bear hunter of the 1900s, Ben Lilly, who had a lot to do with reducing the black bear population, would be distraught to know that now only a few black bears are left in Texas; they roam only the remote reaches of the Guadalupe Mountains and a few other isolated West Texas haunts.

Lone Star folk literature is replete with tall tales about cougar, puma, catamounts, panther, pantha, painters, and mountain lions. As in all good folk tales, there's some substance behind the oft-repeated campfire stories.

Texas claims more species of wild cats than any other place in the United States: six, not counting the domestic type gone feral, the most dangerous of all to bird life. Four of the cats are border residents, slipping occasionally across the Rio Grande from Mexico. All four are on the endangered list: jaguarundi, margay, ocelot, and *El Tigre* himself, the jaguar. Radio-telemetry tracking of ocelots is beginning to reveal the patterns of these beautiful, secretive cats, which inhabit the isolated, dense brush of South Texas. *El Tigre* doesn't visit us any more and the last known margay sortie into Texas was prior to 1850, but we still list these cats as endangered, though *desaparecidos* would be a more accurate classification.

The most numerous of the wildcats is the bobcat, found most everywhere in Texas. He has proved much more adaptable to man's encroachment on his habitat than the

A wild one begins his night's hunt.

other species, and is valuable as a furbearer. He is given an unfair rap for predatory damage to livestock. It's rare that stock pillaging amounts to much, but as Tom Peters said in *Passion for Excellence,* "Perception is everything."

The bobcat's canine opposite, the coyote, can present a threat, mostly to sheep and goats, especially when there's a coyote population explosion. Coyotes are found throughout the state, even close to metropolitan areas. They have especially heavy populations in the South Texas Plains, Trans-Pecos, and High Plains. The coyote's only natural enemies were wolves, but now their sole antagonist is man, and their populations have remained large and well distributed. Coyote hunting is a major sport in many parts of Texas. Hunting is a much more acceptable alternative to control than the poison and trapping approach taken by professional animal control agents.

Raptors—eagles, hawks, falcons, kites, and owls—add immeasurably to the aesthetic experience of Texas sportsmen. Many of these are classified as endangered or threatened, and all others are offered general protection by state law. TPWD reports that the protection this affords is important, because far too many raptors are illegally shot each year either out of ignorance or due to misconceptions of the raptors' impact on domestic livestock and poultry.

Many Texans grew up with the certain knowledge that they had to wipe out any and all "chicken hawks," especially those hovering about the hen house. The certainty of this knowledge is shaken a bit when you learn that there is no such thing as a chicken hawk, but that at least three major species of hawks have been awarded the opprobrium. These are the long-tailed, short, round-winged hawks *(accipiters)*, including the goshawk, sharp-shinned, and Cooper's hawk. In truth, the Cooper's can nail a

Despite unrelenting predator control efforts, coyote populations have remained stable in much of Texas.

chicken in a New York minute and so can the others, but they rarely do. Today's mega-agriculture approach, which provides for huge chicken raising complexes, leaves very few open poultry yards. Anyone whose chicken ranch is threatened by a Cooper's hawk should be innovative enough to protect and shelter the poultry without resorting to killing valuable wildlife.

The larger, thicker looking hawks are often called buzzard hawks *(buteos)*. In the eastern half of the state, you'll find red-tailed, red-shouldered, and broad-winged hawks. In the Trans-Pecos, the graceful Swainson's hawk is common. Harris and uncommon gray hawks inhabit the South Texas Plains. In the confines of the Coastal Plains and Rio Grande Valley, you'll find white-tailed hawks. Visitors to the King Ranch, where fire ecology is practiced, may be regaled by the sight of numbers of white-tailed hawks circling a burning pasture, picking off grasshoppers at 200 feet in the air. The grasshoppers jump up and are caught in the upward thermals from the fire. We know of sportsmen who claimed to have lost a quail shot in the air to a swooping, opportunistic white-tailed hawk.

Buzzard hawks as a group should be considered helpful. They are mighty hunters of mice, rats, weasels, snakes, and large insects. They are protected, and violators are subject to criminal fines and the possibility of civil replacement costs. The latter costs are based on monetary values set by TPWD to recover resources lost, and can range up to more than $5,000 for bald eagles. These replacement costs are over and above any state or federal criminal fines imposed.

The kite is rated as the most beneficial hawk. The Lone Star species include the black-shouldered, Mississippi, swallow-tailed, and hook-billed kites. All are streamlined birds with shapes reminiscent of falcons. They have long, slim, pointy wings and long tails. Kites feast upon snakes, lizards, and all sorts of beetles, crickets, grasshoppers, and other insects that are injurious to crops. Everybody should like kites: naturalist, sportsman, and farmer. The few that don't are in for a rude surprise. The replacement cost for a swallowtail alone will be $500 plus, before the criminal actions. Small kites often run into trouble from overenthusiastic, inexperienced dove shooters.

The only harrier hawk in Texas is commonly called a marsh hawk, and he's also the most populous. The official name for this hawk is northern harrier. One of the most striking hawks is the osprey, a large, ferocious-looking bird which will drive other hawks from its territory.

Also classified as raptors are our many owls, such as the great horned, barn, and screech owls. Their protected status also carries a stiff civil penalty for replacement.

The bird family *Cathartidae* is best known as the "West Texas Sanitation Department." *Cathartidae* is the Greek word for cleanser and is the Latin family name for our black and turkey vultures. The turkey vulture is known for his ugly, red head. He is larger than the black vulture and a better soarer on his longer wings, which can span up to

A member in good standing of the West Texas sanitation committee—the turkey vulture.

six feet. If you are spotting eagles in vulture country, which can happen in late winter, the vulture's wings will be held in a shallow *V* as opposed to the eagle's flat wing.

Vultures are migratory, and late season hunters will often note their absence—they've skipped to Mexico or beyond. The black vultures sometimes venture as far south as Argentina. Both species are on the wane in Texas thanks to rancher and hunter efficiency; fewer dead animals are left for them nowadays.

A third cleanup specialist found from the Rio Grande Valley up into East Texas is the caracara, more commonly called Mexican eagle in the Brush Country. This is the snake-fighting bird you see on the flag of Mexico. Although his carrion eating ways and his looks remind you of a vulture, he's really a falcon. Other falcons include the famous peregrine, the prairie falcon of the Trans-Pecos, and the nearly extinct aplomado falcon of the South Texas Plains. The most numerous of the falcons is the little American kestrel or sparrow hawk, who, contrary to popular belief, rarely eats sparrows or any other type of bird. His diet consists mainly of insects, but, strangely, he's one of the falcons "cleared" for falconry in Texas.

The peregrines found along our Gulf Coast are migratory Arctic falcons; our West Texas peregrines may nest in high places of the Trans-Pecos and could be year-round residents. Between the two, Texas is a hotbed of peregrine research because the world is fascinated by this incredible bird of blinding speed and rarity.

The most spectacular of the raptors are our eagles, the golden and the bald. The golden eagle is an independent creature of western, open country, most particularly mountains and canyons. In contrast, the bald eagle commonly feeds on fish and waterfowl and obviously must be located near seacoasts, large rivers, and big lakes. This need for water has helped reestablish a few eagles in Texas. Our dams and reservoirs, which have cost us some other wildlife habitat, have certainly helped the bald eagle.

While snakes are accomplished predators in their own right, they are a favorite prey of raptors and are often pictured dangling from a clamped beak or clenched talons. Our real problem is not having enough raptors. With about 15 species of pit vipers in the state, Texas can lay claim not only to having the mostest, but also to having the most fatalities. Lone Star reptiles kill more people than snakes of other states, although the bite incidence is highest in North Carolina. These are Texas brags that most of us could do without.

In true Texas fashion we make the most of it. We even have a rattlesnake roundup each spring in Sweetwater, with other communities having their own versions of snake fests. Every so often a participant is killed, but this doesn't seem to deter the macho survivors. Rattlesnake stories enliven our campfires, skins decorate our hats and adorn restaurant walls, and some sportsmen even like to charcoal-broil 'em.

There is a suspicion that much of the brave talk about staying calm near poisonous snakes is just "whistling past the graveyard." Snakes have a way of riveting your attention, and strong men have been known to get a bit flaky in the presence of any kind of snake. Unfortunately, this often results in the untimely demise of some of our more benign species such as the indigo, a nonpoisonous, efficient rattlesnake predator in its own right.

Snakes have also created a lot of controversy with great debates raging over bite treatment techniques, venom potency, and even how far a rattler can strike. The "strike a third of his body length" is an example of dangerous folk lore surrounding rattlers. Some tales would have you believe rattlers can become airborne, such as Audubon's much challenged reference to rattlers chasing squirrels through the boughs of trees. Audubon may have seen a black racer, which will climb trees and slither across treetop branches.

The wise Texas quail hunter will add leggings to his gear when hunting in warm weather, and the sportsman afield for any reason in warmer weather should keep an eye out. Snakes don't stalk humans, but don't tempt them by stepping or sitting on them.

Snakes actually kill very few Texans, although larger rattlers and moccasins can certainly inject enough venom to do the job. And the old saying about coral snakes, "red on yellow, kill a fellow," is true; the coral's venom is like a cobra's—deadly. Most bites occur when some fool picks one up, exclaiming how pretty it is. The coral must chew its way through to the bloodstream, but when it does, chances are you're history.

Principal Texas rattlesnakes include the western diamondback, prairie, Mojave, banded or rock, desert massasauga, western massasauga, western pigmy, black-tailed, mottled rock, timber, and canebreak, a close relative of the timber.

The Lone Star copperheads include the Trans-Pecos, broad-banded, and southern. Our native cottonmouth is the western cottonmouth.

From cougars to coyotes, alligators to moccasins, eagles to rattlers, the wild ones of Texas offer a window onto the wild side, and as such are to be cherished as much as they are cussed.

A favorite meal of the Harris hawk is rattlesnake tartare.

COUGAR INSIGHTS

"We come now to a bloody and unrelenting tribe chiefly distinguished by their sharp and formidable claws which they can hide and extend at pleasure. They are, in general, fierce, rapacious, subtle and cruel, unfit for society among each other and incapable of adding to human happiness."

Oliver Goldsmith
HISTORY OF THE EARTH
AND ANIMATED NATURE, 1774

When our nation was settled, cougars had the most extensive range of any quadruped in this hemisphere. It's obvious many of our settlers shared the view of the good Dr. Goldsmith and almost wiped the American lion off the face of the continent. It's a tribute to the adaptability of this magnificent animal and the changing attitudes of wildlife managers that he is making a comeback in many western states.

The Texas cougar situation is a borderline case, literally. Declining populations are reported across the border in the Mexican states of Chihuahua and Coahuilla—perhaps because, contrary to popular prejudice, cougar meat is palatable, but more likely because ranchers won't

A cougar skulks through concealing brush.

tolerate loss of stock. These states are the source of the *leons* that become Texas lions. They are not protected nor even given game status in Texas, so the squeeze is on in the Trans-Pecos and South Texas Plains, where most of our cougars reside. However, cougar sightings continue in the Big Bend and especially in the Black Gap W.M.A., so wildlife biologists are optimistic.

A typical male cougar weighs 150 pounds and stretches out to eight feet, including about 2½ feet of tail. Females average a foot less in length and weigh, on average, 40 pounds less than males. Coloring is tawny on top, creamy underneath with a light-colored upper lip, giving the appearance of a cat that's been in the cream. "Blue" and

"red" cougars have also been identified, with the upper fur tending to a slate or henna patina.

Cougars use their excellent sense of smell in tracking prey. The cats' habitat is the same as that of wilderness deer; at least 75 percent of the cougar diet consists of mulies and whitetails. The cat's stalk is a skulking, zig zag pattern keeping to cover, avoiding open areas. Even though nocturnal, they often hunt during the day. Cougars are also audiophiles; their sharp hearing enables them to zero in on prey at great distances. But eyesight is the factor that most increases what game biologists call their "PE"—probability of eating ratio. The Texas cougar probably eats 15 to 20 deer a year. Their oversized eyes create a greater focal length. The cougar sees bigger and brighter, like a telephoto camera lens. The back of his eyes reflect light back through the visual cells, giving him tremendous night vision. The cat's eye slit noted in daytime is protection for night vision equipment. Cougars also see in 3-D without having to wear those silly glasses. No wonder he's a good hunter; without moving his head he has a field of view in excess of 280 degrees. About all he can't see is the base of his own tail.

Most game biologists don't really believe that cougars go around selectively knocking off weak and diseased deer. Most would agree, however, that cougar predation under typical deer population conditions does no harm and may have some positive aspects.

Actually cougars hunt deer like sportsmen—for mossy backed bucks and the occasional spike. Like typical Texas hunters, they don't harvest their share of does. Big, old bucks and young bucks are often a little less agile and a lot less smart in the rutting season. Old bucks tend to stay in heavy cover, making them even more vulnerable to cougars.

Cougars and sportsmen share another similarity in that they stake out their hunting range. Depending upon their own local mule or whitetail census, the cats mark out territorial boundaries by scraping up piles of dirt and then urinating on them. Hunters should note that cougars will often pad along in the same direction they were headed prior to making the scrape. A scrape can be a productive place to start a pack of cat hounds. Other cougars respect these scrapes and usually slink off to find their own deer herd. Cougars change their hunting territory when the deer herd population dwindles.

A cougar scream will curdle your blood. It sounds like the shriek of a mortally wounded woman. Most wildlife experts associate the screaming or caterwauling of the big

cats with the female's mating behavior. Actual copulation only lasts 60 seconds. The female initiates the action; her estrus cycle is just over 20 days, with eight days of fertility. Cougars can breed year-round. Gestation is about three months and litters range up to six. Kittens have spotted fur all over and have blackish rings around their tails. In 30 days they have teeth, too.

Contrary to some authorities, it's unlikely that the female cougar is a faithful spouse. If two suitors are around she will mate with the dominant. When the victor falls asleep, exhausted by holding her down by the back of the neck and by his 60-second performance, she's apt to go calling on the vanquished.

Cougar myth has it that they are cave dwellers; they actually prefer dens with good shade cover, such as under a rock outcrop or in dense brush.

The cougar's four-toed forefoot track is distinctive, and if it measures four inches across, he's big. The cougars fifth toe is held too high to imprint. The hind foot is always smaller and you won't see claw marks. These spring out as the cougar leaps upon a deer's back and give purchase as he bites through the neck muscle to sever the spinal cord.

Front

back

Mountain Lion

Cougars usually drag their kills into a secluded area and cover the cache with brush, for the dual purpose of hiding and preserving it. They will feed on the kill, wander off to sleep it off, and typically return until the meat begins to putrify. Cougars won't eat spoiled meat.

BOBCAT INSIGHTS

Bobcats look as if a master painter set out to produce the most artistic and functional of camouflages on an oversized, stub-tailed house cat. Lone Star bobcats tend to be reddish brown with darker blobs of camo spotted all over the hide. You'll also see them amber flecked with dark

Cougars prefer dens under rock outcrops.

brown, but the bay color is the most common. One look at the bobcat's ferocious eyes, set in a witch doctor's mask and topped by tufted ears, tells you this ain't a tabby.

Bobcats most often weigh in at 20 pounds, measure around three feet, and stand 20 inches or so at the shoulder. However, the Trans-Pecos and brush country variety are king-sized, sometimes measuring four feet.

The cats have proved very adaptable. Although bobcats prefer rocky outcrops and canyons for den areas, they'll readily den up in brush piles and thickets. In Texas, the bobcat breeding season begins early in the year, or even in December, and extends into spring. Gestation periods average 60 days with normal litter size at three. There is much debate among wildlife experts on the probability of more than one litter per year. Biologically, this is possible, because bobcats are polyestrus.

Bobcats have adapted to virtually every Texas habitat but pose little threat to game and livestock.

Mature bobcats settle in on the home place and mark their territories much like cougars, with urine-scented scrapes. Unlike cougars, bobcats stay home until prey is pretty well diminished, mainly dining on rabbits, rodents, and 'possums. There are instances of bobcats attacking unwary, bedded deer from time to time and going after small livestock, but basically they are not a predator threat to ranchers.

While most quail hunters go into spasms at the sight of a bobcat, they do little damage to quail populations. Domestic cats gone wild pose a greater threat to all birds, especially quail. You may take another view if your bobcat population is high, your coveys few.

Bobcats are essentially night stalkers, lurking about in their God-given camo until within proximity of their prey, whereupon they are capable of a swift strike. On the rare occasion when they attack a deer, they more often go for

the throat rather than the back of the neck, like the much larger cougar.

ENDANGERED CATS

Among the endangered cats are the beautiful little ocelots, jaguarundi, and super rare margay. The jaguar is still hunted in the mountains of northeastern Mexico. He is truly formidable at seven feet and 200 pounds.

Hunters in the Brush Country could run across the occasional ocelot and implant a bullet, thinking him to be a bobcat. Don't; he is protected and the fine is stiff. The ocelot does favor a bobcat, but his spots are larger and he

Cat tracks   bob cat

has a *long*, slim tail. These are major field marks a game warden will be quick to point out as he writes you up. Also, there is nothing ferocious-looking about an ocelot; most would call him handsome.

The endangered ocelot population is growing in South Texas but these magnificently marked cats are rarely seen.

The same goes for the even smaller jaguarundi, seldom seen as he sequesters himself in the thickest cover the Brush Country can produce. The jaguarundi is unspotted, long tailed, skinny, and appears in gray or red phases. Again, there is no way you can mistake him for a bobcat.

dog tracks coyote Front back

COYOTE INSIGHTS

"The coyote is a long, slim, sick and sorry-looking skeleton, with a grey wolfskin stretched over it, a tolerably bushy tail that forever sags down with a despairing expression of forsakenness and misery, a furtive and evil eye, and a long, sharp face, with slightly lifted lip and exposed teeth. He has a general slinking expression all over. The coyote is a living, breathing allegory of Want. He is *always* hungry. He is always poor, out of luck, and friendless. The meanest creatures despise him, and even the fleas would desert him for a velocipede. He is so spiritless and cowardly that even while his exposed teeth are pretending a threat, the rest of his face is apologizing for it. And he is *so* homely! So scrawny, and ribby, and coarse-haired, and pitiful."

Mark Twain
ROUGHING IT, 1861

In the 20-year span from 1946 to 1966, the U.S. Fish and Wildlife Service proudly reported killing more than 600,000 coyotes in Texas, most with what they liked to call the "humane coyote getter," the cyanide gun. This beauty shoots a load of cyanide into the mouth of coyote, dog, or any other carnivore that happens to chomp and pull on the bait. The "humane" adjective refers to the fact that cyanide kills swiftly, as many a Texas quail dog handler can testify. Toward the end of the 20th century, increasing awareness of wildlife values has led to a re-evaluation of coyote controls, demonstrating that man's best efforts have been not only very costly but ineffective where habitat favors the coyote. Coyote control has been very effective in well-settled ranching areas of the state, to the extent that even hearing a concert is rare.

Coyotes will eat their fair share of sheep, but even this

This coyote has implemented his own wildlife control program.

number is less than commonly believed. In Texas, rabbits are the favored prey, followed by rodents. Coyotes commonly eat fruit, vegetables, insects, and frogs. They seldom eat venison or beef, and proof exists that when coyotes indulge in such delicacies, the meal is carrion rather than from fresh kills. It's a different matter where goats and sheep are concerned, and the West Texas rancher with large flocks has reason to be concerned. The Texas Department of Agriculture (TDA) has a comprehensive predator control training program.

An innovative approach touted by TDA is the use of guard dogs, which, despite initial resistance from ranchers with an instinctive distrust of dogs on their sheep and goat pastures, has proven most effective in deterring coyotes. The dogs don't reduce the coyote population *per se*, but rather run them off the guarded pasture. This may not be viewed as neighborly by adjacent ranchers, so communication and cooperation is important. Lack of communication can also create other problems. One early participant in the program was visited by his rancher neighbor claiming a free steak dinner as reward for having killed "stray dogs" in his pasture—not the way you'd like your expensive Pyrenees to be greeted. The handsome, intelligent Pyrenees are the expert's choice for guard duty, a truly humane way to handle the age-old problem of livestock depredation.

That coyotes always travel in packs is another myth. On the contrary, they are not social animals, preferring to travel as couples. In fact, there is evidence that they stay paired year after year. Coyotes will gather in large packs, as most every Texas sportsman will verify, but such groupings are usually defensive measures rather than the aggressive hunting packs of gray wolves. In fact, one golden eagle can hold several coyotes at bay while he works over a choice bit of carrion.

The breeding patterns of coyotes and domestic dogs are similar. In Texas, coyotes begin breeding at the first of the year, continuing through mid-May. This makes February a good hunting time, when pelts are prime and coyote caution is minimal. Gestation is about two months with litter sizes of a half dozen. Like foxes and badgers, coyotes are den animals. In fact, they often preempt a badger's den, but not while the badger is in residence. Coyotes like brushy areas, rock outcrops, and any well-hidden place. They have learned to hide from man.

Coyotes are frequently mistaken for wolves, which have been extirpated from our state. Coyotes can interbreed with dogs and wolves, but the hybrid would only be clearly identifed by experts, starting with a good dentist. Coyotes, wolves, and dogs have about the same tracks: four toe-nailed toes showing ahead of the pad. The front footprint is the larger, averaging just slightly more than two inches. A gray wolf or large dog track will go up to four inches in width.

Little is known about the coyote despite the many years he's been the target of all-out war. Yet his song is something special for the spirit.

KITE INSIGHTS

The most common kites in Texas are the black-shouldered kite and the Mississippi kite. The black-shouldered variety frequents the Gulf Prairies and Marshes and the South Texas Plains. The Mississippi has a broader range, extending over much of the state, but is rarely seen in the Trans-Pecos. An uncommon visitor to the coastal bend is the swallow-tailed kite; along the South Texas border, sightings of the hook-billed kite are cause for a birdwatchers' jubilee.

BLACK-SHOULDERED KITE The black-shouldered kite has been called the white-tailed kite for more than 100 years, mainly because he does have a nice, long, white tail. Older field guides still use the white-tailed reference. His white underparts and black shoulder patches are easy to spot in flight. However, he is easily mistaken for a falcon. While flying, he displays a graceful power and, unlike other kites, hovers.

Kite flying over West Texas.

MISSISSIPPI KITE Mississippi kites are easily distinguished by their dark tails. They are a dark gray on top, a dove gray underneath. Unusual for kites, they will nest in mesquite trees only a few feet above the ground.

Mississippi kites don't prey on other birds, but will chase off crows and small game animals. Like other kites, they feed on insects, rodents, lizards, and frogs. They are positive contributors to the environment, at least from a human perspective.

SWALLOW-TAILED KITE The swallow-tailed kite is one of the most elegant of all birds in flight. Its black and white plumage provides a distinctive fieldmark. No other large bird is so marked and shaped.

HOOK-BILLED KITE Border patrol agents have the best chance to spot hook-billed kites, identified by a large beak with a vicious looking hook to it. Its head is reminiscent of a small golden eagle. Mature hook-billed kites are mainly black, showing a white band across the tail in flight.

Hook-billed kites are found only along the Mexican border.

HAWK INSIGHTS

Hunters will spot a wide variety of hawks in the course of their Texas adventures. The ardent birdwatcher is advised to acquire an up-to-date, profusely illustrated field reference such as *The Audubon Society Master Guide to Birding*. The *Sportsman's Guide* will only briefly describe those hawks commonly seen in the state.

Long-tailed hawks *(accipiters)* common in Texas include the northern harrier, sharp-shinned, and Cooper's. There are a few sightings of the northern Goshawk and common black hawk. The buzzard hawks *(buteos)* common in Texas include the red-tailed, Harris, Swainson's, red-shouldered, broad-winged, and white-tailed. Only occasionally do we see gray, Ferruginous, and rough-legged hawks.

NORTHERN HARRIER HAWK (MARSH HAWK)
Most Texans call the northern harrier a marsh hawk. They're found anywhere there are wetlands and extensive fields and marshes. These are the hawks that sail close to the ground like helicopter gunships in search of the unwary. Mice and frogs need more than their natural camouflage to survive. Look for the owl face mask. When perched and looking straight at you, the harrier is easily mistaken for an owl. The mature harrier is gray above. Females and immature harriers have streaks of brown on their breasts.

A mature osprey has a wingspan of up to six feet and is an expert fish hawk.

COOPER'S AND SHARP-SHINNED HAWKS In winter months you've got to look sharp to distinguish the sharp-shinned hawk from the Cooper's. The Cooper's has a longer, rounder tail as opposed to the squared-off tail of the sharp-shinned. The somewhat smaller sharp-shinned is a "snowbird," while the Cooper's is a resident. Both immature phases are a buff white underneath with reddish streaks, but the sharp-shinned has bolder striping. The mature Cooper's is almost black on top with a rust flecked breast.

These are the birds that give other hawks a bad reputation. Both hawks find pigeons, songbirds, and chickens tasty. Oldtimers referred to all accipiters as chicken hawks or blue darters, and kept the trusty 12-gauge loaded and handy to defend the poultry yard.

To most Texans the northern harrier hawk will always be a marsh hawk.

OSPREY This ferocious looking customer, known to many Texans as a fish hawk, is dark brown on top and speckled white below. There's a bold, brown stripe running alongside the white crest swept back on his head. In flight, you'll note a similarity to a gull wing, with a crook at the wrist. This is a big bird sporting a six-foot wing span, generally migrant in Texas, and fully protected. When he spots a fish he dives head first, then swings around with uncanny acrobatic ability so that his long, sharp talons are in position. He's a feathered, air-to-surface, fish-seeking missile.

Oldtime Texans call accipiters, such as this sharp-shinned hawk, chicken hawks or blue darters.

BUZZARD HAWKS (BUTEOS) The buteos, or buzzard hawks, a subfamily of *accipitridae*, may easily be distinguished from accipiters by sheer size and body thickness. Buteos are all heavy bodied with broad, rounded wings, except for the pointy wings of the Swainson's hawk. While retaining the buteo portliness, the Swainson's hawks should not be confused with the persecuted "chicken hawks."

Buzzard hawks, such as this red-tailed hawk, are heavy bodied, broad-winged raptors.

RED-TAILED HAWK The red-tailed hawk is the commonest, most widely distributed hawk on the continent, and he's a year-round Texas resident. He is the largest and most powerful hawk, with the exception of his eagle cousins. As you may have guessed, the mature red-tailed hawk has a red tail; he is a nut brown on top. He comes in many variations with the immature showing no tail red at all. In the light phase, you'll see a lot of white underneath. In the dark phase, the white goes to chestnut. This phase used to be thought of as a separate hawk, the Harlan's.

Like all other buteos, the red-tailed hawk prefers to hunt from a high perch, surveying his domain with a wicked looking, sharp eye. He'll also do a lot of slow soaring, especially in lean times. He can spot field mice from several hundred yards in the air. The redtail will migrate southward in the winter to locate better food supplies, and you'll often see several in the same area.

Farmers and ranchers should applaud the efforts of redtails to reduce rodent populations, wipe out snakes—especially rattlers—and take down insects. Very little of their food comes from birds or poultry stock, although they do knock off the occasional clumsy squirrel or rabbit.

SWAINSON'S HAWK The Swainson's hawk, which breeds in Texas, is commonly seen here in spring and fall. Long distance migrants, these hawks winter in Argentina. They prefer the wide open range and prairies of the western half of the state. During their Texas migrations, they congregate in surprisingly large flocks. The Swainson's is another beneficial eater, leaving costly poultry alone, preferring insects and rodents.

The Swainson's hawk is a little smaller than the redtail; its wings are more narrow and come to a point. Light phase birds show a coppery head and neck standing out against buff white breast and belly. In the dark phase, this contrast is not apparent. The bird is generally dark brown all over except for paler tail feathers.

West Texans often see large congregations of Swainson's hawks en route to their wintering grounds in Argentina.

HARRIS HAWK The chunky Harris hawk roams from the Trans-Pecos through the southern portion of the Edwards Plateau to the South Texas Brush Country. This striking bird sports mahogany on top with chestnut bay shoulder chevrons, wing linings, and knickers. His tail is tipped with white, then banded in dark gray, to show white again close to the body. He nests in mesquite thickets and yucca. He loves to nail rabbits and rattlesnakes lurking under prickly pear cactus.

The Harris hawk is a favorite of Texas falconers.

The red-shouldered hawk is an East Texas habitué preferring a cuisine rich in rodents, frogs, and snakes.

RED-SHOULDERED HAWK Operating on the other side of the state in the Pineywoods and Gulf Prairies and Marshes is the red-shouldered hawk. Common year-round in the coastal bend, this hawk is marked like an old freighter, with a rust-streaked brown head above his notable red shoulders. Like all buteos, this hawk prefers to dine on creatures people don't hold in high esteem: bugs, rodents, frogs, and snakes.

Eagles and red-tailed hawks have benefited from the creation of huge reservoirs in Texas; the red-shouldered hawk has not. More than a million acres of East Texas bottomlands have been inundated to construct these impoundments, eliminating his prime habitat.

BROAD-WINGED HAWK One of the smallest of the buteos is the broad-winged hawk common to the Coastal Bend in spring and fall. His wings are proportionately much larger than those of other buzzard hawks, and he displays an off-white underside in both the mature and ad-

The broad-winged hawk is one of the smallest of the buteos.

olescent phases. His primaries are tipped in dark brown and he's a mottled dark brown on top. The immature broadwing is almost identical to the young red-shouldered hawk.

WHITE-TAILED HAWK Visitors to deep southeast Texas may be treated to sightings of the large white-tailed hawk, otherwise rare in the United States. His tail is so short that, when perched, it does not extend beyond the wings, unusual in buteos. The mature hawk has a distinct white tail featuring a band of black, and also has russet wing chevrons which stand out boldly against grayish upperparts. The mature whitetail can display a lot of white on the underparts and wing linings. The immature white-tail hawk is difficult to identify by color alone because his plumage is not as distinct, more dark brown on top, mottled brown underneath.

EAGLE INSIGHTS

"The facts suggest that something is at work in the eagle's environment which has virtually destroyed its ability to reproduce."

—Rachel Carson
SILENT SPRING, 1962

Fire ecology practices on the King Ranch attract unusually large concentrations of the rare white-tailed hawk.

That something that Rachel Carson knew, but could not quite prove with respect to bald eagles, was a chlorinated hydrocarbon—the "savior of mankind"—DDT. Without Carson's attention, DDT would not have saved mankind, but rather condemned it.

As we approach the 21st century, it becomes increasingly clear that Carson's warnings were far more than the rantings of a birdwatcher missing some robins and an eagle or two. Hers was a grim prophecy—the poisoning of our world during our lifetime.

Sportsmen, like all other people, aren't particularly fond of mosquito welts, or of going hungry or being poor because of insect blights to crops. And no one wants to be sickened by insect-transmitted diseases. Obviously there is a place for carefully tested, carefully utilized chemical controls. But it won't just be the birds that are silent if we continue to foul our own nests with toxins through unlimited use of pesticides and herbicides, unchecked air pollution, and radioactivity.

From World War II until the latter part of the century, few of us lower-48 Americans had ever seen our national emblem in the wild. In Texas, that started to change in the last two decades of the 20th century. DDT and other destructive, stable, hard chemical compounds were legislated out of the environment to be replaced with more selective, biodegradable, and hopefully less harmful pesticides. Even the switch to steel shot has had its impact in improving the eagle's future.

BALD EAGLES Ever so slowly, the Texas bald eagle population is growing. But don't expect to see bald eagles by the skyful; Texas populations are still relatively small. Sightings of wintering northern bald eagles are common along the Colorado River north of the Buchanan dam, and there is an increase in nesting sites of southern bald eagles in Southeastern Texas. Eagles in the Colorado River area soar like *Valkyries* into our state on the winds

A Colorado River bald eagle soars to his hunting perch.

of November cold fronts. They find the high cliffs and tall trees along the Colorado ideal perches from which to locate their main entree, dead or dying fish. A scant few southern bald eagles nest in the Gulf Prairies and Marshes during November.

The wing span of a mature female eagle can reach almost eight feet. She will stand an imposing yard tall on her perch and weigh in at over ten pounds. Aerospace engineers should take note that they still haven't approached the strength of an eagle's wing despite all their high tech ways. A female eagle's wings weigh less than two pounds. Not an ounce is wasted in eagle superstructure. Their bones are even hollow, internally crossbraced to add strength and power.

Like man, eagles eat lots of other animals but are seldom eaten themselves. Also like man, eagles are as lazy as they dare to be, and most of them are very daring. They do a lot of scavenging on dead fish and stealing from other hawks such as osprey. With abundant food sources, they work as little as possible, preferring to lollygag about on tree perches, or putting on aerial acrobatic shows for the fun of it.

However, eagles are wonderfully equipped hunters with eyes that can focus with eight times the resolution of human eyes, rough grippers on their huge talons that help them fasten onto slippery fish, and incredible diving speed. They hit prey in the air with the energy release of a rifle bullet. They are great sailplaners, capable of soaring with wings nearly motionless for long periods. Their wings are held flat while soaring. This is one of the ways observers at a distance can distinguish them from vultures.

Although bald eagles commonly eat fish, they rack up an occasional cormorant or coot and a few hapless rabbits or rodents.

Bald eagles mate for life and take exceptional care of their eaglets. Both sexes take turns in feeding and brooding. Nests are often massive structures; some aeries on record weigh more than 2,000 pounds and stand six feet high. These are usually built as high as possible in a tree strong enough to support the weight.

It takes a bald eagle five years to reach maturity, at which time they earn their magnificent white head and tail plumage and begin breeding. They generally lay only two eggs a year, and only 20 percent of all eagles hatched live to maturity, even without pesticide and other chemical poisoning.

The stark white of the eagle's head and tail is set off against the body's dark brown. The wild look is enhanced by the heavy, chrome yellow, deeply hooked beak and wicked looking yellow talons. Immature bald eagles look a lot like golden eagles since they are dark brown all over and, unless they are close in ideal light, it's difficult to distinguish the "gold" of the latter's head. This can give rise to inaccurate bird counts.

GOLDEN EAGLES Mature golden eagles feature a copper-gold helmet reaching to the shoulders and a dark, hooked beak. Immatures can be identified in flight by white patches at the base of the primaries. Otherwise they are very similar to the mature bird. They are about the same size as the bald eagle and the female is the larger.

Golden eagles, although their range spans most of the western two-thirds of the continent, are normally birds of high places. In Texas, they frequent the mountains and canyons of the Trans-Pecos, such as the Chisos, Davis, Glass, and Guadalupe ranges. They breed in these areas, normally at a high elevation, where they stake out a hunting territory upwards of 50 square miles. These hunting grounds are apparently honored by other golden eagles. If competition for food gets stiff from lesser hawks, the goldens pick 'em off, one by one, like gunfighters in a spaghetti western.

The monstrous talons of the golden eagle mean sudden death to rabbits, squirrels, birds, snakes, or any small mammal which wanders by, including lambs and kids.

Immature bald eagles closely resemble golden eagles.

Golden eagles usually favor high places and are frequently sighted in the Trans-Pecos and Edwards Plateau.

The goldens are capable of killing a fawn or young antelope; however, they can only take off with about five pounds of meat, even if they can spring off a ledge. So, tales of lambs being spirited away, dangling from talons, are a bit farfetched. Like other predators, the golden often gets a bad rap by being in the wrong place at the wrong time, feasting off the carcass of a large and very dead animal. They are carrion eaters, too. There's no doubt that golden eagles do some sheep and goat herd damage by killing lambs and kids. The war against the golden eagle goes on because anti feelings run strong in West Texas, though most cattle ranchers have come to recognize that goldens pose no threat, and even help out a bit with snake and jackrabbit infestation.

FALCON INSIGHTS

CARACARA   Brush Country deer hunters are often entertained right at sundown by flocks of caracara settling in perches of the highest mesquite trees in search of food, dead or alive. This large, black-crested falcon looks like a cross between an eagle and a vulture. They emit a grating, croaking sound that goes *cara cara*. The caracara is the famous Mexican eagle, proudly depicted on coins and

The most common South Texas falcon is the caracara, enshrined by Mexico as its national emblem.

flags south of the border. They have a white throat and neck and unmistakable red face.

PRAIRIE FALCON   Trans-Pecos high country hunters are often treated to a sighting of the small prairie falcon. He's a pale, scaly buff on top with white throat and brown streaked, buff underparts. In flight, you'll see distinct dark brown axillaries.

Where the wings of eagles and buteos resemble those of large passenger jets, designed for maximum lift and soaring capability, those of the prairie falcon and his relatives in the *falconidae* are more like the mach-2 design of the Concorde SST. The prairie falcon's wings deliver a rapid power stroke as he cruises at low altitude over his hunting range in search of blue quail, doves, sparrows, and even ducks, which he enjoys blasting in mid-air. He also makes life miserable for rodents and rabbits, lizards and insects.

PEREGRINE FALCON   This endangered bird, called a duck hawk by old timers, is one of nature's wonders. Those who have been privileged to watch peregrines hunt

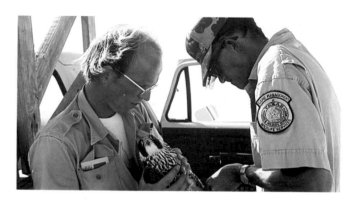

Immature peregrine falcon, found on the Texas coast, is banded by TPWD specialists.

and play, especially in high winds, have experienced one of nature's finest exhibits. When you see this bird in flight, the lack of contrasting axillaries tells you it's a peregrine rather than a common prairie falcon. The distinctive field mark is its black helmet set off by white chin and throat. The back is dark gray. The breast has dark bars against a buff tone. These falcons are loners; beachcombers sometimes see migrating peregrines off Padre Island in the fall cruising at 60 miles per hour. They kill ducks and other large birds by flying like feathered missiles right into them at high speed, knocking the victims out of the sky. Peregrines are also found in the Trans-Pecos, have been spotted in the Chisos Mountains of Big Bend National Park, and are known to nest in the Guadalupes. They like the open header draw country of deep West Texas.

The peregrine adapts to all climate conditions and is trainable and intelligent. Never abundant, the peregrines almost vanished with the DDT onslaught of the '50s and

'60s. Their eggs were as affected as the eagles', with thin shells unfit for protecting embryos.

To many sportsmen, the peregrine falcon is the world's most fascinating bird. He is a world-class traveler, or as the French would say, *peregrinator*. His species has been identified on every continent and most islands.

Falconry probably predates written history. The earliest references are from the 8th century B.C. in ancient Assyria—today's northern Iraq. Today's major buyers of falcons, legally or otherwise, are Saudi Arabians, and some of their purchases come from Texas.

A falcon taken from the nest is called an *eyas*; wild-caught falcons are called *passagers*, as in the seaman's term "passagemaking." They are trapped while migrating. Only the female is called a falcon by falconers. The male, always smaller in size, is called a tercel.

Once fed, the tercel is a showoff. He loves to perform acrobatics for his lady, rolling over and over into the wind, darting, lunging, then swooping skyward for a repeat performance. One can almost see him tip his helmet to the admiring falcon on her perch. A well-fed peregrine will tease other birds, undoubtedly scaring them to death by overtaking them and tapping them on the back as he whistles by. This is called counting coup.

Ornithologist Joseph A. Hager wrote this stirring account of a peregrine watch in 1935:

"He rose to a position 500 or 600 feet above the mountain and north of the cliff. Nosing over suddenly, he flicked his wings rapidly 15 or 20 times and fell like a thunderbolt. Wings half closed now, he shot down by the north end of the cliff, described three successive vertical loop-the-loops across the face, turning upside down at the top, and roared out over our heads with the wind rushing through his wings like ripping canvas . . . the sheer excitement of watching such a performance was tremendous; we felt a strong impulse to stand and cheer."

There are accounts of peregrines diving past small aircraft with indicated airspeeds in excess of 200 miles per hour; some experts are edging the estimate of a peregrine's dive velocity beyond the 250 m.p.h. mark. Only swifts and the aplomado falcon challenge them for the world's natural speed record.

APLOMADO FALCON   Travelers to the South Texas Plains in the early 1900s reported frequent sightings of a spectacularly fast, strikingly beautiful, pointy-winged falcon. The Mexicans named him *apolomadeo* for his steel gray coloring. A modern bird watcher would mortgage his barn to record an aplomado, because they have become one of the most sought-after birds in the world. Unfortunately, they are now rare in Texas. The aplomado may even be faster in level flight than his famed cousin, the peregrine. He is a little smaller than the peregrine, but larger than the frequently seen kestrels and merlins.

The aplomado's steely gray skullcap is boldly striped,

The rare aplomado falcon may even be faster than the more famous peregrine.

as are the adult bird's back and outer wings. The breast is cinnamon or white.

Toward the close of the 20th century, extensive efforts were being made to restore the aplomado to Texas, with some encouraging results. Sportsmen of the 21st century may yet enjoy the performances of this falcon "top gun."

AMERICAN KESTREL   The pretty, diminutive American kestrel is one of our most frequently sighted falcons. He's fairly common over most of the state but very common in the Coastal Bend area from early fall through late winter. Kestrels have a rust-colored topside and tail; the male has distinctive slate gray wings. Twin black stripes on the head give him the ferocious falcon look, especially unnerving to sparrows. The kestrel used to be called a sparrow hawk, for good reason.

The American kestrel, once called a sparrow hawk, is the smallest North American falcon.

MERLIN The merlin also features the fashionable slate gray male plumage that appears more like a top coat. The female of this small falcon group wears a demure bark brown coat; both sexes have brown streaked breasts and underparts. They like to hunt along the edges of lakes, rivers, and marshes. Their former name, pigeon hawk, gives you a clue to dietary preference.

CROW INSIGHTS

While not commonly listed with birds of prey, the crow commands the attention of sportsmen as a source of sporty wingshooting and as a superb resource for training young hunters. Crows are wary creatures requiring great patience and stalking skill when one attempts to sneak up on a murder.

Texas is the best place in America to seek out various species of crows and ravens. We have Mexican crows in the Rio Grande Valley, plenty of American crows throughout Central and East Texas, and both the common raven and Chihuahuan. The latter, found in the Trans-Pecos, is an impressive bird, with his four feet of glossy black wingspan and fan-shaped tail easily marking him in flight.

Crows are omnivorous but are particularly attracted to newly planted crops. They often roost together, and large roosts can pose a real threat to crops. Technically, it is legal to shoot crows only when they are causing a depredation of crops or livestock.

OWL INSIGHTS

Night fighters of the predator air force, owls are among the most beneficial birds to mankind. Some species have been aptly described, for instance, as "flying mousetraps." Yet owls are ranked right up there with haunted houses and other fearful manifestations of the supernatural. Owls are, everywhere on our planet, a symbol of superstition.

Owls are far more numerous in Texas than most would think, because they are so skillful at daytime hiding. Just as skillful at night hunting, they are superbly equipped for silent flight. That's what their fluffy feathers are all about; they act as wind and noise suppressors. If it weren't for their haunting hoots and screeches, we might not suspect these magnificent hunters were about.

That's why sound communication is so important to owls. Most owls are so secretive, so camouflaged, so absolutely still in the day, and so quiet at night while hunting that they not only fool man and other predators, they also would never get together for propagation of the species if they didn't sound off occasionally.

If you think owls have a fixed stare, you're right. Their eyes are fixed in bony tunnels so they can't roll them about, but they can rotate their heads more than 180 degrees to look directly behind themselves. Their eyes are tremendously adapted to night vision. Some biologists claim their eyes contain only rods, no cones, and therefore they have no color vision. There's a myth that owls can't see in the daytime; much like cats, owl pupils scrunch down to emit just enough light to allow them to see better than you in bright light.

Owls can triangulate on sound, and many species can hunt in total darkness if the prey makes the slightest noise. It is thought the disks which frame the owl's face act as a directional microphone or parabolic reflector to focus sound. Other wildlife biologists have determined that the ears of many owls are positioned off line, one above the other, which could further aid in pinpointing a sound source, giving the owl two time-elapsed intervals to plug into his distance-measuring computer.

Owls swallow whole most small prey, such as field mice, then regurgitate the indigestible fur, feather, or bones. These leftovers are in the form of pellets, so one way of locating an owl nesting area is to search for owl pellets. Nesting sites can build up large pellet accumulations, because owls tend to use the same area again and again.

The famous naturalist Ernest Seton, chairman of the committee that established the Boy Scouts of America, dubbed the great horned owls "winged tigers" and ranked them "among the most pronounced and savage of the birds of prey."

GREAT HORNED OWL The great horned owl can be distinguished from the smaller barred owl by both size and his white throat patch. Otherwise, they are similar, with long ear tufts sticking straight up like jackrabbit ears and great camouflage in bars and streaks of dark brown on buff. The great horned owl can stand almost two feet high on a perch, and many have a wingspan of four and a half feet. He's an imposing bird with an insatiable appe-

The great horned owl is nicknamed "the winged tiger" because of his exceptional predator skills.

tite. As long as there are plenty of rabbits around, the great horned owl ignores birds such as quail and ducks, but when food is short this powerful predator will go after most anything, including skunks, snakes, and porcupines. Great horned owls and their nests often smell of skunk. They are said to be the skunk's only natural enemy.

The great horned owl's hoot is the one always associated with owls. It's a deep, resonant bass *who-ho-o-o* repeated up to eight times, and not unlike a foghorn at sea. This is the call that spooks a tom turkey into the nervous gobble that reveals his roost. But, the great horned owl can also shriek a blood-curdling scream if he's mad or hungry enough. Their young will leave their immediate birthplace while the old owls remain on the same roost for years. Great horned owls in captivity have lived several decades.

Although it's true that owls are night prowlers, great horned owls often hunt in the day. They fear no other predators, not even man, but they will fly off the roost at your approach. The silence of their flight is unnerving. You sense the power, but there is almost no wing motion and absolutely no sound, even when they pass close by. Actually, there have been reports of attacks on people, usually those dumb enough to assault an owl nest.

BARRED OWLS The barred owl is a riverbottom dweller and therefore found in Central to East Texas

The barred owl prefers river bottoms and is most often sighted in eastern Texas.

woodlands, where he likes to roost high up. His head is large and round but not tufted. His camo job is similar to the great horned and long-eared owls. He preys on small stuff, even crawfish, frogs, and mice; little birds are delicacies. The barred owl's *who-cooks-for-you, who-cooks-for-you-all* hoot sequence is standard repertoire for much of the East Texas nightsong.

EASTERN SCREECH OWL The interesting thing about the eastern screech owl is that he rarely ever screeches. He's a handsome little "wildcat of the air," usually an overall pale gray. He's tufted like the great horned owl, but much, much smaller. About eight inches high, weighing in at a tough four ounces, he may be the most ferocious predator on earth on an ounce per pounce basis.

A musically inclined observer, more than a hundred years ago, described the love song of the screech owl as "B flat of the middle octave, a soft trill, two or three seconds long and closing with an upward inflection." Hardly a screech. Screech owls also sing melodious tenor/ soprano duets.

Ounce for ounce, the most ferocious predator on earth is the screech owl.

BARN OWL The common barn owl is the culprit in many haunted house tales, and he does screech as well as hiss. He has a heart-shaped face and deep-set dark eyes which stare fixedly out of his snowy white mask. He's also been called, appropriately, the "monkey-faced owl." He's rust-brown on top, buff or white flecked in cinnamon underneath.

Barn owls nest any place they take a liking to as long as it's nice and dark in the day. They're often found in metropolitan areas. Perhaps this adaptability has enabled the barn owl to inhabit every continent with the exception of Antarctica. His world-wide presence is even more remarkable when you remember he's a land-based bird lacking the tremendous speed, range, and endurance of that other world traveler, the peregrine falcon.

Barn owls are one of the few birds
found on every continent.

BURROWING OWL   One of this state's most interesting
birds of prey is the burrowing owl; he's a terrestrial owl
who's right at home on the Prairie Dog Town Fork of the
Red River or any other wide open West Texas prairie. He's
a funny looking guy with long legs and a short tail. He's
got the typical owl camowear, with bold bars and stripes
against buff.

The burrowing owl hunts at night and comports himself like other owls until it comes time to roost. Then he
finds himself a prairie dog, armadillo, ground squirrel, or
gopher hole and burrows there—a most unseemly practice for a bird of prey, but this is how he got the name
"dogtown owl" from oldtimers. He'll use the same burrow
year after year unless rousted by a badger or rattlesnake.

The rattlesnake is the burrowing owl's main nemesis,
and is perhaps the reason why this owl creates such a
good rattler imitation, by rapidly striking his mandibles
together. This sound might not deter a real rattlesnake,
but most other creatures would certainly hesitate before
crawling into a dark burrow from which emanates the distinctive whir of a diamondback's rattle. We would.

Texas settlers knew the burrowing owl as the "dog
town owl" because that's where he was found.

SNAKE INSIGHTS

Killing rattlesnakes would seem to be part of the Code of the West, certainly the code of West Texas. J. Frank Dobie said he grew up with the understanding that "a man even halfway decent would always shut any gate he had opened . . . and would always kill any rattlesnake he got a chance at."

All rattlers are pit vipers, and at least ten different rattlesnakes reside in Texas, ranging from the little and little-known massasaugas to the ever popular, villainous *Crotalus atrox*, better known as the Western diamondback. Atrox does attain seven feet or more and is quite dangerous. He accounts for his share of fangings and deaths in Texas.

Texas also has three copperheads, a water moccasin, and the pretty coral snake, whose neurotoxin makes it the most deadly of all. The copperheads and water moccasins are pit vipers; the coral snake is related to the cobra.

All of the pit vipers have heat sensitive indentations between their eyes and nostrils. These nifty sensors may have been the inspiration for heat-seeking missiles, because pit vipers can zero in at close range on warm blooded prey in total darkness—perhaps a rabbit's burrow or your sleeping bag. Pit vipers also have a keen sense of smell and can track animals and other snakes for some distance. They sense vibrations such as a bootfall, but are believed to live in a silent world, incapable of hearing sound waves transmitted in the air. Their eyesight is inadequate for all but close work.

The western diamondback holds the record for sending Texas sportsmen to emergency rooms.

Sportsmen are aware that snake behavior is affected by weather. Cold snakes are almost in a coma, but the warmer the weather the more you should be on the lookout for snake activity. Don't build too many mesquite fires against old, unmortared stone walls while trying to escape the chill of a blue norther.

Pit vipers den up, often mingling varieties in the same den. Some dens are used year after year. Snakes do give off an odor, and a good place to prove this for yourself is at a well-used den. Ranchers will often know these locations and will gas or smoke out the snakes. As a result, much of the Hill Country is as free of rattlesnakes as Ireland after St. Patrick. But, your rancher might not be as effective as the good saint, so do look down frequently as the temperature goes up.

Male snakes have a two-pronged hemipenis. Not only that, but each of the hemis is covered with tiny spines, and once engorged with blood is textured much like the family planning products oft displayed in roadside men's rooms. The purpose would seem to assure that male and female snakes remain attached long enough for sperm to be deposited in the female's cloaca chamber and remain over the winter. Fertilization takes place in the spring and the young are born in 90 days.

All pit vipers are born alive in a membrane, out of which the young quickly cut their way. They arrive on the scene with fangs, fully capable of immediate envenomation.

Humans constantly shed and replace skin cells, a process which delights the manufacturers of skin care cosmetics. Snakes would not make good cosmetic customers; instead of shedding constantly, they save up for a complete skin changeout several times a year. That's why you'll often come across almost whole dermis. The tip of the rattler's tail accumulates keratin at each shedding. This is the stuff your nails and hair are made of, and it forms the snake's rattles. The older the snake, the more keratin buildup and the more rattles. Since the rattler sheds his skin often, the number of rattles does not directly age the snake. Only microscopic inspection will reveal the correct age.

Snakes can and do hide almost anywhere. Reaching blindly into rock or wood piles, sitting down without looking, or creating warmth in a place where snakes can reach you is inviting an unwelcome event.

The western diamondback holds the all-time record for sending folks to hospitals. In pit viper size, he's second only to the Eastern diamondbacks found in the southeastern United States. A six-foot-long diamondback is not uncommon. He's found throughout most of Texas except the too-wet Pineywoods.

The diamondback's color varies considerably by ecological area from pink to light gray. The diamond outline markings are a very faint white, often difficult to distinguish. If you have time, look for the black and white tail bands.

The Trans-Pecos features seven out of ten of the distinct rattler species, this one being the blacktail.

ground. He's a beautiful snake if you're into such. You'll find him, though rarely, only in the Guadalupe Mountains.

The Trans-Pecos is indeed snaky country, with seven out of the 10 of our distinct rattler species found there. Another species is the northern blacktail, whose range extends eastward into the headers and draws of the Edwards Plateau. He's a shy and retiring little fellow (maybe because of his Yankee-sounding name, a definite liability in Texas) noted for his anthracite-colored tail. Rounding out the snakes of the Trans-Pecos is the fascinating little desert massasauga, once known as the Edward's massasauga. His background color is a creamy, pale yellow splotched over with pale brown patches. Large plates on the head, between the eyes, distinguish the massasauga from all other Texas rattlers except his cousin, the western massasauga. The western massasauga has a higher tolerance for damp, and thus ranges through the Cross Timbers and Prairies, Post Oak Savannah, and Gulf Prairies and Marshes. The western massasauga markings are more vivid; otherwise, the two snakes are much alike.

Along with the heinous *atrox*, the western massasauga bridges Texas rattler species across to the eastern areas of the state. In the Post Oak Savannah and Pineywoods, the ruling rattler is the timber, which can attain six feet. The

Very similar in appearance are the much smaller prairie and Mojave rattlesnakes, with round, brown, blotchy markings on the back. The Mojave also has much wider white tail bands. These small, three- to four-foot rattlers are found only in the western reaches of the Trans-Pecos. Other small Trans-Pecos rattlers include the mottled rock and banded rock. The mottled and banded rock seldom get over two feet. The mottled rattlers also have varying coloration, mainly in pink and gray rock tones. The banded rock rattler has widely spaced, zig zag bands of black, sometimes displayed against a silver gray back-

The western massasauga is actually found in the eastern half of the state.

timber rattlesnake's tail is usually black, and a black saw-tooth pattern with sharp points toward the tail is a distinct field mark. The background color varies and can be cinnamon, brown, or olive-gumbo-colored.

Some herpetologists consider the canebrake rattlesnake to be a subspecies of the timber, referring back to 1935 when it was formally accorded this name. However, most experts believe the canebrake to be just a color variation of the timber. The canebrake favors the dark, wet environment his name suggests.

The timber rattler is also known as
the canebrake rattler in eastern Texas.

We'll also find the occasional western pigmy rattlesnake wandering about in the Pineywoods and hardwoods of East Texas. He's often only a foot or two in length, rarely more than two. He's marked by a series of irregular blackish blotches on the back, and he looks a bit plump as snakes go. One of the myths of the pigmy is that his venom is particularly toxic for his size. Not true. Because of his size, he just doesn't carry enough venom to kill you. Just the same, treat bites seriously. He is a rattlesnake.

Broad, irregular, copper-toned bands mark each of our three copperheads: the Trans-Pecos, broad-banded, and southern. The Trans-Pecos is further distinguished by his dark, laterally streaked and mottled belly. He is only

The broad-banded copperhead is found throughout
Central Texas and is our most common copperhead.

found in the Trans-Pecos, usually where there's water. He's seldom longer than two feet and not nearly as venomous as the diamondback.

Although they should be treated with respect, like all pit vipers, copperheads would seem to be a little less toxic. They are seldom reported as perpetrators of fatal snake bites. But, don't relax too much. They are very dangerous, and bites can cause the loss of a limb or even death, particularly in a small child or dog.

The broad-banded is the most numerous, found throughout the middle portion of the state from the Oklahoma border through the Edwards Plateau. His favorite habitat is deciduous hardwood country, and he can be thick on the ground in the right places. The southern copperhead is found primarily in the Pineywoods, and he favors deciduous woodlands where leafy carpets provide the ideal background for his natural camouflage.

Anyone who's read Larry McMurtry's Pulitzer Prize-winning novel *Lonesome Dove* will recall with horror the death of Sean O'Brien from numerous water moccasin bites incurred during a crossing of the Nueces River. Sean fell into a moccasin den, which in low-water conditions in Texas is not all that uncommon, even today. What is uncommon today is death by moccasin envenomation; the snake is responsible for only about one fatality a year for all of North America, despite its size (up to five feet), a chunky frame, and highly potent venom. They are very dangerous, notwithstanding the low incidence of fatalities.

Cottonmouth moccasins are found in
Texas wherever there's water.

Bayou bass fishermen sometimes have an unforgettable view from below—right into the creamy, fang-bedecked maw of a moccasin dangling from a cypress limb. The more common view is of his brownish, mottled back, featuring wide but indistinct bands and dark blotches. Unlike other water snakes, his head stands out distinctly from the rest of his body. Moccasins are found where there is water, throughout the state east of the Pecos, but rarely in the Rolling Plains.

Finally, our most poisonous snake is the coral because its toxin, like that of cobras, attacks the central nervous system. In lay terms, coral snake venom can be fatal. To repeat earlier warnings, "red and yellow kills a fellow;" the coral's red and yellow bands touch; those of harmless snakes such as the Arizona king do not.

Coral snakes have very short fangs, more like teeth, and must chew through the skin. But, their jaws are hinged to open wide so they can chew on very large objects, such as you.

The once endangered alligator has made a comeback in Texas marshes.

Red and yellow will kill a fellow, because the coral snake's nerve venom is almost always fatal.

The Texas variety of coral snake seems to be a little larger than those of the southeastern U.S., with some close to a yard long, though two feet is the common length. They are numerous over all the state except for the Trans-Pecos, Rolling Plains, and High Plains ecological areas, and they are rare along the Red River. They are common in most of our suburban areas, so teach young children not to pick up *any* snakes.

ALLIGATOR INSIGHTS

Texas alligator tails are back in full swing, thanks to their being placed under statewide protection in 1969. Alligators finally made the federal Endangered Species Act in 1967, after a century of being raw material for purses and shoes, plus handy targets "for a fusillade" of lead, as one writer lamented. It is estimated that 2.5 million alligators were killed in Florida between 1880 and 1884, a good indication of the pressure these reptiles would be under until the 1960s.

For a long time, many said "who cares?" to the fate of the American alligator, unlovely, horny-scaled monster that he is. And, make no mistake, alligators are effective carnivores, capable of snapping up your French poodle or other small mammals. They have done serious damage to large animals and humans and are ferocious in the extreme when coming at you sideways, tail thrashing, jaws agape. The technique is to knock you down with the powerful tail, then chomp on you.

Gradually we became aware of the importance of the alligator in swamp and marsh ecology. Where the 'gators were shot out, for example, gar proliferated, eating all the fry of game and bait fish. Ultimately, all that's left in an alligatorless environment would be gar and other rough fish.

There is a valve in the throat of the alligator that allows it to open its mouth underwater, which in turn allows it to crush whatever morsel it may have acquired while submerged. To gulp down the prey however, the alligator, unlike a turtle, must raise its head out of the water, so he seeks out shallow water or dens to complete his meal unless the prey has been swallowed *in toto* at the first assault. This is easy enough when the prey involved is a duck, squirrel, or tiny toy fox terrier. Alligators can't chew like people so they must rip apart larger prey into what they consider bite-sized bits. Frequently, alligators wedge larger prey in an underwater cache until it decomposes enough to be torn apart and swallowed. The alligator's digestive juices pack a wallop. Talk about an acid stomach. They can digest a horseshoe, and thus find almost any other cuisine easy to assimilate.

Often all you see are eyes and nostrils peeking up while 'gators await prey. The distance between the eyes will tell you the alligator's approximate size. Eyes a foot apart indicate the saurian is sizable. Alligator eyes are great light collectors, so they see well at night and in muddy water. They glow like red-hot coals when spotlighted.

The bellowing call of the bull, a thundering *basso profundo* sound, can reverberate across miles of swamp on a still night. Smaller 'gators have a more mellow sound, closer to the lowing of a heifer.

Alligators create dens known as 'gator holes in pockets of swamp country. The large reptiles feed along the banks and are often seen sunning themselves. Do not be deceived by their apparent slowness. 'Gators can lurch fast enough to catch an unwary animal on the bank.

The female alligator constructs a domed nest from gumbo mud and marsh grasses. She then deposits 30 to 60 eggs, the diameter of hens', but longer. She will defend this nest, so approach at risk. It's not a good idea to chunk a rock at her or otherwise provoke her, because she will attack. If you've come upon an alligator unexpectedly, back away slowly, keeping a close eye on her. If she charges, run. She can't climb a tree. Female alligators rarely exceed 9½ feet in length; 11-foot and longer alligators are always males. You'll want to be skeptical of the hunting partner who claims to have seen a 13-foot female 'gator guarding a nest. He may also tell fish stories.

The American alligator, with an estimated life span of 30 years or more, can attain a length of 19 feet, although 'gators larger than 14 feet are rare. Those taken in Texas have averaged eight feet, with many in the 12-foot range. Their hides are valuable, but because alligator hunts in Texas are strictly controlled, it would be difficult to make a living from the hides. The most favorable economic impact is supplementing guide incomes. Sportsmen should consider a guided hunt. If for nothing else, you'll need help lugging your 12-foot gator out of the muck and stuffing it into your BMW trunk.

With the increase in alligator populations, marsh hunters need to be more careful with camp procedures. More alligators mean more alligators who associate food with humans, such as fish cleaning remains, stringers left in the water, leftovers chucked overboard, or small unwary pets at the water's edge. When alligators lose their fear of man they are especially dangerous. Couple loss of fear with hunger and you have a disaster in the making.

More alligators have also meant more alligator confrontations, and adverse publicity generated from golf course incursions, retriever maimings, and occasional bites on humans. TPWD census efforts confirmed that a population increase was underway in the '70s. By the early '80s, the 'gators were back and a statewide alligator management plan had been adopted to provide for an alligator harvest and to resolve the problem of nongame 'gators.

Although there should be no crocodiles in Texas, the quick distinction is that the croc's teeth stick out when his jaws are clamped shut, while the 'gator's are hidden. The big fourth tooth on the side of the lower jaw slips into a niche on the crocodile's upper jaw, yielding the illusion of an evil smile.

PREPARATION FOR
THE PREDATOR HUNT

The sportsman setting out to explore all possible Texas predator hunting has a formidable task ahead in assembling gear and selecting weapons.

Sportsmen can have a lot of fun putting together the potpourri our state can demand. A usual choice for coyotes is the .243, which is also an adequate deer caliber in most areas. A .222 is ample for bobcats and foxes. Any fast action, such as autoloader, lever, or pump in any .30-caliber, is fine for cougar. Many predator hunters select a pistol, and a good choice would be the effective .357, which also chambers for the more comfortable .38. The six-inch barrel should be minimum. The .357 is a top choice for alligator hunters; some opt for a shotgun and 00 buckshot. Shotguns with #4s are also a good pick for situations where skittish predators are being called to you, such as coyotes or bobcats.

DOG SELECTION In Texas, bobcats are sometimes hunted with dogs. Hounds are also used, though rarely, to track cougar. Good cat hounds are hard to come by for West Texas hunts because they have to be capable of tracking across rocky country. Blueticks, Plotts, and Walkers are among the favorites. Training must eliminate other game trails such as raccoons and ringtails, and those hounds used for cougar have to be able to distinguish between bobcat and cougar, so as not to trail the former.

WARDROBE AND GEAR SELECTION In general, predators are sharp-eyed critters, so camouflage for blending into their environment is essential. This includes using a face net for the twilight hours or the occasional day hunt. Comfortable clothes and boots are required for daytime cougar hunts, which often involve covering a vast amount of terrain.

Since most predator hunting in Texas is done at night, dress like a cat burglar in dark clothing with face concealed *a la* commando. Quiet clothes are also important. Avoid fabrics such as nylon that may crackle when brushed against mesquite.

Texas predator hunting centers around callers and electronic calls. Crow hunters have a couple of calling options, one that replicates the "caw" of fighting crows and another that imitates a hawk. A hawk's shriek signals the crow that the hawk is hunting successfully and dulls the crow's sense of danger, because he knows a hawk is so alert.

The "squeaker" is another effective call, especially when you want to lure a predator a little closer for a clean shot. You mimic a mouse with this call, which can be held between the lips as you squeak, leaving both hands free.

The prime predator call for coyotes, bobcats, foxes, and raccoons is the "wounded rabbit" call. This comes in both cottontail and the deeper-toned jackrabbit imitation. When blowing this call, it helps to have a little "ham" in you. The best callers always appear to be in pain, as desperate as its name implies, even if you have never heard a dying rabbit's squeals and screams. Purchase a cassette tape for practice. This same cassette may also be used for electronic calling.

Commandeer your children's cassette-playing "jam box" for a fair-weather electronic caller. Those with remote speakers are best, as the speakers can be located away from the hunter. The predator will zero in on the sound, increasing your odds of not being detected. Powerful, all-weather units specifically designed for predator calling are also available and they have much more range. Whichever electronic caller is used, the results are likely to be far better than those achieved by an amateur mouth call.

Electronic calling devices are not legal for calling game birds and animals. Nor is artificial light of any form legal for hunting game. If you are utilizing powerful lights for night predator hunting, give prior notice to the local game warden. (For clarification, game animals are those which fall under the state legal code governing the seasons and methods by which the animal may be legally hunted. Predators are not awarded the same protected legal status; therefore, predator hunters are not bound by the regulations that specify season or method for hunting.)

Lights that plug into car batteries have tremendous candlepower. Adding a red lens seems to keep the light from spooking predators as much as the harsh glare of white. When using a 12-volt light, remember that it draws a lot of amps. Many a predator hunter has walked home. We like to leave the light off most of the time, turning it on for a scan after several calls. Or, you can run the light off a separate battery, which can be recharged back at camp. Also very effective is the headlamp used by frog hunters. Tilt the light back on your head—just the glow will pick up predator eyes. Some of the most effective times to hunt predators are the hours just after sunset and before sunrise; often you can hunt without a light.

PREDATOR HUNTER'S CHECKLIST
> (See Falconry and Alligators for additional
> equipment)
> Hunting license

Firearms and ammunition
Quiet, dark camouflage clothing
Black "commando" face concealer
Head net/hat
Dark watch cap
Camouflage gloves
Game stool
Calls: Mouth—wounded cottontail or jackrabbit,
   hawk, crow, rodent squeak
Electronic caller and cassette tape
High-power, 12-volt light
Red lens cover
Headlamp
6-volt belt pack battery for headlamp
Folding knife/skinning knife

TECHNIQUES THE EXPERTS USE

Coyotes, foxes, and bobcats have been hammered by Texas hunters for decades and, consequently, have honed their already sharp survival mechanisms. Yet, most newcomers to predator hunting have a difficult time remembering this. Predator hunting often requires even more skill than deer hunting, especially when it comes to staying absolutely still.

Take your time in setting up and be as quiet as you can. Give yourself a good field of fire. Since you should always call into any wind, you must have some knowledge of the terrain. Are coyotes likely to come from a given area? Remember that at night coyotes are probably in open pastures ready to pounce on rabbits and rodents. Make sure you aren't silhouetted. You must blend completely into your background.

Dark, windless nights provide optimum calling conditions given that you are reasonably sure, through sightings or sign, that predators are in the vicinity. Don't bother to hunt in high winds or a full moon.

Coyotes and foxes will usually come to your call in 30 minutes or so. Calling much longer than this in one place is usually a waste of time. If you are in bobcat country, give it a little longer. Bobcats tend to slip from cover to cover on their way in, taking advantage of their natural camouflage whenever possible. For some reason, they aren't as spooked by scent as their canine counterparts, so instead of a 180-degree scan into the wind, do the entire 360 from time to time when bobcats are probable. Bobcats are small, but one sneaking up on you from the rear is not a comforting thought. At night, if you see eyes bobbing from bush to bush, it's almost surely a bobcat.

If nothing comes running or sneaking, you'll want to relocate. On a still night, move a good distance away. With a breeze working against you, a relocation of several hundred yards may be all that's required to broadcast your call to a hungry predator or furbearer.

If your best chance is a coyote, cut down the frequency of calling since they are wary. If you actually see a coyote running to your call, stop calling. If he hesitates, try a squeak caller or call at much lower volume. Coax him in; don't try to jam-box his eardrums into submission.

Predator calling is a highly suspenseful, exciting, almost eerie sport, especially in Texas where we have so much appropriate habitat. Even if you don't care to shoot, it's a skillful way to see predators in their natural environment, something most sportsmen find fascinating in itself.

ALLIGATOR   Alligator hunting in Texas is highly structured because alligators were so close to extinction for many years. The first modern-era hunt was in 1984. TPWD provides orientation information to licensed hunters to assure their safety and the sportsmanlike harvest of the reptiles. This does not include shooting 'gators off of the bank. They may only be shot after they are fairly hooked by one of four methods.

The great majority of 'gators are taken on rigs that suspend a bait at least a foot above the water. A stout pole is rigged to accomplish this. At least 300-pound-test line attached to the hook is required by regulation; many opt for braided steel, securely attached to a stake or tree on shore. Most use a 10/0 stainless steel shark hook, a vicious-looking weapon resembling Captain Hook's appendage. Other methods, though rarely used, include bows, hand-held snares, and harpoons.

The Murphree Wildlife Management Area near Port Arthur has become a popular public hunting area for alligators. As on most WMAs, hunt permits are allocated by public drawing. The hunts are usually in September; sportsmen need to submit their names to TPWD in July. Alligator populations and hunter permits are on the increase, and sportsmen are likely to find all the excitement they can handle.

CROW   For the hunting purist, crow hunting with a rifle will certainly test skills. A very popular cartridge is the .222, and some even use a scoped .22/250, as 200-yard shots to a crow roost are the norm. Remember, crow shooting is legal in Texas only where landowners have permitted you to hunt to resolve depredation problems.

To tune up for the wingshooting season and perhaps help save a crop, set up a blind near a grain field and call 'em in. Crow decoys are important, and an owl decoy adds a lot of pull to your setup. Complete camouflage is called

A ten-foot alligator can pose logistics problems for the successful hunter.

Perched on the gloved fist of the falconer, this
lanner is *karak*—ready for the hunt.

for since crows are sharp-eyed and wary. Prop up dead
crows on the ground in front of your blind to increase
your decoy spread.

FALCONRY   The most complex hunting regulations in
Texas are those controlling the sport of falconry, though
this does not explain why so little falconry is attempted.
Falconry is, by far, our most difficult hunting sport to mas-
ter, especially if you're not equipped with the patience of
Job and a tremendous will to succeed.

You encounter problems from word one. The sport's
name is even confusing, in that falconers may, under
tightly specified conditions, use hawks and owls as well as
falcons. In fact, two species of buteo hawks are allowed at
the apprentice level. A falconer who uses hawks is known
as an "austringer." The French words contrasting the
wing action of falcons and buzzard hawks are instructive;
"ramiers" translates as "rowers" for falcons, and
"voiliers" as "sailers" for buzzard hawks.

The buteos are far more common in Texas and more
easily trained, thus two species—the red-tailed and red-
shouldered hawks—are specified by regulation as those
for use by apprentices seeking a falconry permit. The
limit is one. The apprentice may also elect as his one

A falcon explodes off the fist
in pursuit of small game.

choice the American kestrel, our smallest and most populous falcon.

An apprentice falconer can be as young as 14, but must be supervised by someone holding a general or master permit. The apprentice is officially sponsored and must spend at least two years in training before he can qualify for the general falconry permit. The minimum age for acquiring the general permit is 18, and the holder is permitted two raptors. Excluded from the raptors allowed in falconry are, of course, all those threatened and endangered under state or federal law, such as peregrines. Also excluded are all kites; osprey; caracara; all owls with the exception of the great horned owl; black, gray, and white-tailed hawks; and golden eagles. The eagle may be excluded for the falconer's own good, although it's just as hard to imagine a great horned owl perched on your arm awaiting removal of his hood.

The master falconer will have spent at least five years at the general level so that his minimum experience is seven years. The regulations state a minimum age of 21, but because of the general requirements, no one under the age of 23 could possibly achieve master. The master can add one more raptor to his air corps, but unless he's issued an exception permit, this must come from the same selection available to those with general permits.

Housing requirements for the raptors are extensive and must be in place before the prospective falconer can even apply for a permit. The rules help assure that the birds will have adequate living space both indoors and out, be protected, and live in a clean environment. Even the material for the floor is specified "absorbent."

For each raptor kept, a long list of equipment must be acquired. Much of this equipment needs duplication, such as hoods for the heads and jesses for the legs, even separate gauntlets and scales for weighing. The reason for duplicate equipment is to minimize communication of bird disease.

All raptor housing must be built and the equipment purchased before the applicant is allowed to take the exam; he must score at least 80 on tests featuring biology, laws, and history, as well as handling. Only then is a permit issued.

Falcons are temperamental birds; if lost, months or years of training is literally out the window as they quickly revert to their wild state. Falconers have been known to act as beaters for their prize raptors, working very hard to scare a rabbit out of cover.

Newcomers to the sport often begin with an *eyas*, a legally acquired falcon taken straight from the nest. Training requires carrying the falcon around on your gauntlet for hours a day, and then more hours are spent whirling a training lure adorned with meat about your head while the falcon makes like a dive bomber. Somewhere in the process, the bird is trained to the hood and to have some tolerance for other humans. All in all, falconry is a major

commitment, which is exactly what TPWD insists be understood before exposing beautiful and wild falcons and hawks to the sport.

THE INJURED WILD ONE

The active sportsman will inevitably come across an injured animal or bird, and the encounter usually poses three questions: legal, ethical, and practical ones.

The issue of legality arises from the fact that without a permit it is against the Texas legal code to possess or transport any game mammal or game bird indigenous to this state that is captured from the wild. This protection is extended by state law to most nongame birds. The U.S. Fish and Wildlife Service has its own umbrella of wildlife protection. The bottom line is that it is against both state and federal laws for unlicensed persons to possess wildlife, even if it is injured or orphaned.

Ethical problems center first on determining whether or not the animal or bird truly needs rescue. General guidelines for attempting rescue would include:
–The animal is very weak, nearly immobilized, or obviously starving.
–It is certain that the parent is dead and the offspring too young to survive.
–The animal is clearly injured.

Unfortunately, there is a strong tendency to overreact, thus "rescuing" an animal which is best left alone. Far too many lovely, spotted fawns are taken home each spring because their rescuers thought they were orphaned. A doe was nearby in almost every instance. This same phenomenon extends to all cuddly little mammals or small birds, most of which have a parent and/or nest close by at the time of "rescue."

There is a misconception that human scent on a young, wild animal will cause the parents to reject it. This is simply untrue and is not an excuse for taking the animal from its habitat.

The classic book, *Born Free*, popularized the idea of keeping a wild animal as a pet. This is not only against the law in Texas, but also potentially dangerous since a wild animal's natural survival instincts lead to unpredictability, especially in captivity.

Raising a wild animal in captivity lessens its chances for survival in the natural environment. A licensed wildlife rehabilitator or veterinarian can provide the specialized care required in a way that maximizes the animal's chances at surviving upon release.

Finally, there is the ultimate ethical concern of when to put an injured animal or bird in the field out of its misery. Here again there are legal considerations. Such decisions are often best left to the judgment of an experienced outdoorsman or wildlife specialist.

The third issue is one of practicality. A cougar with a hangnail may pose a different practical problem than an orphaned cottontail bunny. The rescuer needs to be aware of the threat of rabies, and of the serious wounds a frightened animal can inflict. The typical hawk can exert 50 to 100 pounds of claw pressure. The powerful pully system of the great horned owl's claws can clutch with a strength of up to 150 pounds. This is analagous to having someone drive a nail through your hand. Experience with the strength of domestic cats and dogs under panic should alert the rescuer to the potential for danger from their wild counterparts; keep in mind that the untrained may also be seriously hurt by the forelegs of a deer or the spines of a porcupine.

WHAT TO DO

- Contact a wildlife rehabilitator, TPWD office, or veterinarian as soon as possible. Be prepared to describe the animal or bird in detail and give a lay opinion of the injury.
- A coat or jacket provides good emergency care for hawks or owls with wing injuries. Carefully place the bird headfirst into a coat sleeve. This pins the wings, minimizing damage, and the darkness calms the bird.
- Handle any animal or bird as little as possible. Think through what you are going to do before grabbing.

- For larger injured birds, a large box with air holes, such as a TV set carton, is suitable for transport. Place a towel in the bottom for the bird to grip for security. For smaller birds, a covered box just a little larger than the bird is preferred. Don't forget a few air holes.
- If you must stop at camp or home on the way to a wildlife rehabilitation station, place the bird or animal in a dark, warm, quiet place. Don't allow kids to peek or domestic animals to approach.
- Do not attempt to give water to a bird. What you think is the esophagus is the windpipe. Many a bird has been drowned on dry land by well-meaning rescuers.
- Even if an animal or bird appears to be absolutely starved, resist the impulse to feed it or give it any liquids. It has existed this long and you may well kill or seriously harm the animal by trying to nourish it.

A rescuer, like an urban paramedic, needs to know exactly where to go for emergency wildlife treatment. The key is to have noted veterinarian or wildlife rehabilitation locations in advance, or at the least, to have handy the number of the local TPWD office. We suggest that sportsmen have predetermined locations near the area where they are frequently afield.

LARGEMOUTH
Set the hook when you feel the slightest tug. It takes a hard jerk to push the hook through the worm and into the tough jaw of old "bucketmouth."

SMALL
A great sporting fish! keep the first you catch Release the others PRACTICE CONS

CR

CHANNEL CAT
Not too pretty but one of the best eating fish you can catch.

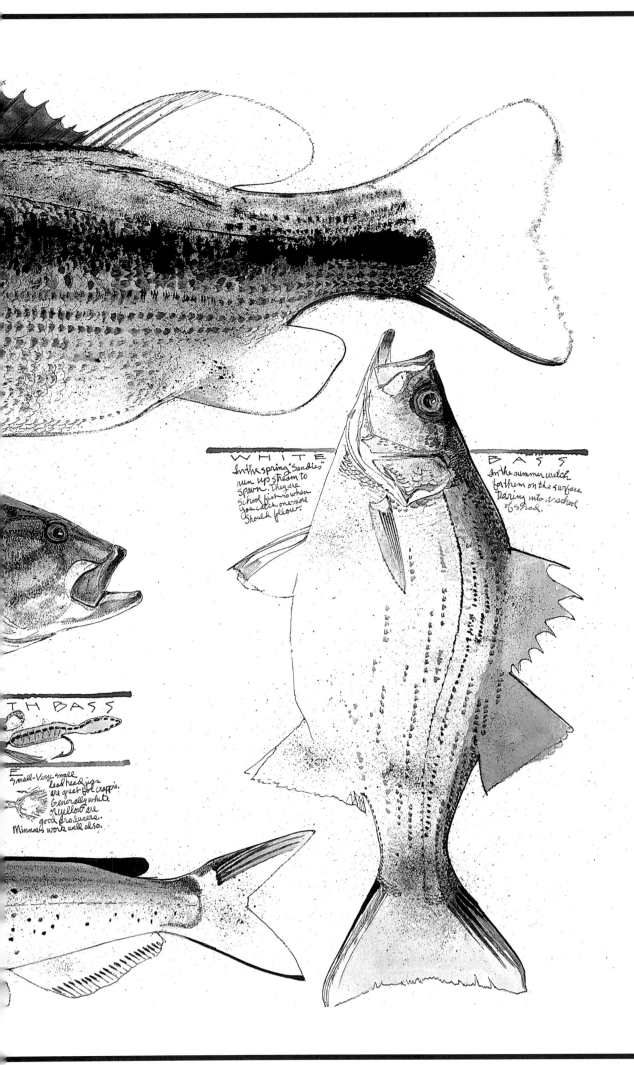

WHITE BASS

In the spring "Sandies" run up stream to spawn. They are school fish so when you catch one more should follow.

In the summer watch for them on the surface tearing into a school of shad.

TH BASS

E Small - Very small lead head jigs are great for crappie. Generally white or yellow are good producers. Minnows work well also.

XII

THE

FISHING

OPTION

THE
FISHING
OPTION

From bluegills to blue marlin, the newcomer to Texas faces a bewildering number of options when he cases his guns and reaches for a rod. We have almost two million acres of impounded water, well beyond that of any other state, and the more than 200 reservoirs involved produce some of the best freshwater fishing anywhere, starring black bass and a host of other top acts.

Immigrants to Texas often think they are moving to a vast desert wasteland when contrasting Texas with a state such as Minnesota, the Land of 10,000 Lakes. Minnesota has 15,000 miles of flowing water; Texas more than 80,000. Although Texas does not have 10,000 lakes, no one has yet counted the stock tanks, which are of paramount importance to sportsmen.

Counting the shorelines of our magnificent barrier islands—such as Padre Island, with the longest protected national seacoast in the nation—Texans have more than 3,300 miles of often spectacular tidal saltwater fishing, with 2.1 million acres of bay fishing alone.

Surf fishing and small craft excursions out to oil rigs that dot the Gulf add to the options, as do party boat trips to the fabled snapper banks. The well-heeled sportsman can troll offshore for big game fish.

It's the options that confound you in Texas. From an elk grazing at 8,000 feet in the Guadalupes to a marlin roaring up from 8,000 feet of blue water, the contrasts are staggering. But, it's what's in between that really counts to Texas sportsmen—black bass and white-tailed deer—more numerous here than anywhere else in our hemisphere.

Black bass, sand bass or white bass, and crappie are the big three of Texas fresh waters; speckled trout, redfish, and flounder are their counterparts in saltwater bay fishing.

Wherever you find fresh water, notably stock tanks, you'll find sunfish, including bluegills, green, and redear. There are four catfish recognized for state record purposes: black bullhead, blue, channel, and flathead. The flathead is also known in Texas as Opelousas and often tops 50 pounds. Redfish have been successfully transplanted to some lakes from their natural saltwater environment. Caddo Lake is well known for its chain pickerel.

Rough fish favored by bow hunters include freshwater drum (gaspergou), bowfin, buffalo, carp, and two kinds of gar, the alligator and longnosed. The alligator gar found in Texas rivers can attain weights of more than 200 pounds.

Saltwater bays and surf feature whiting, pompano, croakers, various catfish, sheepshead, sand trout, black drum, shark, and Spanish mackerel. Sharks are common off our Gulf beaches, but most are not dangerous. There are exceptions, though, and sharks have attacked humans. A fin in the surf should be regarded as reason to head for the beach. Just a bit offshore, you're into the king mackerel, bonito, amberjack, barracuda, grouper, jewfish, red snapper, dogsnapper, spadefish, blackfin and yellowfin tuna, wahoo, dorado, cobia or ling, and various sporty types like tarpon, jack crevalle, skipjacks, blue, and rainbow runners. A little further out and you're in billfish waters with sailfish, white and blue marlin, and broadbill swordfish.

As if our fishing options aren't naturally broad enough, TPWD has seen fit to widen them through the introduction of non-native species that present some of our finest light tackle tests. Making the biggest news ever, since the first stocking in 1972, are strains of Florida bass which are now furnishing state records. It's commonplace for Florida strain bass to be introduced into stock tanks and selected public lakes along with a Florida strain bluegill, the coppernose. The early '70s also saw the initial stocking of the now fabled striped bass, which led to the hybrid striped bass. The hybrid is a cross between the striped bass and the white or sand bass. Many of the large reservoirs are now producing great striper sportfishing, with records being eclipsed regularly.

Here, too, it is important to go very carefully with exotics of any sort, whatever the current compelling argument. White amurs, better known as grass carp, are now not too popular with bass fishermen on Lake Conroe, as they overwhelmed the game fish population. They were imported to check yet another exotic, the aquatic weed hydrilla, which probably found its way here from Florida, where it has destroyed the recreational value of many lakes in that state. There's no doubt that hydrilla is a terrible problem for lakes, but sometimes the cure can be worse than the illness.

The Edwards Plateau area, especially in the Hill Country, has been favored with stocking of smallmouth bass. The program, begun in 1974, has been highly successful where the bass have rocky reservoirs and flowing streams.

During the winter months, TPWD fisheries personnel head for the Guadalupe River below Canyon Dam, the Brazos below Possum Kingdom, and other areas to stock rainbow trout and to test the suitability of other trout strains. The rainbow stocking program is here to stay; another great option for fly fisherman.

Sportsmen will be forever indebted to Bob Kemp, former director of fisheries of TPWD, who died in 1986. Kemp pioneered the introduction of the fish which now bears his name, Kemp bass. Kemp was instrumental in bringing Florida strain black bass to Texas, actually funding the initial shipment out of his own pocket, a risky equivocation of TPWD policy. Kemp was behind the striped bass stocking programs and smallmouth bass, walleye, and the striper-white bass hybrids of the early '70s.

Kemp was also the driving force behind the state's action to declare spotted seatrout and red drum game fish, thereby providing some protection from netters. He courageously led the way toward limits and size restric-

For most Texas sportsmen black bass are the major fishing option.

tions to help preserve the state's fabulous black bass fishing. Without Kemp, the Texas sportsman would have far fewer fishing options today or tomorrow.

"Black bass fishing is changing. At one time it was strictly a contemplative sport in which the angler silently rowed or paddled along the shoreline, tossing a hunk of wood, plastic, hair or feathers towards a likely-looking pocket," wrote Bill Dance, author and professional tournament fisherman.

Dance, in his *Practical Black Bass Fishing*, written with Mark Sosin, states that in the early '70s bass fishing entered "a competitive phase that replaced the contemplative," adding that "competition produces benefits." Dance pointed out that individuals can measure their abilities against others, that competitive bass fishing motivates them to master ever-new techniques and sophisticated equipment, and that competition is also the prime stimulus for the invention of new techniques. Nowhere is this truer than in Texas, where many of our three million plus fishermen have embraced the modern bass boat with its "star wars" strategic initiative capability; nowhere is tournament fishing so widespread. The inherent excitement of skilled game fishing, high stakes gambling, and, above all, competitive appeal are an irresistible lure to thousands of Texas tournament bass fishermen.

Many fishermen in the last decades of the 20th century turned away from competitive bass fishing, perhaps because they began to realize that the warrior-like combativeness of their marketplace or profession had been projected onto a sport that, after all, should be contemplative. No one is more apt to perceive this than a sportsman whose appreciation for all things wild has led to an understanding that it's not man against man in the outdoors, but rather, man in harmony with nature, testing himself against fish, animal, or bird, maybe testing himself against himself. Winning or losing are not really part of it, because the true sportsman always wins on his days outdoors, no matter what.

Though tournament fishing has garnered its critics, it is a highly satisfactory form of weekend recreation for many. To their credit, tournament operators and fishermen are doing much to correct the faults of this organized sport. Corrections were needed as fixing scandals broke out across the tourney scene in the early 1980s. Other remedies were needed to offset the negative public perception that tournaments vacuumed lakes of fish and wasted those harvested. And, for whatever reason, fish populations in many of the large reservoir lakes did decline in the '80s.

Joining a bass club is one of the best ways to learn Texas bass fishing, which, for the bass boat-equipped fisherman, is largely a matter of knowing the Texas lakes and mastering the fine art of structure fishing and pattern recognition. As Dance and others have noted, 90 percent of the fish in an impoundment lake are not along the shore but out there in that big, deep water, which requires a safe boat and specialized equipment such as a depth finder.

Short of revealing their favorite fishing holes, many bass club members are generous in sharing general lake information with newcomers, unless the stakes are really high. Many clubs have a rotating partner system, which can expose the newest members to the expertise of the older hands.

You should also consider hiring a guide if you're new to Texas or unfamiliar with a lake, especially the sprawling monsters of East Texas, such as Toledo Bend.

And, for a modest investment you can collect a portfolio of commercially prepared lake maps worth their weight in fish scales. They'll help in four ways: in locating launch ramps, avoiding dangerous water, not getting lost, and in structure fishing because many terrain features are indicated.

The sportsman views fishing as a natural extension of his enjoyment of all outdoors, and he never forgets fishing can be downright fun. Almost anyone can enjoy fishing, regardless of age or physical condition. If you can hold a pole and hold your mouth right, you can be an angler. Fishing is an ideal pastime and a perfect venue for first introducing youngsters to the pleasures of nature. Getting the whole family involved in catching dinner is a great way to close generation gaps.

Therefore, this guide will focus on fishing tactics that help implement this philosophy. You'll not find much on scientific bass fishing; stock tanks don't require depth finders.

Unless you are on your own land, if you are between 17 and 65 years of age you'll need a license to fish freshwater and a saltwater stamp if you're on the coast. The exception to this would be if you confine yourself to your county of residence and use only a trotline, throwline, or pole without reel. The good buy is a combination fishing and hunting license, typically valid from September 1—dove season opener—to August 31 of the following year. If you're going after rainbow trout, you'll also need a trout stamp. The best bargain is the lifetime license, single or combination. We urge all sportsmen to invest their small fry with this lifelong gift. It's a meaningful contribution to the future of Texas.

There are many other license requirements of TPWD, including those for non-residents and guides. Lake Texoma, the huge impoundment on the Texas-Oklahoma border above Dallas, requires its own special license if you're going to fish both states' waters. Since it's sometimes difficult to tell the Red River channel that separates the states, go ahead and buy one. Texas does have a reciprocal license agreement with Louisiana, allowing resident sport fisherman of either state who are properly licensed or exempt to fish common boundary lakes such as Toledo Bend and Caddo Lake, as well as the boundary rivers.

Many counties and even specific lakes have exceptions to the General Freshwater Fishing Regulations, so it's wise to study the special lake regulations, county exceptions, and complete summaries of regulations for sport fishing in Texas that are available from TPWD.

General regulations cover such things as legal nets, seines, and trawls. For example, gill nets, trammel nets, drag seines, and hoop nets are not permitted. Wire loops, gigs, bow and arrow, spear guns, and spears may be used for taking only rough fish such as buffalo, carp, gar, freshwater drum (gaspergou), Rio Grande perch, suckers, shad, bowfin (grindle), pickerel, mullet, and goldfish.

It's illegal to use noodling poles or snatch hooks. The latter method uses one or more hooks attached to a line that is jerked through the water. It's called snagging and jerking, appropriately enough. All counties prohibit fishing from the road surface or deck of any causeway or bridge maintained by the Texas Highway Department.

Years ago, game hogs discovered "telephoning" to stun fish—employing now antique wind-up telephone generators. Fishing regulations state that it is "illegal to use any explosives, electrical shocking devices, poisons or any other substances which drug, paralyze or kill in the taking of fish from any public waters of the state." As a matter of fact, you can't even have an "electrical producing device" within 1/2 mile of any state water. Most ranchers won't appreciate you blowing up stock tanks either. No sportsman would consider using any such devices.

Limits and size requirements vary year to year so you are urged to count and measure. A ruler is helpful. You may not have in your immediate possession any fish in excess of the daily bag limit while fishing on public waters. The possession limit does not include fish processed and stored at the fisherman's permanent residence.

A separate set of regulations exists for saltwater sport fishing, including the required saltwater stamp. You'll find the rules greatly expanded when it comes to trotlines, nets, seines, and trawls. There are also special seasons and limits for taking shrimp set under the Texas Shrimp and Conservation Act. There is even a license requirement for taking mussels, clams, and naiads. Crabs and oysters are covered under regulations which specifically protect egg-bearing female crabs and oysters, in season, less than three inches across. Scuba divers take note: Saltwater regulations are much freer than those for freshwater. The only fish prohibited are red drum (redfish) and spotted seatrout. When the water is clear from Aransas to South Padre Island, there can be good spearfishing, particularly off the oil rigs and over artificial reefs.

Also worth studying is a condensed version of the Texas Water Safety Act, because under the State Parks and Wildlife Code you can be boarded by any peace officer or game warden. Boats that comply with U.S. Coast Guard requirements will, in general, be acceptable under these regulations as far as equipment is concerned. State regulations are very specific as to safe operation of your boat, and fines are stiff.

PREPARATION FOR FISHING

Sportsmen tend to take a minimalist approach to tackle since they are usually already encumbered with other gear, ranging from cast-iron pots to varmint calls. Lures and terminal tackle vary widely from freshwater to salt, but certain basics can easily be kept at hand. It will come as a total shock to the multi-tiered tackleboxer in the big bass boat set that just a few lures will usually do the trick if the objective is a filled frying pan. And if something special is happening locally, you can almost always locate the hot lure, bait, or system at a sporting goods store or bait shop.

Start off with a couple of good casting rods and reels rigged with the line test you want. Tournament bass folks like 14- to 17-pound test, but most sportsmen believe the lighter the better—10- to 12-pound test for bait casting reels, 8- to 10-pound test for spinning.

Spinning outfits lend themselves well to the majority of stock tank and coastal fishing opportunities that come up during hunting trips. Many excellent spinning rods are available in sections, making packing easier. These rods will throw the lighter lures, which seem to work best in stock tanks and most saltwater flat fishing. Always pack a spare. One of the rods should have a little more backbone to it for bass worming in fresh water and for flounder and bull reds in salt.

There are specific suggestions for each of the basic situations found later in this chapter. But, remember, this is

For more than a million Texas sportsmen the pursuit of lunker black bass is a true avocation.

not intended to be a comprehensive guide to all forms of Texas fishing.

FRESHWATER FISHING

BLACK BASS Modern bass fishing is one of the outdoor world's most complex sports. Aficionados who have dedicated themselves to the pursuit of the wily largemouth have mastered strategies and tactics that rival those of Fortune 500 CEOs.

The constantly growing body of knowledge, increasingly sophisticated equipment, and near professional skill levels of thousands of fishermen have actually put our state's bass population in some jeopardy. More fishermen are catching more bass, putting great pressure on the resource. Sportsmen have long touted the merits of catch and release programs, and future generations will be reliant on how well this concept is accepted by our three million plus fishermen.

To most bass fishermen, and our hundreds of thousands of visitors from other states, Texas means *big* water—huge impoundments with quality habitat. Major tournaments have given many of our reservoirs great notoriety outside Texas, and even Floridians are begrudgingly conceding our preeminence. The race is on to see which state produces the newest world record—Texas, Florida, or California. Texas lakes such as Toledo Bend (186,000 acres), Sam Rayburn (153,000 acres), Falcon (100,000 acres), Texoma (89,000 acres), and Amistad (84,000 acres) are meccas for bass devotees around the world.

Big water fishing demands more scientific methodology than the stock tank fishing favored by many sportsmen, yet the fundamentals remain the same. You must learn bass behavior and how it varies with season, weather, barometric pressure, light, water clarity, and temperature. You need to learn how and where to find bass, how to fish shallow and deep structure, and the principal lures and baits and how to use them. You will be assisted in all this by a welter of exotic, laboratory-created precision instruments and devices that determine temperature, pH, and oxygen content, show and record the underwater structure, signal when bass are present, and even tell you the color of lure to use. You and this high technology are propelled along with rods and tackle at 60-mile-per-hour speeds across vast bodies of water by one of the wonders of the modern world, the high performance, high dollar bass boat.

You really should know engines, trolling motors, and electrical systems and batteries, not to mention navigation, water safety, trailering, and launching under all wind conditions. Watching greenhorns launch new bass boats is like watching a Laurel and Hardy escapade.

With all this effort and expense pitted against a tiny brained, extremely low IQ sunfish, why do you ever fail to bring in a full stringer? Unless you are fishing in a lifeless or bassless lake, the reason usually has something to do with your lack of understanding of how the bass's environment drives his behavior. Although the bass isn't intelligent, his environment is quite complex and his survivalist responses are equally so—therein lies your problem.

Bass Behavior

Bass have a sixth sense that enables them to detect dinner and danger without seeing it. This sense comes from nerve endings emerging through pores along the lateral line down the midline of the fish. The lateral line is a major sensing device of bass and other fish, and it's as important to the fish's survival as eyesight.

Bass have well-developed sight and color perception. Near the surface, bass see about the same range of colors as man, but the deeper the fish are, as underwater photographers have discovered, the more primary colors are filtered out. Bass are extremely light sensitive and manage light intensity by varying their depth or seeking shade. As the sun comes up, they go down or move closer to shady structure. If bait fish descend with bass, they continue to feed. They are most active in the early morning and late afternoon or when weather is overcast. If water tempera-

tures are suitable and light levels are dim, bass prefer 5-to 20-foot depths.

Touch is the next major sense that will confound the ill-informed fisherman. Nerves in the bass's skin can detect temperature changes of $\frac{1}{10}$ of a degree. The bass's ideal comfort zone is 70 to 72 degrees. Finding this zone is a *sine qua non* of bass fishing success. Remember, bass will leave this zone in search of food, like schooling bass on Toledo Bend in summertime, but they will quickly return. When water temperatures drop, bass metabolism slows. You've got to practically drop the worm or jig in the bass's mouth when water temperatures are in the low 50s.

Bass can also hear well even though they don't have ears. Sound is amplified underwater, and bass pick up sound through the bones in their head. Clunky boat sounds can scare them, while noisy lures sometimes attract them.

The bass's sense of smell is keen. He's capable of perceiving certain odors in concentrations of less than one part per trillion. Although there is not a body of scientific evidence to prove it, most experienced bass fishermen believe that smell helps bass locate bait fish or possibly avoid a lure smeared with suntan lotion or beer. And, essential oils have been developed that claim to attract bass and other fish. Bass have a fairly well-developed sense of taste, which, along with texture, can be pretty important to worm fishermen.

Fish behavior is affected by oxygen content, with a range of about six to 12 parts per million considered adequate. The major source of oxygen in a lake is photosynthesis. Wind and wave turbulence adds oxygen, and running water is always oxygenated. Texans are often heard blaming lake turnover as the reason for poor catches. Lakes do turn over in oxygen layers, more noticeably in autumn, and this will affect fishing.

Lakes generally have three discrete layers based on water temperatures. The warm surface water is called the epilimnion, the next is the thermocline, and the coolest layer on the bottom is the hypolimnion. Technically, a thermocline is a stratum in which temperature declines at least one degree centigrade with each meter increase in depth. It is always fairly thin, like the filling in a sandwich. When water temperature at the surface cools, the oxygen-rich surface layer gets heavier and sinks, in turn forcing the oxygen-poor bottom layers upward. In the process, oxygen levels become almost constant at all levels, and the fish scatter. This process can easily take place over several weeks in late fall or early winter.

The most exciting time to bass fish is during the spawn, which is triggered by 62-degree water temperature, about the time the dogwoods bloom. The spawn can last for six weeks or so on our big lakes. Male bass move into the spawning beds first, favoring sand or pea gravel often found under reeds. The bass fan out circular areas which average two feet in diameter. They then try to persuade a female to visit the nest, bumping her with love taps if necessary. After she has deposited 10,000 to 30,000 eggs, the male fertilizes them. The sow stays near the nest for less than a week. The male stands guard for several weeks, not even venturing out for food. These males will attack all interlopers with a vengeance; it's the procreational instinct at work. It's worth making repeated casts in the vicinity of a nest where you've caught the smaller male bass—you just might make a trophy sow so mad she'll tear your bait apart. Weather affects spawn fishing greatly. A blue norther will drive fish down into deeper water. Afterward, the spawn bass scatter again, seeking out their favorite bottom or structure lairs.

The infamous Texas fronts, capable of enough barometric pressure drop to spawn a tornado, seem to affect bass behavior. Sportsmen have noted that when the pressure is dropping rapidly, bass are likely to be feeding; they seem to know something bad is coming. The reverse also appears true—a fast rising barometer will also stimulate feeding. Overall, barometric pressure holding steady in the mid-range has little influence one way or another. Pressures which fluctuate slowly depress feeding patterns. Such pressure patterns are often associated with easterly winds. Winds from east, fish bite least.

How to Find Bass

Whether you're taking on a huge impoundment or a stock tank, you'll have to fulfill the same two tasks in or-

Guadalupe bass are found in the river of the same name and in other rocky Texas streams.

der to be successful: Eliminate barren water and establish a pattern. Essential to these is good local knowledge and a good detailed map.

On large bodies of water, we recommend this approach to eliminate unproductive fishing: Check out each area, perhaps with a variety of lures, but always with a worm, using dark colors on dark days or at night, and light during bright conditions. For example, major points compose a very small portion of a lake. If the fish are there, simply go to every major point on the lake and fish the same pattern you found successful. Regardless of structure type, the structure with the most cover should be fished first. If you're not in a tournament, trolling is an excellent way to eliminate much barren deep water; find the fish, and establish a pattern to repeat.

WHERE	WHEN
1. Flat next to drop offs	Early/late
2. Back of coves	Early/late
3. Secondary points	Early/late
4. Major points	Midday/night
5. Creek beds and roads*	Midday/night
6. Humps and ridges*	Midday/night

*These require a depth finder to locate unless shore signs make them obvious or your map is detailed enough.

On stock tanks or lakes, it's important to remember that catching the first fish is usually no accident. The fish was there for some reason—you just have to be sure you know why. Your next move is to tie down a pattern as

tightly as possible, especially water depth, clarity, temperature, and type of lure. Then you repeat the pattern.

Other structures to explore include the visible tree limbs (stickups) present on many impoundments. In hot weather, seek out those in shade and worm them. Fallen trees should always be tested, with a spinner bait being first choice. Check out timberlines, which are so much a feature of East Texas reservoirs. A crankbait is often a fast way to find action along the timberline. Locate anomalies such as old road or creek beds with a depth finder.

Bass lurking in stock tanks are the rule not the exception. Often you can aid and abet the situation by offering to finance commercial stocking of tanks on your lease and produce great fishing for you and your rancher—a good p.r. move. A compact tackle box should always be at the ready for stock tank fishing, kept right by basic hunting gear. Starting with those dove season hours when the birds aren't flying through the mid-February close of quail season, there's time for a cast or two. The usual result is at least enough fillets for breakfast.

Lures and Baits

Although Florida bass fishermen pioneered plastic worm fishing, usually rigged *sans* sinker, it took a Texan to get it right. The method is properly known as the "Texas Rig," and its "buried hook" technique revolutionized the bass fishing world. Often worm fishing is the most productive way to fill a bass stringer. You'll want an assortment of colors in four-inch, six-inch, and lunker sizes with a variety of bullet sinker weights and worm hooks to match. The hook is embedded in plastic, and a violent yank is required to set it in the jaw of a bass. After feeling the strike, point the rod tip at the fish, then rear back with both arms up and over your head, yelling whatever you desire. That's why rods with more backbone and 15-pound test line are popular.

To fish the worm, retrieve it by first jigging it gently across the bottom, raising your rod tip then reeling down to maintain line tension. Then repeat. Watch the line. It may twitch as the bass picks it up. Bass often hit while the worm is settling back toward the bottom.

If the bass is not headed into heavy structure, we like to give him a chance to swallow the worm, so we'll delay setting the hook for a few seconds. Often, a lunker bass just taps the worm then sucks it into his large mouth.

Topwater lures are the most fun of all and work best on calm mornings and evenings when the water is warm. Actions vary from the floating minnow sort, which can attract best with the slightest twitch, to chuggers that beckon with a loud gurgle.

Crankbaits, which include swimming and diving lures sometimes equipped with "rattlers," are another warm weather favorite. They can run deep to reach bass in their summertime comfort zones.

Jigs, including worm combinations and marabou or other skirts, are effective in colder weather. Bass have slowed down, so when you're jigging, go slow as well. A wintertime bass will hit a jig delicately, so use lighter line despite the risk of break off in timber.

Spinner baits are all-purpose lures along with plastic worms. In the spring, we use bright chartreuse, white, and yellow colors, working them over weedbeds. When buzzed, they provoke angry retaliation, and they can even be fished deep along dropoffs. Flip your rod tip up and down as you retrieve a spinner bait, allowing the lure to drop and flutter.

While we're establishing bass patterns in large water we like to rig three or four rods. Our standards are level-wind bait casting reels with 5½-foot rods, one with a spinner bait, another with a crankbait. A longer, 6-foot graphite rod with backbone is rigged with a worm. Finally, a spin casting rod lets you toss out light, surface lures with ease. Try several casts with each; given common sense, determination, good light, and temperature conditions you'll pattern the bass.

The favorite live bait for bass is large shiners. These can be rigged through the lip with a weedless hook and allowed to free-swim under lily pads or other aquatic plants. Minnows and bobbers dangling from the end of a cane pole aren't a bad deal either.

STOCK TANK BASS FISHERMAN'S CHECKLIST

Fishing license
Light spinning rod and reel
Bait casting rod and reel
Fillet knife
Nail clippers
Needle-nosed pliers
Worm hook assortment
Assorted worms for variable light conditions
Bullet sinkers—³⁄₁₆ and ⅛ oz.
Assorted ⅜ oz. spinner baits, chartreuse, white, yellow, and black
Assorted ½ oz. spinners for buzzing, black and white
Assorted floating minnow lures, orange bellied, lipped to give action on retrieve, and one with spinners
Chugger, black and white
Weedless silver spoon
Jar of pork rind
Deep running crankbaits, shad/pearl and black and orange
Slab type deep runners—dot patterns
Crappie jigs—white
Stringer
Bobbers
Small hooks 1/.0–3/.0
Weights—½ oz. split shot assortment
Small snap swivels
Small whetstone for hooks
Tackle box

Frog gig
Headlamp
Totesack
.22 pistol
.22 ammunition
Alarm clock

Most of this will fit into an amazingly compact box and will basically prepare you for a wide range of fishing opportunities. Although we consider this a "bass box," we've snuck in some lures and bait fishing accoutrements that will enable you to cast for sand bass, capture a few minnows and go after crappie, dig some worms, and fill a stringer with bluegills.

For all but the record seeking fanatics who will be found out at midnight in the dead of winter, the Texas fishing bonanza coincides with the blooming of dogwoods in East Texas. Bass and crappie are spawning and are often easy to find in shallow water. As the days heat up, both scatter, and many sportsmen give serious thought to fishing at night.

Stock tanks often yield a tasty bonus to the night fisherman—lots of frog legs. A tote sack, headlamp, and long gig—they make some in sections—hauled along with fishing gear is about all the preparation you need. We like to add a .22 pistol or .410 for the occasional water moccasin.

Striper fishing has developed a major following in Texas, but many challenge the ecological impact of these imports.

Night fishing is also popular on the large lakes, with an increasing number of tournaments staged in the dark. Night fishing for sand bass and especially striped bass is a way of life for many on lakes such as Texoma. When the sand bass and/or stripers are hitting, Texoma resembles a floating city. Other productive lakes for striper fishing include Toledo Bend, Whitney, Granbury, Travis, E. V. Spence, Amistad, Falcon, Canyon, Livingston, Houston County, Quitman, Possum Kingdom, Sam Rayburn, Buchanan, and Austin's Town Lake and Lake Austin. These are lakes that satisfy the striper's need for cooler water.

Striper fishing has its own nearly cult-like following and sometimes requires specialized gear for deep running, which, in turn, requires a heavier rod and reel combination. In hot summer months, trolling with deep running lures or with lures suspended by means of a downrigger is popular, as is fishing just off the bottom with live bait. Downriggers are a means of fishing a lure at a prescribed depth. We recommend a guide until you get the hang of it.

WHITE BASS Texans call white bass sand bass. Few other freshwater fish provide the chase and cast excitement of these schooling fish in the reservoirs of the north, east, and central sectors of the state. Late summer and early fall usually provide the best schooling action. The best times are early morning and early evening, but sand bass are a most accommodating game fish, available year-round, day and night. Huge sand bass schools will force shad to the surface, where gulls spot them and begin feeding—a signal that declares to fishermen, "Gentlemen, start your engines."

To a Texan this is a sand bass, a great schooling fish in late summer and early fall.

These fish usually don't stay on the surface for more than a few minutes, hence the need for speed. But once the school is located and reached, they are relatively easy to catch. Don't run your boat through the school because the sandies will immediately sound, dropping toward the bottom, and any nearby fishermen will shout unkind words. Stop your engine upwind and drift to within casting distance of the school. Use an electric trolling motor if you have one. Cast along the edge of the school with shallow running crankbaits until the school sounds, then switch to a heavy slab spoon.

White or yellow slabs in a polka dot pattern are excellent choices. Cast out and let the lead slab settle, which it will do in a fluttering motion, all the way to the bottom. Then retrieve slowly, letting the slab bump the bottom now and again until you are ready to retrieve it vertically. Stay alert. Often sandies will follow the slab to hit right at the boat.

In the spring, sand bass move from deep wintering holes toward rivers and creeks, often in the upper areas of reservoirs. Water temperatures in the 55- to 60-degree range signal their migration to the creeks and rivers for the spawn. Bank fishing is most productive at this time. After spawning, the fish return to holes near flats with gravel or sand bottoms. They're likely to hole up for weeks here, guaranteeing great fishing.

Shad is the sandy's principal food, so lures should emulate this bait in size at least. Sand bass are rather indiscriminate, and when they're feeding they'll strike most any small lure or jig. When the schools are scattered, use a rattling type crankbait or small, heavy spoons, which you can fling a mile. These techniques allow you to cover a lot of lake in search of scattered fish.

CRAPPIE When Texas lake waters hit 65 degrees in early spring, the crappie spawn is about to begin. You may be run over on the way to the lake because this is our most popular fishing by a wide margin. This is the time to equip the kids with the time-honored cane pole, rigged with 12

Some of the best fishing action
in Texas is during the spring crappie spawn.

feet of 10-pound test monofilament line, a bobber, a sinker tied to a foot and a half above a 1/.0 to 2/.0 hook, and a bucket full of live minnows. Then start working the nearest brushy shoreline and keep on the move until the crappie are located.

Springtime crappie fishing requires mastering the art of brush fishing. A tandem hook rigged with a fairly heavy weight on the end and two hooks tied on the line works well, because you can feel the weight as it bumps structure. These rigs are widely available prefabbed as crappie rigs. One expert technique is to tie on a $1/32$ oz. white or yellow jig to your main fishing line, usually 12-pound test. Then tie on a separate drop line of less strength, say 6-pound test. Cinch a split shot to this line. The light drop line should extend six inches or so below your jig so you can feel the stumps. If the drop line does snag, you lose only the easily replaced split shot.

Bass fishermen equipped with depth finders who know the location of structure in given lakes can score well on crappie. Crappie are nomads and usually cruise a wide area after the spawn. They avoid the noonday sun by going deep. They'll follow creek channels from deep to shallow water, where they'll feed in late afternoon. Plan to seek them out by continually moving along the structure until you start getting bites.

Our favorite technique is to troll with a jig and minnow combination. We use a drop line with a weight that won't snag easily, such as a nail. Night fishing for crappie is also popular on our clear lakes. Use floating lights wired to a battery other than the one that starts your boat.

As the water warms up in summer, fishing for crappie becomes more challenging because they will suspend more readily than other fish. The problem is they won't necessarily suspend where you think they might. A depth finder can save a lot of time because the crappie are often in open water. You can also troll slowly along dropoffs with baits suspended at various depths until you hit a school. Use a countdown to establish different depths. Remember which line is at which depth and, when fish start hitting, rig all your lines to that depth by using the same countdown. The countdown is also useful when you're attempting to pattern bass while using crankbaits. Count down each cast, varying until you get a hit. Then you should have the formula.

Spawning crappie are the most accessible. Nesting begins in Texas as early as the first week of March, even earlier with a mild winter. As with other species, such as black bass, the male typically establishes the nest area in two to eight feet of water over a gravel bottom, using sand if necessary. Bass will choose sand first. The crappie daddy builds a nest by fanning his tail to clear the bottom. After the eggs are laid, the male then assumes the role of defender.

Various jigs, plastic grubs, maribou, and spinners as well as minnows are popular crappie baits. Hook minnows according to your fishing technique: through the lips for trolling, through the eye socket for jigging, and behind the dorsal fin for bobber fishing.

Submerged Christmas trees, old tires, and pilings attract crappie more than any other fish. Many Texas crappie fisherman build their own fish attractors. Covered and heated fishing docks present good crappie action in the winter as operators use both submerged brush and chum to keep fish in the area.

Winter dock fishing is the perfect place to teach your kids the knit and purl technique of jigging for crappie. Admittedly, women and young children are better at catching crappie this way since their hands tend to be softer and more sensitive. Rather than using an up and down jigging motion, knit and purl involves using your fingers to gently lift and pull the line while twisting your hand around. By handling the line this way you can feel any nibble. A crappie bite is very gentle, and this method enables a young angler to learn to feel the strike.

BLUEGILLS Bluegills, redear, redbreast, warmouth, and other panfish species fill lots of Texas cast-iron skillets. They, too, are quicker to get in the skillet during spawning season. Spawning sunfish prefer shallow bays or sheltered shorelines, such as those at the back of creek arms and coves. Seek coves that are moderately deep at the entrance, about 15 to 20 feet, and that slope up to sand or gravel bottoms with lots of brushy timber cover or weeds. Nesting beds are easily spotted on bright, sunshiny days. Look on the lake bottom for whitish circles about a foot in diameter.

The starting point for many a young sportsman, bluegill fishing in a Texas state park.

Worms, crickets, grasshoppers, and minnows fished with a bobber and light wire hooks are favored by many panfish. Small artificial lures and pieces of plastic worms work well, too. Flyrodders with popping bugs have a ball with these fiesty fish. When hooked, they turn sideways, giving the light tackle angler all he wants in the way of a spirited scrap. They excel in the pan, where, unless they are thicker than 1½ inches, they should be gutted, scaled, and fried whole (but without the head).

Of the more than 100 state parks maintained by TPWD, over half provide freshwater fishing opportunities ideally suited for training and inspiring young fishermen on bluegills. Some of the parks also have big lakes allowing bass boats, but most are cane pole and bobber spots also featuring attractive camping facilities.

GASPERGOU These are definitely some of the best eating fish of our reservoirs. The fact that no one seems to know this amazes us. For centuries, Oriental cooks have been producing gourmet dishes from freshwater drum, the gaspergou.

Drum congregate below dams and are most often caught with bottom fishing techniques. Shrimp, crawfish, and freshwater clams are ideal for bait; the latter is the best of all. Drum are also accidentally caught by bass fishermen using crank or spinner baits. Even crappie fishermen will occasionally nail a drum with a jig rig. Drum often are thrown back because fishermen think of them as rough fish—a culinary mistake. By the way, they *are* rough when it comes to fighting. They give the bass and crappie fisherman what-for on light tackle. They are also legal to take with speargun or bow and arrow.

Bowfishing is a blend of hunting and fishing and an excellent way for bow hunters to sharpen their skills. Targets include gar and buffalofish as well as carp. Experienced bowfishermen wait for the fish to turn broadside and have learned to allow for the optical effect of light refracted through water. Alligator gar can weigh more than 100 pounds and create a lot of excitement once struck with an arrow. There's even a Lone Star bowfishing championship tournament.

WALLEYE Yankees take note. There are walleye in Texas. We snuck them into the state way back in the '60s. They have adapted well and are now found in many reservoirs. The most famous walleye waters are those of Lake

Lunker walleyes in Lake Meredith near Amarillo are one of the state's many fishing surprises.

Meredith, near Amarillo, and Canyon Lake, near San Antonio. An effective fishing method is to troll shorelines with gravel bottoms using shad-type, medium running lures. Jig fishing techniques like those used on sand bass work pretty well, too.

CHAIN PICKEREL A native pike family fish is the chain pickerel, found in Caddo Lake and Lake o' the Pines in northeast Texas. Chain pickerel provide real entertainment, especially in winter when the bass aren't cooperating. Chain pickerel hammer a lure, fighting hard. They're abundant and you'll find them in beautiful surroundings. Although many fishermen won't admit it, it is worthwhile fishing Caddo just for pickerel as a break during the winter months. The cypress trees dripping Spanish moss create an Old South atmosphere not found elsewhere in Texas.

Top water and shallow running minnow type lures are the best bet at Caddo, which is a shallow lake throughout. Look for water lilies, 'coontail, and other aquatic vegetation as pickerel hangouts. Drag your bait along the water lilies or weeds, because pickerel are ambushers.

The only drawback to pickerel is that they are bony. However, they taste awfully good, so we suggest putting up with a few bones.

Chain pickerel are Texas natives worth a winter visit to Caddo Lake.

CATFISH Trotlining can be great sport even if some black bass purists mutter dark imprecations against those who string out hooks in the night. The bad reputation comes from careless trotliners who don't properly tag lines and often leave them abandoned. If not first removed by an angry fisherman or game warden, these lines can easily become entangled in expensive outboards, or at the least, snag a crankbait on the way. But running a trotline at night is excellent family recreation and a good way to teach teamwork, and it can be most productive. If you're running the line in your lease's stock tanks, who's to complain?

The prime targets of trotliners are blue, channel, and flathead catfish. Other cat species include several types of bullheads, including brown and yellow. Bullheads are less favored as table fare, because during our hot Lone Star summers their flesh softens and they develop a muddy taste. Many Texans call them mudcats.

Use extreme care in handling and cleaning all catfish. Their skin is quite slippery, and a puncture wound from their sharp dorsal and pectoral spines can easily become infected. Handling with a glove and using pliers for skinning is recommended.

One or more species of catfish is found in every part of the state. The easiest way we know to distinguish blue or channel cat from the others is by their forked tail. The other tasty cat, the flathead, has a large square tail and is yellowish brown with darker mottlings of brown. Its head

Blue cats are game fish in every sense of the word.

is flattened, and the lower jaw is always longer than the upper.

Several rivers in Texas feature challenging flathead fishing with rod and reel. Flatheads like to lie in wait in sluggish river pools, mouths open for the next sucker that comes along. You'll usually find them over rocky bottoms, such as those found in the Llano and other Edwards Plateau rivers. Large suckers and sunfish make ideal baits when using a rod and reel; throwlines are also used. Make sure the line is stout because it's not uncommon to tie into a 40 to 50 pounder, and catfish can approach 100 pounds.

Juglining can also be effective in lakes. Suspend a baited rig of five or fewer hooks at least three feet apart on a heavy line extended from a plastic jug. Let the jug drift as you follow it by boat. When the catfish hits, handline him in.

You may elect to use limblines, throwlines, or trotlines with 50 or fewer hooks, each end tied to a fixed object. All hooks must be three horizontal feet apart, and each line must be clearly identified with a legible tag bearing your name, address, and the date it was set. Also, no one person can have more than 100 hooks in the water. It's a

good idea to consult the current *Texas Freshwater Fishing Guide* for changing rules on trotlines.

Trotlines are as individual as the characters who run them. We prefer to tie a snap swivel on to each hook line in order to facilitate initial rigging and replacement. This also cuts down on tangling when the fish try to twist free. Also rig a snap for the hook itself. We prefer a treble hook. Our favorite trotline weight is the old window sash, practically a collector's item today. You'll want weights at both ends of the line and the middle, and, depending on overall length, smaller weights placed every 12 hooks or so.

Bait is another highly individual matter and an excellent campfire argument starter as you debate the virtues of blood baits, stink baits, liver, soap, shrimp, cut bait, minnows (dead or alive), grasshoppers, and even Wheaties and orange soda pop, a favorite with the kids. Commercial catfish baits don't seem to be as effective as the homemade variety. To be truthful, making your own bait is one of the fun things about catfishing. Pro trotliners never argue. They let the catfish decide by using different baits on the same trotline, noting the location. When they rebait, it's with the baits that work.

If you know of a poultry processing plant in your area, obtain a jug of chicken blood. Let it congeal in throwaway aluminum pie pans. You can add black sorghum molasses and anise to help ripen the potent concoction; some call this underwater ouzo. Cut the congealed blood into small squares, and you have the near ideal catfish bait for lake fishing.

If you have the stomach for it, the old, original stink bait is for you, and it's a killer on cats. Start with limburger cheese. Rub a piece around the inside of a glass jar, then add some peeled shrimp. Seal the jar and let it sit awhile.

CATFISH FISHERMAN'S CHECKLIST
Fishing license
White plastic jugs
Waterproof ink marker to print name, address,
   and date on jug.
100 yards stout line
100 snap swivels
50 sections (two feet each) of braided line
50 #8 treble hooks
Bucket for carrying all gear
Three heavy weights (sashcord weights)
Additional weights
Pliers—regular, needle-nose, or degouger for
   hook removal
Nail clippers
Fillet knife
Fillet board (drive a large nail through it to
   impale catfish while skinning)
Old gloves
Lantern
Board as base for winding line
Bait (blood/stink/shrimp)
Stringer

TROUT Members of the Fly Fisher's Club of London would probably not spend a whole lot of time pursuing our "put and take" Texas rainbows. But there is no doubt of the special drama of trout fishing and its appeal to the discerning. Many thousands of Texans migrate to other Western states for trout expeditions. We are not all trotliners and bass fishermen.

Texas provides hatchery released rainbow fishing each winter. The principal releases are in the Guadalupe River, Boykin Springs in the Angelina National Forest in East Texas, and in the Brazos River below the dam at Possum Kingdom Lake.

Dame Juliana Berners, the Abbess of Sopwell, wrote a trout fishing treatise which appeared in a 1496 edition of *The Book of St. Albans:* "You must not be too greedy in catching your said game as in taking too much at one time, a thing which can easily happen if you do in every point as this present treatise shows you. This could easily be the occasion of destroying your own sport and other men's also. When you have sufficient mess, you should covet no more at that time."

Rainbow trout are stocked in selected Texas rivers, streams, and springfed lakes.

In those days, every young gentleman was early taught how to hunt and fish, according to Dame Berners, "mainly for your enjoyment and to procure the health of your body and more especially of your soul." Amen.

Although the lady's philosophy applies to every facet of becoming an accomplished sportsman, it fits trout fishing especially well. Since the trout do not reproduce in Texas waters, every one you take diminishes those left for others. Therefore, when we commend you to the special beauties of the Brazos and Guadalupe rivers, keep a rainbow or two in your creel, enough for a shoreside lunch, and leave the rest for others.

Since no trout you encounter will be large, select a lightweight rod and use no more than 4X tippet, about 4-pound test. Streamers, bucktails, and minnow mimics such as the famous Muddler are basic choices. Stay small; a large streamer will scare the scales off our tiny trout.

A basic rod choice would be a 7-weight graphite in the 8- to 8½-foot length, since this is easier to handle than longer or shorter rods. This should handle line weights of 140 to 160 grains. The beginner should elect a double taper (DT) line, which is tapered on both ends, again for ease in learning to cast. You'll need both a floating line and a line with a 20-foot sinking tip for underwater lures. Usually, it's necessary to fill up the reel by use of backing, and 12- to 15-pound test monofilament is good for this. The fly reel is just a device to store line. You don't "reel in" fish as with baitcasting equipment. But, before buying the first item of fly fishing paraphernalia, a combination of study and professional advice is strongly suggested. This is an expensive, complex, all consuming sport. Start out right. Once the fly rod is mastered, you'll be using it on bass, panfish, and ultimately on redfish, which give you almost the same thrill as the fabled bonefish, a little slower but stronger.

Trout fishing in Texas is admittedly limited but well worth exploring. There is quite a bit of trout water in the neighboring states of Oklahoma and Arkansas, and many Texans slip up to Colorado during our blistering summers to cool off in a mountain trout stream.

Before planning a trip on the Brazos or Guadalupe, it's a good idea to check with the Corps of Engineers and make sure they don't plan a water release while you're on the river. This can spoil your day. You might want to consider a canoe float trip in connection with the trout expedition. There are a number of outfitters along the river and arrangements can be made to transport you and your canoe upriver. You then canoe down to the takeout points at one of the bridges crossing the river. Sportsmen have been known to take along seasoned flour, cooking oil, and a portable skillet to prepare an elegant rainbow lunch. Go ahead, leave the heads on and reach for crusty bread and a chilled bottle of a good, dry Texas chardonnay; no gourmet restaurant can come close.

Several state parks are stocked with rainbow trout around the start of deer season each year. These include Buescher, near Austin; Meridian, west of Waco; Bonham, on the Red River; Cleburne, southwest of Fort Worth; Daingerfield, in East Texas; and Boykin Springs, in the Angelina National Forest. Rainbow trout on the deer camp menu would not be bad. These parks offer a great chance to teach youngsters the art and science of fly fishing, perhaps building a lifetime love for one of America's greatest sports.

A freshwater trout stamp is required of all who pursue our hatchery rainbows. This stamp helps fund the trout release programs and experimental programs designed to identify possible strains that can breed in our waters. Regardless of whether you'll make it to the river this year, we urge you, as a sportsman, to buy at least one trout stamp annually as your way of supporting TPWD efforts.

The monies raised through license fees and motorboat fuel taxes are funds that should be dedicated to wildlife and fisheries management. If these funds are transferred into the general revenue fund, as has been suggested from time to time, they could then be spent, as one observer put it, "on anything from social diseases to fine art." It is the sportsman's contention that there would be far fewer social diseases of any sort if we spent more time outdoors. As for fine art, a Hill Country sunset over a carpet of bluebonnets will do nicely, thank you. Letters to your state legislator could make the difference if such "fund transfers" are proposed in the future.

COASTAL FISHING

SPOTTED SEATROUT HB 1000 is not a new shotgun, but rather House Bill 1000, the most significant piece of Texas legislation ever enacted on behalf of inshore saltwater fishing. This bill, passed in 1981, outlawed the sale of red drum, a.k.a. redfish, and spotted seatrout, a.k.a. specks. It set the scene for one of the most dramatic wildlife recoveries of the '80s.

In December, 1983, a devastating winter storm hit the state, freezing as far south as Port Isabel, killing a huge percentage of the trout population. And in 1986, an especially virulent red tide hit the same coast, killing off yet another enormous number of redfish and trout. Yet, both species are back almost as strong as ever. Both are on a definite increase, thanks to the ban on commercial netting and sales. Sportsmen owe a debt of gratitude to the Gulf Coast Conservation Association (GCCA) for its fight to pass HB 1000.

In 1983, further legislation was passed giving the Texas Parks and Wildlife Department the power to set size and bag limits on both species. This legislation will continue to have a positive effect on Texas sportfishing.

The Perry R. Bass Marine Fisheries Research Station at Tres Palacios Bay, which flows into Matagorda Bay, has had a major impact on restoration of redfish and spotted seatrout populations. Although the redfish and seatrout programs are the most vital for sportfishing requirements, the most fascinating research is being done on tarpon and snook. Both species are in full eclipse from their heydays on the Texas coast, although the occasional tarpon may be caught out of Port Isabel, and a rare snook in Lower Laguna Madre. The regal Silver King and hard-striking, great-eating snook may make a comeback before the end of this century. Part of the purchase price of your saltwater fishing stamp goes to the Palacios facility, which is also funded by individuals and organizations.

Spotted seatrout are caught year-round in Texas, although at different places and different times. They are not migratory and remain in schools. They stay pretty much to their home grounds while they are still under three pounds, but they will move from shallow water to deep with the onset of cold weather. They are caught both in inshore bays and surf. The few trout that live past the age of four and attain a weight over three pounds move into deeper, more open water and go it alone except during the spawn. They will travel longer distances along coastlines. Larger trout are often caught in shallow water, feeding alone.

Spring is the best time to go after spotted seatrout, fishing the grassy flats within the bays. In dry weather, hot weather, cold weather, even rainy weather, the salinity of the water tends to drive the trout out of the bays into the passes and channels. They prefer a salinity of 20 parts per thousand. In other words, trout like consistency. The

World-class spotted seatrout are the main attraction of Texas coastal fishing.

spawn usually takes place in May when water temperatures reach the mid-70s. The larger, sexually mature fish school around the deeper passes in the spring. Tidal current is vital to the spawn because it carries the fertilized eggs into protected marsh areas.

One of the most productive trout fishing areas anywhere is in the Laguna Madre, more than 100 miles of narrow, fish-filled lagoon between Padre Island and the mainland, with access via the Inland Waterway and fishing-oriented villages such as Port Mansfield and Port Isabel. Baffin Bay, in the Upper Laguna Madre, and Galveston Bay, south of Houston, are identified as hot spots for big trout weighing over 10 pounds. The average weight for spotted seatrout is two pounds, but those from these two areas average two-and-a-half to three pounds, up to a 50 percent increase in average weight. TPWD biologists report that the trout from these areas are genetically different. Availability of food, year-round warm water, and the high salinity level of the Laguna contribute to extraordinary growth. Texas should have the next world record spotted seatrout.

Most Texas specks are caught on live shrimp, mullet, or pig fish. When using live shrimp, most choose a small treble hook, taking care to thread one of the hooks under the hard-shelled edge along the top of the shrimp's head. Don't stab the black spot just at the back of the head, because that's a vital area. Specks can get greedy, too, and, like ancient Romans, gorge, regurgitate, and gorge again, leaving a slick on the water surface. Fishing these oil slicks can produce a lot of action.

Saltwater flat fishermen are especially ecstatic when a "surfer's nightmare" day dawns. This is a flat, calm, clear

water day with bright skies, creating ideal conditions for specks to spot artificial lures.

Commonly used artificials include plastic bait-tails rigged to lead jigs, feathered jigs, spoons, and mirror finished plugs in pink, gold, red, and white. Top water plugs are seldom productive except at night or very early, and for very big trout. Yellow feathered jigs are effective on a wide variety of saltwater species because they simulate shrimp.

Live shrimp presented on a two hook set up suspended from a popper bobber is one of the deadliest of trout rigs. No need for wire leader—tie a #6 or #4 treble hook right onto your line. Have a small split shot handy should your shrimp be snappy enough to leap out of the water. You want him down just above the grass. These rigs are most successfully fished while drifting over grass flats, casting ahead of the boat, constantly reeling to keep a tight line and occasionally whipping up the rod tip to produce a burble from the popper bobber. Plastic shrimp or bait-tails are often successful substitutes on these rigs.

The most successful trout fishermen wade the flats. Their fishing has a lot of hunting to it, as they must stalk the fish. While wading the flats during warm months, wear jeans or leggings with old tennis shoes and shuffle your feet. The shuffling sends a warning vibration to stingrays, effectively clearing them from your path. During the summer, quite a few waders get speared by cranky stingrays who've been forced out of the wrong side of their beds. If you do get speared, hot water will ease the pain until you get medical attention at a hospital. If you're us-

Wading the saltwater flats is the preferred way to net large spotted seatrout.

ing a boat, your outboard motor's cooling system is an emergency hot water source.

In cooler weather, trout stream waders with tennis shoes over booties are a good choice, because you can then wear long johns. When wading, especially if you are near deep water such as in the surf, it's a good idea to have a long line attached to your fish stringer and/or live bait container, so that any aggressive fish can make the right choice.

Tides, barometric pressure, water clarity, and temperature have a tremendous impact on the quality of your saltwater fishing. Here are a few rules of thumb:

1. Fish in outgoing or incoming tides. If the water has been roiled up and become murky, look for and fish the line where the tide has created clear water on one side. Schools of trout may be feeding along these lines.
2. Fish ahead of or during the early stages of a front, because rapid pressure changes often cause trout to go into a feeding frenzy.
3. When the water is too cold, seek out the deepest holes and fish them until you find the concentrated school. Work a lure or bait more slowly in cold weather because trout, like you, are sluggish, less prone to hit with the verve of spring. They'll pick at their food, so cold water strikes can be barely perceptible.

Fishing the big, wide open Texas bays can also provide some exciting chases out to where the seagulls are feeding. Anytime the gulls start circling, wheeling, and diving, you need to be casting to the school of trout thus exposed. The same cautions apply as those for sand bass school pursuers. Don't scatter the fish by running your boat through the school.

Sportsmen can really take advantage of saltwater flat fishing during waterfowl seasons, not only for trout, but also for redfish and flounder. The action can start in mid-September with the early teal season and continue right on through the various duck and geese seasons, weather permitting. There's nothing like a successful duck hunt early in the morning, capped off by a great trout catch in late afternoon on the spectacular Texas Gulf Coast.

So we urge you to pack up a "coastal box" and keep it with your waterfowling gear. A take down spinning outfit is ideal for travel. Again, we like to have at least two reels and extra spools for both in the event of malfunction. Saltwater fishing can produce its share of stress on rigs, so be prepared.

RED DRUM Few sportsmen call a redfish a red drum, but fish biologists insist that's his name. He has a cousin properly called the black drum, which nobody seems to fish for much, but he is certainly edible. Fame is with the redfish, the second most popular inshore saltwater gamefish.

Symbol of conservation success on the Texas Gulf coast is the comeback of the redfish (red drum).

The redfish is partially a bottom feeder, unlike the spotted seatrout. Reds dine mainly on crustaceans and mollusks, although they sometimes attack bait fish such as mullet shiners with enthusiasm. Crabs, live shrimp when the water is clear, and small live mullet shiners are typical baits. Squid, dead shrimp, and cut mullet are good from jetties. Cut mullet is also a surf favorite along with small, clawless blue crabs and large, six-inch or so live mullet.

Redfish will hit gold spoons, bait-tails fished close to the bottom, and plugs worked slowly in shallow water. You can also fish a live shrimp rigged just to the hook—no other terminal tackle—and cast like a plug. Another technique is to hook live mullet on a two-foot monofilament leader, anchored to a sinker. Run the hook just behind the dorsal fin, under the spine, to keep the mullet alive. Cast to open areas in shallow grass flats and let the mullet swim free.

Like the trout fisherman, the most successful redfish seeker wades. For our big, difficult-to-wade bays, special high-dollar, flat-bottomed redfish rigs have been developed to get the sportsman to his quarry in style, with a knowledgeable guide at the helm. Look for signs of redfish tailing over the sand flats in just a foot or so of water, where the tides have covered the food-rich bottom. Tailing is the bonefisherman's term for the tip of the fin you see as the reds feed head down in the shallows on crustaceans on the bottom. Use great stealth when approaching tailing reds, because they will spook at the sound of a splash. Cast ahead of the red's line of feeding, not on top of his head.

In jetty or surf fishing on the bottom, it's important that the redfish be allowed to take the bait in his mouth and move off. If he feels a sinker or if you strike too quickly, he will not be hooked. The best rigs allow the line with the hook on it to move freely. Big sinkers work well in light current. You may have to rig a heavy pyramid-type bottom sinker to keep your bait from washing ashore; if you do, rig it so the baited hook line is through a sleeve that will let the fish pick it up and mouth it until he's ready to swallow.

Surf fishing is one of the most aesthetically rewarding experiences, a delightful brew of bathing, sunning, exercise, hunting, and fishing. With almost 90 miles of national seacoast at their disposal on Padre Island and hundreds more miles of accessible surfline, Texans are uniquely blessed with space to heave their long lines. Yet few do. One can find solitude approaching that on the far side of the moon by four-wheeling south from the beaches of North Padre Island equipped with several long rods, live mullet shiners, blue crabs or cut mullet, stout terminal tackle, sand spikes—made from PVC pipe if you wish—a light, comfortable chair, and an ice chest for beverages and fish. Four-wheel-drive vehicles are available for rental in Corpus Christi, but call well ahead for reservations. Thus outfitted, the surf fisher is set for many hours of nirvana. The scene is enhanced by breakers, beautiful white sand dunes, and lonely beaches *sans* humans. If you elect to take a swim in the altogether, watch out for safety patrol helicopters.

Major runs of redfish may be expected in the surf beginning in September. Surf fishing for bull reds, those 25- to 40-pound monsters that make your heart pump and your shoulders ache, is a lot like flying—hours of the uneventful punctuated by minutes of sheer panic. But, it's worth it, because even the uneventful is welcome to many harassed sportsmen. If you must, take along a good book and don't forget the sunscreen. Whiting, seatrout, even pompano and flounder can shatter your reverie, so don't get too relaxed. To fish for pompano, jacks, and other surf runners, carry your spinning rod rigged with a yellow feather jig, and when the spirit moves you do some casting.

FLOUNDER The flounder's fine, almost oil-free flesh is an epicure's delight, whether prepared simply with a delicate lemon butter sauce or elaborately stuffed with another of our coastal water treasures, blue crab meat. But, before you order the chilled West Texas sauvignon blanc, you may have a bit to learn, because success with this bottom feeder takes a technique different from nearly all other Texas fishing.

The big difference is in the way flounder feed, lying in wait on the bottom, covered in silt, only eyes showing from the left side of his flat body. He waits, like a spider, for prey to come to him. This tells you that your approach has to first put the bait very near the bottom and, second, cover lots of bottom until fish are located. One way many have solved the problem is to forget bait, pick up a gas lantern, and gig and wade the flats at night.

Most of the flounder caught on the Texas coast are southern flounder; their left-side eyes identify them as *sinistral*. Yankee flounder, found up and down the Atlantic coast, have eyes on their right side, making them *dextral*. When flounder are born they resemble other fish, then one eye migrates to the left or right side and the top takes on a camouflage to match the local bottoms; underside goes fish-belly white.

The very best time to stock up on flounder is during their fall migration from the bays to offshore, where they spawn in the winter. They begin to school around the opening of white-winged dove and early teal seasons and continue right on through most of the waterfowl seasons unless a particularly cold norther comes through, which will chase them out to the Gulf. So pack your flounder gear right along with your 12-gauge and steel shot. At this time, flounder are found schooled up on the edges of channels and passes and around jetties and piers. During the spring and summer they're more scattered, so you have to work pilings, reefs, wrecks, or drift the bays like you would for trout.

Since flounder freeze well, it's a good bet the sportsman may be able to stock all the entrees he'll need during one or two well-planned expeditions. Fall schools of migrating flounder can be awesomely large.

Fall flounder and teal migrations
provide Texas sportsmen with exciting options.

The basic flounder rig is simplicity itself. Tie a #4 treble hook directly to your 30-pound monofilament leader, then rig a weight about a foot up the line. That's it. Live shrimp is the easiest bait to find, but flounder prefer mudfish or small mullet. The latter cut down on the bait nabbing that bedevils coastal fishermen.

Some pros cover more ground by allowing more leader between the weight and the hook, up to two feet. The area covered per cast increases significantly. The secret here is to rig a split shot a few inches up from the bait to keep the bait close to the bottom while the leader swings through its increased radius.

If working piers or other structure, be patient and cover every square inch. Move on to the next piling if you don't get a strike. A flounder's strike is more like hitting a snag until you set the hook and move him off the bottom. Then he'll turn his flat side to test you and your light tackle.

Be careful in taking a flounder out of the water and off the hook, because he has sharp dentures. A net is handy for the former, a degouger for the latter. Don't make like a bass pro and stick your hand in his mouth—you may be headed for the doctor. The flounder has swallowed the bait, and it's sometimes faster to cut off the hook and tie on another, retrieving your hook at filleting time.

One of the many TPWD achievements has been the establishment of several state parks and fishing piers along our coast. These provide a venue for family floundering as well as other saltwater fishing. The major locales are: Bryan Beach near Freeport, close to San Luis Pass; Copano Bay Causeway, between Tivoli and Rockport (camp at Goose Island State Park at the north end of the causeway); Galveston Island; Mustang Island, south of Port Aransas; Port Lavaca fishing pier; and the Queen Isabella Causeway fishing pier near South Padre Island. For a real adventure, try Matagorda Island by boat. This is primitive with zero facilities, so come fully prepared.

COASTAL FISHERMAN'S CHECKLIST
Fishing license
Saltwater stamp
Spinning rod: 6½–7 foot
Spinning reels—10-lb. test line
Extra spools of 12-lb. test line
Long stringer line
Floating plastic bait bucket
Trout stream waders
Tennis shoes
Mirror-finish lures, red, white, pink, gold, silver
Spoons (gold)
Bait-tails (lead head jigs with plastic tails—red and white)
Feathered jigs, yellow and white
Treble hooks—#4, #6
Single hooks—#4, #5
Sinkers
Bottom sinkers, egg- and pyramid-shaped

Popper bobbers, red and white
Assorted 3-way connectors/swivels
Assorted single swivels
Small spool of 40-lb. monofilament for leaders
Degouger (fish hook remover)
Super glue
Sunscreen lotion
Nail clippers
Needle nose pliers
Fillet knife

OFFSHORE FISHING

Offshore on the Texas Gulf coast really means three different kinds of fishing, requiring three different modes of transportation:

1. Small craft to run out to artificial reefs, oil rigs, wellheads. Small boats are also used to fish close in natural reefs for seatrout, king mackerel, cobia (ling), red snapper, jewfish, and grouper. Trout, redfish, and flounder, among other species, may also be caught just outside the surf line on many areas along the coast. Watch the weather. Small craft can get into serious trouble quickly in the Gulf.

2. Large, heavy displacement party boats for excursions to snapper banks and natural reefs well offshore, 30 to 40 miles out, that occur right on the edge of the drop-off of the continental shelf. Party boats depart from Galveston, Freeport, Port Aransas, and other areas.

3. Sportsfisherman's charter. These high-performance boats specialize in fishing outside the 10 fathom line (60 feet plus). It's here that some of the most unheralded billfishing in the northern hemisphere takes place. Sailfish and blue marlin are the stars. Cobia, Spanish mackerel, and jacks begin hitting offshore in early spring, and, shortly thereafter, barracuda, king mackerel (kingfish), dolphin (dorado), bonito, amberjack, wahoo, blackfin tuna, bluefish, and even the occasional swordfish and tarpon. Barring thunderstorms and the summer threat of hurricanes, fishing can be excellent throughout the coastal bend into October and November.

With non-skid deck shoes, Scapalomine for seasickness, a brimmed hat, sunblock with a high sun protection factor, patience, plenty of time, and mayhap some mild pre-trip muscle tone exercises for arms and back, you're more or less ready for offshore fishing. Bring along a Swiss army knife with bottle opener and corkscrew in case you must celebrate a truly grand catch. Many women add bikinis and a book for when they're not in the fighting chair. Women with long hair should remember to keep it pinned up when in the chair, as strands of hair caught in a reel can be quite hazardous and painful. A tape player for listening to good music while you're running from reef to reef is a good idea, too. Oh, yes, don't forget your wallet.

One important aside: If, despite all precautions, you are going to be sick, *tell* someone. A major cause of seasickness is overindulgence the night before or during the trip itself. A classic hangover has contributed to many a seasickness bout. Don't be embarrassed. Remember, you're out of your element, and it's actually the exceptional person who has never experienced at least queasiness from just the wrong combination of sea state, fuel exhaust, and fishy odors.

Most sportsmen either charter offshore fishing trips or participate in the much less costly, but usually more productive, party boat trips. Since a high proportion of these trips furnish tackle, bait, and even a mate to help with boating and cleaning the catch, your main concern should be personal comfort and the ability to *stay* comfortable offshore.

Don't ever roll the dice with unfavorable weather forecasts when headed offshore. Texas is infamous for its changeable weather, so be prepared. Most of the time, you will be able to go out after a prudent wait, but we can often get eight to 10 feet or better seas. When the captain says "No," we quickly agree with him. Gulf seas can give any boat smaller than a 1,000-foot tanker a rough time of it.

When you first come aboard the party boat or other charter boat, check out the "head" facility. Learn how to operate it. It may have a manually operated handle or button to push and perhaps a valve to open and close. Heads are *very* temperamental. Use toilet paper sparingly.

BIG GAME FISH We have known sportsfishermen who have spent years fishing for blue marlin with little or no success. Yet many are always ready to spend another long day in the quest. One has to wonder why. Often it's murderously hot, and almost always there are long, grueling stretches without a strike. In short, you could spend the time much more comfortably, productively, and inexpensively. But more people are turning to deep sea fishing than ever before.

Those of us who return to the sea, again and again, do so for two reasons: the almost hypnotic sense of release and relaxation that comes from just being there, and the totally absorbed sense of the hunt when we're in the chair. Be it blue or white marlin, sailfish, king, bonita, or swordfish, you are on a thrilling hunt for something that will fight back.

Your crew, usually a captain and mate, obviously makes quite a difference in the success or failure of your deep sea fishing experience. Your attitude has a lot to do with their performance. If you are alert for signs of fish—a bill poking through the surface, birds on the horizon, schools of bait fish jumping—you may just spot something they miss.

Texas sportsfishermen have brought blue marlin up to 700 pounds to gaff.

If you are not getting any strikes, the crew should be changing up lures, rerigging bait on the outriggers, changing course—doing many things to find that pattern that produces fish. If they're not, maybe they think you don't care. If they are obviously trying, you should tip generously at the end of the day, fish or no.

Typical trolling lures include feathered jigs, large minnow-shaped plugs, and plastic-headed, skirted lures, invariably in lurid, bright colors. Most sportfishing boats are rigged with two outriggers and two short lines called teasers. Larger fish will usually come on the outriggers. We usually release marlin, sails, barracuda, bonita, and the uncommon tarpon. Most of the others make wonderful eating.

PARTY BOAT FISHING Party boat fishing is quite another matter. Bring a big ice chest for grouper and snapper varieties that may be there in abundance. Hit the right reef with a school feeding on the bottom and you could be taking lots of fish.

Long live the silver king—tarpon fishing provides great sport on the Texas coast.

Red snapper is the featured fish on most Gulf coast party boat excursions.

OFFSHORE FISHERMAN'S CHECKLIST

Sunblock, sunscreen
Camera and film
Windbreaker
Wool sweater in fall
Small towel
Nail clippers
Swiss army knife with bottle opener
Swimwear
Tape player for music
Book
Non-skid deck shoes
Long-sleeved, light-colored shirt
Cotton slacks
Shorts
Long-billed hat
Polarized sunglasses
Seasickness prevention prescription
Ice chest

PREPARATION FOR

FREEZING AND COOKING

Party boat trips are usually on a charge-per-person basis with 20 or more participants, unless you arrange to take the entire boat with all your friends. Otherwise, you're not guaranteed that all the players are, in fact, sportsmen, which can detract from the enjoyment of the trip. Many snapper bank trips take upwards of four hours out, with three or four hours of fishing, and another four hours back, so you're going to spend a lot of time with your companions, sportsmen or not.

If you don't have your own deep sea tackle, most party boat crews usually have rigs for rent. But, before you leave shore, check out the serviceability of reels and the conditions of rods, and especially check the line for nicks or other signs of weakness. Do take a large ice chest, because most trips are productive. The better boats have radar and Loran-C, incredibly accurate in the Gulf of Mexico, and depth finders to locate the fish. They can find their way home with unnerving accuracy, so don't be nervous because you're out of sight of land. Be sure to verify boat rules regarding bringing your own refreshments.

While it's not strictly sportfishing, shrimping, crabbing, and oystering are wondrous ways to spend days on the Texas coast, and the culinary rewards are beyond description. Our coast features some unique varieties of white shrimp not commercially sought. Oysters in the Rockport/Aransas area are world class, crabbing is big around Galveston Bay, and we even have a showing of the toothsome stone crabs on our lower coast.

Perishability is the problem here, and even a stringer of live fish kept in warm water will begin to deteriorate from table quality. The key to keeping fish gourmet-fresh is rapid gutting, removal of all intestines and gills, and getting it on ice. If a fish is dead, look for bright red gills, clear eyes, and a firm body. A fresh fish will also float in water, and it does not smell fishy. You should bleed dark-fleshed fish such as king mackerel to improve the flavor. Get rid of fish if the gills have turned light pink, eyes are clouded, or the fish is soft, limp, and smelly.

Before and after you clean fish, wash your hands thoroughly and make sure your knives and cutting board are impeccably clean. It's quite easy to transfer germs when handling any type of food, but fish are one of the handiest bacteria carriers. Rub your hands with fresh lemon juice to remove the fishy odor.

Most catches can be filleted with a long, flexible-bladed knife or electric knife. Some of the saltwater fish, notably speckled trout and Spanish mackerel, do not need skinning, nor does the tasty freshwater rainbow trout. But most varieties benefit from skinning, a step incorporated in the basic filleting approach.

Of course, if you have a baking-size fish of five to six pounds or more, such as snapper, grouper, or redfish, you may wish to just gut it thoroughly and scale it in the conventional manner—a common dinner fork is ideal for scaling. Kingfish, swordfish, tuna, and wahoo lend themselves to steaking, that is, crosswise cuts about 1½ inches thick; they are excellent choices for the charcoal grill.

BASIC FILLETING TECHNIQUE

1. Hold head of fish firmly and cut down at an angle just behind the gills to backbone. Don't cut through the backbone.

2. Run the knife down the backbone just beyond the vent. On larger fish, angle the knife so as not to cut into the ribs. On smaller fish, go ahead and cut through the ribs, removing bony areas after the fillet is completely free of the carcass.

3. Continue the cut with the knife against the backbone all the way to the tail. Do not cut through the skin as it tapers to the tail. If meat sticks at the rib cage, snip it away.

4. Flip the side of the fish back, hinged at the tail. Hold the skin at the tail firmly and run the knife between the meat and skin.

5. Turn fish over and repeat.

When you're done, rinse the fish fillets in water, then freeze in water for storage. Milk cartons make good freezing containers. When frozen in water, fish will keep for several months.

Texas offers thousands of miles of shore fishing, an economic, efficient, and easy way for every man to fill a stringer.

Gulf Coast and Prairies Menu

Roasted Oysters with Red Sauce
Mesquite Panbread
Baked Redfish with Pecans
Matagorda Ratatouille
Sunday Cobbler

Cypress Valley Sauvignon Blanc

BLUE-EYED GRASS. *Sisyrinchium sagittiferum*. Bluish-purple to purple flowers, singles or clusters at the end of stems, that close in the afternoon. Grows in clumps of narrow, grasslike leaves, although not a true grass. Eight to 12 inches tall in clay or sand-clay pastures, meadows, and open woodlands. Perennial, April through May.

Roasted Oysters

This recipe is best prepared on the coast over an open fire, but you can use your covered grill by utilizing shallow baking pans to keep the oyster juice from stifling your fire. Special equipment is needed: an oyster knife or clean screwdriver and a cloth glove for each person.

6 to 12 oysters per person, depending upon
the occasion

PREPARATION

1. Rinse oysters well in ice chest. Add salt to water after rinsing, since it will make the oysters release last bits of grit.
2. Start mesquite fire.
3. Place oysters in shell on baking pans over fire.
4. When oysters pop open, in 5 to 10 minutes, they're ready to serve.

Shade Tree Red Sauce

1 cup catsup
¼ cup prepared horseradish
squeeze of fresh lime juice
dash sherry pepper sauce (substitute
Tabasco sauce)
dash Worcestershire sauce
freshly ground pepper

PREPARATION

1. Blend all ingredients and taste test.
2. Add more catsup or horseradish to correct and adjust other spices.
3. Store in refrigerator for several hours so flavors will blend.

Mesquite Panbread

SERVES 4 TO 6

1 cup mesquite meal
1 cup whole wheat flour
1 cup water
peanut oil
butter
honey

PREPARATION

1. Mix flours and water to make dough. Pat flat into small patties.
2. Heat thin layer of peanut oil in cast-iron skillet.
3. Fry in peanut oil till brown on both sides.
4. Serve with butter and honey (for breakfast).

Baked Redfish with Pecans

SERVES 4

2 pounds redfish fillets
2 limes
1 cup chopped pecans
4 tablespoons butter or substitute, melted
salt and freshly ground pepper to taste

PREPARATION

1. Preheat oven to 450 degrees.
2. Line baking pan with aluminum foil. Grease lightly.
3. Place fillets on foil, sprinkle with salt and pepper, and coat with 2 tablespoons melted butter and juice of half of a lime.
4. Bake for 20 minutes or grill over mesquite coals until meat flakes.
5. Put remaining butter in separate skillet. Add pecans and brown. Add juice of half a lime.
6. Place redfish on serving platter. Dust generously with pecans.
7. Squeeze lime juice over all and serve with remaining lime wedges.

Ratatouille Matagorda

SERVES 4 TO 6

3 ounces olive oil
1 clove chopped Louisiana "big toe" garlic
(substitute 2 cloves regular garlic)
1 large Texas yellow onion, sliced
1 medium eggplant, cubed
2 tablespoons flour
1 green pepper, cut into strips
1 yellow pepper, cut into strips
4 tomatoes, peeled and sliced
1 tablespoon capers
salt to taste
freshly ground black pepper

PREPARATION

1. Heat olive oil in cast-iron skillet. Saute garlic and onion.
2. Roll cubes of eggplant in flour.
3. Add eggplant and all pepper strips to skillet. Salt and pepper to taste. Cover and cook on low heat for 60 minutes.
4. Add sliced tomatoes and capers. Simmer uncovered for 20 minutes or until mixture thickens. Serve hot or chilled.

Sunday Cobbler

³/₄ cup all-purpose flour
½ cup granulated sugar
½ cup brown sugar
½ teaspoon cinnamon
1 teaspoon baking powder
¼ cup butter
½ cup chopped pecans
¼ cup water
1 1-pound can fruit pie filling
½ cup raisins

PREPARATION

1. Preheat oven to 325 degrees.
2. Combine flour, sugars, cinnamon, baking powder.
3. Cut in butter. Stir in pecans and water.
4. Combine pie filling and raisins in greased, foil-lined Dutch oven.
5. Spoon flour mixture over pie filling.
6. Cover Dutch oven and bake for 25 minutes, or until hot and brown.

BUCKHORN CHILI

INGREDIENTS

6-7 lbs. venison ground for chili

7 onions

5 bell peppers

4 one lb. cans stewed tomatos

1 half lb. can Rostel tomatoes

1/2 tsp. minced garlic or four whole cloves

2 tsp. celery seed

2 tsp. cayenne pepper

3/4 tsp. cominos

6 bay leaves

1 tsp. basil

6 tsp. salt

6 Tbs. chili powder

1 cup flour and water

6 cups water

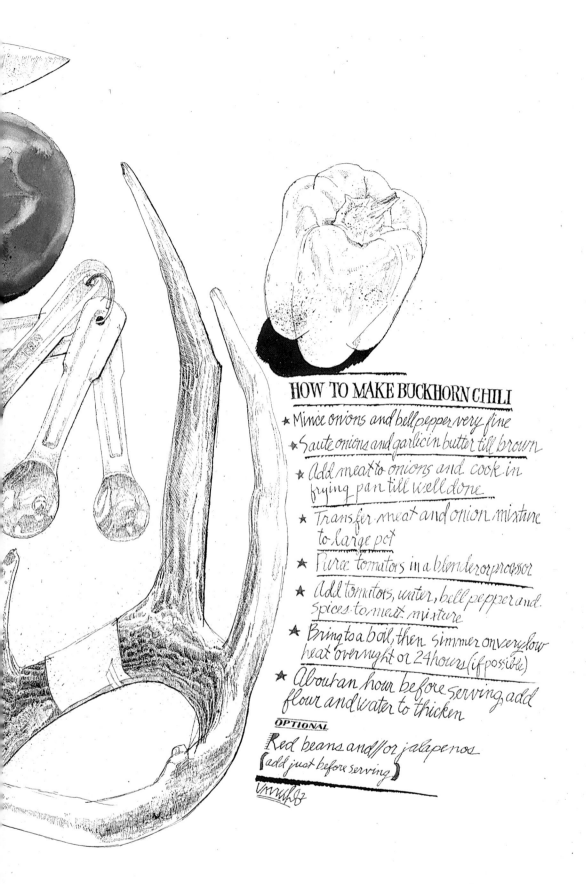

HOW TO MAKE BUCKHORN CHILI

★ Mince onions and bell pepper very fine
★ Saute onions and garlic in butter till brown
★ Add meat to onions and cook in frying pan till well done
★ Transfer meat and onion mixture to large pot
★ Puree tomatoes in a blender or processor
★ Add tomatoes, water, bell pepper and spices to meat mixture
★ Bring to a boil, then simmer on very low heat overnight or 24 hours (if possible)
★ About an hour before serving, add flour and water to thicken

OPTIONAL

Red beans and/or jalapenos (add just before serving)

XIII

THE CAMP

Cooking

and

First Aid

THE CAMP
Cooking
and
First Aid

You can tell a lot about sportsmen by the creature comforts of their camp. The camp will be in a shady location with good drainage in case of rain. If not a cabin, you'll find campers, motor homes, house trailers, even converted semi-trailer "refers." A well-planned outdoor fire pit with a keyhole and a grill are always present, mesquite cut and stacked nearby. A stout game pole is set up, and there's a table for cleaning fish and butchering game. Some sort of outdoor lighting is in place along with comfortable chairs scattered about, occupied by comfortable sportsmen.

While a sportsman may occasionally exert himself in pursuit of game, fowl, or fish, it's against his principles to do so in camp. A well-run camp should be a lazy camp; the few chores shared without undue stress or militaristic assignments. This leaves ample time for poker, guitars, tall tales, and leisurely eating and consumption of beverages after the guns are racked for the evening.

Sportsmen, being ecosystem-oriented, never litter, so the camp is self-policing. Collecting mesquite for the campfire is viewed as no chore at all, usually gathered up on the way back from the hunt. About the only real effort that has to be expended is on dishwashing, so this job is usually rotated among the non-cooks, who tend to use a lot of paper plates anyway. That brings us to the secret of a laid-back, harmonious, downright enjoyable camp—the cook or cooks.

A good cook may have invested a lot of time and money in his gear, but the truth is he cooks because he wants to, he doesn't like to wash dishes, or he likes the recognition. Whatever his motivation, if his cuisine turns you on, let him cook. You eat. Laud his efforts, volunteer as kitchen help or busboy, and wash dishes every once in awhile.

Cooking expert Julia Child has said, "Non-cooks think it's silly to invest two hours work in two minutes enjoyment, but if cooking is evanescent, well, so is ballet." Brava, Julia. Sportsmen have noted a few other evanescent glories, including wilderness sunsets, the lunging strike of a bass through dawn-still waters, the fluid grace of an airborne deer, and the heart-stopping flutter of a covey-rise. And, the evanescence of outdoor cookery generally lasts a little longer; the aromatic smoke of mesquite fire and campmeat tantalizingly whets the appetite and lingers to remind everyone just how good it all was.

The fish and game we harvest is precious. It deserves the very finest in preparation and cooking. It probably will never taste better or be more appreciated than when it is fresh and can be enjoyed with the fellowship of hunting and fishing companions. Camp meals seem especially fine when the entree has been the camp objective, such as backstrap medallions or batter-fried bass. But even if the entree is store-bought, outdoor meals are always special.

The camp cook should plan carefully for the meals he intends to prepare. He must also consider the conditions of his kitchen environment and the tastes of other campers. Planning menus ahead of time ensures easier provisioning and preparation, and better meals. Knowing the tastes and preferences of your campmates is important, because they can range from just flat don't like it to dietary restrictions. So ask before you buy. And, you'll find that if you have regular hunting partners, they come to enjoy and look forward to certain menus, almost as a camp tradition. Many of our most memorable meals are repeated year after year.

Ritual also helps in gently persuading your partners to help out without exerting themselves. Our Llano River Marching Rhythm Band and Pinto Bean Appreciation Society begins the night before the feast with careful bean sorting and soaking in beer. The pot simmers almost all the next day, in readiness for the next evening's meal. It is stirred and liquid is added by anyone who walks by. The firepit or covered grill is tended throughout the day, timed to yield goodies just at dinner time. Salads and vegies are cut at the noon break by those not dressing out deer or other game. They are sealed in plastic and kept on ice. Cornbread or biscuit dough can be mixed in advance and stored in the ice chest. The point is, don't let night fall without being prepared for the evening's meal. The more done ahead of time, the easier it is on a camp full of successful but tired hunters or fishermen. A truly fine camp cook has developed a keen sense of timing so that all dishes are ready for presentation at the proper time. And, ideally, he's flexible and prepared to adapt to a myriad of foul-ups.

Weather can throw a major monkey wrench into any camp meal preparation, especially since most entrees are destined to be cooked outside. If a grill is being used and is covered, fire already going, there is usually less of a problem, although a blue norther blowing on a water-pan-type cooker will cool it to below the cooking point. It pays to have a Plan B that allows you to cook under shelter. A canned ham or a single dish Dutch oven meal, such as chili or stew, frozen and hidden away in the ice chest, can come to the rescue with just a single butane burner for heat. It's also a mistake to rely solely on the prowess of the hunters or fishers for camp entrees. Unsuccessful outings along with those times when a sportsman will be afield without a rod and gun, or perhaps when the traditional work party goes out to get the deer stands in shape, are occasions when the camp chef needs a repertoire of easy to manage, hearty, and just plain wonderful recipes. Common sense, a bit of luck, and hungry patrons will pull you through.

ADVANCE PREPARATION

FOR A QUALITY CAMP

If you have elected to accept the responsibilities of camp cook for a group of sportsmen, preparation is critical, starting with equipment selection.

An all-round excellent camp cook has not only mastered outdoor cooking skills, but also acquired some basic equipment enabling him to cook for a group without the accoutrements of civilization. Matches, tender, and mesquite can suffice, but camp cooks tend to be a little more civilized. They usually pack in propane tanks, burners and grills, and other heavy gear when they're able to reach the base camp by vehicle.

Selecting cooking equipment is very much a function of the type of camping or camp facilities available. In our permanent deer camp, for example, we have a goodly assortment of pots and pans, utensils, and even a complete stock of well-used and well-cared-for cast-iron skillets and Dutch ovens. We handle all serious cooking outdoors on the 55-gallon oil drum and keyhole fire arrangement. Smaller covered pots are good for side dishes, and stainless steel mixing bowls with covers are best for preparation and storage. Most camp cooks acquire cookware over a period of years.

A badge of honor among camp cooks is the black satin patina of well-kept cast-iron skillets. One worked with loving care for a decade or so is slicker than teflon and much more durable; using it is like cooking with a work of art. Cast-iron pots and skillets must be seasoned before use. They rust and pit easily, so manufacturers coat them with a waxy oil that must be thoroughly removed. Wash in hot, soapy water. Dry and coat with a layer of pure, salt-free peanut oil, as this oil will take more heat before smoking. Place the cast-iron item in a 250-degree oven for an hour, wiping it with fresh oil occasionally. After an hour, remove it and wipe completely, then repeat the process. You are burning oil into the pores of the cast-iron, which repels water that might start rust pits. If possible, your first few uses of the new cast-iron utensil should be with dishes cooked in vegetable oil or bacon grease, which provides further seasoning. Later you can employ just about any cooking method without damage to the seasoning. The camp cook will never allow soap to ever again touch his cast-iron—just hot water and paper toweling. Should a Yankee or greenhorn soap up your cast-iron, you must re-season it. However, if you have a home economist in camp who wants the cast-iron a little cleaner, it really won't hurt to first wipe it out with warm sudsy water, rinse well, then coat the utensil with peanut oil and cure it over a campfire or in an oven for 30 minutes at 250 degrees.

There are four categories of cast-iron utensils included in our recommended five-piece basic set.

1. **Skillets**—You will want both a 10-inch and 16-inch. You'll be amazed at how many meals call for two such pans.
2. **Dutch Oven**—Buy the largest you can, usually 16 inches. You want the type with a 1-inch flange around the lid and four stubby legs on the bottom. This allows you to cook with mesquite coals and not burn what's inside.
3. **Deep Pot**—For cooking with large volumes of liquid and frying fish over butane.
4. **Rectangular Griddle**—This is optional but very useful if you have the firepower to heat it and a large camp to feed with slabs of bacon and pancakes.

CAMP COOK'S EQUIPMENT CHECKLIST

Covered grill
Large outdoor 16-inch-diameter cast-iron Dutch oven—with legs and a rim around the top.
16-inch-diameter cast-iron skillet
10-inch cast-iron skillet
12-inch cast-iron pot
Stainless steel wire basket to fit pot
18-quart heavy-duty aluminum stew pot
5-quart heavy-duty aluminum or steel covered saucepan
Set of stainless steel mixing bowls with plastic lids
Large mixing bowls for salad and dough
Measuring pitcher
Wire grill for keyhole fire
Large cutting board
Large can opener
Large meat cleaver
Meat thermometer
Tenderizing mallet
Meat saw
Shovel
Fireplace gloves
Large water pump pliers to remove cast-iron lids
Heavy-duty aluminum foil
Freezer-grade zip-type plastic bags
Large steel slotted spoons
Spatula
Vegetable peeler
Large meat fork
Large steel ladle
Large serving spoons
Large tongs
Large ice chests—for food and game
Two propane burners
Propane tanks
Proper size wrenches for gas connections
Ax and chainsaw for firewood
Canvas tote sacks
Gasoline lantern

A good camp cook is self-reliant. Don't depend on anybody else to furnish equipment or food. We strongly recommend that the cook handle all provisioning, because the potential for error is enormous when you count on others to bring supplies. However, the camp cook should provision only for common meals. This is why planning menus ahead is so important. Let other hunters provide for drinks, snacks, and their personal favorites. Incidentally, we find that a focus on the basics in buying enables us to stock up inexpensively. Our camp meals usually cost less per head than those at home.

A small canvas sack permanently outfitted is fundamental to our camp cooking success. It lives with other basic gear at home and is among the first items packed. Sharp knives, small items, and spices have a way of disappearing, so even if you have a permanent camp cabin you may want to consider the camp cook cache concept:

CAMP COOK CACHE   (Goes with you everywhere)

Thin-bladed boning knife
Long-bladed fillet knife
Paring knife
French-style chopping knife
Sharpening steel and whetstone
Wooden spoons (2)
Tin measuring cup
   (doubles as biscuit cutter)
Bottle opener/corkscrew
Emergency matches in waterproof container

Coarse ground pepper
Garlic powder
Sage
Seasoning salt
Oregano
Tarragon
Sweet basil
Cinnamon
Whole cloves
Dry mustard
Chili powder
Baking powder
Baking soda
Brown sugar
Tabasco sauce
Worcestershire sauce
Bouillon cubes
Vinegar

All knives are sheathed in cases. You can find odd-sized knife sheaths at Army surplus stores or large hunter supply stores.

All of these items fit into a compact tote sack and allow you to work a little magic around camp. Note that staples are not included. They are purchased like any other special condiments and ingredients, as needed, with all other kitchen supplies. The cache is designed as a permanently accessible backup for use in a wide range of tasty recipes, emergency dish preparation, or just for adding some zest to an otherwise ordinary side dish.

Setting up a base camp for a large group of sportsmen is an exercise in logistics rivaling those of D-Day. Even if you have a cabin, be sure staples are not forgotten and that the camp is ready to serve its sportsmen in the customary manner—pampered.

Knowing the headcount is critical, so the well-organized group of sportsmen will have a call-in system to yield an accurate headcount 48 hours before the hunt. Time in the field is the other obvious variable. Menu selection can be limited by refrigeration. If your refrigeration consists of ice chests or coolers, try freezing meats and prepared foods so that they become part of their own cooling system. Don't let foods stand in ice water. For longer trips, consider dedicating a cooler for frozen foods. Prepare this cooler with 20 to 30 pounds of dry ice wrapped in newspaper, placed on the bottom. A 36-quart dry ice cooler packed with frozen food—stuff any spare space with more newspaper—will last a week or 10 days if kept out of the hot sun and opened only when necessary to remove the next entree.

It's hard to beat canvas sacks, those copied from old ice carriers, to transport all dry goods—if you have a place for storing them in camp that's varmint-proof. We take the sacks right into the grocery store and stand at the end of the checkout line, sacking non-perishables and canned goods into the canvas bag while the bagboy handles the cold stuff, which we transfer to an ice chest for transport to camp.

Don't sweat the little things. Some experts will have you counting pieces of bread or calculating the number of servings per person for a head of cauliflower. (One pound of cauliflower serves three, but we avoid such difficult mathematics by leaving cauliflower at home.) Use some common sense, and with staples buy generously, because they can always be used on subsequent hunts. Err on the high side. You'll seldom waste food, although some sportsmen may have to sacrifice and put on a little extra weight to make you look good.

CAMP KITCHEN SUPPLY CHECKLIST
- Dishwashing detergent
- Scouring powder and pads
- Scrub pads and dishcloth
- Bar of soap
- Paper towels (twice as many as you think you'll need)
- Eating utensils
- Extra-wide roll of heavy-duty aluminum foil
- Disposable aluminum cake or roasting tins
- Charcoal briquettes for emergencies

- Lighter fluid
- Large plastic garbage bags
- Large wooden kitchen matches
- Paper plates, bowls, and holders
- Plastic cups
- Table cover
- Zip-type storage bags
- Bathroom tissue

CAMP KITCHEN STAPLE CHECKLIST
- Biscuit and pancake mix
- Cornbread mixes (white/yellow/Mexican)
- Flour
- Cornmeal
- Baking powder
- Baking soda
- White sugar
- Salt
- Pepper
- Coffee/tea
- Pinto beans
- Rice
- Pickles
- Honey
- Peanut oil for cooking
- Wine vinegar

BEVERAGES:
- Fruit juices
- Tomato juice
- Bottled water
- Personal soft drinks
- Mixes, beer, wine**

BREADSTUFFS:
- Sandwich bread
- Crackers
- Cold cereal
- Tortillas

CANNED STAPLES:
- Creamed corn
- Tomatoes/sauce
- Mushrooms
- Jalapenos
- Peas/beans
- Fruit
- Ham (emergency)
- Evaporated milk

PERISHABLE STAPLES:
- Milk
- Eggs
- Butter/margarine
- Catsup*

Mayonnaise*
Mustard*
Jams/jellies*
Salad dressings*

*May not be left in camp without refrigeration after opening. Everything else can be left in a protected grub box. All flour products must be sealed in air- and bug-tight containers.
**When shopping for a group, we prefer to check these out last and separately so that we have a "clean" receipt of the camp-related grocery items from which the cost per person can be calculated for each of the sportsmen involved.

If the equipment, supplies, and nonperishable staples listed above are acquired and either left in camp or kept in a portable grub box, then all the camp cook needs to do is shop for the next hunt. Practically speaking, a certain amount of staple replenishment is usually necessary. We have formed the habit of making a quick review of staples before leaving camp after a hunt, and the cook keeps this with his ever-present camp cache until it's time to buy for the next hunt. The new list would then always start with supplies and staples.

TECHNIQUES AND RECIPES

THE EXPERTS USE

THE CAMP COOK FIRE Fire building and tending is a good source for arguments on the finer points of style, but all Texans agree on the most essential point—the western honey mesquite that has taken over 60 million acres of our state is the finest natural cooking fuel known to man. The hickory and walnut of East Texas and the pecan of East and Central Texas are great cooking woods, but nothing on earth can compare with the fragrance of mesquite; its delectable aroma is a perfect complement to anything grilled or smoked. It may be the only wood with its own active fan club, Los Amigos del Mesquite, headquartered in Austin.

The dense mesquite creates more BTUs than lesser woods. Mesquite coals maintain an evenness of heat at a higher level than store-bought charcoal and almost all other readily available wood fuels. Chunks that are still greenish in the center create good smoke, yet burn well. You can also use a mixture of dry mesquite and a few green fingers to achieve a more aromatic smoke. Small six-inch fingers of fresh cut mesquite tossed into your freezer at home will retain the wood's sap and flavor.

Basic to any camp we've ever established is a keyhole fireplace. The keyhole is a small area surrounded by flat stones extending off the main fire—usually ringed with much larger stones—to hold enough heat for after-dinner guitar sessions, tales of bravery and valor from long-ago hunts, and lies and excuses for today's.

Red hot coals are scooped into the keyhole, which will then radiate a perfectly even heat for cooking atop a heavy wire grill. Dutch ovens may also be placed in the keyhole, stubby legs above the layer of coals, with more coals heaped on the rimmed top.

THE DUTCH OVEN For more remote mountain camps, especially ones with many hunters, you'll probably opt to have butane burners available. Functional homemade burners can be fashioned from the burner rings of old gas water heaters. Still, a camp cook should always have a Dutch oven; it makes you a master on any rough hunt situation. Any baking, roasting, or stewing that you can do at home can be done with a Dutch oven. Cobblers, cakes, pies, breads, and biscuits leave your fellow sportsmen in awe. And if you run completely out of butane fuel, you can still cook with firewood.

The secret of the Dutch oven lies in balancing the amount of heat that is transferred to the bottom, sides, and top. Using your shovel, place a few small, red hot coals in a circular area free of grass and tender, its diameter slightly greater than the oven. Use coals about one inch in diameter, placed two inches apart. Set the oven over these coals with the food to be cooked already in place. For baking, we like to line the Dutch oven with heavy-duty foil or use a disposable cake pan of a diameter less than the oven's, to make cleaning a little easier. We also put a few thin, flat rocks in the bottom as a platform for baked goods to minimize scorching. Level the grill so that no coals actually touch the pot's bottom. Carefully seat the lid. Use your shovel to cover the lid with large chunks of red hot coals, propping a few around the sides. Check the food at about half its baking time. You may want to add or take away coals. If the top is cooking, the bottom is, too. Have ready access to either fireplace gloves or a large pair of water pump pliers—the ones with plastic handles—for lifting the lid.

The best way to roast or stew is to can dig a pit for the oven in the earth around your campsite. Line the bottom of the pit with flat rocks. Avoid those that are really water-logged, because they can explode. This happened to a sportsman we know, riddling both a venison ham and his reputation.

Build a mesquite fire in the pit and let it burn for two or three hours. When you're ready to begin cooking, remove most of the coals with your shovel and set them aside in a heap to stay hot. Be sure you don't catch range grass on fire. If you need to sear meat, place grease in the oven, sear the meat first, then add other ingredients such as vegetables and seasonings, plus liquid. Seat the lid, heap with coals, and place a few more around the sides. Cover the entire Dutch oven with the earth removed from the hole and head out for the afternoon hunt. Pot roasts and stews will be done in less than two hours. Be sure to add enough water to keep the meat from drying out.

Wild turkey will cook at about 20 minutes per pound. If using a meat thermometer, it's done at 180 degrees. Place heavy-duty foil under the fowl and add two cups of water. The water evaporates, leaving the bird's skin a golden brown. Use the foil to lift the bird out of the oven.

Although the earth covering seals heat in, water vapor escapes. Once covered with earth, coals are oxygen starved and begin to die out. However, they retain warmth for six to eight hours, just enough time for you to collect a nice buck, field dress him, return to camp, hang him, and then retrieve the Dutch oven with a nonchalant, "Soup's on."

BAKING Baking in camp Dutch ovens can produce some of the most memorable additions to your meals. You may sometimes singe the bottom while you learn to judge heat, but even so, the rest of the bread stuff will be delicious. Golden brown biscuits, cobblers, cakes, and deep-dish pies will make you the envy of the camp. If you know how to keep and use sourdough, all the better, but sourdough is very difficult for the part-time outdoor chef. One important suggestion: Have handy asbestos-lined fireplace gloves so that you can handle the hot cast iron safely. A large set of water pump pliers is useful for raising the lid to check cooking progress and for removing the lid completely.

BREADS Nothing adds to a meal like a hot, fluffy, tender biscuit dripping in butter. This should be a standard for all camp cooks. Consider double batches, because they go fast, and leftovers can be used to make a bread pudding.

Rescue Biscuits

Although most camps have switched to mixes or even canned biscuits, occasionally somebody goofs and real biscuits are needed. This basic recipe is included to allow you to "rescue" the camp and be a hero.

> 2 cups pre-sifted flour
> 1/2 teaspoon salt
> 1/4 teaspoon baking soda
> 1 teaspoon sugar
> 1 tablespoon baking powder
> 5 tablespoons margarine, or other
>   shortening
> 1 cup buttermilk, or sweet milk
>   Aluminum foil

PREPARATION

1. Preheat oven to 450 degrees, whether Dutch or dude in the cabin.
2. In a bowl, mix dry ingredients thoroughly.
3. Cut in shortening, then poke a hole in the middle of the mixture.
4. Pour buttermilk in hole and stir lightly with a fork until flour is moist throughout.

5. Flour a cutting board. Turn out dough and knead only two or three times. Don't overdo, or you'll toughen it.
6. Mash dough flat, about 1/2-inch thick.
7. Cut biscuits with rim of favorite wine glass, or tin measuring cup from the camp cook cache.
8. Grease aluminum foil with shortening.
9. Bake biscuits for 12 to 15 minutes.

With a Dutch oven, remember to put 3/4 of all coals on the lid to generate heat without burning the bottom or sides. The hotter the better before starting to bake.

Sweet Rolls

For sweet rolls, add one more teaspoon sugar to Rescue Biscuits dough. Roll the dough about 1/2-inch thick in a rectangular form. Spread very soft butter over the dough and sprinkle with cinnamon, brown sugar, raisins, and chopped nuts if you like. Roll longways and seal the edge with a little water on your fingertips. Cut into rounds about 3/4-inch thick, place in a greased Dutch oven, and bake as for biscuits.

OLD-FASHIONED CLOSED PIT COOKERY If you're not using your Dutch oven, food ready for cooking in the ground needs to be very carefully wrapped in heavy-duty foil. A trick to minimize burning is to use two layers of foil, placing four sheets of newspaper between the two layers. Begin by folding the edges of the first foil piece together over the meat or vegetables. Fold the edges tightly one half-inch at a turn. Do the same with the ends. Lay out the second sheet of foil. Place four layers of newspaper on top. Place the foil-wrapped packet face down on the top piece of newspaper. Repeat the careful folding.

Meats requiring fairly lengthy cooking times, such as turkeys, chickens, large game birds, venison hams, feral hogs, and such, go into the pit first. Wrap a loose net of baling wire around the larger items, leaving ends that will stick up from the pit. This helps you find and remove them later. Place the foil packages so they don't touch one another, then shovel back some of your coals to cover them. Cover the whole pit with six inches of earth. A venison or feral hog ham will take four to five hours to cook this way; a large chicken about three and a half hours. Packets of potatoes, corn, and other vegetables can be added in layers. Fresh corn is usually ready in 20 to 30 minutes; potatoes in 30 to 45 minutes. Test potatoes' doneness by squeezing.

In using a more conventional charcoal grill or 55-gallon oil drum on its side, build the mesquite fire at one end and let it burn down before positioning large items that require long, slow cooking, such as brisket, cabrito, hams, venison roasts, or turkey, at the other end. We often add an aluminum pan filled with water or even beer between the meat and the fire to add moisture to the process. A disposable aluminum pan under a turkey or venison roast helps retain moisture. If your grill is too small for good separation, place a cookie sheet or aluminum foil over the fire to deflect direct heat.

PINEYWOODS OPEN PIT COOKERY   If you've taken a feral hog shoat or tom turkey and are ready for a laid-back Big Thicket-type open pit barbecue, dig a pit two-and-a-half to three feet deep, start a large fire in the pit, and let it burn three hours. Any dry hardwood will do, but in most of the state you'll have access to mesquite. You want eight to twelve inches of coals. By this time, the coals won't be giving off smoke, so you'll need to add wood for smoking. In East Texas, hickory will give a sweet, heady taste; pecan and walnut a tangy taste; sassafras a pungent flavor. Pecans, walnuts, and hickory nuts give off aromatic smoke, too. We fudge a little and freeze these during the off season, bringing them to camp and sneaking them into the firepit when no one is looking. Position a sturdy grill above the fire, judging distance by when you want to eat. It also helps to have some sort of windbreak rigged.

In open pit barbecuing, you must keep the meat moist. A baste not only helps provide even heat, but the smoky steam from the constant dripping also imparts flavor.

Open Pit Baste

1 quart water
2 cans broth (beef broth for game; chicken
        broth for fowl)
2 cups white wine, vinegar, or dill pickle
        juice
1/2 cup peanut oil
3 ounces red pepper sauce
2 teaspoons coarse black pepper
2 teaspoons paprika
2 teaspoons rosemary
2 teaspoons savory
2 teaspoons thyme
4 bay leaves
        (Don't add salt—it drys the meat)

PREPARATION

1. Mix all ingredients thoroughly.
2. Using a spoon or brush, apply baste as required to keep meat moist.

Because of the frequent basting required, barbecuing is definitely a stay-in-camp process. Any audience will be driven to the brink of perceived starvation by the fragrance of the baste and aromatic wood smoke. Don't hurry. Enjoy it in the manner of a true sportsman.

WEST TEXAS SPIT COOKERY   In West Texas, they cook on a spit, always over mesquite, using green mesquite twigs for smoke. The game is spread-eagled or trussed to a spit that can be turned manually. The fire is

the same type pit as used for open pit barbecuing. The difference is the turning, which allows the baste to adhere to the meat. Dry seasonings are also sometimes used.

Dry Seasoning Mix

1 part chili powder
1 part crushed red pepper
1 part coarse black pepper
1 part rosemary
1 part savory
1 part thyme

Peanut oil

PREPARATION

1. Mix dry ingredients thoroughly. Add crushed sage if cooking fowl.
2. Place everything in a shaker and have peanut oil handy.

As the meat begins to get hot, baste it with peanut oil to the point that it begins to drip, then sprinkle with the seasoning mix. Once again, the cook is confined to camp with this one. If cooking javelina, add three parts brown sugar. If cooking cabrito (young goat), mix in one cup brandy, two sticks of butter, and baste slowly. Do not allow the meat to blacken too much.

GRILL COOKERY   If there is a suitable grill available, it is much simpler to use than a spit. It is important that the heat be kept constant and that small pieces are not scorched, as this will add a bitter taste to meat. The basic baste can still be used.

The addition of a grill makes it easy to add fish to your menu. Fish can be grilled either whole or filleted. Spreading mayonnaise on the fish, much as you would spread it on a slice of bread, adds flavor, helps hold the meat together, and keeps it from adhering to the grill.

To grill or broil fish, clean, scale, and remove the head—unless you just have to show off—then salt the body cavity, spread it with mayonnaise, and place it on a hot grill with no flame. The initial side down should be almost blackened before turning, but the real test is when the meat flakes away at the touch of a fork. Carefully turn the fish over, and baste with butter and lemon mixture. Sometimes you need to cook on aluminum foil to prevent a complete breakup. If the fish has a strong natural flavor, such as kingfish, or if others in the party are not avid fish eaters, sprinkle it with rosemary. This will not appreciably change the flavor, but it will mask the strong taste. This works for any other strong-tasting meat such as javelina or goat.

The Camp Cook's Marinade

One of the best and easiest marinades is commercial Italian salad dressing, but cooks of distinction prefer creating their own concoctions. We have used a basic recipe for years, making a large batch at the first of the season and keeping it refrigerated.

> 1 pint soy sauce
> ½ pint kosher dill pickle juice, wine, beer, or vinegar
> ½ cup cooking oil
> ¼ cup Worcestershire sauce
> 1 tablespooon coarse black pepper
> ¼ cup blackstrap molasses
> 1 tablespoon dry mustard
> 1 tablespoon dry ginger
> 1 tablespoon meat tenderizer
> 2 cloves garlic
> 1 tablespoon Louisiana pepper sauce

PREPARATION

1. Mix ingredients thoroughly.

This marinade must be used at least 30 minutes before cooking, though overnight is better, and it can be used as a baste.

Camp Ham

An all-time favorite, cooked two to three times each season at our camp for almost 20 years, camp ham is just about failsafe and provides a lot of good eating. It's best prepared in a 55-gallon drum grill with a mesquite fire in one end burned down to coals. Place the ham at the opposite end, never over the flame. Cook for five to six hours and you have a delicious dinner, with more for *manana*. Leftovers make superior breakfast meat; thin slices on rye with Swiss cheese and German mustard make terrific sandwiches. Saw the bone in half and toss it into the social bean pot.

> 10- to 12-pound bone-in cured ham (not fresh)
> Whole cloves
> ½ cup brown sugar
> 2 tablespoons dry mustard
> ½ cup peanut oil

PREPARATION

1. Cut 1- to 1½-inch hatchmarks in ham skin and insert a clove at each intersection.
2. Mix brown sugar, mustard, and oil into a paste.
3. Pat paste over ham.

Mesquite Broiled Chicken

This is a camp favorite in the off season or when we're on a work party at the deer lease. It's really two meals in one with delightfully different flavors. The chicken always turns out juicy and tender, and the leftovers become fajitas.

TONIGHT

> 2 whole young, tender fryers cut in half
> Seasoning salt
> 2 limes or a bottle of lime juice
> 1 white onion, chopped
> Italian salad dressing
> Tabasco sauce
> Sweet-and-sour or hackberry sauce

TOMORROW

> 1 tablespoon peanut oil
> 1 onion, sliced lengthwise
> 1 bell pepper, sliced in thin, long strips
> 1 teaspoon chili powder
> Pinch of cumin
> Flour tortillas
> Salsa

PREPARATION

1. Sprinkle chicken halves with seasoning salt.
2. Marinate chicken at least one hour in lime juice, chopped onion, salad dressing, and dash of Tabasco.
3. Broil chicken skin side up over mesquite coals on covered grill for 30 to 35 minutes.
4. Turn, coat each chicken half with hackberry or sweet-and-sour sauce, and broil another 20 to 30 minutes, or until legs pull away easily. Caution: cooking time varies greatly with temperature of fire and distance from coals. Chickens can be moved to section of grill away from direct heat to cook slowly while the rest of the meal is being prepared.

FAJITAS MANANA

1. Cut remaining broiled chicken into thin strips.
2. Saute in peanut oil with onion, bell pepper strips, chili powder, and cumin.
3. Heat tortillas.
4. Place chicken fajita mixture into tortilla, add salsa, and enjoy.

THE ACCOMPLISHED CAMP COOK

Camp cookery has a rich tradition in Texas. The accomplished camp cook may well add a touch or two of the *nouvelle*, but he won't stray far from the recipes and cooking techniques developed over hundreds of years in Texas wilderness camps. The unknown heroes of these hungry camps collectively created the most diverse cuisine of any place in North America. Depending upon the campsite, early-day cooks learned to prepare meals with whatever was at hand in a style dictated by their cultural background, so we have French gumbo, American stew, and Mexican chili, each dealing with the less desirable cuts of venison, duck, longhorn, or jackrabbit.

The settlers of the Southeast marshes and coast constantly added coots, ducks, geese, oysters, shrimp, fish, frog legs, turtle, and crab to a pot that was kept warm on the back of a wood stove. They made an artform of adding leftovers or almost anything edible to the pot, creating unusual blends of flavors and seasonings.

Gumbo remains one of the best and easiest ways to cook in camp. The base of a Cajun gumbo is the "roux." While it's often secretly prepared in advance at home, it can also be done in camp. Gumbo only gets better with age and can be added to over a long period if it's kept heated or refrigerated. Chili and gumbo cookoffs persist throughout the state as reminders of our past. Some of us believe it would be safer and tastier to have a stew cookoff, but the Terlingua tradition is set.

North of Cajun country, you find the Big Thicket and the hardwood forests of the Pineywoods. A staple game of this region, relied upon by early Anglo settlers, was squirrel. By adding squirrels to the produce from vegetable plots, settlers had the makings of first-rate stews.

The fertile Blackland Prairies and Rolling Plains of Central Texas provide another camp specialty—dumplings. European-stock pioneer women took great pride in their light, thin dumplings, made from scratch. But, dumplings require more skill, equipment, and time than most camp cooks have, and we've found the tortilla to be a speedier alternative.

Frijoles are the heart and soul of a good camp, and who can survive without jalapenos? But, as far as we're concerned, a Texas camp without tortillas and salsa is unthinkable. Some say the popularity of flour tortillas is a consequence of merging cultures in our state. While this may not literally be true, the tortilla certainly makes a noble symbol.

The tortilla has a variety of uses, enabling the basic hunter to dispense with plates and eating utensils if he chooses. A hunter's breakfast can consist of eggs scrambled with onions, nopalitos, and tomatoes rolled into a tortilla. Breast of blue quail spitted and cooked over a small mesquite fire in the wilderness, or pieces of tender venison grilled over a fire with green peppers and onions make a fine dinner when tucked in a tortilla *con* salsa. Tortillas also work as instant energy dog treats, pot holders, and napkins, as well as toast and fritters. You can even use them for burritos, enchiladas, and nachos.

This is why we place tortillas among our essential hunt-

ing gear: gun, ammo, knife, canteen, matches, hat, and tortillas. Of course you can add a lot to the list, but in West Texas, with this basic equipment you can survive just about anything.

PINTO BEANS Beans are a camp's favorite staple. They give you lots of iron and energy, taste good, and stick to your ribs. In Texas, there is really only one bean: the pinto.

Social Pintos

SERVES THE CAMP

2 pounds dried pinto beans
3 cans beer
1 pound ham hock (or ½ pound salt pork,
    cut into ½-inch cubes)
2 onions, minced
1 can Rotel tomatoes
1 jalapeno pepper, whole
2 tablespoons chili powder
1 teaspoon cumin seed
1 clove garlic, minced fine
    Pepper to taste
    Salt to taste
    Louisiana hot sauce

PREPARATION

1. Pick over pintos, culling small rocks and bad beans.
2. Soak beans in beer overnight.
3. In the morning, pour off beer and rinse with cold water.
4. Place beans in large pot and cover with ample water, at least four inches. Bring water close to a boil.
5. Add ham hock or small cubes of salt pork.
6. Add minced onions, tomatoes, jalapeno pepper, chili powder, cumin seed, garlic, and pepper to taste.
7. Reduce heat to "just bubbling" and cook for several hours, until beans are tender.
8. At the very end, add salt to taste and a few dashes of hot sauce. Don't get heavy handed, since you can always add more in the bowl later.

Let camp members stir frequently, adjusting spices to their taste. They will anyway, thus the name Social Pintos. Social Pintos will pretty well take care of themselves in a buried Dutch oven, but be sure to add plenty of liquid and let them cook all day. If beans are too soupy, cook uncovered to evaporate excess liquid.

These pinto beans are a meal in themselves, especially when served with hot cornbread and sliced tomatoes and onions. They go with most every camp meal, and their cooking aroma adds much to the ambiance of your camp.

Refried Beans

To prepare refried beans, simply mash leftover Social Pintos, then add them to a cast-iron skillet already bubbling with butter or fat. Stir occasionally so the beans don't burn while they thicken. Serve these up when they reach the mushy consistency you prefer and top with white cheese, chopped onions, cilantro, and other condiments of choice.

CHILI Further west is the next camp specialty: chili. Cowboys and sheepherders spread its fame. Their duties kept them out from bunkhouses and ranches many nights. They had to travel light and live off the land. Along with their pistols and carbines, they carried a stew pot, a packet of dry seasoning, and a canteen of water so they could always count on a hot supper, often made with the ever-available jackrabbit.

Jackrabbit flesh is tough and stringy when broiled or fried. But, it's pretty fair when it's cut into bite sizes, browned with suet or salt pork, and mixed with seasonings, water, and some red beans in a chili recipe.

Camp Chili

Venison chili cooked over an aromatic fire on a cold night after a hard hunt is a satisfying meal that will be long remembered. This recipe is a wonderful adaptation with a Mexican influence.

> 4 pounds deer meat, chopped, not ground
> 2 pounds chorizo (Mexican sausage),
>   chopped
>   Peanut oil
> 2 medium onions, chopped
> 2 cloves garlic, minced
> 1 teaspoon oregano
> 1 teaspoon ground cumin seed
> 6 tablespoons chili powder
> 1 can tomatoes, mashed
> 2 jalapeno peppers, chopped
>   Salt and pepper
> 2 cans beer

PREPARATION

1. Brown meat in peanut oil with onion and garlic.
2. Add the remaining ingredients.
3. Bring to a boil, then simmer for two hours.

Our camp cook reminds us that you should use full-strength beer, not the lite varieties, and never, ever add beans; "Beans are beans, chili's chili."

We won't touch the chili with debate; it rages beyond the realm of political or religious issues. Instead, we simply enjoy the repast, passing swiftly over the subject to a discourse on other legumes and vegetables vital to camp cuisine.

GOURMET GONE WILD

There are a number of edible plants in Texas that provide the camp chef with opportunities to treat fellow sportsmen to flavors seldom enjoyed in the city. Among the most versatile are the ubiquitous prickly pear cactus and honey mesquite.

PRICKLY PEAR CACTUS Young pads picked in the spring are called *nopalitos*. Pick them before they form long spines. We use water pump pliers and a thin-bladed knife to harvest. Singe the pads over an open flame to remove the hairlike needles, then scrape off all remaining spines with a knife. Rinse and double check for spines.

PRE-PREPARATION

1. Slice the carefully scraped pads into thin strips.
2. Boil for 10 minutes.
3. Drain and rinse.

Fried Nopalitos

SERVES 4

> 1 cup nopalitos, sliced and prepared
> 1 cup flour
> 1½ cups corn meal
> 2 teaspoons chili powder
>   Salt and pepper
>   Peanut oil

PREPARATION

1. Put dry ingredients in paper sack, then add nopalitos and shake to coat the strips.
2. Heat peanut oil in cast-iron skillet.
3. Fry strips till brown.

PRICKLY PEAR TUNAS Prickly pear fruit is ripe when it's a deep, magenta-red. Pick with pliers, dropping the tunas into a paper sack. Watch out for rattlesnakes under the prickly pear clumps. Scrape or burn off the hairy needles and peel. These can be eaten raw or roasted whole.

Prickly Pear Jelly

> 24 ripe and denuded prickly pear fruits
>   Pectin powder or Sure-Jel
>   Lime juice
>   Sugar

1. Cover fruit with water and boil for 20 minutes.
2. Squeeze juice from fruit, then strain through cheesecloth.
3. Measure juice yield. For each cup, use 1½ tablespoons pectin, 2 tablespoons lime juice, and 1½ cups sugar.
4. Pour cactus juice into pot, add pectin, and bring to rapid boil, stirring constantly.
5. Add lime juice and sugar, then bring to a rolling boil.
6. Skim and cook for three minutes, or until jelled.
7. To check for jelling, set aside a teaspoonful of liquid to cool for a few seconds. Pour it back into the pot. If the liquid forms a sheet, sliding off the spoon, it's properly jelled. If the liquid runs off in a single stream, cook another minute or so and test again.
8. Pour into sterile jars.

NOTE: You can substitute muscadine or other wild grapes for a delicious variety of camp condiments.

PREPARING JELLIES AND JAMS FOR STORAGE

1. Wash and rinse glass jelly jars and closures (lids and rings).
2. Immerse in water. Boil for 15 minutes. Leave in hot water until ready to use.
3. Ladle jelly into hot, sterilized jars. Leave ½-inch head space.
4. Wipe jar rings clean of any jelly spill.
5. Place lids on jars with sealing compound next to glass.
6. Screw on metal bands.
7. Cool jars on cooling rack or towel.
8. Test seal on metal lids by pressing on center. Lids stay down when properly sealed.
9. Label jars.
10. Store jelly in a cool, dark, dry place. Once opened, jars must be refrigerated.

Persimmon Jam

Central Texas has an abundance of native persimmons. The fruit is a distinct reddish-orange to orange color, about two inches in diameter. Contrary to myth, a frost isn't necessary to make them sweet, but they must be ripe, soft, and mushy to the squeeze.

3 cups persimmon pulp, seeds removed
2 cups water
2 tablespoons Sure-Jel
2 cups sugar
2 tablespoons lemon juice

PREPARATION

1. Put pulp and water in pot, and simmer for 5 minutes.

2. Squeeze pulp through coarse sieve to remove skins.
3. Place squeezings in clean pot, add Sure-Jel.
4. Heat to rolling boil.
5. Add sugar and lemon juice, stirring constantly.
6. Skim, then pour jam into sterile jars. (See instructions for Prickly Pear Jelly.)

This should jell in the refrigerator overnight. If not, boil again, adding a little more Sure-Jel.

Pequin or Jalapeno Mint Jelly

This wild taste combination is best when you use wild mint and pequin peppers, but jalapeno peppers are the norm, even though they are not usually found in the wild. This jelly is the ideal complement to venison sausage and other rich game meats.

½ cup jalapeno peppers, chopped (less if you use pequin)
2 cups bell pepper, chopped
1½ cups vinegar (6 percent acid)
½ teaspoon salt
½ tablespoon butter
7 cups sugar
6 ounces Sure-Jel
Dash of green food coloring (consider using red coloring for another batch)
Crushed mint leaves, or ½ tablespoon mint flavoring

PREPARATION

1. Seed and chop peppers.
2. Liquify peppers with vinegar in blender.
3. Place in saucepan. Add salt, butter, and sugar.
4. Boil 5 minutes. Add Sure-Jel.
5. Boil 2 minutes, then add food coloring and mint.
6. Skim, test for proper jell, then pour into jars and seal. (See instructions for Prickly Pear Jelly)

Hackberry Sauce

This is great on camp pancakes. The fruit is red to brownish-red and small, about ⅓-inch in diameter.

1 cup hackberries
2 cups water
2 tablespoons lemon juice
¼ cup sugar

PREPARATION

1. Remove stems and wash fruit.
2. Bring water to boil.
3. Boil fruit for 30 minutes.
4. Mash and strain fruit through sieve to remove seeds and bits of skin.

5. Put strained sauce in pot. Add lemon juice and sugar.
6. Heat to a boil. Simmer and stir continuously until mixture thickens, about 10 to 15 minutes.

HONEY MESQUITE RECIPES Mesquite trees are among the world's great survivors, and they are prepared to return the favor. For centuries, Indians in arid zones used mesquite pods as vital food sources during the usually dry summers and early falls, but you don't have to be desperate to enjoy the fruit of these sweet trees. You may have to sample a few pods to locate the sweetest, then remember that tree for hunting seasons to come. Break open the dry pod and suck out the pulp to test.

Mesquite Meal

1. Collect a sackful of the sweetest pods you can find.
2. Dry the pods in a 175-degree oven for 2 hours until brittle.
3. Break up pods and grind. (Hopefully in a food processor.)
4. Sift fragments through coarse sieve. The seeds will have separated.
5. Regrind the seeds and other large fragments. Sift again.
6. You should now have a bowl of meal and a bowl of seeds and shell fragments. Throw away the fragments.
7. Seal the meal in an airtight container for use in the recipe found on page 274.

OUTDOOR FIRST AID SUPPLEMENT

IMPORTANT WARNING

This supplement is intended for application to persons over the age of 10. It is not intended as a complete major emergency first aid text, and we urge inclusion of a quality first aid manual in your camp gear. If you plan to take an infant or small child into a camp environment, we urge additional preparation.

Major medical emergencies can occur at camp, and with the exception of some Trans-Pecos camps, this puts the vast majority of sportsmen within an hour's drive of professional medical care. If you regularly hunt or fish in one area, such as your deer lease, make it a point to stop by the nearest hospital, obtain the emergency room telephone number, and, if it's a little complicated to get there from camp, draw up a simple map complete with phone numbers, best driving route, and estimated driving time. Post this notice in camp. Although the camp itself will rarely have a phone, there is almost always one at the rancher's house. Know where this elusive phone is.

In addition, sportsmen should master basic first aid skills, especially CPR (cardiopulmonary resuscitation). We strongly suggest that all members of your regular hunting/fishing group spend the few hours required to learn CPR and other first aid techniques from a local hospital, Red Cross, or Heart Association program. (Such programs usually teach other basic skills needed in emergency situations.) Your family doctor will know the best local source for such training. At the very least, make sure your tetanus vaccination is current so you are not the one who has to go into town just because of a minor puncture wound.

The incidence of major medical emergencies in camps is probably no greater than that in urban areas, but the likelihood of something discomforting happening is greater. Your tender hide is no longer protected by the amenities of an air-conditioned home or high-rise office. Texas terrain can jump up and bite, sting, blister, puncture, and, on occasion, freeze you. Most of these occurrences are of relatively minor consequence, especially if properly and quickly treated. But, environmental emergencies can include envenomization by poisonous snakes or spiders, ingestion of poisonous plants, severe allergic reaction (anaphylaxis), and many other situations which may require emergency first aid and professional medical treatment. Regardless of the specific problem, take time to observe and evaluate before taking action. *Do not take unnecessary risks.*

PLANTS THAT POISON Texas has three plants that wreak havoc with skin, and many that are extremely poisonous to ingest. The contact poison plants are:

1. **Poison Ivy**—It always has a cluster of three leaves in low shrub or vine. In spring and summer, the leaves are a distinctive shiny dark green. In the fall, leaves will turn red, then yellow, but are still poisonous. The poison may be spread in smoke if plants are burned.
2. **Poison Oak**—Similar to poison ivy, its leaves are rounded at the tip rather than pointed.
3. **Poison Sumac**—It's a bush that resembles staghorn sumac, but with smooth-edged, narrow leaves and whitish berries that form in clusters where branches fork. The Pineywoods and Big Thicket are greatly blessed with this plant.

TREATMENT: Wash affected areas with soap and water ASAP. Rinse and rinse again. Gently pat on calamine lotion. Partial immunization is possible if you are a frequent victim.

Many Texas plants are poisonous to eat, and we advise sportsmen to eschew chewing any wild plant unless you find it in one of our recipes. Don't succumb to the temptation of wild mushrooms, no matter how they may appeal to the romance in your soul.

Highly Toxic Wild Plants
Reactions to ingestion of toxic plants vary widely, and rapid first aid can often lessen the chances of serious illness. Except for jack-in-the-pulpit and May apple, which will be discussed separately, the best first aid is to induce vomiting if less than two hours have elapsed since the plant was eaten. If the person has not vomited naturally, Ipecac followed by water (never milk) is recommended. Ingestion of any of the following plants can cause symptoms ranging from nausea and diarrhea to vomiting. Those toxic enough to be fatal are so noted, but fatalities are extremely rare.

Bagpod—Legume-like seed pods mark these herbaceous plants, which reach 12 feet. Found in the Pineywoods, Gulf Prairies, Post Oak Savannah, Blackland Prairies, Cross Timbers, and South Texas Plains.

Wild Balsam—Vine creepers with small yellow flowers and yellow-orange fruit. Found in the Gulf Prairies.

Black Locust—The locust tree can reach 100 feet, and is noted for spines at the base of leaf stalks. Found in the Pineywoods, Gulf Prairies, Post Oak Savannah, Blacklands, Cross Timbers, and High Plains.

Black Nightshade—An annual, it may spread on the ground or from a short, two-foot-high bush. Look for small white flowers, mature black berries. Found in all ecological areas.

Texas Buckeye and Red Buckeye—The red buckeye has red flowers; the Texas yellow. The fruit is a leather-like

poison ivy

poison oak

poison sumac

Bag pod

Wild Balsam

Black Locust

Black Nightshade

Texas Buckeye

capsule enclosing up to three larger brown seeds. Found in the Pineywoods, Gulf Prairies, Post Oak Savannah, Blacklands, Cross Timbers, Edwards Plateau, and Rolling Plains.

Buttercup

Buttercup—These bright yellow flowers are a low herb, commonly seen covering entire pastures and scattered through marshes. Found in every ecological area.

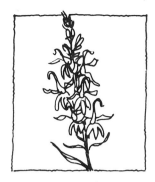

Cardinal Flower

Cardinal Flower—Deep red flowers mark this perennial, which can reach five feet. Found in the Pineywoods, Gulf Prairies, Post Oak Savannah, and Blacklands.

Carolina Horsenettle—Pale violet flowers become bright yellow berries. Nettles cover stems and leaf veins. Found in the Pineywoods, Gulf Prairies, Post Oak Savannah, Blacklands, and Edwards Plateau.

Carolina Horsenettle

Carolina Jasmine—A climbing vine that can reach 20 feet with bright yellow flowers in early spring. Found in the wild in the Pineywoods and Gulf Prairies.

Carolina Jessamine

Coyotillo—Also known as wild cherry because of reddish brown or black berries, it's a shrub that can reach eight feet. Its flowers grow in small green clusters. Found in the Gulf Prairies, South Texas Plains, Edwards Plateau, and Trans-Pecos.

Coyotillo

Death Camus—Yellow-white flowers bloom through February to early April on a short one-foot stalk. The bulb found at the base of the stalk is most toxic, although, despite its name, death camus is not lethal. Found in the Pineywoods, Gulf Prairies, Post Oak Savannah, Blacklands, Cross Timbers, and Edwards Plateau.

Death Camus

Elderberry—Most often a shrub, it can be a tree with small, purple-black berries after small, white flowers. Never eat fresh ripe berries, even though elderberry wine, jams, and jellies cause no ill effect, because cooking eliminates the toxicity. Found everywhere in the state except for the High and Rolling Plains and the Trans-Pecos.

Elderberry

Jimsonweed—This annual herb can reach five feet. Flowers are white and trumpet-shaped; fruit covered with sharp spines. Found everywhere in the state except the Blacklands.

Jimson Weed

Mescal Bean or Texas Mountain Laurel—An evergreen shrub, it can reach tree height of 35 feet. Pale lavender flowers are very fragrant. Seed pod contains up to four bright red seeds. Apaches used to chew the seeds for a narcotic high, proving how tough Apaches really are, since ingesting one seed can cause a fatal overdose. Found in the Gulf Prairies, Blacklands, South Texas Plains, Edwards Plateau, and Trans-Pecos.

Mescal Bean

Mistletoe

Mistletoe—Parasitic shrub that grows on deciduous trees and above doorways at Christmastime. The small white berries are killers; the leaves are bad enough. Found in the Pineywoods, Gulf Prairies, Blacklands, Cross Timbers, and Edwards Plateau.

Moonflower—It can reach three feet and has large, white, trumpet-shaped flowers that only open in the dark. Found in the South Texas Plains, Edwards Plateau, and Trans-Pecos.

Moon Flower

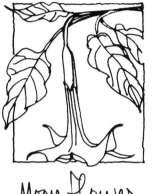

Peyote

Peyote—A small, three-inch-diameter cactus, hemispherical in shape, with no spines. Small pinkish flowers grow from the top. Indians chewed the "buttons," the aboveground portion of the plant, to experience psychedelic effects. Alkaloid mescaline and other related alkaloids are what produce hallucinations and can lead to serious psychotic aftereffects.

Poison Hemlock—"The hour of departure has arrived and we go our ways—I to die, and you to live. Which is the better, God only knows." Socrates on the subject, and he should know. The biennial plant grows to six feet with lacy, triangular leaves. The entire plant is poisonous, and the alkaloids do most of the damage. Found in the Gulf Prairies, Blacklands, Edwards Plateau, and Trans-Pecos.

Poison Hemlock

Pokeweed

Pokeweed—A native perennial herb, it can reach nine feet. In season, it's marked by long, dangling clusters of small white berries. Despite its strong odor, some persist in cooking and eating it. If you're going to brew up a mess of pokeweed for the camp, parboil it first, throw out the water, then cook it as you would greens, throwing out the last water, too. If your guests' gullets burn and they yawn a lot, you didn't boil the pokeweed enough. Found everywhere but the High Plains and Trans-Pecos.

Purple Rattlebox—A perennial that can reach 10 feet. Red or purple flowers are in long clusters. Seed pods are produced in mid-summer. Found in the Pineywoods, Gulf Prairies, and Post Oak Savannah.

Purple Rattlebox

Senna Bean

Senna-Bean—Can be a small tree up to 20 feet with long clusters of golden flowers. In summer, seed pods turn from green to dark brown at maturity. Human and livestock fatalities have been attributed to the plant. Found in the Pineywoods, Gulf Prairies, Post Oak Savannah, Blacklands, and South Texas Plains.

Silverleaf Nightshade—A perennial weed that can reach three feet. Violet flowers turn to black berries at maturation, but are the most toxic when green. Found throughout the state.

Tree Tobacco—A perennial evergreen that can reach 20 feet. Yellow tubular flowers. Fruit is egg-shaped seed pod. Leaves have a waxy, gray quality. Found in the Pineywoods, South Texas Plains, Edwards Plateau, and Trans-Pecos.

Virginia Creeper—A climbing vine that produces small, blue to black berries that can cause death. Found everywhere but the High Plains and Trans-Pecos.

Water Hemlock—Also known as cowbane and poison parsnip. The root of this plant has been mistaken for ginseng by sex-starved greenhorns and for wild carrots by misguided nature lovers. It contains a poison that is a potent convulsent, and nibbling on a piece as small as $3/8$ of an inch may cause death. Found in the Pineywoods, Gulf Prairies, Post Oak Savannah, Blacklands, Edwards Plateau, and Rolling Plains.

TREATMENT FOR ALL OF THE ABOVE: Get medical help immediately or call the nearest poison control center. (Texas poison control centers are located in Galveston, (409) 765-1420, and Houston, (713) 654-1701. Collect a sample of the plant. Determine how much of the plant was eaten and the time since ingestion. To assist the doctor, know the age and weight of the person poisoned, as well as the symptoms. Victims in remote camps should drink lots of water, then induce vomiting repeatedly. Two tablespoons of Syrup of Ipecac followed by a glass of water will also induce vomiting. Repeat the dose only once. (Your doctor can recommend proper dosages for all family members.)

Jack-in-the-pulpit—The plant may reach three feet. Clusters of half-inch-diameter red berries attract the unwary. However, one bite is usually enough, because chewing causes immediate pain to mucous membranes in the mouth. *Do not induce vomiting.* Rinse the mouth with water and head for a hospital; a tracheotomy may be necessary. Found in the Pineywoods and Gulf Prairies.

Mayapple—A ground herb with large, deeply lobed leaves; the fruit turns from green to yellow. *Do not induce vomiting.* Get to a hospital for relief of severe abdominal pain. Found in the Pineywoods, Gulf Prairies, and Post Oak Savannah.

Space does not permit full descriptions and photographs of even a minimal number of the many poisonous

Silverleaf Nightshade

Tree Tabacco

Virginia Creeper

Water Hemlock

Jack-in-the-pulpit

Mayapple

wild plants of Texas, and there are surely others not covered above. We recommend using this list as a guide to learn more about each plant if you are interested. This list should at least convince you that the risk is great.

INGESTED CORROSIVE POISONS

TREATMENT: Get medical help immediately. If the victim has swallowed lighter fluid, gasoline, or a corrosive poison such as drain cleaner, ammonia, or lye, *don't* induce vomiting before consulting a physician. It's a good idea to have noted a poison control center phone number in your first aid kit and/or in your camp cabin.

CARBON MONOXIDE POISONS

Sportsmen run a higher than normal risk of carbon-monoxide poisoning because charcoal fires, camp stoves, and lanterns can give off a dense concentration of this colorless, odorless gas. It kills without warning, but can be prevented by sufficient ventilation in cabins, tents, or motorhomes. Symptoms include nausea, headache, dizziness, and weakness. Look for a bright pink tinge around fingernails and lips.

TREATMENT: Get the victim in open air immediately. Begin artificial respiration if not breathing. Rush to the emergency ward and have someone call in advance to have oxygen ready.

SPLINTERS AND CACTUS

Carry tweezers into the field. In camp, the best practice is to sterilize a needle and the tweezers in boiling water. Wash around the splinter. Work the splinter or spine out with the needle, grasp it with the tweezers. Wear leggings in cactus country if you must walk a lot.

INSECTS THAT BITE

A good insect repellent is an item of immense value in certain Texas hunting and fishing situations. Most marsh hunting, especially early teal, cannot be tolerated without repellent because of mosquitoes. Pre-freeze dove and quail hunts can tick- and chigger-bite a person near to desperation. Take time to spread sulfur around the campsite in all but the winter months. A clean camp *sans* garbage piles will cut down all pests, including poisonous insects.

TREATMENT FOR TICK AND CHIGGER BITES: Wash the bitten area thoroughly. Application of clear fingernail polish will often make the rascals let go. Smearing bites with a petroleum jelly also works. Do not simply pluck off a tick. As a last resort, try to work its head loose with tweezers. Rocky Mountain fever is a real and present danger in Texas, and tick bites should be observed for any sign of swelling. Seek medical aid if the bite reddens, swells, or if a fever develops.

STINGING INSECTS

Honeybees, bumblebees, paper wasps (also known as yellow jackets), and fire ants are found in goodly numbers in the Texas outdoors. Wasps are found especially in deer stands that haven't been checked out for some time. One of the preseason deer lease assignments should be to remove wasp nests and beehives from stands and the campsite. Carefully. Wear long sleeves during this operation.

Fire ants can devastate you; the best protection against them is to take care where you're standing. They build mounds 18 inches in diameter up to a foot high. They can stab repeatedly with a posterior stinger while attached with pincers to your hide. Colognes, fragrant cosmetics, and soaps will attract stinging insects and repel game animals, so leave them in your kit until nightfall.

TREATMENT: Ants and bees can cause severe allergic reactions. Symptoms include shortness of breath, weariness, and hives. Any sportsman who is allergic to any of the various insect bites and stings should have his doctor prescribe an anti-anaphylaxis injection kit, carry it with him, and know how to use it. We would advise telling fellow sportsmen of your allergic reaction, where you keep the kit, and how to use it. The commonly prescribed medication is epinephrine.

Don't pull out a bee stinger. Often the venom sac goes into the hide with the stinger; pulling may squeeze more joy juice into your victim. Scrape the stinger away with your folding knife blade. Ice packs can help. A water paste of unseasoned meat tenderizer is very effective on mosquito, bee, and ant bites. Carry a supply of the tenderizer with you in a waterproof container. You'll use it frequently to ease discomfort. As noted above, carry an anti-sting kit if you are known to have allergic reactions to bee stings.

POISONOUS INSECTS

Poisonous insects include black widow spiders, brown recluse spiders, scorpions, tarantulas, and puss caterpillars. Use gloves while picking up firewood or other objects and you'll cut down on bites and stings, especially from scorpions. It can be a mistake to bug bomb a woods cabin in the summertime—the insecticide may just cause scorpions to become hyperactive, and you'll wind up sleeping outside. Shake out clothes and boots before donning. A vigorous shake of a sleeping bag is a sensible bedtime habit. Many spider bites are on private parts because victims sit down without thoroughly checking out the prospective derriere site. Look under the outhouse seat!

Black Widow Spider

The female of the species is deadlier than the male, about two-thirds of an inch longer, and bears a red hourglass on her black belly. Don't worry about the male; more than likely, she's already killed and eaten him. The male is also venomous, but at a much lower level. The female's initial bite is not too painful, but if she injected a lot of venom into you, muscle cramps and pain will occur, especially in the cheek, back, and stomach. Nausea and even paralysis can follow.

TREATMENT: Take the victim to a doctor immediately.

Bring the spider whenever possible. Apply an ice pack to the bite en route.

Brown Recluse Spider

This little, less than ½ inch, tan to dark brown fellow sports a violin-shaped mark from eyes to swollen abdomen. He can put a tissue-toxin hurt in you that can be fatal, usually only to the very old and very young. The initial bite doesn't feel like much, but two to three hours later you may notice reddening, some pain, and blistering.
TREATMENT: Take the victim to a doctor immediately. Bring the spider.

Scorpion

Although worldwide there are some 6,000 species, the Texas critter is the common striped scorpion, averaging about 2½ inches long, featuring a five-segment tail that looks just like the constellation. The poison gland is on the end of the tail, a little bulb. He's fronted by pincers but it's not the pinch you worry about. The sting feels like you'd imagine a red hot nail would feel entering your hide. Numbness and tingling often follow. Allergic reactions are possible, with swelling and respiratory problems within the hour.
TREATMENT: Unless the allergic reaction sets in, just let the pain dissipate and watch out next time. An ice pack should help reduce pain.

Tarantulas

We've got both bird and wolf tarantulas, the latter truly ferocious in appearance. These hairy monsters are the stuff from which nightmares are made, but they are not as deadly as they look. If provoked, they'll fang you, injecting a mild venom similar to that of a wasp. A bacterial infection can occur from the bites, but otherwise Texas tarantulas are much less harmful than their scary looks indicate. Much more poisonous tarantulas are found in Mexico, so don't get too chummy with these insects.

Puss Caterpillar

A small, two-inch, chocolate brown caterpillar known to many Texans as a tree asp. The spines of this little devil are venomous; its bite will make you think the cook threw hot grease on you. You may have dermatitis at the site of the sting for several days.
TREATMENT: Apply ice. If ice does not reduce pain, take an over-the-counter pain reliever such as aspirin or an antihistamine. If this doesn't help, see your doctor.

VENOMOUS SNAKE BITES Statistically, sportsmen in Texas run the highest risk of fatal snake bites in the nation. Prevention is key, and every sportsman should carefully study the section on poisonous snakes found in Chapter XI. A visit to a top-flight zoo like those in Dallas/Fort Worth, Houston, San Antonio, and Brownsville is helpful because pictures sometimes don't suffice in teaching positive identification. In addition to pit vipers and coral snakes, bites from many other Texas snakes can cause bad infections, so all snake bites should be treated as potentially serious, particularly if there is not a 100 percent identification of the perpetrator.

Texas sportsmen should develop habits that call for checking out bedding, campsite areas such as woodpiles, even boats before casting off. Never sit down in the woods without a thorough check and don't reach into dark places.

Fang puncture wounds are not a sure check on envenomation. Fang marks may be no larger than teeth marks. However, on larger snakes there will be no mistake, and the snake may have hit several times. Early symptoms include pain, swelling, blisters, weakness, faintness, sweating, thirst, nausea, vomiting, and diarrhea. There may be bleeding from fang wounds, nose, mouth and gums, rectum, urinary tract, and vagina. Coral snake bites can produce neurotoxic symptoms including a blocking of some muscles of the upper body. All these symptoms can ruin your day. No more comforting is the fact that both the first aid treatment and surgical techniques are among the most controversial issues in medicine, and Texas is right at the center of the debate. In first aid the debate centers on two issues: (1) local cuts and suction to remove venom and (2) administration of ice packs. The weight of medical opinion is that you should do neither because both procedures can delay transportation and both have, in past instances, caused serious complications.

TREATMENT:
1. Reassure victim, place him in recumbent position.
2. Apply a constricting band, 1 to 1½ inches wide, just tight enough to slow the spread of venom. You should be able to fit two fingers under the bands after they're in place. Don't apply bands around fingers, toes, neck, or torso.
3. Transport victim to hospital emergency room. Keep patient still and reclining en route. Try to keep the wound below heart level.

The best treatment is a set of car keys. Don't let anything delay getting to the hospital. If other camp members are available, here are two more important assignments.

1. Kill and bring the snake to the emergency room for positive identification.
2. Call ahead to the emergency room to alert the staff of an incoming snake bite victim. This may save valuable time when the victim arrives.

ON THE WATER The area of outdoor recreation that presents the highest degree of risk as measured by fatalities is boating. A significant number of drownings could be prevented by the simple expedient of donning an approved PFD—personal flotation device. An inordinate number of native Texans have never learned to swim, a skill easily acquired at any age. Many bass boats are inherently unseaworthy and overpowered. Such boats are frequently piloted at unsafe speeds in flooded timber or in dangerous wind and wave conditions in defiance of small craft warnings. Another defiance of common sense includes too many boaters who consume as much alcohol as gasoline—a deadly combination on water or asphalt.

SALTWATER MARINELIFE INJURIES Our first aid suggestions exclude shark, turtle, and Moray eel bites, all of which can be extremely dangerous, nor will we cover the damage that can be done by the likes of barracuda or reef dwellers such as the porcupine fish and sea urchins. Sportsmen planning reef-dive scuba trips or shark fishing expeditions should familiarize themselves with these and other marine dangers.

The dangerous marinelife most frequently encountered by sportsmen are stingrays and the venomous coelenterates such as Portuguese Man-O-War.

Stingray Envenomation

Wear sneakers and leggings; these plus the shuffling of feet offer the best prevention. When you step on a stingray, the barbed tail tears into your tender hide. Pain is intense and may cause paralysis, nausea, and complete collapse.

TREATMENT: Usually the foot or lower leg is punctured. Submerge in hot water for up to an hour. The venom is unstable in heat and is thereby deactivated; the heat will also reduce pain. After this initial treatment, the wound will require a doctor's care.

Coelenterate Envenomation

Our summer Gulf beaches are amply supplied with coelenterates, better known as jellyfish and Portuguese Man-O-War. The moon jellyfish and hairy stinger jellyfish will cause a stinging sensation. The sea wasp and Portuguese Man-O-War are more serious, and extensive stings can cause unconsciousness, muscular cramps, paralysis, and death. The Man-O-War stings can leave permanent scarring and the venom remains potent for several days, so don't poke at those seemingly dead on the beach. The sea wasp is a free-swimming jellyfish with a four-cornered bell shape; tentacles are attached to the corners. It actually swims by pulsations of the bell.

TREATMENT FOR MAN-O-WAR AND SEA WASP: First protect your hand, then pull off tentacles. Flush wound with rubbing alcohol, then cover with unseasoned meat tenderizer to neutralize the toxic effect. The minor skin irritation caused by other jellyfish can also be soothed by flushing with rubbing alcohol; again, meat tenderizer helps diffuse the milder toxins.

WEATHER DAMAGE Texas weather can abuse your hide and cause life-threatening conditions for the unwary and unprepared. Reasonable foresight can forestall almost any weather-related health problem short of a tornado. Here are the most prevalent villains:

Sunburn

There really is no excuse for suffering sunburn any longer. Cosmetic companies, dermatologists, and the Surgeon General have long publicized the long-term cancer risk of ultraviolet (UVB and UVA) radiation exposure. Sunscreens are widely available and the higher sun protection factors create a virtual sunblock. Use them.

Sun protection factor (SPF) indicates the increased length of time you can remain in the sun when contrasted with normal, no-protection burn time. If your skin begins to appear barely pink in 30 minutes, an SPF-8 should allow four hours in the sun without burning. Note that SPF protection is reduced or even eliminated by sweat or swimming, and that individuals taking drugs such as tetracycline, sulfa, and barbituates may be very sensitized to ultraviolet exposure and should avoid it.

TREATMENT: Mild cases will benefit from an allergy tested, fragrance-free moisturizer. Cold water cloths, tea bags or baking soda baths also help. Roasted victims should receive medical attention because they may have second degree burns.

Heat Exhaustion and Stroke

Texas summers can record triple digit weather for weeks at a time, so heat exhaustion and its more dangerous form, heat stroke, are real threats. Avoid these risks by seeking shade whenever possible. Heat exhaustion is marked by headache, pale skin that's cold and clammy to the touch, and dizziness; internal temperatures remain near normal. Heat stroke victims have high temperatures, up to 105 degrees or more, and their skins are red, dry, and hot to the touch.

TREATMENT: A heat exhaustion victim should lie down with feet elevated, cold towels on his head, and a chilled orange juice to sip. Ideally, he, too, should visit a doctor and avoid any further camp work. We have had many cases of heat exhaustion at our camp, all making miraculous recoveries when work is done.

A heat stroke victim should be taken to a hospital ASAP, but first put him in the shade and try to cool him off quickly. A water hose or buckets of cool water from the camp spring help greatly. Soak down a sheet in water from your ice chest and wrap him in it for the journey to the emergency room.

Hypothermia

Texas waterfowlers and early season bass fishermen run a risk of overexposure, particularly if they fall overboard. In hypothermia, the victim will be drowsy, numb, may have difficulty seeing, and may stagger. The conscious victim should be put in a warm cabin and wrapped in warm blankets. Coffee or hot soup will help. No booze. The unconscious victim should be wrapped in warm blankets and rushed to the hospital. Keep checking his breathing.

HYPOTHERMIA TIME CHART

WATER TEMPERATURE (F)	TIME BEFORE EXHAUSTION OCCURS	EXPECTED SURVIVAL TIME
32.5	Less than 15 min.	Less than 15 to 45 min.
32.5–40.0	15–30 minutes	30–90 minutes
40–50	30–60 minutes	1–3 hours
50–60	1–2 hours	1–6 hours
60–70	2–7 hours	2–40 hours
70–80	3–12 hours	3 hours to indefinitely
over 80	Indefinitely	Indefinitely

WIND CHILL CHART

THERMOMETER READING (F)

EST. WIND SPEED/MPH	50	40	30	20	10	0	−10	−20	−30	−40	−50	−60
	EQUIVALENT TEMPERATURE (F)											
0	50	40	30	20	10	0	−10	−20	−30	−40	−50	−60
5	48	37	27	26	6	−5	−15	−26	−36	−47	−57	−68
10	40	18	16	4	−9	−21	−33	−46	−58	−70	−83	−95
15	36	22	9	−5	−18	−36	−45	−58	−72	−85	−99	−112
20	32	18	4	−10	−25	−39	−53	−67	−82	−96	−110	−124
25	30	16	0	−15	−29	−44	−59	−74	−88	−104	−118	−133
30	28	13	−2	−18	−33	−48	−63	−79	−94	−109	−125	−140
35	27	11	−4	−20	−35	−40	−67	−82	−98	−113	−129	−145
40	26	10	−6	−21	−37	−53	−69	−85	−100	−116	−132	−148
DANGER FACTOR	Slight					High						Grave

ASSORTED SMALL WOUNDS The sportsman is subject to nicks, cuts, bites, fish finnings, scratches, abrasions, and skin punctures, all of which should be treated immediately so they do not become infected. This is no time to be macho, because wounds inflicted in the camp situation where you may have cleaned fish or game often run a much higher risk of infection and potential exposure to serious diseases such as rabies, tularemia, or tetanus, to mention a few.

TREATMENT: Wash your hands first then wash the area around the wound, working away from the wound itself. Flush out the wound with soap and water and pat dry. Apply antibiotic salve and cover the wound with sterile gauze secured with tape. For deep punctures, flush the area for five minutes with soap and water, then apply an ice pack. If the puncture was caused by an animal bite, especially a wild one, take the victim to the doctor immediately; rabies is a possibility. Domestic animals should be brought in to be observed for rabies. Under most circumstances, the wild animal should be killed and taken in for an autopsy.

Fishhook injuries also plague the clumsier sportsman. In most cases, run the hook on through until the barb is exposed, clip it off, then pull the shank out of the wound.

A butterfly bandage is very helpful for holding together the edges of gaping wounds. Of course, if the gap is too wide, sutures will be required, and off to the emergency room you go. To make a butterfly bandage, fold a piece of tape, and cut off both corners at the fold. Unfold the tape to view your "butterfly." The narrow part goes over the wound, wide parts to adjacent skin.

EYE INJURIES Eye protection is important around camp, from shooting glasses to protective goggles for use while cutting firewood, sawing boards, and hammering nails into a deer blind. Keep protective goggles with your tools.

TREATMENT: If a speck of wood or steel flies into your eye, pull down the lower lid and peel back the upper. If the speck is on a lid, remove it with a clean, damp cloth. If on the eye, head for the doctor or emergency room. Place a sterile pad over the injured eye; a bandage covering both eyes is recommended so the "bad" eye will not move in conjunction with the "good" eye, minimizing further damage.

BLISTERS AND SPRAINS High-top, lace-up, broken-in walking boots are the best available prevention against blisters and sprains. On long treks, it's a good idea to carry a packet of simple adhesive bandages along with a tube of antibiotic ointment, as well as an elastic bandage to wrap minor sprains. The latter also makes an excellent tourniquet, sling, or spare tie-down.

TREATMENT: If you can, leave the blister alone; it's the best protection against infection. If it breaks open, wash the area, apply ointment, and cover it with a sterile bandage. For more severe sprains, elevate the injured joint and apply an ice compress. (Cold compresses which activate chemically on demand are available; they're handy for the camp first aid kit.) At some point, a doctor should check the sprain for broken bone.

BROKEN BONES AND DISLOCATIONS
TREATMENT: Keep the broken bone ends or dislocated joint from moving. If the fracture is compound, that is with the bone showing outside the skin, and there is heavy bleeding, stop the bleeding, *but never try to push the bone back under the skin*. Do not move the victim if you suspect the break involves the skull, neck, back, or pelvis.

In a camp situation, victims with less serious breaks, such as an arm or leg, may need to be transported to an emergency facility. A splint may be required to prevent further damage and pain to the victim.

1. Find a suitable splint, such as a board, small tree limb, or broom handle. The splint should be long enough to reach beyond the joints above and below the break.
2. Fasten the splint with a belt, duct tape, elastic wrap, or even your shirt sleeve. Don't allow duct tape to contact bare skin.

3. Don't try to clean the wound. You may relieve pain caused by dislocation by applying an ice pack.
4. *Leave the bone or dislocation setting to a doctor.*

MINOR BURNS Handling cast-iron pots, campfires, and grills, the sportsman has his share of minor burns.
TREATMENT: Avoid ointments, grease, butter, and baking soda, no matter what your mother told you. Soak the burned area in ice cold water immediately. If the area can't be submerged, apply ice-water cloths. If the skin blisters, cover it with sterile dressings. Don't break the blisters.
CHEMICAL BURN TREATMENT: Use a hose or water bucket to flush if eyes are burned with any alkaline such as acid or lye. Rinse gently for 20 minutes. Then treat as a major burn.
MAJOR BURN TREATMENT: Keep the victim recumbent because shock is likely. Cut away burned clothing, but do not pull it away from burned skin—*if it sticks, leave it.* Cover the burn with a sterile dressing. *Don't apply ointment, antiseptic, grease—nothing. Rush to the emergency room.*

STOMACH DISORDERS Much common camp stomach distress—G.I.'s, *tourista*—can be prevented by common sense. Texas heat can turn ice chests into lively bacteria cultures and quickly spoil food left out, and the result can be one of many serious gastrointestinal infections, the most common being staphylococcus. Symptoms usually appear within two or three hours after eating, up to six hours. The victim will have cramps, nausea, and diarrhea. Other parasites and infectious agents can cause even more serious consequences, fever, chills, and persistent diarrhea, requiring a doctor.

Another source of mild distress is improperly cleaned cooking gear. Dishwashers should be diligent; the best camp cooks use boiling water for a final rinse. Camp water sources should be suspect until checked. You can arrange for an analysis at any commercial laboratory. You will need to obtain special sterile containers from the lab, collect a water sample, and return to the lab within 24 hours for bacteriological analysis. Even if the water is deemed drinkable, you may wish to pack in drinking water; nothing upsets a stomach faster than a change in water.
TREATMENT: With high fever, persistent diarrhea, or symptoms of appendicitis, get the victim to the emergency room immediately. Otherwise, the *tourista* will run its course in about 24 hours. If afflicted with this minor but discomforting malady, modify your diet accordingly. In the first stages, drink only clear liquids, such as broth, soda water, or apple juice. Fluid replacement is important with diarrhea. Avoid all dairy products and high-acid fruits. Gradually add potatoes, rice, cooked lean meat, and cooked vegetables to your diet. Avoid booze and spicy foods.

If there are no signs of fever, severe cramps, or blood in stool, a mild anti-motility agent, available over the counter, may be used. Popular prescription drugs including Lomotil are also standard issue with most sportsmen. In severe cases, a physician will probably want to treat the symptoms with his choice of various antibiotics; hospitalization may even be necessary.

MAJOR MEDICAL EMERGENCIES The following first aid procedures are for persons more than 10 years of age.

This supplement is not intended as a substitute for a complete emergency first aid manual. (See our recommendation in the First Aid Kit Checklist.) We list the following procedures only to give the reader an armchair familiarity with emergency action so that if the unfortunate incident arises, he or she will not be wholly uneducated with regard to the appropriate course of action.

What To Do First with a Major Accident

Send a companion to the nearest phone with an urgent request for medical assistance. Have him return ASAP so you will know if help is on the way, and perhaps how best to handle the first aid. Frequently, sportsmen have to provide makeshift ambulance service. If you are *absolutely* sure you can move the victim without further injury, it might be wise to start immediately for the nearest hospital.

Moving the Victim

Be certain there are no neck or back injuries. If the victim is conscious, see if he can move his fingers. If he detects any numbness or tingling in hands, arms, or shoulders, this would indicate a broken neck. If he can't move his toes and has numbness and/or tingling in his back or neck, the back may be broken. *Stop. Don't move him or let him move, as this could paralyze him.*

Unless moving the victim is absolutely necessary to save his life, don't change the position of the victim with head or neck injuries. If he *must* be moved to save him from further injury, carefully work a blanket or sleeping bag under him. Then support his head and neck and pull him to safety, head first and lengthwise. If he must be lifted, you'll need help, and preferably a door or stretcher. Slip the victim, again head first and lengthwise, onto the door, and then carefully into your vehicle.

While waiting for the doctor, keep the victim lying down. If you are positive there is no neck or back injury, and he has vomited, turn him on his side to keep his airway open. Put on your best bedside manner, calmly reassuring him. Don't give water to a semi-conscious or unconscious victim. Water in the windpipe may suffocate him.

If the Victim Is Not Breathing

1. Check his airway. Don't move the head or neck if there is any chance of spinal injury. Firmly lift the

victim's jaw; make sure the tongue does not block airway and that the passageway is clear of all debris. Wipe out with a cloth. If there's no chance of neck or back damage, place your palm on the victim's forehead and tilt the head back. Place the fingers of your other hand under the victim's chin and lift to bring it forward. Clearing the airway may restore breathing.

Place your cheek by the victim's mouth. You should feel exhaled air. If not, use your thumb and forefinger to pinch the victim's nostrils shut, maintaining the airway tilt. Place your mouth over the victim's. Give *two full* breaths, inhaling between, allowing the victim to exhale. The victim's chest should rise and fall. If not, the airway may still be clogged.

2. Check his pulse. The carotid pulse in the neck is the easiest to find. Feel for the Adam's apple, and gently slip your index and middle finger into the groove between the Adam's apple and the muscles of the neck. Either side will do. Touch gently, don't compress. If a pulse is present, repeat mouth-to-mouth procedure, breathing vigorously into the victim's mouth 12 times a minute. Remember to allow the victim to exhale. You should see his chest rise and fall.

If the victim has a pulse but is still not ventilating—no rise and fall of chest—his airway is blocked. Use the Heimlich maneuver. The victim should be face up. Kneel astride his hips and, with your hands on top of one another, place the heel of your bottom hand on the victim's abdomen between the navel and rib cage. Press with a quick thrust. Resume mouth-to-mouth breathing.

If the victim still has no pulse, a paramedic must start cardiopulmonary resuscitation, CPR. *CPR warning—* Cardiopulmonary resuscitation may inflict serious damage. It should only be used by trained personnel, preferably professional paramedics. If no one in camp is trained and qualified to administer CPR, there is a grave risk in attempting it.

Control Obvious Bleeding

There are four arterial pressure points which an amateur can usually find and use, two in the upper arms and two in the groin. *Don't apply arterial pressure on head, neck, or torso wounds.* On other wounds, place a sterile gauze pad or any cloth at hand over the wound and press firmly with the palm of your hand. Elevate the victim's head, neck, arm, or leg wound if there is no suspected fracture. Tie the sterile pad firmly in place using anything at hand, such as a bandana.

Treatment for Shock

Assume that the seriously injured victim will go into shock. If there are no neck or back injuries, raise his feet and cover him if the weather is cold. Keeping the victim warm and as comfortable as possible is the assignment.

Treatment for Electric Shock

The electrical power must be stopped immediately. Be sure to stand on a dry surface, so you don't electrocute yourself in the rescue attempt. Turn off the main power switch or use a non-conducting stick such as a dry tree limb or wooden tent pole to remove the power line. Check airway, breathing, and pulse. See p. 298 for appropriate action to take.

Heart Attack

Out-of-shape sportsmen should not overextend themselves in the retrieval of downed game, climbing, and other such activities for which they may not be in aerobic condition. Preseason conditioning, including at least 30 minutes of aerobics daily, is strongly advised. Get that weight off, too. But, don't be macho in the field. Go for help rather than risk a heart attack.

Know the symptoms of a heart attack: hard pain under the breastbone, possible pain in the back and left arm, shortness of breath, extreme weakness, paleness, sweating, and nausea.

With a suspected heart attack, seek medical help and make the victim comfortable. If he is in pain and lying down, let him assume whatever position relieves pain most effectively. Loosen tight clothing and don't give him anything to drink.

Heimlich Maneuver for Choking

Is the victim choking? It could be a heart attack. Take time to be sure. If the victim puts his hand to his throat and looks panicked, ask, "Are you choking? Nod yes or no." If he nods "yes," start the Heimlich maneuver.

See above for procedure when victim is lying down. For a sitting or standing adult victim:

1. Ball one hand into a fist.
2. Standing behind the victim, put both arms around the victim's waist.
3. Place the thumb side of the fisted hand into the victim's stomach above the navel and below the breastbone.
4. Grab the fisted hand with your other hand.
5. Press upward with force. Don't squeeze with your arms. Keep your arms bent.
6. Repeat until the airway is cleared of obstruction.

NOTE: If you are taking an infant or child under the age of 10 into a camp environment, we strongly advise that you and your spouse have your pediatrician show you how to eject a foreign object from a child's windpipe.

FIRST AID KIT CHECKLIST

Fishing tackle box marked with bright red cross

Detailed medical guide book (We recommend
   Medicine for the Outdoors by Paul S.
   Auerback, M.D., Little, Brown & Company,
   ISBN 0-316005929-3)
2-inch-square sterile gauze pads
4-inch-square sterile gauze pads
Assorted adhesive dressings
Assorted butterfly bandages
Roll of 1-inch adhesive tape
Roll of 2-inch adhesive tape
Moleskin
2-inch-wide gauze bandage roll
Tube of antibiotic salve
Small jar of petroleum jelly
Calamine lotion
Unseasoned meat tenderizer
Syrup of Ipecac
Scissors

Tweezers
Cotton swabs
42-inch-square cloth for triangular bandage
Safety pins
Packet of needles
Oral or headband thermometer
Instant chemical cold packs
Buffered aspirin
Antacid
Decongestant
Antimotility coating agent
Hard-backed razor blades
Sterile eyewash
Eye dropper
Sterile eye patches
Supply of quarters for pay phone
Wrapped bars of hotel guest soap

Epilogue

By the year 2000, the world could be losing one species of flora or fauna every hour of every day. By that same year, Texas is projected to have a population in the 20 million range: At least four million of those people are expected to purchase hunting and fishing licenses, but will they have anything to hunt or fish?

Fortunately, as we approach the end of the 20th century public awareness and interest in wildlife conservation and management has never been higher. It's going to take a lot of awareness, interest, and money to retain the word "wildlife" in our vocabulary. Awareness, then, is the first step. What are the major negative forces? Are they real threats or environmentalists' panic? Can the facts be supported? Can we do anything?

The satirical cartoon character Pogo, fittingly a 'possum, said it best: "I have met the enemy and he is me." That 20 million population estimate may be scary, but there's little reason to doubt its accuracy. The corresponding loss of wildlife habitat will be staggering, as lands give way to development, highway construction, creation of reservoirs, and urban sprawl. Another 21st-century threat is the move of city folk to exurban and rural areas encroaching on the remaining wildlife habitat. This trend has most recently been played out in the Sunbelt, where a weekend visit to any big lake invariably brings the reaction, like Custer's, "Where did they all come from?" Renewable resources are in a tight race with population pressure.

The population shift to the Sunbelt and our growing birthrate cannot be reversed. And yet, some conservationists may be overly negative. Like music critics they have pointed out our discordances, an invaluable service in itself, but they write no new music, only the repeated refrain of doom. In a mid-'80s public lecture series in Boston entitled "Extinction: Saving the Sinking Ark," paleontologist David Jablonski postulated, "Our species, then, is on the brink of causing, single-handedly, the worst mass extinction in 65 million years."

Forty years earlier, the great Aldo Leopold expounded in *A Sand County Almanac*, "Man always kills the thing he loves, and so we the pioneers have killed our wilderness. Some say we had to. Be that as it may, I am glad I shall never be young without wild country to be young in. Of what avail are forty freedoms without a blank spot on the map."

Blank spots on the map *are* getting harder to come by. We still have some in the Trans-Pecos, which has been designated by the Texas Nature Conservancy as a "mega-site of critical importance." The long-range plan for this area is to create a vast biological reserve that would combine federal, state, and private ownership, a project that will extend well into the 21st century. The conservancy already has acquired the 10,000-acre Big Brushy Canyon, in the Dead Horse Mountains between the Big Bend National Park and the Black Gap Wildlife Management Area. Fully 30 percent of our Texas natural heritage could be preserved through this project. Of the more than 2,000 rare Texas plants and animals identifed by the Texas Parks and Wildlife's Natural Heritage program, 736 are recorded in the Trans-Pecos.

That a project of this grand scope can even be considered is a tribute to Joseph M. Heiser, Jr., one of Texas' most distinguished conservationists. He was a founding governor of the Nature Conservancy, Life Trustee of the Texas Conservancy, and was the individual responsible for the designation of the mockingbird as our state bird.

We need many more Joe Heisers. As always in America, the answer lies in individual action. Authorities on endangered and threatened species state that neither state nor federal government funding is likely to cover the expenditures required in purchasing both land and the services of wildlife specialists needed to forestall the loss of biological diversity. Not only that, but it was just a few years ago that gaining access to new domestic energy sources outweighed the need to preserve the American wilderness. (Then-Secretary of the Interior James Watt was strongly advocating that national wilderness lands be leased for oil exploration and drilling.) Government can and does serve an essential purpose in enforcing conservationist practices, but making conservation the government's priority rests with the individual, and we believe sportsmen should lead the way. Public-private partnerships are the most viable alternative. Despite the efforts of the Texas Nature Conservancy and bills such as the Endangered Species Act of 1973, sportsmen need to remember that a "let George do it" attitude with regard to federal programs won't get the job done in Texas.

Unifying sportsmen and environmental lobbyists in their efforts to protect our wilderness is, sadly, not without its difficulties. It would seem American sportsmen will never live down the acts of a greedy few game thieves. Despite the fact that the majority of Americans have a favorable attitude toward hunters and fishermen, the leadership of many conservation groups continues to aim right between the eyes of modern sportsmen, laying accusations and blame for the loss of passenger pigeon, buffalo, Merriam elk, wolves, prairie chicken, et al. Sportsmen did not extirpate these species. Market and degenerate hunters did. Custom and law eliminated market hunting. We still have degenerates, but fortunately, not enough to tilt the ecological balance.

The Last Extinction, a book which grew out of the aforementioned Boston conservationist meeting series, is one of the most thought-provoking modern environmental works. However, key contributors James D. Williams and Ronald M. Novak, writing on "Vanishing Species in Our Own Backyard: Extinct Fish and Wildlife of the United States and Canada," indiscriminately slammed all hunters, even the prehistoric, even the Comanche. "Deliberate killing by human hunters," Williams and Novak concluded, "was for many years the leading known cause of extinction." The Indians hunted buffalo for millenia.

Their hunting and deliberate prairie fires were an integral part of the plains ecosystem.

Some conservationists seem to have been sealed in a vacuum since the 1900s, at least so far as hunting and fishing is concerned. There are no stauncher advocates of wildlife conservation today than those who hunt and fish, even if we do plan to kill and eat a wild turkey or redfish. No modern sportsman of my ken is engaged in a war against wildlife; quite the reverse. The loudest voices against unchecked predator control come from the ranks of sportsmen, while government-fueled predator eradication programs persist to this day.

Nationwide, sportsmen's purchases of licenses, excise taxes on arms and ammunition, purchase of federal and state migratory bird, fish, and nongame wildlife stamps provide almost 80 percent of the annual income of state wildlife agencies. In Texas, the contribution is closer to 90 percent. Because of this support Texas has a superior parks and wildlife management program. Our game wardens are highly trained, required to attend a Game Warden Academy for several months, where they learn far more than state park and wildlife codes and enforcement. They are equipped to teach hunter safety and water safety, and they present public education programs, especially programs for youth. Project WILD is such a program, made available free of cost to teachers and designed to help young sportsmen learn to evaluate environmental problems and "take intelligent and constructive action to conserve the wildlife and natural resources of Texas."

But sportsmen need to acquire more conservation insight, because it is a complex field with problems much broader than the depredations of slob hunters. The world ecosystem is at stake. The very existence of our earth is threatened by the extinction of each tiny species and by such diverse and seemingly remote events as the disappearance of rain forests in the Amazon basin or the Antarctic ozone hole. The balance of nature is a delicate but formidable one, and disturbing it can have consequences beyond our immediate understanding.

Who really cares if seemingly insignificant species perish? Who cares if a periwinkle becomes extinct? Maybe all of us. The Texas Nature Conservancy points out that more than half of today's medications can be traced to wild organisms from wild ecosystems. "Thanks to drugs prepared from a tropical forest plant—the rosy periwinkle—a child suffering from leukemia today has four chances in five of remission," says the conservancy. In 1960, the odds of leukemia remission were only one chance in five.

Biologists have not come close to discovering, let alone naming, all species on earth, nor have the pharmacologists. The penicillin of the 21st century may well be tucked away inside an as yet undiscovered bit of Amazonian or Texas wildlife. At least 18 species of Texas plants, from Texas wild rice to black lace cactus, are close to extinction. What other organisms, unknown to us, depend on the survival of these endangered plants for their own survival? Again, even the loss of one species can disturb the ecological balance of a large area.

John Steinbeck's *The Red Pony* told of a wagon train pioneer who, once settled in California, lamented the end of the crossing. "Then we came down to the sea, and it was done.... Westering has died out of the people. Westering isn't a hunger anymore. It's all done." We believe the westering instincts of frontier America are still with us, still shaping our national character, even if the frontier itself is gone, its ecosystems never to be completely restored. At first we didn't understand the ecological necessity for predators, so bears, wolves, and cougars were persecuted as deer and elk were protected. Exotic flora and fauna and comfy recreational facilities catering to the ultra-mobile campers of modern America proliferated so that what you see in today's national park system is but a pale reflection of the robust wildlife and native plant ecosystems of the early 19th century. Westering need not stop with the coastline; exploration of new frontiers is not its only component. Today's reference must include developing new frontier out of the old, especially through preservation.

Recently, zoos were described as the "last arks," and their keepers the "riders of the last ark." The Texas Nature Conservancy's approach is to expand the ark with carefully selected sanctuaries, managing them in a way that they may one day reveal their biological secrets. The objective is to preserve nature's diversity and the balance of natural selection.

Yet preserving nature's diversity is not just a matter of protecting existing species from man-made poisons; it also involves protecting them from the introduction of natural and wildlife exotics. Fully half of the extinct fishes in America were extirpated by exotic organisms. Generally recognized biological pollutants include exotics such as English sparrows, starlings, Norway rats, grass carp, and Asiatic clams. Nutria should be added to the list. On their way to Texas are so-called killer bees. Projected to arrive in Brownsville via Mexico between November 1989 and March 1990, these Africanized bees produce little honey, drive out other honeybees, and don't pollenize as well as European varieties. Genetic engineering and pheromone stimulation are among the control methods, in themselves harbingers of an exotic future for the human race.

Sportsmen should learn more about the consequences of introducing exotic big game animals to our state. Exponents of Texas safaris point out with pride that there are now more varieties of game to be hunted in Texas than any nation on earth. Some lists include more than 50 exotic animals to hunt in Texas. Often named are axis deer, fallow deer, blackbuck antelope, sika deer, blesbok, eland, Grant's gazelle, various ibex, waterbuck, oryx, sable, roan antelope, wildebeast, gemsbox, Catalina goat, mouflon sheep, Corsican sheep, and Barbados sheep.

But there is concern about unknown disease and health problems with exotics. It's certain that exotics compete more effectively for food than whitetail, making an exotic population explosion a real danger. There may be an abundance of livestock to *shoot*, but what game will the sportsman have to *hunt*?

Should one think an explosion of exotic game, particularly the ungulates which find our pastures so comfortable and tasty, to be unlikely, remember that we have already had explosions of exotics. They were called longhorns and mustangs. Granted, that's a part of Texas history, but do we want history to repeat itself with blackbuck and sika? Can we afford the consequences of an unsuccessful experiment, given our dwindling land resources?

The so-called exotic game safari is popular in Texas. The killing of these animals is profitable to landowners, many of whom need the money, but at what expense? At the very least, let's find out. Let's learn more about the impact of free-ranging exotics on existing biological communities.

The really sad thing about exotic game ranch hunting in Texas is the emphasis on high-dollar "no game, no pay" deals and on quick hunts for busy executives. Vehicles are commonly used to run the exotic game to ground; game fencing effectively pens animals for slaughter, much the same technique used a hundred years ago to wipe out antelope. Fair chase is unheard of here.

There is yet another dimension to the problems facing Texans and their environment. Conservation is not always a tidy affair of good versus evil, or ignorance versus enlightenment. Sometimes it's a matter of choosing the lesser of evils. We are now facing just this sort of choice in the handling of our water resources.

Seven major and a dozen minor aquifers flow under Texas, the Edwards Aquifer of Central Texas being the largest entirely within the state. The water-saturated limestone and sandstone rock strata which form these aquifers are like huge water-soaked sponges—and they're being wrung dry. Not enough water is percolated into them to replace that which is pumped out.

Currently, three quarters of all ground water pumped in Texas comes from the Ogallala Aquifer in the High Plains, which took ten million years to form. Since it has been pumped for irrigation, particularly in the High Plains and Rolling Plains, where most major ancient springs have dried up, it may be exhausted in less than 100 years. Gunner Brune, a 33-year veteran of the U.S. Soil Conservation Service and a seven-year employee of the Texas Water Development Board, believes most of the water in the Ogallala Aquifer will be gone by sometime in the 21st century, because it cannot be recharged from Rocky Mountain runoffs. By the year 2020, if you believe a 1982 federal government report, five million acres of irrigated land will be dry.

The Texas response has been to dam more rivers and capture more runoff; an answer that is a double-edged sword to wildlife, but necessary to support all life in the state. One of the great dam projects in Texas, the Amistad at Del Rio, was a mammoth effort to balance the needs of agriculture and population growth with the ecosystem of the Rio Grande. Expert ecological attention has been focused on a small fish known as the Amistad gambusia of Goodenough Spring. The gambusia was killed off when the Amistad Dam flooded the spring, but the immediate problem was that Goodenough Spring was not good enough. It could not supply the water needs of the area. Surely, a great deal of wildlife habitat is lost forever each time a dam is built, but man's survival created the need for dams—not callousness about endangered wildlife. Rational man knows that water and aquatic resources are finite. The Texas Water Commission forecasts a critical water shortage by 2000, so man and wildlife alike are seriously threatened. Most Texans spend quite a lot of time praying for rain.

Since Rachel Carson's publication of *Silent Spring* in 1962, great strides have been made to control chemical pollution of land and water. There is now a national consciousness about chemical poisoning of the environment and the effluvium from our cities and factories. There is increasing government and community support for control of groundwater pollutants. Both state and federal legislation has been passed intended to reduce the pollution of our environment by toxins, carcinogens, and birth defect-causing chemicals. The 21st century will see a proliferation of state legislation introduced under the heading "clean water." Americans will no longer tolerate the poisoning of their homeland, but we must insist on rational remedies.

Compliance and enforcement activities consume millions of dollars annually. As taxpayers and consumers, each of us supports the cost of these programs, and we must remember that the public tax base is also an endangered resource. It is extremely important that the efforts and tax dollars dedicated to environmental protection be wisely used in carefully planned, scientifically based programs to provide maximum public and wildlife protection from realistically identified hazards. Protection of the environment is too important to permit its becoming embroiled in inefficient, high cost, pork barrel projects and meaningless paperwork. It would be easy to relax and leave the guardianship of our land and water resources to the federal government, but no bureaucracy in a free society should be left without public scrutiny, which means informed eyes and ears on a state and individual level.

Similarly, while Texas' blank spaces are attractive to those who must dispose of nuclear and toxic wastes, our state can no longer continue to accept these poisonous wastes just because we have the room. The Texas Panhandle near Hereford was one of three blank spots targeted by the U.S. Department of Energy (DOE) under the Federal Nuclear Waste Policy Act for the nation's first nuclear waste dump, expected to be in use by the early part of the 21st century. Other original dump site choices were in Nevada and Washington State. Millions of dollars in federal incentives, referred to by some as bribes, were offered to these states to accept the dump. (The DOE also approached various Indian tribes; it's not enough that we've taken most of their lands, now we seek to pollute the few remaining reservations.) The Texas site would put the dump astride the Ogallala Aquifer, raising concerns about pollution of the state's major source of groundwater. The safety of the Waste Isolation Pilot Plant (WIPP) near Carlsbad, New Mexico, thirty miles from the Texas border, has been challenged because of the dangers of brine seepage. The issue of nuclear waste disposal in the 2000s is not yet resolved.

YOU CAN MAKE A DIFFERENCE

The typical Texas sportsman is well educated; nearly half in Texas have college degrees, in comparison to a statewide average of one in three. The typical sportsman is also twice as affluent as the average Texan and can, therefore, articulate his beliefs and put his money where his mouth is on conservation issues. Given the chance, he will become active in an organization or volunteer to help out. TPWD biologists had no problem establishing a volunteer angler program composed of citizens who kept elaborate fishing diaries to provide TPWD with data on bass size and lake populations. Organizations such as the Gulf Coast Conservation Association, Texas Independent Bird Hunters Association, Texas Wild Turkey Federation, Lone Star Bowhunters Association, Ducks Unlimited, Pheasants Unlimited, and Texas Bighorn Society are well funded and supported in our state. By actively participating in clubs and organizations, by speaking out, by funding conservation programs, we can assure fair chase and a fair environment.

Sportsmen's dollars are also indispensable. Present your children and grandchildren, even yourself with a Lifetime Texas Hunting and Fishing License. For only a few hundred dollars each, you fund the programs that will assure a place for your offspring to hunt and fish and revel in the wilderness.

We recommend that you contribute to the Texas Nature Conservancy. As noted earlier, it is actively acquiring the land that shelters remnant native ecosystems. Conservancy members aren't taking you on a guilt trip, nor have they set up an administration that pockets the lion's share of donations. They are acting in the most meaningful way of all to preserve nature, using a practical, businesslike, results-oriented approach. For membership information, write Texas Nature Conservancy, P.O. Box 1440, San Antonio, TX 78295–1440.

The *Sportsman's Guide to Texas* began with the concept of fair chase. Loss of habitat, endangered wildlife, dwindling water resources, environmental pollution, exotic infestations, and many more people could make fair chase history in our state. Fortunately, you, the sportsman, are our greatest resource. You can make the difference.

Mary-Love Bigony, with *Texas Parks & Wildlife* magazine's staff, has been one of the most eloquent defenders of the faith for many years. She has written thousands of moving words about the wild flora and fauna of Texas. From her, the last words in the *Sportsman's Guide to Texas:* "As the 21st century approaches, this is the challenge facing all who love Texas and its land: to preserve it when possible, restore it when needed, and strike a balance between its economic uses and aesthetic value. We will determine whether Texans of the future will revere this land as their ancestors did, this land that is our heritage."

Acknowledgments

To be complete, our acknowledgments would cover a 40-year span and thousands of sportsmen, be they hunters, fishers, birders, environmentalists, outdoor writers, or wildlife scientists. Writing the *Sportsman's Guide to Texas* has meant adventuring through their sometimes widely varying thought processes and beliefs. The contrasts were many and as great as those of a state known as "The Land of Contrasts."

The often self-taught lessons of the past four decades were used as benchmarks for most of the information in this book. And, on a few occasions, practical observation had to stand in absence of scientific proof, for by no means are all things wild and wonderful completely understood.

A great effort has been expended on this work to achieve technical accuracy with the freely given assistance of some of this nation's most expert wildlife specialists, all from the Texas Parks and Wildlife Department. They are:

Bobby Alexander, Wildlife Division Field Operations Director;

Mary-Love Bigony, managing editor, *Texas Parks & Wildlife* magazine;

Jim Cox, contributing editor, *Texas Parks & Wildlife* magazine;

Phil Evans, TPWD Regulatory Coordinator;

Ron George, TPWD Program Leader for Migratory, Shore, Upland Game Birds;

Steve Hall, TPWD Hunter Education Coordinator;

Bob Jessen, TPWD Waterfowl Program Leader;

Charles Winkler, TPWD Big Game Program Director;

Don Wilson, TPWD Upland Game Program Leader;

Dale Witt, TPWD Migratory, Nongame, and Endangered Species Director;

Bruce Thompson, TPWD Program Leader for Nongame, Endangered Species, Furbearers, and Alligators.

A special accolade is warranted for the outstanding work of our state game wardens, who patrol millions of acres of public and private property to ensure proper game law enforcement.

We are deeply indebted to an army of wildlife photographers whose specific photo credits appear at the end of the book. They, along with master birders, are among the most highly skilled sportsmen. One hundred years ago, the serious student of wildlife, particularly of birds, never went afield without his shotgun. Today, the shotgun is replaced by finely ground optical lenses, even though it's still easier to obtain results with your double barrel.

We are grateful for the contributions and advice on

Texas flora and wildflowers from Dr. David Northington, Director of the National Wildflower Research Center, and Herb Neimann of the Texas Department of Highways. And a special bouquet to Rosario Baxter for her research assistance and both delightful and botanically correct illustrations.

Thanks also to Cammie Vitale for her culinary expertise.

Sharing their insights were:

Joe Krieger, first world-champion bass tournament winner and sportsman/television personality;

Jake Guarino, tournament bass fisherman;

Sonny Baughman, waterfowl expert at Los Ganzos Lodge;

Dick Grimm, of CAT scan fame, another waterfowl expert;

Rainie Bishop of the Texas Nature Conservancy;

Dennis Smith, master falconer;

Herb Wagner, outdoor writer and expert cast-iron cook;

Randolph and **Lillie Mae Leifeste,** ranchers at Castell, whose families have lived on the Llano River for almost 150 years;

Don Coney, gynecologist and owner of a trophy deer ranch;

Mike Windsor, for his wonderful words of wisdom, "Hold your fire until you see one with his horns way outside his ears."

Few authors amount to much without a great editor, and we were no exception. First to Bobby Frese for having faith in us, and substantial credit to Dominique Gioia who, while learning a great deal about the outdoors herself, honed and refined this work to make it more readable and certainly a great deal more brief.

And, of course, our own informed hunting group, the Shade Tree Sportsmen themselves, without whom there would be no book. Patriarch of the Shade Tree Sportsmen is Jack Ogilvie, of Websource, whose sporting exploits are legendary throughout Texas. The *Guide's* first draft was replete with Ogilvie stories, but all agreed that they would make a future book unto themselves. A prime force in the book has been Shade Treer Carl Lively, whose four decades of hunting, fishing, and cooking game in Texas has only been interrupted by his becoming one of the state's leading graphic designers. Our technical editor, Dave Baxter, guided us through the Texas outdoors. Above all, we owe special thanks to Jack Unruh for allowing us to see Texas wildlife through his aesthetic perspective.

—DALLAS, TEXAS, 1988
Dick Bartlett
Joanne Krieger

Index

Page numbers in **bold face** indicate illustrations.

Photo Credits

FRANK AGUILAR pp. 3 (upper right); 14; 77 (upper right); 99 (left); 230 (left)

GRADY ALLEN pp. 3 (left); 47 (left); 61; 73 (left), (upper right), (lower right); 74 (left), (upper right); 75 (left), (lower); 77 (upper left); 78 (right); 80; 82; 96 (left); 102 (left); 201; 202 (left); 204; 221 (lower); 225; 226; 232 (upper); 233 (right); 234 (left)

STEVE BENTSEN pp. 48; 77 (lower right); 101 (upper); 155 (left), (upper right), (lower right); 224; 231 (lower right); 233 (left); 236 (lower right); 240

MIKE BIGGS pp. 180; 228; 242 (lower left), (right)

ED DUTCH pp. 229 (right); 272

GWEN FIDLER p. 238 (left)

MARTIN FULFER pp. 63 (upper left); 196 (right); 200; 202 (right); 205; 239 (lower right)

BUDDY GOUGH pp. 259 (left); 264; 268 (right)

MADGE LINDSAY p. 20

WYMAN P. MEINZER pp. 35; 59 (upper), (lower right); 74 (lower left); 114; 116 (upper left); 131 (right); 135; 142; 145; 146 (left); 152 (right); 178; 179; 181; 198 (right); 199 (right); 203; 221; 222 (left); 231 (upper right); 255

GLEN MILLS pp. 4; 9 (left); 17 (upper), (lower left); 24; 34; 38 (lower left); 60 (lower left), (upper right); 62; 71; 99 (right); 118; 132 (left); 146 (right); 150; 152 (left); 154 (lower); 171; 172; 193; 194; 197; 199 (left); 220; 223; 227 (left); 230 (lower right); 232 (lower); 234 (right); 236 (upper right)

RICHARD MOREE p. 163

GILBERT PALMER p. 230 (upper right)

TATE PITTMAN p. 239 (upper)

BILL REAVES pp. 2; 3 (lower right); 13; 26; 27; 30; 38 (upper); 41 (upper left), (lower right); 47 (right); 48 (upper left); 51; 79 (upper right); 96 (right); 97 (lower); 102 (right); 103 (upper), (right); 104 (upper); 121; 128; 130 (upper left), (lower left); 132 (right); 143; 147; 148 (upper), (lower); 149; 151; 153; 154 (upper left); 184; 192; 196 (left); 198 (left); 229 (left); 231 (left); 241 (upper left), (lower); 243 (right); 246; 257; 262; 266 (left), (right); 267 (right); 270 (upper right), (lower right); 271

RAY SASSER pp. 72; 97 (left); 100; 101 (right); 131 (left); 167; 169; 242 (upper left); 253; 259 (right); 261 (left); 263

TOM J. ULRICH p. 103 (left)

VINYARD BROS. PHOTO p. 78 (left)

JIM WHITCOMB pp. 227 (right); 235 (left), (right); 261 (right)

LEROY WILLIAMSON pp. 9 (right); 31; 98; 104 (right); 116 (lower); 211; 238 (right); 243 (left); 247 (upper), (right)

About
the
Artist

JACK UNRUH opened his first studio with Lee Schwarz in Dallas in October 1958. Since then, millions of sportsmen have seen his work in such publications as *Sports Afield, Outdoor Life, Sports Illustrated, Field and Stream,* and *National Geographic.* His work has appeared in national exhibits including the New York Society of Illustrators (regularly since 1967), C. A. Art Annual, and "200 Years of Illustration."

His corporate clients include Twentieth-Century Fox, Time Inc., NBC, Exxon, ITT, American Airlines, and Hyatt Hotels. Major paper companies with decidedly environmental concerns have also enlisted his talents as one of this country's leading wildlife artists, as have the National Park Service and Ducks Unlimited. Jack's mastery of fine detail and his subtle watercolor and ink technique make his original wildlife paintings highly sought after by collectors and sportsmen alike.